TOR!

TOR!

THE STORY OF GERMAN FOOTBALL

ULI HESSE

POLARIS
PUBLISHING

POLARIS PUBLISHING LTD
c/o Aberdein Considine
2nd Floor, Elder House
Multrees Walk
Edinburgh
EH1 3DX

Distributed by Birlinn Limited

www.polarispublishing.com

ISBN: 9781913538743
eBook ISBN: 9781913538750

British Library Cataloguing-in-Publication Data
A catalogue record for this book is available on request from the British Library.

Designed and typeset by Polaris Publishing, Edinburgh
Printed in Great Britain by MBM Print SCS Limited, East Kilbride

CONTENTS

Uli Hesse is an editor at *11Freunde*, Germany's biggest football monthly, and has been published on five continents. He is a long-standing contributor to *FourFourTwo*, the *Blizzard* and *When Saturday Comes* and has written more than 400 columns for ESPN FC. His first English-language book, *Tor! The Story of German Football*, was shortlisted for the William Hill Sports Book of the Year award, while two of his German books have been nominated for that country's Football Book of the Year prize. In June 2017, he was appointed a member of the German Academy for Football Culture. His book, *Building the Yellow Wall: The Incredible Rise and Cult Appeal of Borussia Dortmund*, won Football Book of the Year at the 2019 British Sports Book Awards. He lives in Berlin.

This book has always been dedicated to the memory of Walther Bensemann.
It is now also for David Wangerin and Bernhard Carl Trautmann.

GERMANY

- Towns and cities of significant football interest
- - - - BUNDESLÄNDER (federal states)
- · - · - Former border between West and East Germany

SCHLESWIG-HOLSTEIN

Kiel

Rostock

Hamburg

MECKLENBURG-WESTERN POMERANIA

Bremen

POLAND

LOWER SAXONY

BRANDENBURG

NETHERLANDS

Wolfsburg

Berlin

Hanover

Braunschweig

Magdeburg

Münster

Bielefeld

Cottbus

NORTH RHINE-WESTPHALIA

SAXONY-ANHALT

Gelsenkirchen

Dortmund

Oberhausen

Bochum

Halle

Leipzig

Duisburg

Essen

SAXONY

Mönchengladbach

Düsseldorf

Dresden

Leverkusen

Aachen

Cologne

Jena

Chemnitz

Bonn

THURINGIA

Zwickau

BELGIUM

HESSE

Frankfurt-am-Main

LUXEMBOURG

Offenbach

CZECH
REPUBLIC

RHINELAND-PALATINATE

Herzogenaurach

SAARLAND

Kaiserslautern

Fürth

Nuremberg

Mannheim

Saarbrücken

Karlsruhe

Stuttgart

BAVARIA

FRANCE

BADEN-WÜRTTEMBERG

Ulm

Freiburg

Munich

SWITZERLAND

AUSTRIA

N

0   50   100   150   200   250   300 Kilometres

INTRODUCTION

THIS IS THE FOURTH edition of this book, and I'm beginning to struggle with these introductions. There will be people who are reading *Tor!* for the first time, at least that's what we all hope, and they deserve some background. On the other hand I don't want to repeat myself and bore our season-ticket holders with tales I've told before. For instance about a reporter whose name I still cannot recall. He was interviewing me on BBC Radio 5 Live in September 1998 about a game in the Champions League, and I happened to mention a few things in passing that seemed utterly perplexing to him. It was the first time I realised that many people, even professionals, simply assumed German football was pretty much like English football, only played by Germans.

I'm not sure how much this has actually changed since the first edition of this book came out, which was in 2002. To give you just one example: Barely a week before I sat down to write this new introduction, the editor-in-chief of an excellent magazine announced on social media that the latest edition of his publication would be devoted entirely to Bayern Munich. In his post, he referred to the Munich giants as 'a club that, until 1970, had just two Bundesliga titles'. Er, no. Actually, they had lifted only one, in 1969. Because when Bayern won their first national championship, in 1932, the Bundesliga was still more than three decades in the future, and with it professionalism.

This was precisely what had caught the BBC guy off guard back in 1998. He asked me: 'You mean Germany won the 1954 World Cup without professional players?' I replied: 'Well, we didn't even have a nationwide league.' He gasped: 'But that's incredible!' That was the moment I got the idea for a book aimed at non-German football fans with an interest in the German game. (This also answers one of the questions I'm most often asked, namely if this is a translation of a German original – no, it isn't.)

But like I said, enough of those tired old stories. Let me instead share something with you I've never told anybody before. Namely that the book you're reading is a shameless rip-off.

See, in the early 1990s, I became obsessed with baseball, not least because the literature on the game is amazing. However, some baseball books really test the delicate boundaries between exhaustive and exhausting. Which is why I was bowled over by a one-volume, 388-page book published in 1991, simply entitled *Our Game*. It was written by a 57-year-old Distinguished Professor of History at Ohio University called Charles C. Alexander. In one fell swoop, Alexander told me everything I wanted to know and gave me all the names and numbers I needed to know, without being dry, academic and pedantic or superficial, rash and cursory. I can't put it any better than the reviewer for *Spitball* magazine, who said: '*Our Game* goes down as easily as a cold one on a hot day in the bleachers.'

Back then, I had no intentions of ever doing a book about sport myself, but I was already dabbling in some non-professional writing, which is why *Our Game* also left a deep impression on me in terms of, for lack of a better word, technique. How could the author cram all this information into one book and still remain conversational? It's a mystery I still have only partially solved.

Which is why this book can never be as good as *Our Game*, although I do hope that some of you come away from it with the same feeling I had back in 1991, namely that you've just read a fairly long book about history which is, in contrast to what we've all learned in school, not totally boring.

A word of warning, though. For the sake of continuity, I felt forced to disregard certain aspects of, note the lower cases now, our game. The most glaring omission has always been women's football. You have to take my word for it that this is not because of prejudice (for many years I used to work with one of Germany's most legendary female goalkeepers on her homepage) and that I'm painfully aware of this oversight. One day, I'll have a glorious idea of how to incorporate women's football into this narrative. It's on my list for a future edition.

While we're talking about old and new editions, let me point out the most important and obvious change. For almost two decades, *Tor!* was published by *When Saturday Comes*. Over all these years, Mike Ticher, the original manuscript editor, Andy Lyons and Richard Guy have become friends. I'm not sure if I've ever properly thanked them for their interest, encouragement and help. So, at last: *Vielen Dank*!

Uli Hesse, March 2022

PROLOGUE

THE SUMMIT

IT IS NOT YET seven o'clock on this Sunday morning. Lake Thun is calm, waiting for the first rays of sun to warm its waters. The tourists, all but one of whom are still asleep, will be flocking to the beach before midday.

Hardly a cloud is visible in the sky which is coloured a deep red by the sun rising over the foothills of the Bernese Alps. Some of the peaks here measure well over 6,500 feet – a deeply impressive sight to anyone coming from a place offering nothing taller than smokestacks or church steeples, but less than half the height of the fabled Matterhorn.

The Matterhorn lies 50 miles due south. It was first climbed by an Englishman, Edward Whymper, on July 14, 1865, a mere three years after the publicist Hermann Alexander von Berlepsch had declared it 'invincible'. Whymper later said that 'after the mountain had been defeated with astonishing ease, it took dreadful revenge', referring to the fact that four of his five companions died during the descent.

A man is standing on the balcony of a hotel, silently watching the scenery. He has almost certainly never heard of Whymper and his thoughts are not revolving around mountain climbing. At least, not in a literal sense. Instead his gaze is fixed on the skies, as if trying to will something to appear there. He remains in this position for a few minutes, his lean, muscular body seemingly untouched by the beauty around him. When the sunlight finally finds an opening in the mountains, as it always does, and bathes the lake in a golden light, he turns around and walks back to his room in disgust.

It's not as if he is insensitive. He is a simple man, that's true, a man who is running a dry cleaners and will soon, unsuccessfully, try his hand at a cinema. But on any other day, the sun, the lake and the mountains would warm his heart. This day, however, is unlike any other day. The man lies down to get another two hours' sleep. At nine o'clock he's back on the balcony. Now the sun is fully up, the lake shimmering, the mountains an immovable confirmation that the day is going to be beautiful.

Disappointed, the man joins his brother, who manages a petrol station back home, and his group of friends for breakfast. All morning, he will return to the balcony at regular intervals only to find his hopes dashed again. But he's not giving up. At half past eleven he believes he can make out a few innocent clouds in the distance, and his heart misses a beat. At noon, some scattered drops touch his straggly black hair. He goes down for lunch with renewed confidence.

At exactly half past 12 there is a sudden stir in the dining room. A somewhat sturdy but wiry fellow, co-owner of a modest lottery kiosk in his home town, comes storming down the corridor, grinning broadly. 'It's raining,' he says to the first man. 'It's raining!' The man allows himself the biggest smile he can reconcile with his cautious, introverted nature. Then he puts his share of chicken breast back on to the plate in order to verify this piece of possibly priceless information.

It's true. Ugly, fat raindrops are falling from what is now a grey mass above Lake Thun, driving tourists away from the beach. They promise wind and cold and mud. 'Now nothing can go wrong,' says the man.

It is July 4, 1954. The man's name is Fritz Walter. In four and a half hours' time he will be playing a game of football against what is indisputably the best team in the world. In little more than six hours' time he and his companions will be living legends.

One day later Elvis Presley enters Sun Studios to record his first single. Life has never been the same since.

ON THE TURN

GERMAN FOOTBALL'S STRUGGLE FOR RESPECTABILITY

LET'S PRESUME THERE IS a non-German football fan who, at this moment, is reading a newspaper. Let's further presume this person comes across results from the various European leagues, pausing for a moment to contemplate the German Cup, the DFB-Pokal.

Let's say, just for the sake of argument, that our fan is English, male and lives in Nottingham. He will be familiar with the city's claim to host two of the oldest football clubs in the world, Notts County (formed in 1862) and Nottingham Forest (1865). Something strikes him as irritating. He knows the Germans have a knack of adorning clubs' names with the year of their foundation, as in 'FC Schalke 04'. How, then, to account for the fact that there seems to be a team universally known as TSV München 1860? And what about this other club, a few lines further down, that is called SSV Ulm 1846? Our fictional reader puts the paper away. Since I made him up, I can read his mind. He is thinking: 'Those Germans! Not content with the automobile, communism and printing with movable type, now they're claiming they invented football too.'

In fact, neither Ulm nor Munich maintain they started playing football before the last decade of the 19th century. The reason they carry such impressive dates in their names simply marks one of the fundamental differences between German football clubs and their English counterparts, a difference which is not only still relevant today (you won't encounter the very modern buzzword '50+1' again for a few hundred pages, but its roots are right here), it will also lead us to the beginnings of football in this country.

German football clubs are never solely that. They are, without exception, multi-sport associations which offer their members a variety of athletic activities. At 1860 Munich you can play basketball and tennis and may even bowl, box or wrestle. Stefan Effenberg's sisters played softball for St Pauli. SSV Ulm 1846 go several steps further, collecting 22 different sporting departments under the club's banner, among them such crowd-pleasers as competitive dancing and, guess what, cricket. Even those German clubs carrying the familiar letters 'FC' in their name do things besides kicking a ball: Bayern Munich FC used to lay claim to the best chess team in the country, 1. FC Köln have table-tennis players. Many of today's clubs were formed with the explicit intention of playing football but later added other sports to their roster. But more often it was the other way around. Thus the TSV Munich of 1860 created a football division in early 1899. And today's SSV Ulm 1846 is the result of a complicated and long-winded series of mergers that involved, among others, a football club formed in 1894 and the TSG Ulm of 1846.

The clue as to the origins of this system is the letter 'T' in both TSV Munich and TSG Ulm. It stands for *Turnen*, which can only be translated as 'gymnastics', but which carries with it a mass of connotations which the English word does not. Long before football arrived, physical training in Germany was dominated to an astonishing degree by the gymnastics movement. The German obsession with the teachings of these stern contortionists goes a long way towards explaining why sport (as opposed to *Turnen*), and especially professional sport, had such problems taking root in Germany. In fact, the influence of the gymnasts still permeates German sport and has haunted the footballers in particular since the first ball was kicked by Germans in Germany, which was probably in Braunschweig in 1874.

Three men were primarily responsible for the rise of the gymnastics associations in 19th-century Germany. But, as so often happens, the true catalyst was a terrible hiding. Actually two of them, both at the hands of the French. In 1806, Napoleon's troops annihilated the Prussian army on the battlefields of Jena and Auerstedt. These devastating defeats would prove to have long-lasting effects on the German psyche. They cost Prussia all its estates west of the River Elbe and put the kingdom under French influence, which in turn led the defiant Prussians to develop the concepts of freedom and nationalism – until then two virtually meaningless terms on German-speaking territories.

The most immediate effect of Jena and Auerstedt, however, was to provoke reform of the Prussian army. This task fell to General Gerhard David von Scharnhorst, who decided to open the higher military ranks to members of the middle class and establish universal conscription. In order to make his recruits fit for the task, he strongly advised secondary schools to introduce physical education according to the teachings of Johann Christoph Friedrich GutsMuths.

GutsMuths was a teacher and philosopher, who in 1793 had published a book called *Gymnastik für die Jugend* (Gymnastics for Young People). It bemoaned 'the physical decline of humanity' and proposed the ideal of a 'perfect man', to be achieved through a unity of mind and body. The term 'perfect man' may sound a bit ugly, but GutsMuths was fairly liberal (for the times) and belonged to an educational reform movement known as Philanthropinism. He originally wanted to bring to the bourgeoisie what until then had been a privilege of the aristocracy, namely the resources to indulge in healthy and uplifting physical activities. In the wake of the wars against Napoleon's French empire, though, he became progressively nationalistic and militaristic.

His visions were put into practice by Friedrich Ludwig Jahn, who in 1811 began organising gymnastics events that included swimming and hiking in addition to the usual gyrations. At first, Jahn was perceived as a subversive element by the authorities, because he made it clear he wanted physical education everywhere and for everybody, and that sounded too much like revolution to some. He was arrested in 1819 and would have faced the death penalty if he had been convicted. As a result, many German gymnasts fled to Switzerland, and there the movement took hold. Gymnastics festivals became national events and, as soon as Jahn's home country realised the gymnasts were not anarchists but in many cases deeply patriotic idealists whose goal was to create a trim and healthy people, Jahn turned from outcast to leader. He even pursued a career in politics and was a member of the 1848 Frankfurt National Assembly which attempted to create a unified German nation out of the various kingdoms and principalities.

As far as Jahn was concerned, 'gymnastics' and 'sport' were not the same thing at all. In fact, they were diametrically opposed. Sport was whatever the decadent English did, games like billiards, cricket, golf or even hunting and horse racing. For Jahn they were elitist activities that only existed to divide the world into winners and losers, individualistic affairs of no communal value, devoid of any ethical or philosophical grounding. But gymnastics! Ah, here Jahn's long, flowing beard would tremble with the excitement only righteous moralists can feel, while he embarked on yet another speech extolling the virtues of the pure and honest. Gymnastics was for the people. It created unity, not separation. It existed for the good of the whole, not for the self-esteem of a select few. Jahn usually had to say nothing more once he mentioned that in England some people bet money on sports. Money!

Such was Jahn's fervour that he insisted on dumping the widely accepted term *Gymnastik* and replacing it with a word derived from a Germanic stem: *Turnen*. (Traces of the original surface in the English 'tournament'.) This is the point where an unpleasant odour began to waft through the gymnastics movement, as Jahn was no longer interested in GutsMuths's 'perfect man' but instead wanted the 'perfect German', physically prepared for life – and war. Soon the once carefree, jolly and relatively casual associations mutated into tight custodians of a dulled nationalistic spirit and joined hands with the notoriously conservative student fraternities to build a bulwark against all things foreign.

The first national German gymnastics festival took place in Frankfurt in 1841, and they have been held more or less every five years since. Each of the early conventions inspired members to go out and form clubs, so that the years 1847 to 1877 are marked by avalanches of local associations all over the country. These clubs performed some particularly German functions, quite apart from creating an environment where the popular habits of drinking beer and singing could flourish. They proved to be the perfect vehicle for two German character traits which at first appear mutually exclusive: gregariousness and suspiciousness. One could be fostered with club members, the other marshalled against those who were not.

They also satisfied the need for a sense of belonging, which was important when you consider that Germans in the first half of the 19th century had little or no picture of what today we would call 'a nation'. In addition, a club allows Germans to organise things and keep them tidy, something we tend to do with gusto. Finally, to leave the realm of clichés, clubs played an explicitly political role for the German middle classes. For them it was a great thing to be allowed to form a club in the first place. Freedom of association was seen as a cornerstone of legal equality, something they had fought long and hard to achieve.

The clubs we are talking about all worked under the same principle. Members of the local petty bourgeoisie came together to provide their community with an opportunity to steel the human body and while the time away, be it through *Turnen*, running, swimming or whatever else seemed feasible. They drew up statutes in which they went on at length about the pureness of their intentions, the importance of physical education for young people and the undeniable greatness of whichever Kaiser, King or Prince was ruling them, until they got down to business.

Their club was open to everybody willing to pay a small fee. This money bought him or her access to all facilities and the right to elect the all-important officials: the president, the secretary, the treasurer and the other worthies. Then this organisation would apply for inclusion in the official club register at the county court. This stamp of approval usually meant the club had the right to use municipally owned buildings and playing fields (which helps to explain why for a long time very few German football clubs owned their own grounds) – and the not inconsiderable right to obtain tax relief.

Not all of these original gymnastics associations are still recognisable when you look at today's German football league tables. In the Bundesliga, only VfL Bochum leaps out, because this club lists 1848 as its year of foundation, and perhaps TSG

Hoffenheim 1899 (a gymnastics-only club until 1926). But in one way or another, all of the most famous German football clubs have a connection to these ossified and peculiarly Teutonic organisations. Some are still a part of them, others the product of a hostile split. All of them, however, were cast in the same mould: public, for the common good, non-profit making. And that includes Bayern Munich.

The task of pinpointing the date when football came to Germany has weakened many a stout heart. Contrary to popular belief, the game reached these shores fairly early. So early, in fact, that at the time even the English had not properly defined the various codes of football. Many of the earliest accounts we have of 'football' on German playing fields actually refer to something that would look more like rugby to the modern eye.

This ambiguity persisted for quite a while. In 1878, the German Football Club of Hannover was formed, an organisation which is often bestowed with the posthumous title 'first ever football club in Germany'. What they were playing, though, was rugby football. Even 22 years later this confusion of terms was still widespread. On May 4, 1900, 18 young men from Franconia came together to found a club that would become one of the most legendary in German football history, collecting more national championships than anybody else until Bayern Munich finally equalled the record in 1986. Those youngsters, however, initially set out to play with an oval ball – and did so for the first 14 months of the club's existence. And yet, from the beginning, it was called 1. FC Nürnberg – the first football club in Nuremberg.

In the late 19th century the ties between England and Germany were close, not least thanks to the marriage of Queen Victoria to Duke Albert of Saxe-Coburg and Gotha. There were

English schools in almost every larger German city for the sons of the wealthy, but there were also many workers from England, dealers and craftsmen plying their trades in the Hanseatic towns and elsewhere. These people, especially the students, brought the game that would split into rugby and football to Germany in the middle of the 19th century. The first known accounts mention a private school in Heidelberg and then, around 1865, the cities of Neuwied on the Rhine and Bad Cannstatt near Stuttgart. The first had an English boarding school, the second, a spa town, attracted many overseas tourists.

One of them was William Cail, who would later become president of England's Rugby Football Union. 'The youth of Stuttgart,' Cail noted, 'derived great pleasure from the ballgames.' That certainly must have held true for at least one boy in Neuwied. Ferdinand Hueppe, born in 1852, was so intrigued by what the English did on the fields of his home town that he followed the development of their game over the next four decades, finally becoming in 1900 the first president of the *Deutscher Fussball Bund* (DFB), the German Football Association.

In 1872, the first German club explicity devoted to rugby football saw the light of day in Heidelberg (the other sport the members practised was rowing). The story of association football in Germany began two years later, in 1874. In March, a club was founded by Englishmen living in Dresden – the Dresden English Football Club, which would remain undefeated for almost exactly two decades (and not only because opponents were few and far between). And six months later, on September 29, 1874, Germans enter the picture thanks to a leather ball casually thrown to the ground.

It lands among a group of grammar school pupils in Braunschweig, who have absolutely no idea of what to do with it. The man who threw the ball is called August Hermann. He and his friend Konrad Koch are teachers at the school in question.

Both are men who are willing to try something new, especially if it keeps their charges interested. They have heard about this new game on the other side of the channel, and Hermann has ordered a football from England simply to try it out. (What he got sent was actually a rugby football, but in all likelihood Hermann didn't know the difference.) He has no masterplan, in fact he is only familiar with the most basic of rules, and the bustle he causes is chaotic to say the least.

Still, Hermann's act is noteworthy. First, because it marks the first recorded instance of the use of a football in Germany that involved no Englishmen at all. His 'throw-in' is thus regarded, according to the great German football historian and author Hans Dieter Baroth, 'as the moment when football in Germany was born'. Second, this experiment must have made a deep impression on Hermann's sidekick Konrad Koch. He would soon be recognised as one of the two main pioneers of German football.

A year later, in 1875, Koch published the first German-language version of football rules. He also set up what was later called the first club, though it was more like a student association comprised of about 60 pupils – and it played a game that was still very much like rugby. It wasn't until about 1882 that Koch's pupils stopped carrying the ball entirely. The second edition of his rules, published in 1885, explicitly differentiated between rugby and 'association football' rules. A year later, in 1886, Koch's school – the *Martino-Katharineum Gymnasium* – played a grammer school from Göttingen, probably the first away game in German football history.

We are still years away from the first organised football games in Germany but, with hindsight, a pattern was already emerging. The people interested in the new English sport were generally well-off schoolboys. They had the time and the facilities to try something new and they were young enough to get away with unruly behaviour. In an age dominated by Prussian ideals of discipline and order, English ball games were viewed with disdain. That is precisely what fascinated rebellious adolescents bored brainless by the stifling rigours of gymnastic drills. Often it took only a slight impetus to arouse their enthusiasm, an impetus provided by a handful of progressive men like Koch. (Who also invented a precursor of team handball. His colleague August Hermann would introduce basketball to Germany many years later.)

The first true German football club still in existence today is FC Germania Berlin, founded on April 15, 1888, by four teenage brothers. (The name 'Germania' would prove to be annoyingly popular.) Six weeks later, a Hamburger FC comes into existence. It, too, is still with us, in a way. About a year later, in June 1889, Viktoria Berlin was founded, already the fourth club in the capital and one that would soon become famous. (Not least because it managed to break the winning streak of the Dresden English Football Club in March 1894.)

It can be an arduous task to trace the life of a German football club. In England most of the famous clubs were formed and named, and then that was that for the next hundred years or more. It has never been so easy in Germany, despite our supposed love of discipline and order. Take for instance the famous Hamburg club, the Hamburger Sportverein. If you consult a modern football reference book, you will find the club's date of birth given as September 29, 1887. This would make it the oldest club in the country, but the reality is otherwise.

What happened was this. In 1919, three Hamburg clubs severely weakened by the First World War came together to join forces under the name HSV. They were FC Falke (founded in 1906), the above-mentioned Hamburger FC and the Sports-Club Germania (again) of 1887. With a single stroke of the pen the latter's year of foundation was adopted for the new entity. But on what grounds? While it's true that Hamburg's Germania fielded a strong football team during the 1890s, the club was originally an athletics association that didn't even play football until 1891, when six Englishmen joined the runners and immediately demanded a ball. The explanation HSV offer for insisting on the year 1887 is that the club, as already noted, is not limited to football: they also harbour track-and-field athletes and thus they can somehow trace their history to Germania's sportsmen of 1887. It also sounds better.

Here is an even more bizarre case. It's complicated, but it typifies early German football history. In the summer of 1894 (a good year for club formations), amateur actors founded the Football Club Germania (yes!) in Frankfurt. Five years later, a few of Germania's members walked out in protest over something or other and created their own club, Victoria Frankfurt. A couple of weeks later there was another new kid on the block, Kickers Frankfurt, whose ranks were swelled early on when more disgruntled Germanians deserted. In 1911, Kickers and Victoria merged into FV Frankfurt. Nine years on, the ancient gymnastics organisation TG Frankfurt 1861 joined FV Frankfurt to form yet another new amalgamation, the TSG Eintracht Frankfurt of – quick, guess! – 1861. (In fairness, however, Eintracht Frankfurt today list their birthdate more honestly as March 8, 1899 – the day Victoria Frankfurt were founded.)

The oldest of the truly well-known clubs who have not resorted to such artificial means of elongating their history is Hertha BSC Berlin, formed on July 25, 1892. Until the 1920s, however, Hertha played only a minor role, not only in German football in general but even in Berlin itself. The reason for this is that Berlin was the undisputed centre of football in this country from roughly 1888 (when, as mentioned, FC Germania Berlin were founded) to about 1909, and the city had so many good sides that Hertha were only small fish in a large pond.

Berlin led the way not just because of its rapid growth since being made the capital of the young nation in 1871. There was also a very practical aspect. The nascent footballers had to overcome many obstacles: there were no balls and no boots, and they faced considerable harassment from the public. Yet the most pressing problem was to find a place to play. There were few sports fields in Germany, and most of these were controlled by the gymnasts, who refused to share them with the kicking traitors to the Fatherland (that's not a joke – footballers were really described and treated as such). The gymnasts also had access to most of the public parks, and they used their clout to persuade the authorities to drive away footballers. That left military parade grounds, which were spacious, unused on Sundays and less bumpy than open meadows. Berlin, with its Prussian heritage, had many of them and that's where a lot of footballers went to play.

The second island of football in an ocean of gymnastics was the Bremen-Hamburg area, where Konrad Koch spread the gospel, laying down the first rules and encouraging youngsters. The third was Stuttgart and by the beginning of the 1890s the game had spread further south, to the region of Baden and the city of Karlsruhe. The man almost solely responsible for making Karlsruhe into the football power that would one day overtake Berlin was Germany's other pioneering giant, Walther Bensemann.

Bensemann was born in Berlin in 1873, one year before Hermann and Koch introduced their football to Braunschweig. He was educated in Switzerland, where he became so fascinated by the English game that he formed a club in Montreux in 1887, aged 14. He changed schools and moved to Karlsruhe, taking the game with him. That year, 1889, he founded something called the International Football Club, the first in the southern part of Germany that played according to association rules. The members were German schoolboys and more than a dozen Englishmen living in the area.

Bensemann was not a good player, even by the standards of the time. He was short-sighted and definitely on the portly side ('the Man-Mountain', the English called him), but he was an incredibly active missionary. In 1891, he broke with the International Football-Club and started FV Karlsruhe (a future national champion). Two years later, he founded a club in Strasbourg. And in 1899 alone, he first urged five Mannheim clubs to found a city association, which later led to the formation of VfR Mannheim, German champions of 1949. Five months later he pulled off a startling coup by bringing a representative team of English professionals to Germany to play four games against local combined teams.

Bensemann loved England and must have spoken the language exceedingly well even as a young man. In 1901, he moved to Britain to teach French and German at public schools in, among other places, Staffordshire, Bedford and Liverpool. During what was supposed to be a brief stay home, in the summer of 1914, war broke out – and Bensemann couldn't go back to England. His travels had deepened his disdain for nationalism ('The place where a man is born is as unimportant as the place where he dies,' he wrote) and Prussian small-mindedness.

His fellow pioneer Konrad Koch became so exasperated with the public calling his beloved game 'un-German' that he published a list of German football expressions in 1903. So it was almost 120 years ago that people first began to refer to a forward as *Stürmer* and a goal as *Tor*. Until then, football devotees had simply used the English words, and some in the German-speaking world still do – while Germans talk of the *Eckball*, the Swiss and Austrians still refer to it as a corner.

Bensemann never had time for such nit-picking. There was one British expression he was particularly fond of. In 1893, he started a short-lived club modelled after Corinthian FC which he called Kickers Karlsruhe. And shortly before the turn of the century, he co-founded Kickers Frankfurt (who, one might remember, are today Eintracht Frankfurt). Finally, in 1920, he founded a football paper and named it with the same English term. Bensemann, whose father was Jewish, went into exile when the Nazis took over and died in Switzerland in 1934. However, his *kicker* magazine (these days never with a capital letter) is still with us.

Besides Berlin, Stuttgart and Karlsruhe, football had also reached Leipzig by the beginning of the 1890s. In the first year of that decade, a handful of young sportsmen discovered the game, and since they would one day be able to call themselves the first football champions of Germany, it seems appropriate to follow their history for a moment. These young men liked athletics and as good underlings of the Kaiser they were members of a gymnastics club which allowed a little running and a bit of football on the side, the Allgemeine Turnverein (General Gymnastics Club) Leipzig of 1845. In 1893, no fewer than four distinct football clubs came into existence in the city, one of them, the Leipzig Ball-Club, initiated by three Englishmen, and another one known as the 'Sports Fraternity'.

The kicking gymnasts of the Allgemeine Turnverein stayed with their parent organisation, though life there was not easy. To say they had to beg the club's officials to be allowed to play is not an exaggeration. The *Turner* ordered the footballers to attend regular gymnastic drills and only then – maybe – did they get the go-ahead to use the club's facilities for football. But that was only the bureaucratic aspect of it. Much worse was that the footballers slowly became lepers at their own club. Other members either ridiculed them or suspected them of unpatriotic, subversive activities, even though German football was still the exclusive domain of reasonably affluent, conservative middle-class people and students. But this was the world of the reactionary, xenophobic *Turner*.

There was only one solution. In December 1895, the footballers of the Allgemeine Turnverein played the English-dominated Leipzig Ball-Club. Something about this contest must have convinced them it was time to become independent. Less than six months later, on May 13, 1896, they withdrew from the gymnastics club and formed VfB Leipzig. (They later incorporated the 'Sports Fraternity', which is why the club's official year of birth is now given as 1893.) It was a story happening all over the German empire at the turn of the century. In Munich, the football-playing members of the MTV (Men's Gymnastics Club) of 1879 asked the club to register the football division with the recently formed South German Football Association, but the MTV balked and stalled. On February 27, 1900, the football aficionados (among them the well-known German-born British sculptor Benno Elkan, who would flee Germany in 1933) decided they had had enough and walked out on the MTV. Their own club was christened Bayern München FC.

Life outside the haven of the gymnastics clubs was less suffocating, but not much easier. First, there were the pitches. Werder Bremen, formed in 1899, played on a cow pasture – alongside the cattle. The football club of Frankenthal used a rubbish dump. Meidericher SV (later MSV Duisburg), formed in 1902 when students convinced footballing gymnasts to leave their parent club, turned out near a cemetery, and more than once play had to be stopped to allow coffins to be carried across the field. In Cologne, a shepherd called the police because the local football club used his grazing land, thereby ruining the grass.

Sheep had already halted football's progress in Stuttgart in 1895, where footballers frightened the poor beasts so much that the authorities threatened to punish them. The sheep would continue to be a problem. A chronicle of football in Mannheim says of 1901: 'The parade ground was leased to a sheep farmer, and as football grew he became more and more unpleasant. The threat of a ban hovered over the clubs, especially since the military also complained about their discarded water bottles. Much pleading was required until the football players were at least tolerated on the premises.'

In 1899, Preussen Berlin FC became the first club to boast a permanent ground of its own, with fences and a wooden stand. (Naturally, it was a Briton who owned the site and built the ground.) The rest of the country, however, usually had to make do with removable goalposts which would be carried from one part of town to the next for games or training. At Germania Berlin, they even laid down exact rules as to which player was responsible for which part of the equipment: 'The left-winger takes the corner flags for the left side. The right-half takes the corner flags for the right side. The goalkeeper carries the ball and the gimlet.' Prussians.

Equipment, clearly, was the second big problem. One of the founders of FC Cannstatt, the American-born Philipp Heineken, remembers of the early 1890s: 'We didn't own an air pump, so those members with powerful lungs had to attend to the inflation of the ball.' In 1899, some of the people who would later become known as VfL Osnabrück played with bicycle tubes. And the founders of Germania Frankfurt first ran about barefoot.

The third, and by far the gravest, problem was that football remained an underground game, still suspect in the eyes of many Germans. The gymnasts referred to it as 'the English disease' and in 1895 the educationalist Otto Heinrich Jaeger wrote: 'If one wants to give expression to feelings of disdain, one kicks the thing which he hates. We kick a vicious dog, and it is because this dog-kick plays such a huge role in football that I loathe the game, also because of the pitiful, crouching stance in which the players chase the ball.' Many schools, especially in western

Germany, forbade students to participate in football games, even in their spare time. And in 1898, the gymnast and teacher Karl Planck published a diatribe against, using his vernacular, the 'foot-louts': 'We permit our-selves to regard this anal [sic] English sport as not just nasty but absurd, ugly and perverted.'

It is true that the parochialism of people like Jaeger and Planck may be viewed as typically German. But such stereotyping is itself narrow-minded. After all, there were other Germans, too. When Planck put his poison pen to paper, a game between Viktoria Berlin and Germania Hamburg had already attracted 5,000 spectators, and there were other signs that the new game was here to stay.

Competitive matches for regional or citywide championships began in 1891, of course in Berlin. The new 'German Football and Cricket Association of Berlin' organised these fixtures, and after Viktoria Berlin 89 had won two of the first three titles, the Association felt it would help the game's development to invite a team from the south to a final for the 'national championship'. They chose 1. FC Hanau 93, but Hanau's players couldn't afford the trip to the capital. Logically, therefore, Viktoria declared themselves German champions of 1894. (Hanau were finally ready 113 years later. In the summer of 2007, the club asked Viktoria to 'settle the matter once and for all in the interest of sport' and challenged them to a two-legged final. Viktoria won 3-0 in Hanau and drew 1-1 at home.)

Also in 1894, eight clubs from the Hamburg area formed an association and began a league programme. The same happened in Leipzig in 1897, and in October of that year footballers from Karlsruhe founded the first association reaching beyond city limits. It was called the South German Football Association and had members in six different towns and cities.

The football of these early German teams was rudimentary, but they were willing to learn from the masters. In 1896, a team from

Duisburg went to England to play four games. They returned after failing to score a goal and conceding plenty. Two years later, a member of Preussen Berlin stayed in England for business reasons and spent most of his time analysing the professionals' style of play. He urged his club to trap balls instead of 'speeding them across the field in high arcs'. His comrades heeded the advice: Preussen did away with the long ball, began developing a passing game – and won the championship of Berlin.

Then there was the miracle pulled off by Walther Bensemann in 1899, the historic first appearance of professional English football players (supported by selected amateurs) on German soil. These rugged men, idolised beyond belief by the German pioneers, played a combined Berlin XI, winning 13-2 and 10-2. Then they moved on to Prague and beat a team of Austrian and German players 8-0. Their last stop was Karlsruhe, where they escaped with a 7-0 victory. (A Berlin correspondent suspected that the results got better from a German viewpoint mainly because 'most of the Britons were somewhat exhausted' by the heavy drinking bouts that followed each game.)

Football may still have been an outcast in the Kaiser's empire, but those few who already believed in the game treated their English guests like royalty. They were taken by horse-drawn carriages from the railway station to the Hotel Monopol in Berlin. As the professionals entered the hall, a band struck up *God Save the Queen*, and Bensemann gave a heart-warming speech in both languages.

The first of these encounters marked, according to the late Dr Heiner Gillmeister of the University of Bonn, 'the first international match ever played by an English representative team outside the British Isles, and the first truly European one into the bargain'. Of the football itself, a chronicle of the Berlin game says: 'One marvelled at the peerless Bassett on the right wing, the legendary defender from Aston Villa, Crabtree, and Bach from Sunderland, the tall centre-half Stanley Briggs, Forman on the left wing, the small Holt and the splendid Chadwick. These encounters completely reversed our views of the game, as one naturally attempted to do like the masters and keep the ball on the ground.'

Germans attempted to do like the masters off the pitch, too. On January 28, 1900, envoys of 86 clubs came together in Leipzig, among them Walther Bensemann, representing Mannheim, and Ferdinand Hueppe, representing Prague. (Prague was the capital of Bohemia, then part of the Austro-Hungarian empire, but it had a large German population and had had a German club, DFC Prag, since 1892.) This collection of delegates formed the *Deutscher Fussball Bund*. Hueppe, at 47 the oldest person present, was elected president. The official set of rules, published a few months later, mentioned that 'no player is allowed to lie down to rest' during the course of a match.

The DFB itself, even though it wasn't much more than a word on a piece of paper at first, did not rest until the game had become respectable. In March 1901, Preussen Berlin became the first German side to beat a team from England, winning 8-3 against an amateur team contemporary sources referred to as 'Surrey Wanderers' (not the famous Wanderers FC, it would seem, as they had been dissolved at this point). Later that year, a combined team of Berlin footballers was sent to England to meet a handful of professional clubs. They lost 5-1 to Southampton and 6-2 to Aston Villa. Encouraging results, considering the circumstances. A year later the DFB decided it was time to get serious. The Association declared that 1903 would see the first official games for the national championship of Germany.

2

NAMING RITES

SPVGG AND OTHER MYSTERIES

HERE ARE TWO TYPICAL German club names in their full, official glory:

FC Bayern München 1900 e.V.
BV Borussia Dortmund 09 e.V.

As you can see, both are made up of five elements. Other names have less, some even more. The order in which they appear is rather arbitrary, but knowing roughly what each element stands for will enable you to decode similar names – and will also tell you more about the club in question than you probably thought was there.

Beginning at the end, the innocuous abbreviation 'e.V.' is a mere technicality, meaning 'registered club'. Any club playing in an organised league in Germany has to be officially recognised as a public, non-profit making, sporting society, so adding those two letters was rather superfluous. Indeed, many clubs didn't use them in their letterheads, though Bayern Munich even carried them in their club badge until 2000. Why Bayern eventually deleted them will be covered in more detail in the chapter that deals with the drastic changes German football underwent towards the end of the 20th century. (At which point you will also encounter some of the catchphrases that have become famous outside of Germany lately, for instance '50+1 rule' and 'fan ownership'. Their meaning and implications become much clearer when you know how we got there.)

Preceding 'e.V.' is usually the date of the club's formation, an often misleading piece of information, as we have seen. (Bayern and Dortmund, however, were indeed founded in 1900 and 1909, respectively.) Making the foundation date a part of the club's name – another legacy of the gymnastics associations – is always a matter of great pride. Bayer Leverkusen, for instance, whose full name is TSV Bayer 04 Leverkusen, were known only as Bayer Leverkusen or even only as Bayer throughout the 1980s and most of the 1990s. But then they began referring to themselves as 'Bayer 04' and it stuck.

That was a calculated decision. For a long time, Leverkusen were considered an oddity because they are one of the very few German clubs directly connected to a commercial enterprise. The forerunner of today's club came into being in 1903, when 170 employees of the chemical company founded by Friedrich Bayer signed a petition asking Bayer's directors to allow the workforce to take part in organised gymnastic activities. The company gave the green light and even promised to support the venture. The following year TuS Leverkusen saw the light of day, evolving in a roundabout way into today's TSV Bayer 04.

The fact that the club was backed by a private concern rendered them a bit dubious in the eyes of traditionalists. Indeed, the club's name alone raised eyebrows. Who ever heard of fans urging their team on by chanting the name of a company? And so Leverkusen have decided to challenge this image by pointing out that the club actually has a long (if undistinguished) history. And they are certainly aware of the similarities between 'Bayer 04' and 'Schalke 04', the latter being a synonym for tradition in Germany.

There are exceptions, of course, clubs which do not officially list their birthdates. Some of them are simply rather recent arrivals and prefer to conceal that, like VfL Wolfsburg (founded in 1945) or Hansa Rostock (1965). And then, as always, there is Bayern. They could use a boost in the tradition department, because many German fans still regard Bayern as arrivistes, claiming that Munich 1860 are a much more tradition-laden club. That is simply not true. Bayern are only one year younger than the football division of Munich 1860, and they won a championship long before their rivals did – in 1932. Still, they steadfastly refuse to play this trump card. As mentioned, their club badge used to say 'e.V.', but it never said '1900'. I can only explain this by presuming that they just love to be the bad guys. Sceptics are urged to read later chapters.

In front of the year of formation, you will usually find the name of the city the club represents. That poses no problem when you are dealing with Munich or Dortmund, but it becomes a trickier affair when you encounter teams representing districts, such as FC St Pauli 1910 (a part of Hamburg), FC Schalke 04 (Gelsenkirchen), SG Wattenscheid 09 (Bochum) or KFC Uerdingen (Krefeld). Each of these four, and many more like them, has its own unique story, but of course this is hardly an exclusively German phenomenon. As a kid, I always wondered why I couldn't find the city of West Ham on a map, let alone Aston.

Schalke are officially called FC Gelsenkirchen-Schalke, which goes back to a time when Gelsenkirchen pleaded with the club to alter its name to lend more prestige to the city. Schalke relented, but even though they have long since become the club of all Gelsenkirchen, they never refer to themselves by that name.

Wattenscheid 09, now fallen on hard times but once a mainstay in the top two divisions, were formed when their locality was still a village, distinct from Bochum. It was later incorporated into the city, a hostile act that people from Wattenscheid still attempt to erase from their memory. It helps that their club was never called anything other than just Wattenscheid.

The next element in German club names (still counting from the rear) is the often flowery expression which many teams prefer to be known as. The founders of the earliest German football organisations were often middle-class students at some of the more liberal educational establishments, mostly secondary schools with a bias towards Latin and Greek, and the people growing up in such an environment consequently had a taste for fancy-sounding names of Roman origin.

Great favourites with those founders were names carrying a patriotic connotation, because in those days footballers would do everything they could to convince the world of their loyalty to the Kaiser. Hence the popularity of Germania, Alemannia and even Teutonia. It was also deemed fitting to express solidarity with your local region or county. That gave us Westfalia Herne, Preussen (Prussia) Münster, Schwaben (Swabia) Augsburg, Sachsen (Saxony) Leipzig, Bayern (Bavaria) Munich and a host of others. A special favourite was Borussia, because that term combined education with local patriotism: Borussia is neo-Latin for Prussia. (Not Latin, as you sometimes read. Obviously, there was no such thing as Prussia when Latin ceased to exist as a spoken language.) Such patriotic names, it must be noted, do not mean that the clubs in question were made up of political nationalists. For instance, Germania Hamburg's team in 1904 included three Dutchmen, a Spaniard, an Austrian, two Englishmen and only four Germans.

Other names of Roman origin include Fortuna and Viktoria (the goddesses of fate and victory, respectively), Concordia (a symbol for harmony) and Britannia. The latter expression was widespread during the last century to honour the inventors of the game, and many larger cities had at least one club bearing this name. Most of them hurried to change it at the onset of the First World War.

These slightly pretentious names, however, were not always chosen by cultured men engaged in erudite conversations. The founders of the Dortmund club picked Borussia because their inaugural meeting took place in a pub where a large enamel plate advertised the products of the Borussia Brewery. And the people who formed Fortuna Düsseldorf were, recent research indicates, borrowing the name from a local chemist's shop.

Those who were short on imagination simply decided to name their club after their colours: Rot-Weiss, Schwarz-Weiss or Blau-Weiss, say. (Red-and-white, black-and-white, blue-and-white.) Still others came up with more individual solutions. The founders of Hertha Berlin borrowed the name of a pleasure steamer on which they had spent a leisurely afternoon. The Bremen club played on a meadow known as the City-Werder, for Werder is an old Germanic term for any large piece of land next to a river.

That should leave only a few names unexplained you may have come across, for instance: Eintracht Frankfurt or Braunschweig, Hansa Rostock, Energie Cottbus, Dynamo Dresden, Erzgebirge Aue and Arminia Bielefeld. Oh, and Greuther Fürth. Of these, Eintracht is German for 'harmony', while Hansa refers to Rostock's former place in the medieval Hanseatic League of port cities. Energie and Dynamo mean what you think they mean and have their roots in the eastern bloc's preference for charming sobriquets which refer to the particular industry or branch of government associated with a club. (More about that in a later chapter.)

Erzgebirge translates as Ore Mountains and refers to the club's location. Arminia is a bow to the warrior Arminius, who in AD 9 annihilated three Roman legions, leading the Roman historian Tacitus to call him 'the liberator of Germania'. The site of the slaughter was a forest near Bielefeld. Finally, the word Greuther that precedes Fürth is just an idiosyncratic bow to the fact that this club is the result of a merger between the famous Fürth team you will soon meet with a side from Vestenbergsgreuth, a hamlet 50 minutes down the road.

No, I have not forgotten the club in the Bundesliga that insists on being called (and spelled) *RasenBallsport*. However, this is an entire story in itself we'll have to come back to, so let's now move on to the confusing mass of characters you often stumble over at the front of the name of a German football club, the unwieldy 'VfL', 'TuS' and so on. Usually, they are shorthand for what it is the club exactly does. They may look like ingenious CIA codes, but in fact they are fairly easy to decipher. After all, there are only so many different sports you can perform.

Thankfully, most Germans call a club a Club (the correct spelling would be with a 'K', but you seldom find that). The German word for a club is *Verein*, or sometimes *Union*. So whenever you find the letters 'C', 'K', 'V' or 'U', you know you are dealing with a club. More rarely you might see a 'G' for *Gemeinschaft* (group or community), as in TSG Hoffenheim.

So, what sort of club? The other letters will tell you. 'S' is as general as it can get – it simply means *Sport*, or sometimes *Spiele* (games). 'T' has already been touched upon – it stands for *Turnen*, gymnastics. And the first two mysterious names have been decoded right there. The TSV Munich of 1860 or the TSG Hoffenheim are 'clubs for gymnastics and sports'.

An 'L' in a name often stands for *Leibesübungen* (physical exercises), while a 'B' either denotes *Bewegungsspiele* (physical games) or *Ballspiele* (ball games). Thus the BV Borussia 09

Dortmund is a club for ball games. Sometimes you'll also notice small letters inserted into such abbreviations, normally an 'f' or a 'u'. The first simply means 'for', the second 'and'. The VfB Stuttgart is 'a club for physical games'. The VfL Bochum is 'a club for physical exercises'. In other words, more or less the same thing. Possibly the most baffling abbreviation is FSV – *Fussball-und Sportverein* (as if football isn't a sport). The ugliest is is 'SpVgg', not very short for *Spielvereinigung* or 'playing union'.

That should not leave too many inexplicable names you might have read somewhere, sometime. MSV Duisburg are a 'sports club from Meiderich', the district of Duisburg where the club has its home. SSV Reutlingen and SSV Ulm burden their name with a second 'S' to make it clear you are facing people who know how to swim, too. KFC Uerdingen are a 'football club from Krefeld', based in the suburb Uerdingen. And if you see an 'R', as in VfR Aalen, it will tell you that such a club plays games on grass, as it stands for *Rasenspiele*. I kid you not.

Finally, there is the club which came into being in 1902 as the swish Berlin Society for Tennis and Ping-Pong Borussia. The name was shortened to Tennis Borussia Berlin when the worthy gentlemen gave up ping-pong and decided to concentrate on football. That was in 1903, the year Germany crowned its first national football champions.

3

THE CLUB, 1918–30

ALL ROADS LEAD TO NUREMBERG

THERE'S A FOOTBALL TEAM waiting for a train, and it might just be the best team in the country. The train leaves, the players are not on it, and they will never know what might have been. That team was FV Karlsruhe in 1903, champions of the South German FA for three years running and a club that beat anyone who crossed their path. They had just defeated Amsterdam and VfB Leipzig in friendlies. A year earlier they had made fools of DFC Prag, winning 9-0. On this day they were meant to be playing Prague again, in what later generations would call the semi-final of the first national German football championship.

Actually, the simple term 'semi-final' doesn't do justice to the confusing set-up. Six teams survived the qualifying contests of their respective regional associations and were supposed to meet in knockout rounds to decide who would become the inaugural title-holders. Though six is not an ideal number for a quarter-final, matters were made worse by the discrepancies between the individual associations. Britannia Berlin and FV Karlsruhe, who came out on top of the Berlin and South German qualifiers respectively, had overcome formidable opposition, while Prague were technically members of the Austrian FA (!) but were admitted on past merits.

Luckily for the DFB, the quarter-final between Karlsruhe and Prague was difficult to stage, because neither wanted to play the game at the other's ground. And so the DFB simply allowed both clubs into the semi-final (which elegantly solved the six-team problem). The match was to be staged at a neutral ground, in Leipzig. That is why the members of FV Karlsruhe had already gathered in their clubhouse, suitcases packed for the train journey, when a telegram arrived. Captain Hans Ruzek read it and said: 'You can unpack.' According to most sources, the dispatch simply read: 'Match in Leipzig postponed. FA.'

Such cock-ups were not uncommon in those early days. (The 1903 final would be delayed by 45 minutes because the only ball to be found on the premises was damaged beyond repair.) So the players of FV Karlsruhe went home to wait and see what would happen. Meanwhile, the players of DFC Prag were waiting, too – in Leipzig, for their opponents. When Karlsruhe didn't show up, the DFB declared Prague the winners and even spared them the trials and tribulations of a semi-final. Well, someone had to go straight to the final, since three teams are not easily accommodated in semis. To this day, people in Karlsruhe are trying to find out who sent that false and fateful telegram. (The most common theory puts DFB president Ferdinand Hueppe at the centre of the conspiracy. He was also Prague's chairman.)

The either lucky or cunning German Bohemians of Prague faced VfB Leipzig in the final, held at a parade ground in Hamburg on May 31, 1903. The playing field was defined by ropes, and people went around with plates, asking the spectators for donations. They collected 473 Reichsmarks. It seems likely that it was this sum that has led some researchers to claim there were only 500 people in attendance, but the official figure is still

2,000. Not many newspapers covered the game, and those that did printed only brief accounts, two days after the event. A piece which appeared in a Berlin daily used the English words 'goal', 'halftime' and 'score' to describe what happened, noting that 'VfB Leipzig secured the title of championship club of Germany with a lovely victory of seven goals to two over the German Football Club Prague'.

The Leipzig club received a statue slightly less than the height of a small boy, made of zinc and copper, portraying the Roman goddess of victory. The Victoria, as this trophy would come to be known, seemed chaste enough: she was clad in a long, falling robe, her gaze contemplative rather than inviting. But she did bare one shoulder, and a year later it turned out to be a cold one.

Because there were no German champions in 1904. Again mighty FV Karlsruhe were dealt a cruel blow when the DFB ordered them to play their quarter-final against Britannia Berlin in Berlin, even though the rules stipulated neutral grounds. Karlsruhe lost 6-1. Britannia went on to beat Germania Hamburg in the semis and were preparing for the final against VfB Leipzig, when FV Karlsruhe at long last filed a protest with the DFB. Less than five hours before the scheduled kick-off, the officials cancelled the final. This led to further protests, and finally the DFB just called the whole thing off.

Things could only get better in 1905, and they did – just. VfB Leipzig again qualified for the knockout rounds, but the club didn't have the funds to send the players across the country and thus bowed out. Schlesien (Silesia) Breslau got through the first round, beating Alemannia Cottbus 5-1, but then couldn't make the trip for the semi-final to meet FV Karlsruhe. Poetic justice at last? No. Karlsruhe lost the deciding game to Union Berlin (not the same club as today's Bundesliga team 1. FC Union Berlin), although the team from the capital benched its regular goalkeeper because he'd had one too many on the evening before the game.

The score was 2-0 and the attendance figure was 3,500, which would prove to be the biggest crowd for a final until 1910.

Obviously, German football was still fighting for survival in 1905. Organisational problems were manifold, the public largely apathetic and the authorities always suspicious. And yet, in retrospect, things took a turn for the better that year. I regret to say this, but again it all had to do with the military.

On April 29, 1905, it was Germania Berlin's turn to receive a telegram. It said: 'His Imperial Highness the Crown Prince will arrive at 5.30 today for the football competition.' Those words sounded a lot more suspect than the ones delivered to FV Karlsruhe two years earlier, but this time around the telegram was genuine. The Kaiser's son, Crown Prince Wilhelm, did indeed show up to watch Germania beat an English amateur side 3-2, and he even presented the winners with a silver cup.

'After this display of interest on the part of the Prince,' noted a club representative, 'even the highest military circles suddenly took notice of the sport.' Dietrich Schulze-Marmeling, Germany's premier researcher of football's social history, says Wilhelm's visit – and the fact that his brother played football – brought the game 'general social acceptance' and made it popular with the army and especially the navy.

And yet few could have predicted in 1905 that the nation would go football crazy within one generation. And no one had any idea that the West German Playing Association, formed as the Rhineland Playing Association in 1898 but still exceptionally weak, would soon rise to become a major force, battling the South German FA for supremacy both on the playing fields and at negotiating tables. The main reason behind both developments was that football began to appeal to the working man.

The evolution of football in Germany closely mirrored the journey of the game in England. In both countries, the sport was initially played and ruled by middle-class students and educated gentlemen flying the lilywhite banner of amateurism. Then, roughly 20 years after the formation of a national FA, workers took to the game and quickly made it their own, and a further ten years on came demands for the legalisation of professionalism.

The difference between the two countries was that this process unwound some 40 years later in Germany. Two factors determined this delay. First, the industrial revolution gathered steam later. In 1830, four out of five Germans were still working on the land, and it wasn't until the 1850s that machines truly changed the social fabric of the country. Second, working-class politics in Germany took a more militant form than in Britain, striking terror into the hearts of the rulers and fostering paranoia in their minds at the spectre of communism.

When German workers began to show signs of developing a class consciousness by establishing the General Workers' Club in 1863, the Social Democratic Workers' Party in 1869, and amalgamating those into the Socialist Workers' Party of Germany in 1875, the Kaiser and his Imperial Chancellor Otto von Bismarck smelled revolution. In October 1878, Bismarck enacted the so-called 'Socialists Law', which made left-wing parties and unions illegal. The law survived until 1890, and while it could only slow but not stop the communal spirit within the proletariat, it created a sharp-edged rift between the middle and the working class.

Earlier in this book, I said that the original German gymnastics clubs were 'open to everybody willing to pay a small fee'. That was not strictly true. Because while those bourgeois organisations had no statutes prohibiting workers from joining, they were closed societies nonetheless. Usually they would find a way of discouraging any enterprising person they didn't deem worthy from approaching them. But that was rarely necessary. Most workers had little time for elaborate socialising in clubs and no use for gymnastic drills.

All that would change for good between 1918 and 1923 with the gradual establishment of the eight-hour day. By that time, football had already made impressive inroads into the lives of working-class people. Probably the first German football club founded by workers was Lipsia Leipzig in 1893 (Lipsia is Latin for Leipzig). The men who brought Lipsia into being were artisan apprentices. According to the chronicle of their regional FA, they formed their own club 'because private physical exercises were only possible in gymnastics associations, and then only indoors and under the constraint of stringent discipline'.

But it was the Ruhr area in western Germany, loosely defined as the collection of cities between Oberhausen and Dortmund, that would prove to be the birthplace of football as the working man's game. This region was a rural hinterland, forgotten by everyone, until the machine age. Machines lived on coal and steel, and the Ruhr could produce those in abundance. In 1850, there were only 13,000 miners working in this relatively large area, and Schalke was a village of 400 inhabitants. Only two decades later, well over 80,000 people were ruining their health in the underground darkness. By the start of the 1890s, ever more human labour was in demand, resulting in mass migration from the east. Families fled the impoverished parts of East Prussia, Silesia and Poland to work for the Ruhr steel barons, as well as in northern France, Belgium and other big German cities. They gathered in housing estates, miniature settlements fuelled by a strong sense of community, which would soon spawn football clubs and create the strong local rivalries so typical of the Ruhr. (They would also eventually make German national teams full of players with names like Szepan, Szymaniak, Kwiatkowski, Tilkowski or Libuda.) By 1914, more than three million people lived in the whole Ruhr area, roughly 400,000 of them miners.

In 1904, a bunch of teenagers, most of them the sons of miners, formed Westfalia Schalke. The club would remain 'wild', that is, not playing in officially organised leagues, until 1912. This has led romantics to create a myth of Schalke's renegade beginnings. As recently as 1995, a journalist explained that 'the bourgeois DFB would not tolerate self-governing "workers' gangs" in its ranks', thus denying the future Schalke 04 entry into the West German FA. That's true. But equally true is that the kids of Westfalia plainly had no idea of how to apply for official status.

In 1907, the club that would evolve into Rot-Weiss Essen saw the light of day, to the extent that it was visible behind the clouds of coaldust. This club, too, had no interest in matching its skills with posh gymnasts and steered clear of the FA. And in 1909, members of a Christian youth club got in trouble with the local parish by refusing to give up using a pub as their meeting room. The hard-drinking youths decided to form their own club, though they did not play organised football as Borussia Dortmund until 13 months later.

That same year, 1909, dominance of German football was decisively wrestled away from Berlin and Leipzig, when Phönix Karlsruhe beat Viktoria Berlin in the final of the national championship. The game was watched by 1,500 people, but before long gates for finals would move into five figures, as the south began to flex its muscles. First in Karlsruhe, then in Fürth. And then, most dramatically, in Nuremberg.

Unlike comparable structural changes later, this first power shift in German football had neither political nor economic reasons – it just happened. And it wasn't sudden or drastic. FC Freiburg (still in existence today, but not to be confused with the Bundesliga club) had brought the first championship to the south as early as 1907, though clubs from the north would continue to be a threat. After all, Viktoria Berlin, Holstein Kiel and VfB Leipzig lifted the trophy in the years 1911 to 1913. But

German football in the 1910s and 1920s was shaped, defined and regulated to a large degree by the clubs south of Frankfurt, and the South German FA became the driving force behind how the DFB thought and acted.

If a reason has to be put forward to explain why the southern clubs improved so fast, it might have to do with Walther Bensemann and his willingness to pass the domestic game into the most capable hands – English hands. In 1893, Bensemann urged six clubs to form the South German Football Union (a forerunner of the South German FA). A British military chaplain by the name of T. Archibald S. White became its chairman. And when two clubs founded by Bensemann, the International Football Club and FV Karlsruhe joined forces in 1894, an Englishman known as Captain R. Cooper was appointed as coach.

This cosmopolitan approach proved influential in the south. In 1908, Bayern Munich won the championship of Southern Bavaria under the tutelage of one Thomas Taylor. A year later FV Karlsruhe lifted the national trophy with more than a little help from William Townley, a former Blackburn Rovers and England player. In April 1911, Townley then joined the eight-year-old SpVgg Fürth, teaching the young club what a historian labelled 'the Scottish passing game' and creating one of the future superpowers of early German football. (Five weeks after his arrival, Fürth put in a sensational performance against Newcastle United, losing only 2-1. Though it may have played a role that the game was officiated by Townley.)

Nuremberg, too, went looking for outside expertise. The Franconians learned the finer points of the game from an ex-Britannia Berlin player, Fritz Servas, who had joined them in the summer of 1901, only weeks after Nuremberg's renunciation of rugby. One of his successors was the former Leeds and

Huddersfield player Fred Walker, whose German according to legend amounted to little more than 'Beer good!' For the 1913-14 season, the club briefly secured the services of Fred Spiksley, who had been with Sheffield Wednesday for 13 years, gaining fame as the man who won them the 1896 FA Cup final against Wolves. But Spiksley's career in Germany was rudely interrupted by the First World War, and by the Nuremberg footballers' soon-to-be legendary aversion to coaches of any nationality.

Notwithstanding this sense of independence, the Nuremberg players were aware they could only get better by coming into contact with the very best, even if that meant a drubbing. Beginning in 1909, Nuremberg played English professional clubs on a basis which, considering the times, could almost be called regular. That year, they lost 8-3 at home to Sunderland. In 1912, it was 5-1 against QPR. Twelve months later, Middlesbrough humiliated them 7-0. Then, on May 6, 1914, a sell-out crowd of 8,000 graced Nuremberg's new and club-owned 'Zabo' stadium in order to watch Tottenham Hotspur. The game ended in a 1-1 draw and the spectators gave both sides a standing ovation.

But less than eight weeks later, the Archduke Franz Ferdinand of Austria and Hungary was shot dead by a Serbian gunman in Sarajevo, and Europe began preparing for war. Suddenly, the adored sportsmen of Tottenham and the impeccable Mr Spiksley were no longer playing partners and teachers, but cursed enemies. And SpVgg Fürth, having learned most of what they knew from William Townley, would remain the German champions for a long and bloody time to come. On May 11, they had won the 1914 final against VfB Leipzig, 3-2. The game was still level after 30 minutes of extra time, and under the rules of the day the teams were forced to play on until there was a decision. Fürth scored the third goal in the 153rd minute. One paper commented that Leipzig 'fought bitterly' despite being 'wounded and weakened'.

In Germany, the war was seen as a long-overdue catharsis because of confusing inner conflicts. The strongest political party were the Social Democrats, but the nominal rulers of the country were the royal family, while the true economic power lay in the hands of middle-class businessmen. The country showed all signs of a nascent class war, until the bigger war served to unite the feuding elements.

Among the first young Germans to enlist happily, naturally, were the *Turner*, who had always held that their sport was meant to prepare for war. The footballers, viewed as being subversive for so long, didn't stand back either. 'The clubs had worked hard and tirelessly to make our people, and especially the young, realise the value of athletic education in developing physical and spiritual powers for the good of the self and the country,' explained a history of VfR Mannheim. 'Now is the time for German sportsmen to act in the first passage at arms.'

Almost immediately, most clubs lost large numbers of players to the great cause. Modern, critical German sports historians have a pet theory that says our early football had such strong patriotic undertones that games were allowed to continue during the war to boost morale. Christiane Eisenberg wrote: 'One of the main characteristics of German football is an orientation towards the nation,' adding that organised football 'was less concerned with the clubs and local identification than with the national team and "Germany".' She supports her claim by saying that league games still took place during the First World War, that games took place between representative city teams, and that even soldiers in the trenches played football.

As much as I sympathise with any thoughtful approach to football, I don't believe the facts bear this out. There's no denying that German footballers as a whole were as reactionary, nationalistic and subservient as the rest of the country. However, at the time in question, the national team was something of a joke and had only been playing occasional games for six years, while club football was already a matter of feverish local patriotism, especially in the south. Games between the sister cities of Nuremberg and Fürth were habitually marred by crowd riots, beginning with a pitch invasion in 1910. And whenever Nuremberg and Fürth players were chosen to represent Germany, they tended to put club before national pride by making a point of ignoring each other. In 1920, Fürth's Hans Sutor was even forced to change teams, simply because he married a woman from Nuremberg.

That league football was played during the war is true, but it was completely in tatters and had nothing whatever to do with a championship. In late 1914, the South German FA created a trophy called the 'Iron Football' and allowed participating teams to field whoever they wanted, as most clubs didn't have 11 registered players left. A proud team like FV Karlsruhe couldn't even come up with a patchwork side and didn't play officially for three years, while arch-enemies Kickers Stuttgart and VfB Stuttgart joined forces in order to be able to drag a complete team on to the pitch – and if that isn't a sign of meaningless, makeshift games I don't know what is.

It wasn't only the armed conflict which brought German football to its knees during the war. When Britain began the sea blockade, living conditions in Germany deteriorated fast and food became scarce. Some historians claim that close to 750,000 Germans lost their lives between 1914 and 1918 not because of bullets and grenades but hunger and cold. The Kaiser issued an edict saying that all public open space should be used to grow potatoes. Now the football clubs had neither players nor pitches.

When the war finally ended, the chaos and misery it produced led to political upheaval, the end of the monarchy and the creation of the Weimar Republic, marked by divisions between the nominally strong left, a conservative centre and a smaller but vocal and revanchist right. Its sporting effect was a burst of interest in anything that provided a means of escape, especially football. The last final before the war had been watched by a crowd of 6,000; the first final after the war would attract six times that number.

The war did not hit Nuremberg as hard as other clubs. Most of the young men who had played in the team that drew with Spurs returned from the front as early as 1916. Nuremberg won the Iron Football that year, and they even had a foreign player-manager, the Swiss Gustav Bark. At this time people in Bavaria had already taken to calling Nuremberg 'the Club'. It may sound like they were suffering from a bizarre lack of imagination, but in fact the name was born out of respect for Nuremberg's sophisticated and self-conscious appearance both on and off the pitch.

One of the club's founders, Hans Hofmann, claimed the term was used as early as 1907, though it seems very unlikely people outside Bavaria then would have known who it referred to, as Nuremberg made their first appearance in the latter, knockout stages of the national championship only after the war. However, they were clearly the best team in the south during the war years, and it must have left an impression, because by 1919 'the Club' had become a widely used nickname. (It is pronounced like the German *Klub*, with the 'u' sound as in 'look', though it's always spelled the English way.) Even Nuremberg's numerous followers were now referred to as *Clubberer*, just as if no other clubs existed in the country. Seldom has a nickname been more appropriate.

On July 22, 1919, Nuremberg played MTK Budapest, one of the strongest continental sides at the time. Nuremberg lost 3-0, but immediately snatched the opposing centre-forward Alfréd Schaffer from the Hungarians. Schaffer was a footballing wanderer at a time when most players preferred to die in the house they were born in, and he only stayed five months at Nuremberg as playing coach. That was enough, however, to teach his team-mates some secrets of MTK's success. He didn't make the Club a new team, but he must have delivered the little something that turned a very good side into a great one.

Eleven months after the Budapest game, 1. FC Nürnberg reached the first postwar final for the championship of Germany. During qualification – which consisted of league games in their district, then matches for the South German title, followed by a quarter-final and a semi-final for the national title – they drew only once, with FSV Frankfurt. Losing? Not in the Club's dictionary. From July 1918 to February 1922 they would remain unbeaten in official matches, no fewer than 104 of them.

The 1920 final in Frankfurt was the first football match for which the German rail system put on special trains, as it pitted Nuremberg against their local rivals SpVgg Fürth, defending champions since 1914. Over 35,000 people saw the game, many of them perched on buses and lorries parked alongside the ground. Nuremberg won 2-0 and an era had begun. The following year, the hapless victims were Vorwärts Berlin, outclassed 5-0. A DFB representative commented: 'Nuremberg played with the class of a top English league club.' In other words, as far as the rest of Germany was concerned, they were not of this earth.

Football became a mass spectator sport during these first years of the 1920s, since many working people now had the freedom and more time to look for entertainment, especially on Saturdays. Consequently, footballers emerged as figures of national interest. There had been great players before the war, people like Max Breunig, the midfield maestro of FV Karlsruhe. Hugo Meisl, manager of the Austrian *Wunderteam*, later said Breunig was the best European centre-half of his generation. Some English professional clubs supposedly tried to sign him. Certainly Blackburn Rovers knew enough about him when they came to Karlsruhe in May 1910 to intentionally give away a penalty for handball, because they wanted to find out if it was true that Breunig never missed from the spot. (It was true – Rovers won 7-1.) Yes, this footballer was a legend. But only in his own circles. Most people on the streets had never heard of him. During the war, Breunig was wounded and never played again.

But now peace created heroes. There was the tall, blond and handsome Otto 'Tull' Harder from Hamburg, who got his nickname from the English professional Walter Tull he was said to resemble. In any case, he had a great name for a centre-forward. Unfortunately, Tull Harder was a giant only when donning football boots and it was bitterly ironic that he was nicknamed after one of Britain's first black footballers. However, all that would not be revealed until a new and even more terrible war came along.

There were the *Clubberer*, prominent among them the robust centre-half Hans Kalb and goalkeeper Heiner Stuhlfauth. Stuhlfauth had few equals, possibly not even the legendary Spaniard Ricardo Zamora. He was renowned for his ability with his feet, often clearing balls from yards outside the area. When Germany beat Italy in Turin in 1929, the crowd yelled that he was 'the Devil', as his saves began to demoralise the home side. In 1998, a group of self-styled football experts placed Harald Schumacher ahead of Stuhlfauth when naming the greatest German goalkeepers of the century. That was enough to render the voting irrelevant. That even Andreas Köpke came higher was beyond words.

While the players acquired mythical status, the same held true for the games they played, such as the epic 1922 championship final between Nuremberg and Hamburg. The date was June 18, the place Berlin. The sides were level at 2-2 after 90 minutes and so the 22 men played on. And on. And on. 'They were staggering across the pitch, near a complete breakdown,' said a match report.

'Nobody had any strength left for a shot on goal, but nobody was willing to give up, either.' Besides being a strenuous game, it was also a ruthless one. Many Hamburg players were carried off the field – and denounced as 'actors' when they returned a few minutes later – while Nuremberg's defender Anton Kugler lost five teeth thanks to Tull Harder's fist. After three hours and nine minutes, the referee, an exhausted Dr Peco Bauwens, called the ordeal off on account of darkness.

The replay was scheduled for August 6 in Leipzig, and almost 60,000 squeezed into a ground that could hold only 40,000. They didn't come to watch a picnic. Nuremberg's Willi Böss was sent off during the first half, because, according to Bauwens, 'he raised his leg against a Hamburg player lying on the ground'. This was a euphemism: Böss had viciously kicked Albert Beier in the stomach and he was suspended for more than six months by the DFB.

The Club went ahead, but Hamburg equalised 20 minutes later. During the first period of extra time, Nuremberg's Kugler had to be taken off. Substitutions were for sissies in those days, so the defending champions were down to nine men. In the 100th minute, Bauwens felt compelled to send off another Franconian, Heiner Träg. 'His act was so mean,' noted Bauwens, 'that I came close to ending the match right there.' He didn't – yet. Instead, he asked the teams to change ends a few moments later. During the interval, Luitpold Popp collapsed, and suddenly Nuremberg had only seven players left. Bauwens informed the captains that this was against the rules and stopped the proceedings.

Months of legal wrangling ensued. Hamburg considered themselves winners, but the DFB felt this was a terrible way to decide a championship. Nuremberg argued Bauwens had disregarded the statutes by calling off the game during the break. The half-time interval, the ingenious argument went, is not legally a part of the game, thus the referee had no authority to enforce his decision at this point.

The debate dragged on until November. During its annual meeting, the DFB granted HSV the championship – whereupon the club's board declared to 'not lay claim to this year's title'. What seemed like a great sporting gesture may have been the result of behind-the-scenes dealings. HSV later claimed that the DFB had urged them to decline the title. If proof was needed that the South German FA were the power behind the DFB during these years, here it was. Nobody won the Victoria in 1922.

Hamburg didn't have to wait long for their revenge. In 1923, they beat the Berlin club Union Oberschöneweide (a precursor of today's 1. FC Union Berlin) to win their first official national championship. But mighty Nuremberg were only gathering breath. In 1924, history granted them revenge of their own, when they easily disposed of Hamburg in the final to collect their third Victoria, thereby catching up with VfB Leipzig in the silverware department. One year later, the Club overcame FSV Frankfurt to win the title for the fourth time in five seasons (not counting the Never-Ending Story of 1922).

This 1925 final marked the beginning of the lingering end to Nuremberg's fairy tale. Like many southern sides, the Club favoured a slow, considered style of play centred around good technique and the stringing together of passes. The whole point of their game was to draw the defence out of position and create openings for their small, lithe and hard-shooting inside forwards. But opposing teams had learned how to organise while Nuremberg were indulging themselves in slow build-ups. And then, in 1926, the offside rule was changed so that two rather than three defenders had to be between the attacker and the goal, which helped quicker teams more than the stolid Franconian strikers. In the north, most clubs stuck to what contemporaries called either the 'English' or the 'Flying Hussar' style, based on pace and directness. Fast, furious wingers dashed to the byline and sent high crosses in towards the head of bustling centre-forwards like Tull Harder.

The 1927 final, in which Nuremberg beat Hertha Berlin, was notable for being the first match to be covered live and in full on national radio (football having made its German radio debut in November 1925, for a match between Münster and Bielefeld). It was Nuremberg's fifth trophy since the beginning of the decade, but age was catching up with them and the team which had helped to make football a national game in Germany was already passing into the realm of legend.

One of the teams that would challenge them came from an old football stronghold, Berlin. Like Nuremberg, Hertha Berlin had survived the war relatively well. In 1915, 1917 and 1918 they won the championship of Berlin-Brandenburg with an almost intact team, which led their rivals Preussen Berlin to grumble that 'due to exemptions from military service, some clubs are fielding virtual peacetime sides'. Hertha made an effort to take advantage of their rise in status by merging with the rather refined Berlin Sports Club in 1923. The reason behind this move was that, in contrast to staunchly working-class Hertha, the BSC had money – which was used to buy a ground in their local district of Wedding. The uneasy partnership ended in 1930, but Hertha kept the ground and the 'BSC' initials in their name.

Hertha already had business sense during those early unprofessional years. In 1919, they invited MTK Budapest for a friendly, and many Berlin fans secured tickets in advance to make sure they would see the Hungarian masters. But MTK called off the match at short notice. Unwilling to pay back the money, Hertha simply substituted another Berlin team for the Magyars and cunningly forgot to inform the spectators about this slight change of affairs. Predictably, the crowd was not amused and Hertha were temporarily suspended by the Berlin FA.

On the pitch, though, Hertha proved less imaginative, until 1925. That was the year Johannes 'Hanne' Sobek joined them from Alemannia Berlin. If ever one man turned a club around, that man was Sobek. Before he became a Hertha player, the club had only once got as far as the preliminary rounds for the national championship (in 1906). After Sobek joined them, no national final would be complete without Hertha.

Sobek was a tall inside-forward with a renowned first touch, who scored goals or created them while orchestrating the midfield in his spare time. So versatile was he that the Hertha side somehow managed to combine the technically accomplished football of the southern teams with the northern 'Hussar' style. What they lacked were nerves – and luck – in losing no fewer than four finals in a row between 1926 and 1929. The last of those was a vicious battle against Fürth, in a hostile atmosphere in nearby Nuremberg. Fürth's Ludwig Leinberger almost broke Sobek's leg, but 'Hanne' scored twice regardless. It wasn't enough. Fürth's winner came in the dying minutes, by which time Hertha had been reduced to ten men when defender Gerhard Schulz had to leave the pitch. He fell into a coma during the evening and the doctors diagnosed a fractured skull. As Berlin's team trudged off, many of its members in tears and certain they would never win a final, the spectators jeered and laughed. That was the game that convinced the DFB that finals should henceforth be held only at neutral grounds.

Remarkably, Hertha pulled off their first title win the following season, after a tempestuous 5-4 victory over Holstein Kiel in Düsseldorf, though again almost the entire crowd of 45,000 favoured their opponents. They were finally silenced by Hans Ruch's 87th-minute winner, though Sobek would later say his team had never felt as lonely during a football match. On their way home, the Hertha bus was hit by rocks and rotten fruit.

A year later Hertha became the first German club to adopt Herbert Chapman's WM system and won another title with it, beating Munich 1860 (coached by Max Breunig) 3–2. It was the very least fate owed them. Sobek and his team-mates had been subjected to abuse and hatred for three finals in a row – in Hamburg, Nuremberg and Düsseldorf. What was it that provoked these instances of proto-hooliganism, decades before we ever heard that term?

To answer this question, let us go back to the replay of the 1922 final between Nuremberg and Hamburg. That game, too, had seen trouble on the terraces, largely caused by the Nuremberg fans. Their club may have been founded by future lawyers and businessmen, their great team of the 1920s may have included two doctors, but by now most of the fans were industrial workers. During the long train journey to Leipzig, they were informed that no beer would be sold at the ground, which led to a massive pre-match drinking binge. The stadium in Leipzig was hopelessly overcrowded and hundreds of supporters broke through the barriers to position themselves on the cinder track. The makeshift stand for the Nuremberg fans was too small and offered hardly any view of the pitch. The combination of alcohol, heat, excitement and disastrously bad planning created a tense and explosive atmosphere.

Here's how one of those Nuremberg fans recalled the day two years later: 'I can still see in my mind's eye the splendid brick scaffolding in Leipzig, erected especially for the Nuremberg proles, the tremendous crush behind the monument for the Battle of the Nations, and the jolly fight with water bottles between those in the back rows and the people in front. It was good sport to see the ladies in their white summer dresses seeking shelter from enemy missiles in the black mud.'

The people to whom 'proles' was a badge of honour rather than a swear word had arrived at football grounds for good, and they viewed games not as opportunities to show off middle-class virtues but as emotion-filled occasions to settle scores. They were rowdy. White summer dresses meant nothing to them. And they would soon find themselves represented not only off the pitch but also on it.

In 1932, Bayern Munich beat Eintracht Frankfurt 2-0 to become champions of Germany for the first time. It was the 23rd final since 1903, and in all those attempts not one single true workers' club had ever made it that far – unless you count Hertha, who certainly came from a working-class district but were led by a bank clerk for more than two decades. In addition, only one club from western Germany had ever played for the trophy, Duisburger SV in 1913. But this time it was close, as Frankfurt narrowly defeated Schalke 04 in the semis. It was the last hurrah for the old guard, as Schalke fielded a team that would soon dominate German football. It was a team made up of miners with weird-sounding Polish names and a team that in August 1930 had been expelled from the DFB when the officials found out that Schalke paid their players money for wearing the royal blue shirt.

The issue of professionalism was a running sore throughout the Twenties and early Thirties. In the middle of 1931, the German national side was demolished 6-0 by the Austrian *Wunderteam*. Shocked DFB officials feebly mumbled in excuse that, after all, amateurs had been playing against professionals, but few swallowed the bait. 'Many Austrian professionals,' one Cologne paper pointed out, 'wish they were German amateurs!' And the magazine *Fußball* bluntly stated: 'The DFB's statute about professionalism is masking reality.'

This statute, included in the original 1900 constitution of the DFB, stipulated: 'Every regional association or local club can become a full member of the DFB, provided none of its members are professional players.' So strong was the anti-professional stance within the regional and national governing bodies that Walther Bensemann found himself kicked out of the

South German FA for organising the famous tour of English players in 1899. The rules, Bensemann was told, even forbade sharing the same pitch with morally corrupt professionals.

The German FA's officials, most of them successful businessmen and academics, propagated high standards indeed. Their righteousness rested on three pillars. First, they were ideologically still rooted in the black-and-white world of the gymnasts, where a middle-class code of honour had created a new ethical elite, justifying itself not through descent but through the pureness of its values. Second, the FA's damning of professionalism also helped curtail the influence of the potentially dangerous working class. The 'Socialists Law' of 1878 had, for all practical purposes, introduced a modern class system to Germany that was less rigid than the old principle of serfdom but pronounced nonetheless. Third, Pierre de Coubertin's noble theories of amateurism, exemplified by the Olympics, had spread like wildfire through Germany's educated upper middle class. The most influential Olympic figure was Professor Carl Diem, director of Bremen's University of Physical Education and in this capacity a man whose voice was heard and whose service was needed within the DFB.

Peculiarly, these high morals didn't prevent the DFB from charging admission to both club and international games. And the profits were hoarded rather than reinvested. During the first years of the national team, players had to bear the travel costs out of their own wallets and when the DFB did begin paying expenses, these excluded loss of earnings. The clubs argued equally loudly from an equally lofty podium. But when they had to act, they stepped down and began to whisper. Because it goes without saying that the best players were rewarded for their efforts, especially in a country in which local patriotism often came before morals and always before national pride.

When Tull Harder left Eintracht Braunschweig in 1913 to join Hamburger FC (later to become HSV) he went from a good team on the move to second-stringers. Eyebrows were raised, but immediately lowered again when it became known Harder had opened an insurance company in Hamburg. Everybody knew who had paid for the establishment of this business, and no one blamed Harder for using his talents to secure his future – apart from a few hot-blooded Braunschweig fans who congregated on the railway platform to physically remove him from the train to Hamburg.

The important thing when it came to circumventing the amateur rules was to not get caught. Or rather, to avoid acting so blatantly that the DFB could no longer look the other way. This system worked for as long as it involved people who had the riches and the clout to distribute donations among players who were willing to keep up the facade. It stopped working when it began to involve people who couldn't understand what was wrong with a fair day's pay for a fair day's work.

Those people came from western Germany, most of them from the Ruhr, where the local football clubs had gained strength during the 1920s thanks to the workers who played the game and paid money to watch it. Schalke had opened their own ground in 1928 and frequently drew over 30,000 spectators. The squad included famous future internationals like Fritz Szepan and Ernst Kuzorra, simple and hard-working miners living in an area hit hard by recession, inflation and unemployment. In 1930, 67 per cent of workers in Gelsenkirchen were out of a job and the future seemed hopeless. Football was the only way out of the pit or off the breadline for people like Szepan and Kuzorra. And of course the club let them take a share of its revenue.

The lid blew on August 25, 1930. The West German FA issued a statement saying: 'First team players have been receiving expenses greatly in excess of what is acceptable.' The officials declared 14 of Schalke's footballers professionals and excluded them from the West German FA and thus organised play. Schalke's treasurer Wilhelm

Nier, who was responsible for the under-the-table payments, broke under the pressure and shame, and committed suicide.

But the ones who had really overstepped the mark were the bureaucrats. The whole region rose as one to condemn the decision and even Schalke's rivals joined in. 'With one stroke of the pen,' spat a newspaper, 'a syndicate of pedants has destroyed a club that was unparalleled with regard to organisation, commitment and pioneering work.' The West German FA, caught unaware by the public uproar and thinly veiled threats of a breakaway league, gradually relented. One year later, Schalke were back on the map and Szepan and Kuzorra back on the pitch.

'A law which you can only live under by breaking it undermines itself,' wrote the journalist Gerd Krämer later. 'Either the conditions have to be changed until they fit the letter of the law, or the law has to be changed. The DFB doesn't want the first, because it would mean the provincialising of our football and a weakening of the DFB's position. And the majority of officials can't find the courage to do the second.'

The result of the Schalke scandal was a deepening rift between the regional associations. The West German FA, home to all the working men's clubs of the Ruhr, became convinced the only solution to the mess was official recognition of professional footballers. The associations representing North, North-east and Central Germany were opposed to any alterations in the rules. The Berlin and South German FAs opted for playing blind man's buff, saying that 'all players should be categorised under the neutral term "footballers".'

Finally, it was agreed to settle the matter once and for all during the course of a general meeting on May 25, 1933. But this all-important ballot was never held. Because on January 30, 1933, President Paul von Hindenburg appointed the son of an Austrian customs officer as Germany's new chancellor.

4

THREE MEN ON A MISSION

THE NATIONAL TEAM GETS SERIOUS

MORE THAN HALF A century of telling and retelling the tale had honed Fritz Becker's oratorical skills to the point where he knew better than to begin the story about how he achieved everlasting fame with the glorious day itself. Instead he first related a small incident that had happened a few weeks before the date in question. Becker, then 19 and in the final year of Grammar School, had been caught kicking a ball by his school headmaster, who had solemnly lectured the youngster on the depravity of football before giving him three hours' detention.

At this point, Becker would pause and smile to give his listeners time to marvel at the cruel justice of history: nobody remembers the name of the stern headmaster, but the disobedient pupil who loved football more than he feared teachers has gone down in history. Then Becker would fast forward to a day in early April 1908. He would describe how forlorn he felt on the platform and how he was beginning to have second thoughts about this whole trip. He would explain how, only minutes before departure time, a tousled, panting man he had never seen before handed him his ticket and gave him directions to the train and his compartment. He would recall how he spent the journey silently listening to conversations between strangers, while the people he was supposed to be travelling with congregated in a different coach.

And then, finally, Becker would relate what had happened on the rainy day after this doubt-filled train ride. It was a few minutes past three in the afternoon, Becker said: 'The goalkeeper didn't move. He thought the shot was wide. Well, he was right, it would have missed the target. But he didn't know how fast a runner I was. After all, I used to compete in relays for my school's track-and-field team. So I got to the ball before it could go into touch and deflected it into the net.'

Even if one admits that it took agility of mind and legs to score this goal, it was by no means a beauty. Moreover, it was of little consequence, as Becker's team lost 5-3. And yet there was a reason why he would spend large parts of his later life recounting the occasion. It was Germany's first international goal.

Or was it? At first glance, Becker's claim to fame seems watertight: Switzerland v Germany, on April 5, 1908 in Basel, is listed in every reference book as the first official game of a German national team. The key word here, however, is 'official'. Official records are kept by a sport's governing body, and the criteria employed to determine what constitutes a true international game can appear elastic at times. (We will later encounter a famous game which undoubtedly took place, even though both parties involved have chosen to erase it completely from their recorded memory.) In the case of Fritz Becker and his team-mates, this governing body is the DFB. It recognises an international as official when it involves a team representing not the country, whatever that precisely may be, but itself – the DFB. That is why Fritz Becker has become 'the first man to score a goal for Germany', despite the fact that there had been international games before April 5, 1908, even before the DFB's formation in 1900.

As early as December 1898, the ubiquitous Walther Bensemann had taken an all-star team, of sorts, to Paris to meet The White Rovers, a club founded by Englishmen, and a Paris select XI. This proto-national team consisted of players from Berlin, Hamburg, Karlsruhe and Strasbourg (Alsace was German between 1871 and 1918). They played in all black and beat the English 7-0, the Parisians 2-1. This side, which described itself as 'a team compiled from all German regions' in a note to the Kaiser, included Bensemann himself, one of the Jestram brothers who had founded Germania Berlin in 1888 and Ivo Schricker, who went on to become general secretary of FIFA.

And a mere week prior to the 1908 game between Switzerland and Germany, a combined Berlin team had lost 5-1 at home to an England XI. This encounter, too, never made the archives as a true international because it only marginally involved the two FAs. Still, as far as the idea of 'Germany' is concerned, Bensemann's side and the Berlin team were just as representative as the motley crew of utter strangers which travelled to Switzerland in order to make history.

This digression is not meant to challenge or even discredit Fritz Becker. It only serves to show that the early history of the German national team was anything but 'efficient' or 'well organised', to use terms later generations would invariably associate with everything German. Rather, the whole affair was often marked by haphazard player selection and confusion about the scheduling of the games. Of course, that was the case with almost every footballing nation during the first decades of the century, but the situation in Germany was made much worse by two factors which would prove to be stumbling blocks for years and years to come.

First, there was local instead of national patriotism. The DFB had joined FIFA the very day it was formed — by telegram on the evening of May 21, 1904 – clearly with an eye towards participating in international games. But while the DFB liked to think of itself as a centralist governing authority, German football was in fact firmly in the grip of the regional associations, who jealously guarded their own rights. The lack of a national league put more power into their hands, since the DFB had no reliable way of finding out who were the best 11 players in the country. Thus the matter of selecting the national squad, ostensibly the task of the DFB's playing committee, was largely left to the regional FAs.

The problem with this set-up was not that there was no national coach – after all, the English had a similar system and it seemed to work for them – but that each regional association attempted to get at least one of its players into the squad. The thing to be avoided was not a weak team but over-representation of one region. That explains why the players forming the inaugural team of 1908 represented 11 different cities. It may sound peculiar to a modern football fan, but during the first three decades of German international football, the enmities between, say, the South German FA and the Berlin-Brandenburg FA were far stronger than any rivalry between Germany and England (or any other country).

One of the effects of this parochialism was that nobody could agree on a settled line-up, let alone grant it time to knit together. Germany's first nine games saw seven different goalkeepers, a trend which would carry on well into the 1920s. And on April 4, 1909, there were even two official German teams playing on the same day. A side featuring six Berlin players drew with Hungary in Budapest, while a Karlsruhe-led XI beat Switzerland 1-0 on home soil.

The second problem the DFB had in creating a truly national team was its insistence on a rigid definition of amateurism. Many good players could not afford to leave their jobs for the two or three days needed to participate in an international game. The incomparable Max Breunig appeared in only 9 out of 22 matches between 1910 and 1914, because he worked as a teacher and was unable to take holidays just to help his country win at football. Still, Breunig's was one of the less bizarre cases. In March 1909, Germany played England Amateurs at Oxford. The team lost 9-0 and featured the 18-year-old forward Willy Baumgärtner, who was chosen primarily because he lived in England at the time.

Self-inflicted weaknesses of this variety would prove to be a staple of German football for decades to come, but a particularly tragic climax was reached in 1932-33, when Germany were in dire need of a striker to replace Bayern Munich's consistent goalscorer Josef Pöttinger, who was plagued by injuries. They found such a man in the young and exceptionally talented Oskar Rohr, also a Bayern player. Rohr made four appearances for his country and found the net five times. Then he signed a professional contract with Grasshoppers Zürich – and was never picked again. Rohr knew turning professional would put an end to his international career and ruin his reputation in Germany. (What he didn't know was how dearly he would pay for this move after the Nazis took over.) That is why his choice was not one widely emulated. Far more typical were cases in which players turned down offers to become full-time footballers without so much as a moment's hesitation.

One of the earliest such instances concerned Paul Eichelmann, a small but fearless goalkeeper. Eichelmann had kept goal for the Berlin XI put together by Walther Bensemann when English professionals came to Germany for the first time, in 1899. Two years later, he went to England for the return matches and endeared himself to the hosts by playing hard and drinking harder. (He was the goalkeeper Union Berlin benched for the 1905 final because he got drunk the night before the game.)

Aston Villa offered him a contract. Eichelmann, however, laughed off their approaches and returned home. He was later rewarded by being picked to represent his country in Germany's second and third official internationals: a 3-2 defeat at the hands of Austria on June 7, 1908, and a match against England, played on April 20. This England game is recognised by the DFB but not the FA. That's because England only dispatched their amateur team, although that did not mean it was a weak side. It included the Tottenham centre-forward Vivian Woodward, who scored two in England's 5-1 win, and much the same team would win the Olympic title six months later.

Thus the first year of the national team ended with a record of three straight defeats. The next season saw Germany's first victory – 1-0 over Switzerland – but celebrations proved premature. Germany won only five of its first 32 internationals. What's more, three of those five victories came against Switzerland, fast becoming the one opponent Germany were looking for when they began to feel depressed. Granted, there was one impressive result. In April 1911, Germany drew 2-2 with England Amateurs in Berlin. The hosts were even ahead until Hull City's Gordon Wright equalised in the 65th minute. But the match was played in driving snow and judging from their future performances, the conditions probably helped the Germans to achieve a fluke result.

There were no two ways about it – the early German teams were well below the highest international standards. The DFB, setting a precedent for the future, only decided to do something about the sorry state of the team when a big international tournament came along. In this case, it was the 1912 Olympics in Stockholm. The DFB revoked the powers of the regional FAs to influence team selection, thus making the Playing Committee – and especially its chairman, Paul Dreyer of Hamburg – solely responsible for the national side. The 22-man squad they nominated included eight players from Karlsruhe and looked good on paper. Though less good in practice.

The 1912 Olympics are remembered by Germans for their side's record-breaking 16-0 victory over an inexperienced Russian team. (A persistent rumour says the Russians were not only inexperienced but also inebriated.) Gottfried Fuchs scored ten of the goals; another record, but also the beginning of another tragic story (Fuchs was Jewish). However, defeats against Austria (5-1) and Hungary (3-1) gave a more accurate indication of where Germany stood.

The DFB reacted by appointing three so-called *Bundes-Fussball-Lehrer* (National Football Instructors), who were supposed to find and nurture talent in the part of the country allotted to them. However, the war intervened, and so only one man took up the job. His name was Richard Girulatis, and although he had little influence over the make-up of the national team, he has gained moderate fame as the first German football coach. In 1919, he would publish the first systematic German textbook on football and probably coin the phrase *Elf Freunde müsst ihr sein* – you have to be 11 friends. (Although this oft-quoted line might have been engraved in the original base of the Victoria, which was replaced in the late 1920s and is lost.)

But theory was not the problem, it was practice which was causing headaches. In 1913, Germany lost four out of four, including an embarrassing encounter with the hardly awe-inspiring Belgians, who hit the net six times.

In fact, so miserable was the Germans' international reputation that Girulatis had to inform the press that the English, the masters from whom everyone wanted to learn, had told the DFB that their Amateurs would no longer play Germany annually and would prefer it if future games took place in Germany, as English crowds just weren't interested enough. 'They said our performances are too modest,' explained a sad Girulatis. He would have been even sadder had he known that the encounter between Germany and England in March 1913 was to be the last meeting between the two countries for 17 years.

'Our sport, which gave the most noble blood to this disastrous war, which gave the beloved Fatherland its best sons, will weld us together in these dark hours. Our sport pays homage to you who are returning home and offers you incomparable gratitude.' That is how German football papers welcomed the veterans returning from the battlefields of the First World War. But as a result of the bitterness engendered by the war and the Treaty of Versailles which set down the terms for the peace, 'the beloved Fatherland' quickly became an outcast in the world of diplomacy – and sport.

While German domestic football rose to unexpected heights in the years following the war, both in popularity and playing strength, the international game lay dormant, unable to capitalise on the great things happening in Nuremberg and Fürth. Germany's wartime enemies refused to play football against them and in 1920 England even attempted to have Germany expelled from FIFA. For three years, that left Germany with only four countries to play – its wartime allies Austria and Hungary, Finland, which owed its sovereignty in part to Germany, and ever-honourable, neutral-to-a-fault Switzerland.

For the second but not the last time, Switzerland put Germany back on the footballing map by agreeing to play a friendly on June 27, 1920, two years after the war had ended. This grand gesture almost led to a serious split in Swiss football, as the regional association representing the French-speaking part of the country threatened to break away from the Swiss FA should the game go ahead. In the end, it allowed the match to be played but discouraged its own players from participating.

'The only one from western Switzerland who did take the field against us was Oskar Merkt of Servette Geneva,' said

Nuremberg's international Hans Kalb many years later. 'And he got expelled from his club for it.' Before the game, Felix Linnemann, the deputy chairman of the DFB, reminded the team how important the match was and urged them 'to behave in a genteel manner'. 'We obviously took those words to heart,' noted Kalb drily. Germany lost 4-1.

The 13 years that followed were full of ups and downs. The domestic football boom did nothing to dispel the stubborn attitudes which had plagued the national team before the war. On the contrary, the emergence of Nuremberg and Fürth as the country's premier clubs led to an intensification of local patriotism bordering on the absurd. In April 1924, the German team travelled to Amsterdam in two different railway carriages. One housed the Nuremberg players, the other carried those from Fürth. The two parties refused to speak to each other. When Fürth's Karl Auer scored the only goal of the game to secure Germany's first win over Holland, the Nuremberg players did not even celebrate.

Amateurism was still there, too. The DFB decided in late 1924 that this noble spirit was of such overriding importance that it even forbade playing against professionals. Unfortunately, Hungary and Austria had sanctioned payments, which meant that two of the few countries which did not boycott Germany were now boycotted by Germany.

It is hardly surprising, then, that the national team's progress was faltering. Its limitations – some self-inflicted, others beyond the control of the football authorities – offset even the most progressive innovations. And there were some of those. The team was now regularly made up of the best players available, regardless of what the regional FAs wanted, thus often resembling a combined Fürth/Nuremberg XI. And in 1924, Max Breunig, who had spent the past two years coaching in Switzerland, was made the team's official 'adviser', which was a significant move towards installing a national manager. There were many writers and fans who clamoured for such a post, especially since Hugo Meisl was having great success with the Austrian team, thereby proving that one man's vision could work, provided he was in sole charge. The men running the DFB, however, felt that a national coach would be the first step towards insidious professionalism and were not in favour of the idea – with one exception.

Felix Linnemann, the official who had briefed Hans Kalb on how to behave back in 1920, was one of the younger members of the DFB's executive board. In 1921, on the occasion of a friendly with Finland, he took aside a player who had made his debut that day, scoring twice. Linnemann told him that a German University of Physical Education had been founded in Berlin, that this institute would teach ambitious young men how to become coaches and that one day the German national team would have an official coach. This was of the utmost importance, Linnemann said, to make the team competitive.

The novice player listened intently, as he nurtured the dream of one day becoming a football instructor himself. His name was Josef Herberger, he was playing for Waldhof Mannheim and he already had a role model to follow. Otto Nerz also hailed from Mannheim, was a fatherly friend to Herberger and was about to join that same University of Physical Education to study sports (and listen to Richard Girulatis teach football). Thus began the formation of a triangle that was to alter drastically the course of German football.

Linnemann, Nerz and Herberger did not have too many character traits in common. In fact, in any other walk of life they would probably never have got along. Linnemann was a police inspector who believed in discipline and order, and like many such men he was often calm, understanding and friendly but could sometimes burst into rage. Nerz came from a working-class family but had climbed the social ladder, not through guile or genius but thanks to willpower and hard work. He had studied to become a teacher before the war, and would later obtain his doctorate in medicine and attempt to become a professor. Herberger was brought up poor, too, but what made him upwardly mobile were exactly the qualities Nerz lacked: street smartness, an uncanny knowledge of human nature and a talent for playing football. Linnemann and Nerz would be interned after the war, and both were dead by the time Herberger became the greatest legend in German football.

The three men's journey to despair and glory began in 1925, when Linnemann became head of the DFB. Knowing the conservative nature of his fellow officials, he decided to act swiftly. Without consulting the DFB's board, he declared that from July 1, 1926, Germany would have a national coach and that the coach's name was Otto Nerz. Nerz looked exactly like the man one would expect to coach a German team in the 1920s and 1930s. He had a clean-cut, stern face, wore his hair extremely short and watched the world suspiciously through steel-rimmed glasses. He never smiled, had no time for niceties and valued discipline, conditioning and strategy. 'As a player, Nerz's performance was built on power,' remembered Herberger much later. 'He was an athlete focused on destruction and prevention.' A grafter, then. But such players often make good coaches and, regardless of his lack of vision, Nerz was always willing to learn. Above all, he wanted to learn from the English.

So great was Nerz's fixation with England and English football that he wholeheartedly embraced Herbert Chapman's revolutionary WM system and doggedly worked at implementing it in Germany. He found significant resistance, as most clubs and players saw no reason to fix something they felt was not broken. It took Nerz many years to convince the rest of the country he was right, but finally he succeeded. Which set another precedent for decades to come. Here was a German football person who was anything but a pleasant man, yet one had to admire his determination.

Nerz's scientific approach yielded results. At the 1928 Olympics, Germany dismantled Switzerland 4-0, with three goals coming from the future star Richard Hofmann. In 1928, Hofmann was still playing for Meerane (a small town in western Saxony), but soon the English coach Jimmy Hogan would take him to Dresden, where he blossomed into one of the best players ever seen on a German pitch. The next match was lost, thus ending Germany's chances of a medal, but it was regarded as a moral victory to have given Uruguay, the best team in the world, a good game. To this day it is popularly believed that Germany might even have beaten the mighty South Americans if only the Egyptian referee had stopped the Uruguayans from kicking their opponents to pieces. Instead he sent off two Germans, Hofmann and Nuremberg's Kalb. Never before had a German international been dismissed, let alone two. Both were banned from the team for a year as a punishment for losing their tempers. Kalb never played for Germany again.

A year later, Germany won 2-1 in Turin. It was the country's first victory over Italy, achieved entirely by an unbelievable fighting spirit and tremendous goalkeeping from Heiner Stuhlfauth, whose heroics gripped the country's imagination, because this game was the first German international to be broadcasted live on the radio. Two months after that, Germany played Sweden in Cologne. They had not beaten the Swedes since 1911 and had lost five of the previous six games against them. But this time the roles were reversed: the rehabilitated Hofmann scored three, had another three disallowed, and Germany won 3-0.

Then, on May 10, 1930, came the big day. England had not only agreed to lift the ban on Germany and travel to Berlin for a friendly, they were also finally sending their professionals. After 20 minutes, they were practically down to ten men, as Billy

Marsden of Sheffield Wednesday broke a cervical vertebra in a collision with a team-mate. (Amazingly, he wasn't taken off until half-time. The injury ended Marsden's career.) Still the English dominated the game. Birmingham City's Joe Bradford put them into the lead and, after Richard Hofmann's unexpected equaliser, the same player made it 2-1 to England. After the break, however, the Germans played like men possessed. Hofmann levelled the scores four minutes after half-time and scored Germany's third on the hour. A sporting sensation of spectacular proportions hung in the air until seven minutes from time, when Arsenal's David Jack made it 3-3.

Twenty-two years after their first official international, the Germans had held their own against the masters. True, England were handicapped, but the same went for Germany's new folk hero, Richard Hofmann. Hofmann had lost his right ear in a car accident only two months before the game that made him an icon. He played with a bandage over his head, a picture that captured the public imagination and led to the newspaper headline: *King Richard, the Lionheart.*

This match with England was the high point of Germany's football history so far and would remain so for many years. The following seasons proved to be anti-climactic. Particularly grim was 1931, when Germany lost to France in Paris, a game that was eagerly awaited as the two sides had never previously met. Then the elegant Austrians, led by the 'Paper Man' Matthias Sindelar, humbled their neighbours twice: 6-0 in Berlin, 5-0 in Vienna. Suddenly Nerz came under heavy criticism for his obsession with athleticism and theory.

Schalke's Fritz Szepan, many observers felt, was a football genius on a par with Sindelar, but he seemed to be paralysed when playing for Germany. At his club, the team did everything to make Szepan's magic work. But under Nerz, Szepan had to follow orders and run in straight lines. Was Germany's power football stifling grace? Was it producing runners instead of artists? Such questions concerned the public, but not Nerz. No one had denounced his methods when they had helped to get a draw against England, he felt. What counted was not the debate between flair and power, but results.

Results, though, were hard to come by now. In the wake of the Great Depression, desperation and disheartenment had set in everywhere, and the national team was no exception. Even Nerz seemed to lose interest and concentrated more and more on his studies. In mid-1932, six million Germans were out of work (an unemployment rate of 44 per cent). One of the lucky few who got a job was Josef Herberger. On August 1, he became a coach with the West German FA, partly on the strength of a letter of recommendation written by Nerz. 'Herberger was admitted to the German University of Physical Education, even though he did not meet the usual requirements [the equivalent of A-levels],' Nerz wrote. 'When he finished his studies, he was given the institute's highest honour.' Herberger's task was to select and train this very large association's representative team. It was a dream come true for him to be allowed to earn a living in the only field he really cared about – football. Little did he know that only five months later life would dramatically change again. For him, for his country and for the world. For football, too.

5

ANGST AND ANSCHLUSS

FOOTBALL UNDER THE NAZIS

ON OCTOBER 20, 1929, Germany played Finland in front of a 20,000 crowd in Altona (Hamburg). At half-time the score was 0-0 and fans were grumbling that the coach Otto Nerz had underestimated the Finns and was pushing his luck by giving international debuts to no fewer than six players. Yet it was one of those newcomers who broke the spell after 52 minutes, setting the stage for a comfortable 4-0 win. In the eyes of many that was only fitting, as young Fritz Szepan seemed to be an expert in spells. Back home they said he was not a player but a magician.

With hindsight, this game against Finland and the fact that Szepan scored on his debut signalled change. Not so much because of Szepan as a person but rather what he stood for. 'Back home' to him meant Schalke, the working-class district of Gelsenkirchen and home to FC Schalke 04. Szepan was already the second player from this club to be called up to the national team, and Schalke fans saw his selection as proof that their club was on the rise. They were right, but they could not have imagined how far that rise would take them.

And there was another thing about the Finland match. Four days later Wall Street crashed and the stock market collapsed.

The Great Depression destroyed economies and ruined lives in almost every country in the world. But nowhere tasted the grapes of wrath quite as bitterly as Germany. The main reason for this was that the diffuse and unstable political situation prevented the country from coming up with a workable concept to fight the crisis. The nominally strong left exhausted itself through trench warfare between its communist and social democratic wings, thus denying the working class a unified voice. The moderate conservative parties were too divided to help create anything but confusion. The so-called Weimar Coalition, made up of the Social Democrats and two liberal democratic parties, lost its absolute majority in parliament as early as 1920. By the end of the decade, politics had descended into a desperate scrabble among the increasingly ineffectual democratic parties to hold the centre. Power changed hands on an alarmingly regular basis. Between late 1920 and early 1933, Germans found themselves governed by 12 different chancellors of the Reich, one of whom led the country on two different occasions, while four others were not even affiliated to a party.

The national election held on September 14, 1930 brought an entirely unexpected result. One of the obscure splinter groups on the extreme right, which called itself the National Socialist Workers' Party of Germany (NSDAP), became the second strongest party in the country by raising their percentage of the vote from less than three to more than 18. Two years later they more than doubled that result and suddenly their leader was in a position to demand the post of chancellor. On January 30, 1933, President Von Hindenburg relented and Adolf Hitler was asked to form a cabinet.

The Nazis termed January 30, 1933 *Tag der Machtergreifung* (the day of seizing power), which has led many people – including Germans – to believe that during the first weeks of that year, almost the whole of the country embraced Hitler as the strong man to lead them out of desolation and followed him with blind obedience. That, however, was not at all the case. At the time, it seemed to many that the NSDAP was still just one of many parties in the parliament struggling for support, and Hitler was just another chancellor destined to lose his post before long. There was a widespread conviction that the Nazis would go away as quickly as they had appeared.

There were good reasons to believe it. The economy had improved during the latter part of 1932, whereupon the NSDAP almost immediately lost over four million votes in the national election and suddenly found itself on the defensive in numerous municipal elections. This trend continued into March 1933, two months after Hitler's appointment, when Germans were asked to vote in yet another election. The Nazis were confident they would win an absolute majority, but since they were not willing to leave anything to chance, they sent out their ruthless gang of thugs the *Sturmabteilung* (SA – Storm Troopers) to beat up or otherwise intimidate democratic voters and politicians, which robbed the left of many potential votes. Yet despite such systematic terrorism, the NSDAP still only collected 44 per cent of the vote and had to seek a coalition partner.

Alas, what should not have happened in theory did happen in practice. Historically, January 30, 1933 is indeed the day the Nazis seized power. Once democracy had got Hitler where he wanted, he made sure it would not last long enough to remove him. The burning of the Reichstag on February 27 gave him an excuse to annul the constitution, which in turn allowed the Nazis to arrest communists and social democrats at will. After the March election, he presented parliament with the Enabling Act, which basically meant that the government would henceforth issue laws and regulations just as it liked. The Act was passed because more than 100 elected representatives could not be present at the ballot. They were in jail or on the run from the SA.

The reasons for Hitler's subsequent acceptance by the German people go beyond the scope of a football book. But there were far too many among the population who would be labelled 'fellow travellers' 12 years later, people who considered themselves apolitical without realising that such a thing was no longer possible. Some of them, like Felix Linnemann, already had nationalistic leanings and found nothing inherently wrong in a dictatorial system. Others, like Otto Nerz, were susceptible to the prejudices the Nazis turned into a racist ideology. (Nerz, a former Social Democrat, joined the SA in 1933 and published a series of anti-Semitic diatribes in the summer of 1943.) Still others, like Josef Herberger, thought of themselves as too simple to understand events outside their own small, private world. In his case, that world was football, but it did not remain private for long.

In his book *Hitler's Olympics*, the British journalist Duff Hart-Davis said: 'On June 2, 1933, Dr Bernhard Rust, the Minister of Education (no less), gave instructions that Jews were to be excluded also from youth and welfare organisations, and that the facilities of such bodies were to be closed to them.' It was decrees like this one that would later lead our clubs to claim that what happened during the Nazi years was a result of the *Gleichschaltung* (forcing into line). Put differently, they said their hands were tied because of regulations demanding that every club member had to prove themselves to be of so-called 'Aryan' descent, that all juvenile members had to join the Hitler Youth and that the club was to be put into the hands of trusted party people.

The *Gleichschaltung* was an extension of the party doctrine that said no sphere of life should remain beyond the grasp and the influence of the NSDAP. In fact, the Nazis' initial plan had been to do away with the old clubs altogether and to replace them with new, artificial and centrally ruled 'local sporting groups'. It was a goal the Nazis never lost sight of, and they did indeed force quite a few clubs to disband or merge with others, as when they created VfL Bochum in 1938 by combining three separate clubs. However, the war prevented this typically grandiose plan from being carried through on a larger scale, and so most traditional German clubs kept their name and an outward appearance of normality throughout the fascist years.

That did not really worry the Nazis. Because while they may have initially suspected that subversive things were going on at those places where people played English games and sometimes even spoke of dreaded foreign things like 'professionalism', most such organisations left little or no doubt as to where they stood ideologically. Because most German sporting organisations and clubs had sprung into action long before men like Rust issued directives. In fact, at this stage of the unfolding tragedy, the party had very little interest in forcing Jews out of the clubs, precisely because of 'Hitler's Olympics'. In April 1933, the strong Jewish tennis player David Prenn was barred from the German Davis Cup team, which led to international protests. From then on, the Nazis tried to avoid such high-profile cases, because they feared that they would lead to countries boycotting the Olympics that were only three years away. However, most sporting functionaries were falling over themselves to insinuate themselves with the new masters (or satisfy their own racist leanings) and were faster and more radical than the party probably expected.

Of course, the *Turner* were first. In late March 1933, the Saxony Gymnastic Circle asked the sport's governing body to introduce a so-called Aryan paragraph. This means nothing less than that the gymnasts introduced this paragraph before the party did! (The first time the Nazis ever used an 'Aryan paragraph' in a law was April 7, when it was put into writing that Jews could not be employed in public service.) On April 3, the German Boxing Federation excluded Jews. In May, the German Rowing Association followed suit. In June, the German Ski Association. And so on. Before the Nazis had even decided how to handle sports, most sports bodies had already chosen the path they wanted to follow.

The DFB and its affiliated clubs were no exception. On the contrary. Perhaps fearful of the old 'English disease' tag and its implications of being unpatriotic, the footballers were among the first to display their obedience. On April 19, 1933, the DFB used *kicker* magazine (which, remember, was founded by the Jew Walther Bensemann) to make an official announcement stating that 'members of the Jewish race, and persons who have turned out to be followers of the Marxist movement, are deemed unacceptable'.

The local associations and some individual clubs had acted even earlier. After 27 years as a member of FV Karlsruhe, the former international Julius Hirsch left his club on April 10, when he read of the plan to expel Jews from all sporting organisations and learned of anti-Semitic sentiments against him. The club sent him a letter that said they were sorry to see him in distress and that Karlsruhe still considered him a member as they had not yet received explicit orders to expel him. However, that letter was dated August 4 – almost four months after Hirsch's resignation – which makes you wonder how sincere the club really was. Also in April, 1. FC Nürnberg expelled their Jewish members and 14 clubs from the southern part of the country published a letter of intent, among them many clubs founded by Bensemann and also Eintracht Frankfurt – until then often referred to as a 'Jews club' because of their many Jewish members and benefactors. The letter said the clubs would act swiftly and 'remove the Jews'.

Thus, the often-heard excuse 'We were only obeying orders' masks the frightening fact that the Nazification of German clubs was forced through by people who were willing to carry out those orders before they had even been voiced. The DFB and its clubs acted long before there were regulations. And their coldness becomes the more numbing when one realises that in a few isolated cases people proved you could at least attempt to swim against the tide.

In Munich, FC Bayern were on the rise when the Nazis took over. The club had won its first national championship in 1932, thanks to a goal by Oskar Rohr, and the club's president Kurt Landauer had reason to hope the future would be bright. However, like very many of Bayern's leading members (and fans), Landauer was Jewish. In March 1933, he was forced to step down. He later spent time in a concentration camp and escaped to Switzerland in 1939, where he survived the Holocaust – in contrast to four of his siblings.

So far this is a typical story. What makes it noteworthy is that Bayern never made a secret of the fact that they stood by Landauer and were accepting orders from above only under protest. As late as November 1943, the whole team gave their regards to their former president and greeted him warmly after a friendly in Zurich, even though the German secret police had explicitly instructed the players to not acknowledge Landauer's presence in any shape or form. Furthermore, the club proved adept at installing new presidents who only went through the motions of toeing the line. Naturally, this approach cost Bayern dearly in the long run. The Nazis clearly felt 1860 Munich was the more trustworthy club (besides having the working-class touch so cherished by the fascists) and turned the Blues into the 'flagship club of the Nazi era,' according to historian Anton Löffelmeier. After the war, it would take the Reds at Bayern more than two decades to regain the strength they once had.

Kurt Landauer returned from his exile in 1947 and was again elected president of Bayern Munich. His was a rare fate, however. Gottfried Fuchs (the man who had scored ten goals for Germany in one game in 1912) fled to Canada in 1937 and never again set foot on his native soil. Julius Hirsch stayed in his home country, hoping things would turn out all right. He was murdered in Auschwitz.

Bearing in mind this backdrop of prejudice and fear, dull nationalism and mindless militarism, one might expect the actual football during the Nazi years to be described in terms similar to those of the Soviet Union and GDR sides of the 1970s – 'well organised but lifeless', 'robot-like' or 'lacking individualism'. And yet the dark 1930s produced two of the most famous teams in German football history, neither of which can be accused of lacking flair. There was the national side of 1937, nicknamed the *Breslau-Elf* (Breslau XI) and – above all – there was the Spinning Top.

The term 'spinning top' (*Kreisel* in German) may seem a bizarre choice for describing a style of play, but contemporary writers felt it perfectly evoked how the players of Schalke 04 dealt with their opponents. They never moved upfield by belting long balls and chasing them. Instead, they strung together an often bewildering succession of short, quick passes, always keeping the ball on the ground, always looking for the better positioned man. At its best, it left the other team reeling, never certain of where the ball would be played next.

Schalke's defender Hans Bornemann would later argue that this marked the first time in football history that it was not the man with the ball who determined the direction of play but his team-mates running into space – who never asked for the ball, but demanded it. 'It was only when there was absolutely nobody left you could pass the ball to,' said Bornemann, 'that we finally put it into the net.'

This description is reminiscent of the Austrian *Wunderteam* of the same period, which in 1932 almost became the first foreign team to win in England, over 20 years before the Hungarians. And indeed Schalke hired an Austrian coach in 1927, Gustav Wieser, to help them perfect the Spinning Top, though its roots go back to what was then called the 'Scottish Passing Game', which the brothers Hans and Fred Ballmann had imported from Britain. Unsurprisingly, some German experts doubted the efficiency of this method. 'Schalke's love affair with the ball is restricting and unproductive,' argued one magazine in the late 1920s. Seldom has a prophecy been wider of the mark.

The club reached its first national final in 1933. This was a symbolic game for many reasons. It took place less than six months after Hitler had been named chancellor and for the first time ever it was an entirely western affair – the venue was Cologne, the finalists Schalke and Fortuna Düsseldorf. Fortuna won 3-0, led by the great Paul Janes, who would soon captain Germany and, in 1941, become the country's record international appearance maker. (Janes held this honour for a staggering 29 years, until Uwe Seeler finally surpassed him.) This result was something of an aberration, however. Schalke had beaten Fortuna only weeks before the final and while Düsseldorf would never win another national championship, there was now no stopping the miners from Gelsenkirchen.

They were back for another shot at the title only a year later, facing Nuremberg in Berlin. Two minutes from time, the Franconians led 1-0. Moreover, Schalke's two most important players were ineffective: Fritz Szepan couldn't get past the Nuremberg defence and Ernst Kuzorra was barely able to walk due to a hernia. Then a corner sailed over the heads of the momentarily disorganised Nuremberg backline, and Szepan was there to knock the ball in from close range. It was 1-1, and extra time seemed inevitable. But in the final minute of play, Kuzorra mustered all the energy left in his pain-ridden body, held off a defender and fired a left-footed shot into the far corner. Shortly after, Kuzorra broke down and lost consciousness. When he woke up, he was told he could now call himself champion of Germany.

It was a fittingly heroic end to this final. Because regardless of all the titles Schalke would come to collect, the most lasting legacy of this side was the creation of a concept (a myth, if you like) that permeates German football and especially the Ruhr to this day – that of honest, close-to-the-people, proletarian football. Nearly all the Schalke players had been raised in or near Gelsenkirchen, and the majority had known each other since early childhood. Most had worked either down the pits or at the steelworks, and many continued to do so while winning championships in their spare time.

As if that weren't enough to make them a close-knit group, they were also family in a very literal sense. Fritz Szepan was married to one of Ernst Kuzorra's sisters, reserve player Fritz Thelen to another. The wives of Ernst Reckmann and August Sobotka were cousins. In 1931, Ernst Kuzorra married the daughter of the man who ran the club's pub. Winger Bernhard and goalkeeper Hans Klodt were brothers (though they only played together for a few years).

This footballing clan won the regional championship of western Germany 11 times running between 1934 and 1944, easily overcoming strong local opposition such as Herne, Bochum and soon-to-be fierce rivals Borussia Dortmund. These teams played in the so-called *Gauliga Westfalen* (league of the district of Westphalia). The *Gauligen* were created by the Nazis, who restructured organised football in 1933 and divided the country into 16 *Gaue*. (The word *Gau* was an old, seldom used Germanic term for 'region' and had distinct tribal connotations, which the Nazis loved.) Under this system, the 16 winners of the *Gauligen* were divided into four groups. The group winners then went on to play in the semi-finals of the national championship. This set-up had to be altered slightly when new *Gaue* were inconveniently added to the Reich due to Hitler's expansion policies. It was replaced during the last years of the war by less logistically demanding knockout rounds.

Schalke dominated the national championship, winning five titles between 1934 and 1940. Their only failures came in 1936, when Nuremberg beat them in the semis, and in 1938, when they lost 4-3 to Hannover 96 in a replayed final after a 3-3 draw, one of the biggest upsets yet seen in German football history. In 1939, they reached their sixth final in seven years, and this game was as one-sided as the Hanover matches had been tense. Adolf Urban scored, Otto Tibulski scored, Kuzorra scored, Szepan scored. Oh, and Ernst Kalwitzki scored – five times. But from a historical point of view, it was not so much the 9-0 scoreline that made the 1939 final special. Rather it was the name of Schalke's opponents, Admira Vienna. And, of course, it was the last final in peacetime.

When Schalke won their third title, with a 2-0 revenge victory over Nuremberg in 1937, the stage was set for another first. Because that same season, the *Königsblauen* (Royal Blues) also lifted the Cup, thus becoming the country's first official Double winners. This, however, needs some explaining, especially when one considers that the first round of the Cup was played in late August, two months after Schalke beat Nuremberg, and that the final was not held until January 9, 1938.

The competition that later became known as the *DFB-Pokal* (German FA Cup) was introduced as late as 1935. One would tend to think that some sort of cup tournament would be the easiest thing to organise and should thus historically precede any form of league football. Indeed that was the case in most other countries, including England, of course. That the Cup was a latecomer in Germany was a corollary to its failure to develop a national professional league.

As easy as a knockout competition may appear, the one thing it involves is travelling, and in a country as large as Germany that means extensive travelling. Not only did amateurism's double-standard bearers feel that it smacked of semi-professionalism to while away hours on a train, it also presupposed you had any interest whatsoever in forsaking a chance to play your local rivals in favour of meeting a strange team from the far north or south. The regional FAs mostly felt they were doing fine in their own little worlds. And the way the national championship was organised meant that, unlike in England, Spain or Italy, the title winners were decided in a one-off, set-piece match in a neutral stadium. By incorporating some elements of a cup competition in its later stages, it made the need for a separate competition seem less pressing.

There was a cup, but it involved representative teams of the various local associations. The Crown Prince Cup (named after the son of Kaiser Wilhelm II, who established it) saw the light of day in late 1908 and more or less lives on, under another name, to this day as a tournament contested by the best amateurs from each region, though it never captured the public's imagination. And so the story of the German FA Cup really begins with the Nazis, and in particular a balding, hard-partying official whose name no footballer or gymnast had ever heard before he became head of German sport. Hans von Tschammer und Osten was named *Reichssportkommissar* (later *Reichssportführer* according to the fashion of the time) in April 1933, and less than two years later he donated the trophy which bore his name until the end of the war – the Von-Tschammer-Cup. 'The competition is open to every one of the 14,000 football clubs,' he explained, 'but only teams from the top two levels [the *Gauligen* and the district leagues below them] are obliged to enter.' The idea was to keep players in shape during the close season, hence the peculiar scheduling, which would only be altered once Von Tschammer was as dead as the self-styled Third Reich.

Hans von Tschammer und Osten was one of those strange men German fascism either produced or was built upon. He possessed personality in spades, but apparently no character. Helmut Schön remembered him as 'a good-looking, conceited, pompous man', but most of the sports people who met him described Von Tschammer as jovial and clubbable, someone who loved to tell anecdotes while downing glass after glass. He knew next to nothing about sport, but got on well with many footballers and often made sure the party would not interfere with his charges too much.

This nicer side of the man has led some people to presume that he was not only out of place in his post but that his appointment had actually been a mistake and that it was Von Tschammer's older brother, a major, who was originally intended for the job. However, the likeable *Reichssportführer* was more than willing to forgo his live-and-let-live philosophy when he got an order from above. He was not only a socialite but also a First World War veteran and stout SA man, often strutting around in full military gear, who had built a secret police force intended to persecute, torture and murder communists and social democrats.

He survived in his job partly because he talked a good game, but mainly because most ideological and organisational duties were taken off his shoulders by football officials eager to please. Felix Linnemann worshipped the ground on which Von Tschammer walked, and the DFB's press officer Guido von Mengden rose through the ranks until he became a highly influential man in German sport, doing all the things Von Tschammer couldn't or wouldn't do. 'National Socialism,' Von Mengden wrote, 'has restored the meaning of sport,' adding that 'footballers are political soldiers of the Führer'. With willing men like that to be found within the DFB, Von Tschammer could rest easy and channel his efforts into wine, women and song.

Meanwhile, his cup competition flourished. More than 55,000 saw the first final, won by Nuremberg over Schalke, and 72,000 were on hand a year later when Szepan and Kuzorra beat Düsseldorf to claim that first Double. Yet the Cup final of 1938 (held in January 1939) was watched by only 36,000 fans. In part this was down to the abysmal weather conditions – a mixture of snow and rain that drove people away. It didn't help, however, that the match-up held little glamour for Berlin football fans. The eventual losers came from Frankfurt, yet they weren't the strong and popular Eintracht, who had missed out on the 1938 championship semi-finals only on goal average, but the much less fancied FSV Frankfurt. And the winners weren't even Germans: Rapid Vienna hoisted the trophy.

On March 12, 1938, German troops marched into Austria, according to Hitler because the new head of the Austrian government, Arthur Seyss-Inquart, had asked him to 'take the country back to the Reich'. Austria was referred to in Nazi Germany as the *Ostmark*, another of those ancient terms, meaning a region east of the border but one that was still considered part of the national territory. And indeed, following the First World War a large number of Austrians had demanded that their country become part of Germany, a notion vehemently rejected by the victorious powers. Now, less than 20 years later, hundreds of thousands of Austrians lined the streets to welcome the German soldiers and cheer Adolf Hitler, the man who had grown up in Linz and Vienna before moving to Munich so that he could evade the draft.

Naturally, the story of the *Anschluss* is more complicated. Fascism was clearly on the rise in Austria, with anti-Semitic and pro-Nazi sentiments widespread, and since the early 1930s the country's strongest ally had been Mussolini's Italy. But not all of Austria welcomed Hitler with open arms – the problem was that there was no choice. The closer Hitler and Mussolini grew, the more hemmed in Austria felt, and when hints grew that England was willing to swallow whatever Hitler did with his home country, Austria's fate was sealed.

Quite a few of the people whose arms remained firmly folded across their chests when the Germans started goose-stepping around happened to be footballers. There was, for instance, Hakoah Vienna, the Jewish club (Zionist, even) which had not only been the first continental club side to win a game against English professionals on English soil (in 1923 at Upton Park) but also winners of Austria's first fully professional league in 1925. Other clubs in the capital, most notably FK Austria and FC Vienna Wien (usually called 'First Vienna' in English), had many Jewish members and players, too – which wasn't surprising considering that the city boasted a Jewish population of more than 200,000 in the 1920s.

But even non-Jewish footballers and fans were not at all happy to be ruled by new masters. For many of them, this had nothing to do with politics or morals, it was a footballing problem. The country was very proud of the legacy of its *Wunderteam*, the legendary side born in May 1931, when Austria first beat a proud Scotland team 5-0, then demolished Germany 6-0. In December 1932 that team played England at Stamford Bridge and, despite losing 4-3, the Austrians mightily impressed their hosts. The *Daily Mail* declared Matthias Sindelar, Josef 'Pepi' Smistik, Walter Nausch and Adolf Vogl to be among 'the greatest players in the world' and detected 'genius'. After 1932, however, the *Wunderteam* slowly fell apart, and the results were never as good again. Yet, as the social historian Wolfgang Maderthaner noted: 'The myth of the *Wunderteam* as a synonym for idealised Viennese virtues was to survive for decades.'

That myth centred around the team's Danubian style of play, or what the Viennese fans lovingly referred to as the *Scheiberl* game. Call it combination or passing football (there is certainly no direct translation), mention the words 'ballet' and 'grace' – or simply say the Austrians played not unlike Schalke but added considerable flair to the mix. Whatever it was, it wasn't what the world regarded as typically German. In fact, many Austrian players felt only contempt for German football. 'They play strictly according to army regulations,' Rapid Vienna's Hans Pesser allegedly quipped. 'It's their strength-through-kicking football.' He must have said that before Schalke made a laughing stock of Admira in the 1939 final, but the fact remains that the Austrian players carried themselves with some aloofness and had little use for the Germans who were suddenly supposed to be their fellow countrymen, their brothers-in-arms and – perhaps the most annoying aspect for the Sindelars and Pessers – their team-mates.

The Germans felt much the same way. One might have expected their players and coaches to be intrigued by the prospect of incorporating the fabled Viennese wizards into their national side. However, history played a trick on Germany that it would repeat some 50 years later. Territorial expansion opened new possibilities, but they soon turned out to be problems rather than solutions. First, the German players disliked the Austrians almost as much as the reverse. They considered the Viennese stars to be not a little stuck-up as people and dainty to a fault as footballers. Second, over the previous ten years Germany had, after many sorrows and bitter defeats, finally managed to create a national side the country was almost as proud of as the Austrians were of their fading *Wunderteam*. It was a line-up football history knows as the *Breslau-Elf*.

Considering how thoroughly Schalke dominated German domestic football during the 1930s, it would have seemed logical for national coach Otto Nerz to build his team around players from Gelsenkirchen. There was only one problem: Nerz didn't like Schalke. To be more precise, he didn't like their style of play. A spinning top was for children, he figured, something that turns around *ad infinitum* but never goes anywhere. What Nerz loved was English football – fast, physical and always heading towards the opponents' goal. Ernst Kuzorra and Fritz Szepan were without any doubt among the greatest players in the country, but Nerz could not figure out how to use them and, almost as importantly, how to treat them. Or maybe he never really tried. Where others marvelled at the vision and technical ability of the two players, he fretted about their lack of pace and fumed at their tendency to disregard his authority.

In late October 1933, Germany were about to play Belgium in Duisburg (where Herberger oversaw the development of the West German FA). Kuzorra had played in five of the previous nine games and he was in very good shape. The papers were convinced he would start against Belgium, and Kuzorra must have been pretty certain of it himself. He even spoke in an interview about the tactics Nerz should employ. In fact, he kept talking to reporters while the other players were assembling for a team meeting. As he belatedly entered the room, Nerz announced the side. When Kuzorra heard the name of Düsseldorf's Willi Wigold in the forward line, he knew he was out of the team.

Herberger, who was present, later noted: 'I think Kuzorra never understood what he had done wrong.' As always, Herberger was right. Many years after the fact, Kuzorra told a journalist that it had been his own decision not to play and that he had feigned an injury: 'Truth be told,' he said, 'I withdrew because my brother-in-law Szepan, with whom I normally played, was only a substitute.' That was far from the truth, of course, but for a man as simple, stubborn and proud as Kuzorra, his own version might have become 'the truth' through re-telling, his way of coming to grips with a development he couldn't grasp. Or not fully grasp, because he understood the other part of the problem between him and Nerz very well, the one that had nothing to do with Kuzorra the obstinate man but everything to do with Kuzorra the Schalke player.

With something approaching glee, Kuzorra recited to a journalist an illuminating dialogue between him and Nerz which had indeed taken place, albeit not on the occasion of the game against Belgium. 'Nerz said to me: "Let me tell you something, your odds-and-ends football at Schalke, all that passing around, doesn't impress me one bit. If you and Szepan play together it'll be just fiddling and dribbling around, anyway."' Kuzorra would play only two more games for his country, one in 1936 and one in 1938.

Thankfully, Nerz was more patient with Szepan, if only reluctantly. In his third appearance for Germany, a 4-2 win over Denmark in 1931, Szepan set up three of the goals, but felt very uncomfortable with his surroundings. First there was the coach who never stopped grumbling about 'how slow Szepan is'. On top of that, the other players, especially Richard Hofmann, made a point of ignoring the proleterian rebel from the Ruhr. After the final whistle, Szepan stormed into the dressing room and frantically began packing his bag. 'There is going to be a banquet,' Nerz informed him. 'I'm going home,' Szepan shot back. 'You'll certainly not see me again in this team. In the future, I'll only play for Schalke. You know, there I've got ten mates, and that's important for playing football. Mates, you understand?'

Nerz never forgave Szepan for that scene, and the player's self-imposed exile lasted for two and a half years, during which the coach made no attempt to lure him back. Then, however, the 1934 World Cup in Italy was approaching. Nerz could do without Kuzorra, as he had more than enough capable forwards – Edmund Conen (FV Saarbrücken), Ernst Lehner (Schwaben Augsburg) and Otto Siffling (Waldhof Mannheim) were all outstanding talents. But there was a shortage in the creativity department, and so Nerz decided to eat humble pie for once and literally knocked on Szepan's door.

'We plan to adopt Arsenal's WM system for the World Cup,' Nerz said. 'What do you think of that?'

'Well,' a sceptical Szepan replied, 'if that means that the whole team defends, with only three forwards, that's not my idea of football.'

'We will build from the rear, based on a solid defence,' Nerz explained. 'But it's not going to be stereotyped. We want to score goals. We want to play. A modern, flexible system with a stopper. Make sure you'll be there.'

There were too many key words in that speech for Szepan not to relent – words like 'play', 'modern' and 'flexible'. What he didn't know, and what Nerz wisely withheld, was that he was supposed to be the stopper.

Germany had declined to take part in the 1930 World Cup, had in fact even refused FIFA's offer to stage the tournament. The reason was typical – it could not be expected of morally incorruptible Germans, argued the DFB, to share pitches with teams that fielded professionals. (Austria, incidentally, had also been identified by FIFA as a possible host nation, but it didn't possess sufficient stadiums.) Four years later, however, things had changed. As we have seen, many German football people, Sepp Herberger among them, considered the DFB's anti-professionalism stance increasingly anachronistic, and even those officials drenched in the Corinithian spirit had begun to accept that playing against professionals was neither contagious nor outrageous.

The main reasons behind Germany's participation in the 1934 World Cup, however, had little to do with the amateur problem. First, there had been no football at the 1932 Olympics (hockey and water polo were the only ball games on offer in Los Angeles) and everybody – players, coaches and fans – was thirsting for real, competitive matches. Second, football in Germany was no longer a matter even of chauvinism and patriotism. It had become much more important than that – it was propaganda.

Germany had left the League of Nations in October 1933 and now it was down to ambassadors everywhere – those in suits and those in shorts – to prove to the world that the country was nonetheless still civilised and peace-loving, while at the same time asserting its superiority, for instance through winning football matches. To that end, the Nazis solved the tiresome question of professionalism by insisting that all athletes had to be pure amateurs, while at the same time turning a blind eye whenever money changed hands. Naturally, the national team suddenly got all the help it needed. Whereas the side had only played 53 internationals between 1923 and 1932, in the next ten years it played 106 – exactly twice the previous amount – and no regional association or club voiced any protest.

Adolf Hitler, the vegetarian who wanted his youth to be 'firm as steel, tough as leather and quick as greyhounds', understood that sport was good for keeping a nation in shape and that football victories boosted the population's morale and Germany's image. That, however, was all he understood about sport. He didn't even have a personal interest in gymnastics, the classic Teutonic exercise, and only ever attended one football game in person. (Perhaps two, but more about that later.) A historian once explained the Führer's aversion to sport, a character trait he shared with Winston Churchill, by arguing Hitler had once commented he 'couldn't afford to participate in something he wasn't the best at'. Put differently, that simply means he hadn't the foggiest notion what sport was about and how it worked. That left the football experts some breathing space, but it also put them under huge pressure.

At first, Nerz coped exceedingly well with that pressure. Between March 1933 and June 1934, his team didn't lose a game, winning seven and drawing two. Luxembourg were soundly beaten (in Germany's 100th official international) to assure qualification for the World Cup, and at the tournament proper a young German team stormed to new heights. The Italian press, at this point still hostile because Mussolini had threatened Germany with war if Hitler invaded Austria, had portrayed the side as 'one of the weakest in the tournament'. Yet Germany beat Belgium 5-2 and Sweden 2-1 to reach the semi-final against Czechoslovakia.

So far, Szepan had indeed played in the stopper position, pretty much against his will. During the Sweden match, however, striker Karl Hohmann, who had scored both goals, suffered an injury that ended the World Cup for him. Back home, Sepp Herberger told Aachen's Reinhold Münzenberg: 'Now Nerz is going to call you up.' And he was thinking: 'Münzenberg will play stopper, and Szepan will finally become the inside-left he really is.' He was to be proved right again, though not immediately.

Nerz did tell Münzenberg to postpone his wedding and come to Italy, but Felix Linnemann insisted on not changing the basic set-up of the Sweden game for the semi-final. Still, Germany might have won a close, intensely fought match in which the Czechs finally triumphed 3-1, had it not been for three mistakes by the Dresden goalkeeper Willi Kress. So taken were the victors with their opponents that the head of the Czech delegation, a man by the wonderful name of Professor Rudolf Pelikán, later remarked that 'this was the best German football team since the great days of Nuremberg'.

History's punchline was that Italy beat Austria in the other semi-final with a single, highly controversial goal. That meant a *Wunderteam* in distress and drained by a heavy Milan pitch would meet Germany in the third-place play-off. Apart from all the political implications of that encounter, there was also the matter of those 6-0 and 5-0 defeats in 1931. There had been a few upheavals in the German squad during this tournament that had only indirectly to do with football. Defender Rudi Gramlich (Eintracht Frankfurt), a leather trader in his day job, had gone home before the semi-final because his Jewish employers needed his help – they were beginning to feel the effects of the Nazi-inspired boycotts. And the Bavarian Sigmund Haringer had left the squad on account of sickness. ('Caused by beer shortage,' his team-mate Conen was convinced. Haringer had already run foul of Nerz by eating an orange, which was forbidden because the coach thought tropical fruits, just like too much water, were bad for players' stomachs. So perhaps he beat it to pre-empt a ban.)

The most important changes for the match with Austria, however, were motivated by footballing reasons. Hans Jakob (Jahn Regensburg), destined to become the next German legend between the sticks after Stuhlfauth, replaced Kress in goal. Münzenberg was installed at the heart of the defence and Szepan played, at long last, in attack. Lehner scored within the first minute and the Viennese stars, lacking the injured Sindelar, never managed to come back. Germany won 3-2, returning home as the third best team in the world.

Or that was the theory. Because two very strong teams had been conspicuous at the World Cup through their absence. The title-holders Uruguay had pulled out and England had withdrawn from FIFA itself in 1928 over the issue of amateurism, after a brief and almost reluctant four-year spell as members of the world governing body. Thus December 4, 1935 was an important date for Germany, as they met England for the first time since 1930 and for the first time as representatives of a fascist regime.

Germany had played 16 games within the previous ten months to prepare for the 1936 Olympics in Berlin. Most results had been very good, including victories over Holland, France, Ireland and Czechoslovakia. The only two losses of the year had come against Spain in Cologne and Sweden in Stockholm. But the England v Germany match had, at least initially, very little to do with sport.

As had been the case with the game against France in Paris, the Nazi organisation Strength Through Joy (a subsidiary of the labour union German Work Front, if 'union' is indeed the right word for it) saw to it that German fans would travel with the team in unprecedented numbers. At least 5,000, probably more like 10,000, Germans were expected to be among the crowd of 50,000 at White Hart Lane, and liberal and left-wing groups in England were appalled at what they considered a political rally if not outright propaganda on the streets of London. The Home Office declared it would not allow German political demonstrations and urged the DFB to reduce the number of travelling fans. Hitler himself ordered Germany's ambassador in Britain to let it be known that if the hosts were having problems with the visitors' support, the FA could and should withdraw its invitation and cancel the game. But that was well nigh impossible, for organisational and political reasons, and so the match went ahead.

Sepp Herberger was sitting in the stands that day with his close friend Georg Knöpfle, also a football coach. His account of the events, which he confided to his diary, is remarkable. For once, Herberger, who was and always would be a fanatical football man before anything else – be it husband, citizen or voter – did not limit his report to what happened on the pitch. In fact, the football aspect of the encounter seems to have been of little interest to him. 'The national anthems rang out,' Herberger wrote, 'and following ours, again and once more, the

Horst-Wessel-Lied.' Horst Wessel was a Nazi who had been killed by political enemies in 1930, and the song that glorified him as a martyr was the semi-official NSDAP hymn, though not a part of the national anthem. The officials at White Hart Lane had agreed to the band playing the song after members of the German delegation insisted upon it.

It seems very peculiar that Herberger would note this in his diary and that he would use the tautological insertion 'again and once more'. But he must have felt extremely uneasy, to the point that he and Knöpfle tried to hide from their neighbours the fact that they were Germans. 'We have such a subtle feeling for how to create embarrassing situations,' he added with not a little irony and sadness. England won 3-0, but some of the German players stunned the hosts, especially goalkeeper Hans Jakob and Fritz Szepan, the latter immediately nicknamed 'Snowball' due to his flaxen hair. 'If he were English,' said the *Daily Telegraph*, 'the transfer sum for him would be considerable.' Oh yes, and Reinhold Münzenberg marked a young winger from Stoke out of the game – Stanley Matthews.

But the result wasn't the most important thing about this match. The British press pointed out that it had been a very clean struggle, very much in contrast to the so-called 'Battle of Highbury' against the world champions Italy the year before. And the *Daily Sketch* concluded: 'We don't think there has ever been a more noble demonstration for the understanding between two peoples.' Germany's footballers had lost, but Germany's 'political soldiers of the Führer' (in Von Mengden's words) had won. Maybe Herberger had known all along that he was not going to see a football match but a propagandistic charade.

Eight months later, however, the days of playing more for the national image than for results were over. The Berlin Olympics began, and nothing short of triumph was expected of Nerz's team, especially in the absence of professional teams – Britain patched together an untrained amateur squad, and Italy and Austria also sent over their amateurs. However, Nerz had to do without Szepan, who as a member of the banned Schalke team of 1930-31 qualified under Olympic regulations as a former professional. Still, that seemed only a minor irritant. Germany scored nine without reply against Luxembourg in the first round of the knockout tournament, which brought up Norway as the next opponents. It was a side coached by the former Hamburg player Asbjörn Halvorsen and a team Germany had never lost to in eight matches so far.

Hitler was making plans for the day of the game, trying to determine which competition he should grace with his presence. Rowing, that would be to his liking. Polo, whatever it was, sounded nice, too. That was when the *Gauleiter* of Danzig, Albert Forster, suggested football. 'The team will win gold,' Forster told the man who had never seen a football match in his entire life. And so Hitler went to Berlin's Poststadion on August 7, 1936. And not only the Führer. The propaganda minister Joseph Goebbels, the head of the Luftwaffe Hermann Göring, the deputy party leader Rudolf Hess, the interior minister Wilhelm Frick and the education minister Bernhard Rust were all there to lend support to Otto Nerz and revel in the glory of goals to be scored by Ernst Lehner, Otto Siffling or August Lenz, a young player from Dortmund and that club's first international.

Four days earlier, Hitler had watched the 100 metres in the nearby Olympic stadium, accompanied by the Reich Youth Leader Baldur von Schirach and Hans von Tschammer und Osten. To Hitler's horror, the race was won by the black American Jesse Owens. 'I shall not shake hands with this negro,' the Führer growled. Von Tschammer und Osten raised the objection that Hitler should act 'in the interests of sport', while Von Schirach had the guts (or, as Duff Hart-Davies wrote in his account of the Games, the naivety) to mention that Owens was 'a friendly and educated man'. Hitler shot back: 'Do you really think that I will allow myself to be photographed shaking hands with a negro?' According to Von Schirach it was only the second time in over a decade that Hitler had yelled at him. Hart-Davies concludes: 'What Schirach could not see was that Hitler was entirely cynical. Hitler was merely using the Games as a means of gaining prestige and time.' One wonders how many people within the German football camp really knew how much was at stake for the team.

At the risk of sounding repetitive, Herberger, for one, knew it. Or at least he sensed that Linnemann was making a mistake by demanding Germany should play 'a few young talents' to rest the first team for the later, more taxing matches. Nerz, too, felt uneasy with this plan, especially since Paul Janes had sustained an injury during one of the squad's daily 400-metre runs. Linnemann, though, was adamant, insisting: 'I am responsible to the *Reichssportführer*.'

With six minutes gone, the *Reichssportführer* looked ashen. Norway surprisingly took the lead and Goebbels noted: 'The Führer is very agitated, I'm almost unable to control myself. A dramatic, nerve-racking fight.' Twice the young Lenz missed easy chances, then Nerz ordered even the defenders into attack. The context forbids using the term 'siege', but Norway hardly managed to cross the halfway line. However, when they finally did so, in accordance with one of football's many unwritten laws, it decided the game. Five minutes from time Magnar Isaksen, a man with a strangely Jewish-sounding family name, caught Germany on the break and made it 2-0. Hitler immediately rose to leave the ground.

Herberger, meanwhile, had watched Italy v Japan and returned to the German camp to find it still deserted. He was in the process of devouring that most typical of German dishes, knuckle of pork with sauerkraut, when Georg Knöpfle entered the room.

'How was it?' Herberger asked. 'Two-nothing,' Knöpfle replied, before pointedly adding: 'Lost.' Herberger put down his knife and fork. He never ate knuckle of pork again in his life.

Elimination from the Berlin Olympics was a catastrophe for German football, but in a sense it may have sown the seeds that would bloom after the war. Naturally, the manager was blamed for the defeat, and possibly not without reason. The team lacked match practice, having played only one friendly, against Everton, during the three months leading up to the tournament. Moreover, many players had clearly been tired by Nerz's rigorous, military-style training and round-the-clock supervision. ('We didn't even have time to take a shit,' Karl Hohmann said pointedly.) But of course Nerz was not officially sacked. The DFB would not sully their hands with such a disgraceful measure for another 48 years and the Nazi worthies had lost too much faith in a sport so unpredictable that you sometimes actually lost despite all the pre-planning. For them, demanding Nerz's head wasn't worth the bother. Yet the DFB wasn't unhappy that Nerz had declared all along that he would slowly step down after the Olympics to concentrate on his lectures at the Reich Academy for Physical Education.

Nerz's natural successor was Herberger, and consequently he was named sole supervisor of the team for the international with Poland five weeks after the Norway debacle. But Nerz had indeed intimated he intended to step down 'slowly', and for the next 18 months the situation was muddled. Nerz wanted to work in tandem with Herberger, while Herberger felt too indebted to Nerz to start the row that would clear the air and the DFB didn't know what to do. But Herberger's influence increased with every day Nerz was away on academic duty, and during 1937 the German national team was gradually becoming his.

In May 1937, both Linnemann and Nerz joined the NSDAP. On their recommendation, Herberger had done so a lot earlier, but there is no recorded instance of him defending or spreading the party line. At a training camp, he even sent high-ranking SA men off with a flea in their ear after they suggested he should employ the same quasi-militaristic drills as their comrade Nerz had. Later, he outwitted the SS (*Schutzstaffel*, the secret police) to make sure his players were exempt from the obligatory reservists' training. But these examples should not be taken to mean that Herberger opposed the Nazis in any coherent ideological or political fashion. Both were terms with next to no meaning to this intensely private, solitary man who only cared about football and who had now come so close to reaching his ultimate goal – being the sole man in charge of the best football team his country could muster.

Beginning in late 1936, Adolf Urban and Rudi Gellesch of Schalke 04 became mainstays in the German team, supporting their club-mate Fritz Szepan and creating a subdued version of the Spinning Top game. In the vernacular of those days, Germany's football became less 'English' and more 'Scottish'. The next year began with four victories and a draw, before Germany met Denmark in Breslau (now Wroclaw in Poland) on May 16, 1937. The Danes had a good side, and so Nerz and Herberger were anxious about keeping the run going. Two weeks before the match, Nerz gave Herberger a sheet of paper with his proposed line-up. Herberger made three changes, Nerz nodded his head, and the team that would become known as the *Breslau-Elf* was picked:

Goalkeeper	Hans Jakob (Regensburg)
Right back	Paul Janes (Düsseldorf)
Left back	Reinhold Münzenberg (Aachen)
Right half	Andreas Kupfer (Schweinfurt)
Centre half	Ludwig Goldbrunner (Bayern)
Left half	Albin Kitzinger (Schweinfurt)

Right wing	Ernst Lehner (Augsburg)
Inside right	Rudi Gellesch (Schalke)
Centre forward	Otto Siffling (Mannheim)
Inside left	Fritz Szepan (Schalke)
Left wing	Adolf Urban (Schalke)

Only two teams in the whole of German football history are more famous than the *Breslau-Elf* – the 'Miracle of Berne' side of 1954 (for sheer mythical presence) and the 1972 team that beat England at Wembley and won the European Championship (for pure perfection). Because when the 90 minutes against Denmark were over, it suddenly seemed as if the ball thrown by August Hermann in 1874 had at long last landed, as if Germany had finally arrived at their own brand of football, a cross between the Danubian style of the south and the 'Flying Hussar' brand of the north, or between England's long-balls-and-tackles variety and the passing game of the Scots. However, in contrast to quite a few later German teams, the foundation was not athleticism but exquisite technique and an eye for combinations.

Of course the *Breslau-Elf* didn't come into being overnight. Almost the same team had played Scotland in Glasgow the previous October and had done so well that one Scottish paper claimed this was the best continental team ever to set foot on British soil. (Still, Germany lost 2-0, after a Gellesch goal was dubiously ruled out and Siffling hit the post.) The football historian Karl-Heinz Huba even traces the nucleus of the side back to the team that beat Austria at the 1934 World Cup. In fact, history agrees that most of the credit for the *Breslau-Elf* is due to Nerz, as it was he who had found, nurtured and taught most of the players. Football sometimes is as ironic as this. Nerz, the Teutonic disciplinarian with that England fixation, will primarily be remembered for shaping a team that was decidedly un-Teutonic and un-English.

Another noteworthy detail of the *Breslau-Elf*, sadly sunk into oblivion since, was that not all the positions were as fixed as they should have been in a pure WM formation. Siffling, nominally the centre-forward, was an elegant, lithe footballer, not a classic target man, and indeed he played as an inside forward at his club. Herberger had him lying deep, sometimes behind Szepan and Gellesch, which meant he eluded the grip of his Danish marker Henry Nielsen and created space for himself to run into. In other words, he did exactly what Nandor Hidegkuti did 16 years later at Wembley, when Hungary beat England 6-3 employing this supposedly revolutionary idea.

With seven minutes gone in Breslau, Lehner volleyed home following a clever move down the left flank. Then Otto Siffling, the lad from Herberger's home town Mannheim (whom Nerz viewed with suspicion because Siffling's throat instantly felt rough whenever he passed a pub), scored five times within barely 30 minutes. The fourth of these came after Lehner had delivered a breath-taking pass that travelled for 55 yards before landing at Urban's feet. Urban himself scored the seventh with a long-range screamer, and finally Siffling set up his captain Szepan to make it 8-0. There were still 12 minutes left, and the players began showboating, until Herberger walked to the sideline to tell them off.

Huba, who covered the game for *kicker*, had seen Norway v England and Czechoslovakia v Scotland on the previous two days. He concluded that Germany were superior to England and the Czechs, rivalled only by the Scots. And all contemporary accounts that we have bear him out. 'The robot style people like to pin on Germany sank into the realm of legend. Artistic football triumphed,' wrote the journalist Gerd Krämer.

Three days later, Schalke 04 convincingly won 6-2 against Brentford, a team that had finished the 1935-36 season in fifth place in the First Division. Suddenly the future looked rosy. So euphoric was the country in the wake of Breslau that the Nazis might have had second thoughts about football. Maybe the game wasn't that volatile an affair after all, maybe the Norway match had really been only an aberration? Didn't Germany win the remaining four matches of 1937, and didn't the team greet the new year that would bring another World Cup in the knowledge that there was now no opponent it had to fear?

But irony was to strike again. Just as the Nazis were finally presented with the successful football side they had wanted for propaganda, they themselves relegated the *Breslau-Elf* to history and set the stage for embarrassments that would surpass even the Olympic debacle. If the use of football parlance is permitted, the *Anschluss* proved an own goal. Today, Germany's main football feud is with Holland, but that did not take off for real until the 1970s. Whereas quarrelling with the Austrians goes back a long way.

At the 1912 Olympics in Stockholm, Germany led Austria 1-0 when, early in the second half, goalkeeper Albert Weber of Vorwärts Berlin collided with the goalpost. Austria then scored twice past a visibly dizzy Weber, whereupon Germany asked their opponents for permission to substitute the badly hurt goalie. Under the rules of the time, the Austrians could refuse the request – which they promptly did. Weber then also suffered a heat stroke and had to be carried off the pitch. (It's safe to say it wasn't his day.) An outfield player went in goal, and Austria ran out 5-1 winners.

Twenty-two years later, the third-place play-off at the World Cup in Naples produced a comic but telling situation – both Germany and Austria appeared in the same kit (white shirts, black shorts). And both teams refused to change, unwilling to relent even in trivial matters. A few minutes into the game, the Italian crowd voiced its displeasure at not being able to tell the teams apart. Referee Albino Carraro stopped the game and, after lots had been drawn to determine who would have to budge, told the Austrians to wear pale-blue Napoli shirts.

There were two other incidents in that match that neither side would forget. With the score 2-1 to Germany and the Austrians apparently getting the upper hand, Edmund Conen lost the ball to defender Karl Sesta (Austria Vienna), a dear friend of the absent Sindelar. Instead of passing the ball, Sesta ridiculed Conen by momentarily sitting down on it. Three minutes before the interval, he tried the same trick again. But this time the fuming Conen sensed what was coming. He stole the ball from under Sesta's backside and crossed it to Lehner, whose shot decided the match.

One World Cup later, both Conen and Sesta were still internationals, only this time they were told they would play for the same country. The Nazis could have sent two strong national teams to France, as both Germany and Austria had qualified. And indeed that's what Sepp Herberger at first thought was the normal way of proceeding. 'It would have been child's play,' he wrote. 'Anyone who knows about man management and team management would have agreed.' But in late March, the Austrian FA had informed FIFA of its dissolution, thereby waiving the right to field an autonomous team. To make matters worse, Felix Linnemann told Herberger that 'on instructions from above' his order was not just to build a pan-German squad but to pay attention to parity when picking the team. Six Germans and five Austrians or six Austrians and five Germans, that was to be the rule. 'In our sphere as well as in others,' Linnemann reported, 'a visible expression of our solidarity with the Austrians who have come back to the Reich has to be presented. The Führer demands a 6:5 or 5:6 ratio. History expects this of us!' With that, Linnemann and Nerz – both unpleasant people but no fools – mumbled something about 'occupational demands' and went on leave. Herberger wrote in his diary: 'Me: lonely and deserted on the edge of a steep rock.'

Herberger knew his mission was impossible, but he tried to make the best of it. He couldn't cure the hatred between the two camps, but he might be able to, as he put it, 'get the Austrians down from their heaven of supposed superiority'. To that end, he organised a practice match between teams from the 'Old Reich' and the *Ostmark*. The Germans won 9-1, which did dampen the Austrian aloofness a bit, but added rancour to antipathy.

A few days later, the two groups sat in the dressing room and engaged in a staring match. Suddenly the fabled Viennese technician Josef Stroh took a ball and began juggling it with various parts of his body. The Austrians exaggeratedly applauded Stroh. 'Pepi is a wizard,' they said, 'he's got some touch.' The Germans got the message, and their eyes wandered over to Szepan. The Schalke player rose and asked Stroh for the ball. Then he imitated the Austrian's moves and tricks with uncanny exactness. As an encore, Szepan volleyed the ball against the wall, only inches above the heads of the Austrians. A cold silence covered the room. Then Szepan whispered: 'You arseholes.'

Herberger was distraught, complaining that his captain 'had added fuel to the fire'. The coach began taking long walks with individual players, Germans and Austrians, to talk them into overcoming their squabbles for a common good. Then he went to see Matthias Sindelar, the legendary 'Paper Man'. However, the sensitive star of the *Wunderteam* begged Herberger not to select him for a pan-German World Cup team, claiming he was too old and unfit. 'He proved to be the fine fellow I had known him to be,' a disappointed but understanding Herberger noted. 'As I tried again and again to change his mind, I gained the idea that he had some other reasons to decline. I almost had the impression it was down to feelings of uneasiness and rejection to do with the political developments that weighed on his mind and caused his refusal.'

Despite occasional reports to the contrary, Sindelar was not of Jewish heritage, but the Gestapo (secret police) did have a file on him that labelled him 'a social democrat and a Jews' friend'. While this didn't stop him from buying a cafe at a good price after the original owner, a Jew, was dispossessed, it can be said with some certainty that Sindelar despised the Nazis and had little use for Germans in general. That some of his team-mates at Austria Vienna, for instance skipper Walter Nausch (whose wife was Jewish), were forced to emigrate after the *Anschluss*, didn't help matters.

Fittingly, his last appearance in an international came on April 3, 1938 in Vienna, a match that pitted Germany against Austria for what was supposed to be the last time. This 'Alliance Game', as the Nazis dubbed it, was intended as a propagandistic display of unity and brotherhood. The circumstances surrounding the match are somewhat unclear to this day. For instance, it does not appear that the teams were under any orders to settle for a draw, but there are still people who claim the Austrians were told not to score.

They strangely missed a few golden opportunities in the first half, that's true, but after the break Sindelar and Sesta made it 2-0, and the 'Paper Man' did a dance of joy directly in front of the VIP rostrum that was covered with swastikas, as 60,000 fans frantically cheered what used to be their team. The Austrian academic Michael John wrote of this day: 'A certain ambivalence came to light. Irrespective of the social realities, namely that a considerable part of the Austrian population was favourably or even euphorically disposed to the *Anschluss* with Hitler's Germany, wild choruses of "*Österreich!*" (Austria) could be heard repeatedly.' Neither the DFB nor the Austrian FA lists this match as an official international.

If that game was embarrassing to Herberger, the future held something a lot worse. First, however, there was a ray of light.

As of May 12, 1938, Otto Nerz officially stepped down from all national team duties, leaving the side solely to Herberger. (It took Nerz over two weeks to inform Herberger personally, though. The relationship between the two men had deteriorated over the past few years.) Two days later, England came to Berlin. This was the game in which Stanley Matthews and his teammates infamously lifted their right arms in the Nazi salute to greet their hosts, though unbeknownst to the English, Hitler wasn't even present. He had had enough of football. Then they beat a lifeless, disappointing German side 6-3.

Herberger's best man on the pitch was Hans Pesser – the only Austrian, as there had been some confusion prior to the match about which sort of team Herberger was supposed to field. Nerz had told Herberger that an all-German team would play England, while an all-Austrian side should face Aston Villa a day later. When Herberger consulted Felix Linnemann about this, the president of the DFB had to admit utter ignorance. 'It was becoming increasingly obvious,' wrote Herberger's biographer Jürgen Leinemann, 'that only the sports politicians had the say. The truth was that Linnemann and Nerz were no help to him. They had no right to vote and little influence. And they were always willing to agree. And he, Josef Herberger, wasn't even asked.' Chaos reigned. Chaos and absurdity. Since the Austrians were professionals, they had to be given fake jobs to keep the amateur sham alive. Thus the city of Vienna pretended to employ (and pay) the players – for instance as butchers or old people's nurses.

A week after beating Germany, England surprisingly lost in Zürich to Switzerland, coached by the Austrian Karl Rappan, employing his famed 'Swiss bolt' tactics (one of the first systems to use a sweeper). That was an ominous portent for the pan-German patchwork team, as the Swiss were to be their first-round opponents at the 1938 World Cup in France. The game was scheduled for June 4, and ill-feeling hung palpably in the air. Little Switzerland, always the country Germany liked to play the most, had developed a strong antipathy towards its large, now fascist neighbour. A year before, in May 1937, near-tumultuous scenes took place when Germany came to Zürich. The Swiss threw rotten fruit at travelling German fans and tried to destroy every swastika flag they could get hold of. Now, in Paris, the French followed suit, at one point hurling broken bottles at the German players.

Still, Josef Gauchel put Germany ahead, but Switzerland equalised before half-time. Herberger's team included five Austrians, as stipulated, and the longer the game lasted the more conspicuous it became that, in the words of the German journalist Christian Eichler, 'Germans and Austrians prefer to play against each other even when they're in the same team.' The second half and 30 minutes of extra time yielded no further goals – but a sending-off for Hans Pesser, who was spat at as he left the pitch.

Five days later, there was a replay, these being the days before group matches or penalty shoot-outs. Again, Herberger picked five Austrians (not three, as Brian Glanville says in *The History of the World Cup*), but made seven changes to the line-up. That seemed to save the day, as Germany took a 2-0 lead after less than half an hour. But then the roof fell in. In what might well be the greatest 60 minutes in Swiss football history, Rappan's team rose to the challenge, led by striker Georges Aeby, who suffered a gaping wound to his head and even lost consciousness but returned with a bandage covering his stitches to lead the attack. The Swiss scored four times against a German team that disintegrated under the pressure. The combined forces of the *Breslau-Elf* and the *Wunderteam* were eliminated before the World Cup they had set out to win had really begun.

Who was to blame? Easy. 'The Austrians have to learn a lot,' Herberger informed Linnemann. 'During a game they prefer to give in, instead of fighting for victory.' Herberger was angry, dejected, even briefly desperate. But one of his character traits was the willingness to learn from whatever happened to him. The 1938 drama taught him quite a few things – about who has to be in command and what sort of player is needed to achieve success – that he would later put to astonishing use.

As 1938 turned into 1939, Germany collected three 4-1 wins in a row, against Poland, Romania and Belgium. In each of these games, a young novice from SC Dresden scored, who had learned the finer points of the game from the English coach Jimmy Hogan. His name was Helmut Schön and his biggest footballing idol was Matthias Sindelar.

Two days before Schön scored against Belgium, his fifth goal in his fourth international, the same Sindelar visited his new girlfriend, an Italian Catholic with a Jewish background, Camilla Castagnola. It was January 23, 1939. The two probably emptied a bottle, had drunken sex and then fell asleep. What they didn't know was that one of the chimneys in the block in which Castagnola had her flat was defective. Her neighbours had complained of carbon monoxide-induced sickness during the previous days, but nothing was done, and the chimney still emanated fumes – which proceeded to kill the greatest Austrian footballer of all time in his sleep. (Castagnola died a few hours later in the hospital.) This is the most banal but still the most likely explanation for Sindelar's death. There are competing theories, though, including murder at the hands of the Nazis or a suicide pact. While these two seem absurd, it can't be ruled out that Castagnola's well-established ties to the Viennese underworld somehow triggered a tragedy.

While Austria mourned and Herberger tried to find a team for the 1940 Olympics – beating Norway 4-0 to take revenge for 1936, then losing honourably to an Italian side that seemed invincible – Hitler moved closer towards his personal goal. In

September 1938, Neville Chamberlain agreed to grant Germany the Czechoslovak Sudetenland in return for the promise to stop making territorial demands. But six months later, Slovakia first declared its independence, then its virtual entry into the German Reich. A day later, the Czechoslovak head of state, Emil Hacha, was ordered to Berlin and forced to sign a treaty that put the fate of all Czechs into the hands of the German Führer. Immediately, German troops occupied Bohemia and Moravia. Chamberlain now realised what was happening and assured Poland that any form of German attack on the country would result in war. France followed suit.

On September 1, 1939, Herberger and his wife Eva were taking a stroll in the streets of Berlin. They were passed by a convoy of cars, and Herberger could make out Hitler and Göring sitting next to each other. The Führer was on his way to a radio station to speak to his people, but Herberger would only learn that a few minutes later when he stepped into a cafe to hear Hitler announce that the country was at war with Poland. Two days later, English and French diplomats entered the Reich chancellery to present formal declarations of war to the German government. A perplexed Göring, who like many others had never expected Chamberlain to carry out his threat, slowly said: 'If we lose this war, the heavens have mercy on us.'

6

A MATTER OF SURVIVAL

HERBERGER AND SCHÖN AMID THE RUINS

'IF YOU VOTE FOR Hitler, you vote for war!' That's what Annelies Gräfe's father had said again and again. Her family, stout democrats, was one of the few that not only detested the Nazis but had been certain almost from the beginning that the fascists would plunge the country into a bloody and probably hopeless war. That is why, on September 1, 1939, Annelies shook with fear on hearing Hitler announce that Germany had invaded Poland.

Her new boyfriend was less pessimistic. He came from a middle-class, liberal family who were still renting out a flat to a Jewish publisher and had no intention of ending the arrangement. He had no truck with the Nazis, but he was also young, a ladies' man and a footballer. Carefree, as such people tend to be, he believed the trouble with Poland would develop along the same lines as the Austria and Czechoslovakia affairs. Little did Helmut Schön suspect that September 1 would ultimately result in his physical and psychological uprooting, and in a night dreadful beyond imagination.

As of now, he even considered himself lucky, given the circumstances. During the first weeks of the war, football came to a complete halt, as most players were immediately drafted into the army. By September 5, Sepp Herberger had already lost nine members of his squad to the military. But Schön was invalided out due to recurring knee problems, an injury he had first sustained shortly before the 1936 Olympics. His friend, the actor Hans Hansen, quietly said: 'Can't you give me that knee?'

As early as November, however, Hans von Tschammer und Osten declared that the football championship should be continued. The non-aggression pact between Hitler and Stalin (August 23, 1939) meant the Nazis could disregard their potentially largest front, to the east, and they now correctly presumed that their armed forces, more than three million strong and prepared for war since at least 1936, would meet little resistance. In less than a year Denmark, Norway, Holland, Belgium and France fell. Hitler sent his peace terms to England, but the new prime minister Winston Churchill didn't even reply properly. That upset the plans of the Nazis, who had hoped to close down all fronts, especially the African one, to prepare another breach of a treaty by invading the Soviet Union. And so, in August 1940, the German air force began their major attack on the country that had invented football.

Three weeks before the Luftwaffe came down on England, Schalke 04 had won their fifth title, against SC Dresden. Dresden were a club on the up and one that stood in marked contrast to Schalke. First, they were very different cities. Gelsenkirchen was, and is, no beauty but a hastily constructed, single-minded industrial town. Dresden, on the other hand, was one of the country's most gorgeous cities until the war. The poet Johann Gottfried Herder had called it 'the German Florence' and that was certainly no poetic excess. Second, while Schalke bred simple men like Szepan and Kuzorra, Dresden produced sophisticates like Helmut Schön (whose father was an art dealer) or flamboyant stars like Richard Hofmann. Yes, 'King Richard', who had scored three against England in 1930, was still active and still in good shape. However, he was no longer an international. In 1933, he had posed for a cigarette advertisement in return for 3,000 marks, whereupon the DFB unceremoniously expelled one of the country's best players. Hofmann was pardoned 18 months later, but never played for the national team again and missed the 1934 World Cup. The reason for all this was the pay, of course, not the product. Hofmann was a non-smoker.

The 1940 final was a drab game that a superior Schalke side won 1-0 because only Ernst Kalwitzki could put the ball past Dresden's strong goalkeeper Willibert Kress (he of the mistakes in the 1934 World Cup semi-final), but the quality of matches was no longer of real concern. What counted was that they took place at all. Football, already a propaganda tool, now became an undertaking in the interests of war as well. Matches distracted and entertained the people in hard times, and, what's more, they proved to the world and to Germans themselves that the nation had nothing to worry about. So the English Football League had suspended competition on September 2, 1939? Well, that only befitted a weak and timid nation.

'German football closed the championship season of 1939-40 with a powerful demonstration of its inner strength and closeness to the people,' trumpeted the magazine *Fußball* after the final, as if to make English ears ring. 'Berlin's Olympic Stadium was sold out, with close to 100,000 enthusiastic spectators inside – just like in the most tranquil peacetime.' These 'enthusiastic spectators' had angrily demanded 'Play football!' during the second half, but never mind the details. The days of empty rhetoric had arrived. 'The men in action can be proud of sport's efforts on the home front,' concluded *Fußball*, 'and sport is proud of the army under whose protection it can develop so splendidly.'

Not all sportsmen felt the benefit of that protection. While Dresden progressed in the Tschammer Cup to compensate for the defeat against Schalke, Oskar Rohr despairingly tried to find a way to hide from his own people. The player who had scored five goals in his four internationals during 1932-33 was called a 'traitor to the country' by *kicker* and 'a gladiator who sold himself abroad' by *Fußball* for having moved to France and become a professional seven years previously. The newspapers even speculated that Rohr joined the French Foreign Legion when Germany invaded France (which appears to have been true). After France's capitulation, he moved to Sète, in the deep south, but was eventually arrested, probably in late 1942. He was deported to Germany, where he spent two months in a concentration camp, before being sent to the death trap that was the eastern front. But Rohr survived. (His great-nephew, Gernot Rohr, made more than 350 appearances for Girondins de Bordeaux and then worked as a coach in France and Africa.)

Dresden lifted the Cup in 1940, through an extra-time golden goal (not such a Nineties novelty, after all) against Nuremberg, having beaten Rapid Vienna en route to the final. Their main target, however, was the national championship. The next year, they won 20 of the 22 games in their regional *Klasse* – the word *Liga* having been outlawed by the Nazis because it sounded too much like the English 'league' – and cruised through the group stage of the finals to reach the semis. But there they met Rapid again, and this time the Austrians ran out 2-1 winners. The other team in the final was, who else, Schalke.

After eight minutes, the serial winners from the Ruhr were 2-0 up, and it seemed as if Rapid might do even worse than their city rivals Admira, who had lost 9-0 in 1939. Rapid's star striker

Franz Binder even missed a penalty, but somehow the Viennese managed to avoid further damage until the 60th minute, when Heinz Hinz made it 3-0 to Schalke from an impossible angle. Instead of deciding the match, however, this goal merely prepared the stage for the most stunning nine minutes German football has ever seen at this level.

Two minutes after Hinz's goal, Georg Schors pulled one back for Rapid, and that suddenly brought Binder to life. Binder, by the way, is often credited with being one of the very few players who scored over 1,000 goals in their careers. Three of them came now – a direct free-kick from 18 yards (63rd minute), a penalty (65th) and another free-kick that whooshed into the left-hand triangle (71st). From then on, Schalke were in the driver's seat again, but it was too late. Those crazy six minutes had made Rapid the first, and only, non-German champions of Germany.

Reading that account, one will hardly be surprised to learn that Schalke fans all over the country whispered the words 'fix' and 'orders from above'. Two penalties! And those free-kicks, were these really fouls? The Nazis, said the rumour-mongers, wanted a champion from the *Ostmark* for political reasons. This belief was nourished by reports that Hitler had watched the game from the stands, though the source materials are not in agreement on this. Most authors say Hitler only ever saw one football match and we know that he was at Germany v Norway in 1936, so Schalke v Rapid would constitute a second offence – and another German defeat.

Like all good conspiracy theories, this one has never been proven – just like the one that Admira's fans had brought up two years earlier after their team had conceded nine goals. However, there are a few points that shouldn't go unnoticed even by one-eyed Schalke supporters. First, Rapid were a good team, as simple as that. They boasted the former or future (German) internationals Rudolf Raftl, Franz Wagner, Stefan Skoumal, Willy Fitz, Hans Pesser and, of course, Franz 'Bimbo' Binder. These guys were no pushovers. Second, just after Schors had made it 3-1, Rapid's Leopold Gernhardt had to clear the ball off the line with a desperate, last-ditch effort, not to mention that Schalke hit the post in the closing stages. Who knows, it might have been just one of those days.

One person who firmly believed 'those days' didn't exist for Schalke was their forward Adolf Urban. He was convinced that his team had been robbed and swore he'd be back next year to take revenge. Neither the conviction nor the oath was easy to make, as Urban was not on the pitch at Berlin's Olympic Stadium with his team-mates on the day of the final. And he wasn't at home, either. He was lying in the dirt and mud of a godforsaken trench somewhere very far indeed from Gelsenkirchen. Adolf Urban was fighting the Soviet Union for his Führer, listening to the match and a lot of white noise on the radio.

In late 1940, Germany's supposedly swift and clean war had begun to show signs of being neither. The bombers that were meant to force England to her knees were vulnerable, because the Nazis' fighter planes had to refuel too often. Thus, anti-aircraft guns shot down well over 2,000 defenceless bombers. And not only did the English refuse to give in despite massive civilian losses, they also managed to cause the Italians in north Africa enormous headaches. Hitler was forced to send troops to help his ally. Not content with now having two problematic fronts, he also decided to occupy Yugoslavia and Greece in April 1941. That proved easy, but it cost time and would ultimately result in the undoing of the seemingly invincible German war machine. Because when German troops finally invaded the Soviet Union, on June 22, 1941, the day of the Schalke v Rapid final, the Russian winter was already drawing breath.

A few months after the invasion of the Soviet Union had begun, Germany played Sweden in Stockholm and lost 4-2. 'Some of our players don't have the stamina that is needed to beat opponents such as this one,' noted Sepp Herberger. 'The war and its attendant circumstances, the army duty, guard duty, night duty, air-raid warnings and so on, do of course unfavourably affect the players' stamina.' It was a sensible assessment, but only Herberger could have added this afterthought: 'I detect, however, that these things are starting to become a place of refuge for flimsy excuses on the part of our players.' He then listed a few names in his diary, names of players he suspected of being less than completely committed to football, one of whom was Helmut Schön.

As was so often the case with Herberger, one doesn't know whether to pity the man or to marvel at him. His was a single-mindedness you find either in the greatest of men, or in the lowest. He never seems to have felt really deeply about anything but football, as you would expect of a man who leaves the world 361 thick files full of notes which almost never touch upon anything other than the names of players, their strengths and weaknesses, accounts of games, copies of discussions about football, or recorded thoughts concerning tactics and strategy. Granted, we know that he once came to the help of a Jew who was being attacked on the street and that he always stuck by his family doctor, who was married to a Jew and ostracised by almost everybody else. But whether these acts were inspired by a deep-seated moral conviction rather than a footballer's simple sense of honour and solidarity we don't know. He never told us, not once in 361 files. (Incidentally, one of the scholars who would spend months and years sifting through Herberger's extensive estate in the Nineties, after the death of his widow, was Wolfgang Weber, the former international.)

We also know that he took very good care of his international players, that he did everything within his power to make life easier for them. In the autumn of 1941, Herberger was involved as a consultant for the making of a football film, *Das Grosse Spiel* (The Big Game) – he also played a small part himself. He managed to have no fewer than 19 of his internationals called back from the front to appear as extras. Of course, this made the match sequences more credible, but artistic considerations hardly ranked high on Herberger's list of priorities. His main interest was to safeguard his players, and later that year he proved he was willing to risk a lot to achieve this.

Preparing for a game against Slovakia in December, he tried to obtain leave passes for those players, by now the majority, who were at the front. On learning that passes were handed out mainly to combatants who had been decorated, Herberger simply invented a few medals in his letter to the command. 'Considering the negative developments at the front, I conducted myself moderately with regard to the awarding of decorations,' he wrote, 'handing out one Iron Cross I, three Iron Crosses II and a Storm Badge.' This sounds innocuous, and you can visualise Herberger's smiling, wrinkled face as he wrote it, but make no mistake: it was forgery of a document that cheapened honours which were of profound importance to the Nazis and the military hierarchy. Many people saw the inside of a concentration camp for lesser things. Still, as brave as this act was, would Herberger have done anything like that for somebody who did not happen to be good at football?

One man who was very good at football and who would soon become Herberger's favourite player, in fact something like a surrogate son, was the best player Germany would produce until Franz Beckenbauer – and there are more people than you would think who would still put him above the 'Kaiser'. Fritz Walter was born on October 31, 1920, in Kaiserslautern, 40 miles west of Herberger's home town Mannheim, in the slightly remote, slightly backward region of Pfalz (Palatinate).

Walter's father, a boxing fan, worked as a lorry driver until he lost an eye in an accident, then opened a restaurant that would become the de-facto clubhouse of 1. FC Kaiserslautern. He had spent some time in America, but returned home before the First World War and married a Berlin woman. This may sound like a halfway cosmopolitan surrounding, but people from Pfalz have a reputation for being reticent and mistrustful, while fostering the strong sense of family common among countrymen and women. This would cause Fritz Walter a few problems later on, when he married a gorgeous Italian who was viewed with suspicion both by his family and by Sepp Herberger. But it also made for tightly knit groups and deep friendships. Fritz and his two younger brothers, Ottmar and Ludwig, lived near two boys called Ernst and Werner Liebrich. Ernst went to the same class as one Werner Kohlmeyer. All six kids loved football, all would play for 1. FC Kaiserslautern and four of them would win the World Cup. (Ludwig Walter's brief career – two *Oberliga* games – was ended by an injury received during the war.)

Before experiencing the World Cup, however, Fritz Walter first got his share of a world war. He made his international debut in July 1940 against Romania, playing as centre-forward and scoring three goals in Germany's 9-3 win. 'I'm happy, Fritz,' smiled Herberger afterwards. 'You didn't disappoint me. You can come again.' That was easier said than done because, like most other sportsmen, Walter was drafted into the army in late 1940, when things got serious on the various fronts.

Walter the soldier would march, drive or fly through France, Sardinia, Corsica, Elba, Bohemia and Romania during the following years. That wasn't unusual for a member of the *Wehrmacht*. But Walter the footballer also saw Slovakia, Hungary, Yugoslavia, neutral Switzerland, Sweden, Finland,

Croatia and Bulgaria. Because, incredibly, Herberger's national side played another 25 matches, often chaotic, haphazard affairs, until late 1942, when everything collapsed. And Walter, even more unbelievably, missed only one of them. (Helmut Schön, who was not drafted into the military, played just five; the next most consistent man after Walter was the veteran Paul Janes with 19 appearances.)

That was only possible because Herberger was so enamoured of Walter that he tried every trick in the book to get the young player away from the mortal danger of the front and back to the safety of a football pitch. 'Herberger feinted, wooed and plotted,' says his biographer Jürgen Leinemann, 'to guarantee some sort of shelter for the protection and nurturing of the football genius amid the increasingly menacing turmoil of war.' But posting Walter and the others home and detailing them for football duty became more and more difficult.

Germany's internationals during the war were all but worthless games against weak opposition, either allies or occupied countries (and, of course, dependable Switzerland), with two possible exceptions worth remembering. In April 1941, a brilliant German team beat Hungary 7-0 in Cologne, bringing back memories of the *Breslau-Elf* (whose star, Otto Siffling, had died of pleurisy at just 27 years of age, shortly after the outbreak of war). For the return match in Budapest, on May 3, 1942, the wounded Magyars meant to restore some pride and deservedly led 3-1 at the interval, having thoroughly dominated their opponents. 'Don't let this become a catastrophe,' a pale Herberger warned his men at half-time. Led by young Fritz Walter, the Germans not only restricted the damage but managed to turn the game around, eventually winning 5-3. Three years later, his performance in this match would save Walter's life; 12 years later, it helped win the World Cup.

As 1942 drew to a close, Herberger's strikers scored 15 times in three matches against Switzerland, Croatia and Slovakia, the latter an ugly affair marked by aggressive play and a hostile crowd in Bratislava. For 1943, games with Sweden, Spain, Italy and Hungary had been scheduled, but they never happened. News reached home that things had gone badly wrong on the eastern front.

On December 11, 1941, a few days after Pearl Harbor, Hitler declared war on the US to support his Japanese ally. Around that time, Germany slowly began to suffer visible marks of the war. Leinemann evokes the shift in mood by noting the changing colours: 'The windows of buses and trams were painted a blue shade that seemed to deaden all colours. And the atmosphere, too. Berlin's Victory Column was painted black, so as not to shine in the lights of headlamps. Since September, Jews had been forced to wear the yellow star.' Food and clothing became scarce, the air-raid alarm sounded ever more often.

Yet, during the first part of 1942, General Erwin Rommel advanced to El Alamein, near Alexandria in Egypt. In the Soviet Union, the German troops had managed to ride out the first winter and were quickly progressing towards Moscow. The mood brightened a bit. When the famous fighter pilot Major Hermann Graf, a former goalkeeper, paid a visit to Herberger's squad he jovially declared: 'I always feel good when I'm around footballers.' Herberger replied: 'Perhaps I will remind you of this one day.'

Graf had just been honoured for having brought down his 200th enemy plane and Hitler would soon send him to France to instruct trainee pilots. The plane that Graf had shot down to earn the Knight's Cross with diamonds had crashed on to the frozen earth near Stalingrad. There the German troops had been halted and became involved in a desperate attritional battle. Hitler forbade them to retreat and during November the Red

Army encircled the aggressors. Two months later, the Germans surrendered. Only 6,000 of the 235,000-strong army ever saw their homes again.

Rommel, meanwhile, had wisely begun to withdraw (ignoring orders to the contrary) in the face of British and American offensives, and the *Afrika Korps* would capitulate in May 1943. The war was effectively lost, but it was far from over. On February 18, 1943, Joseph Goebbels gave a speech in Berlin and asked if the country was willing to engage in 'total war'. The selected party people present enthusiastically replied: yes. Two days later, the precise meaning of 'total war' was laid out in writing. Sepp Herberger only studied those parts that were of importance to him.

'International sporting competitions are to be cancelled until further notice,' the newspapers explained, 'because front soldiers are no longer available and people doing labour service will not be granted leave of absence.' It meant Herberger was out of a job, and worse, without an aim in life. But at least there was to be some football, as the papers also noted that 'sporting competitions of a local character are to be carried through in order to sustain the work ethic'. When hundreds of letters written by soldiers begging for football at home arrived at the ministry, this concession was partially extended to nationwide contests as well.

While the national championship continued through the months and then years of growing chaos and anxiety, the scheduling of games became more and more difficult. Travelling turned into an uncertain adventure due to fuel rationing, and the trains were increasingly commandeered for transporting military personnel (not to mention concentration camp victims). Even playing itself came to be a problem when ever larger numbers of young men and adolescents were sent to the crumbling front lines. In 1942, there was still a semblance of regular league competition, because some clubs had at least a few players stationed nearby. Schalke's Szepan and Kuzorra, for instance, did service at an airforce base in Gelsenkirchen.

Still, that year is marked by the mass appearance of sides like Air Force Sports Club Pütnitz or Sports Union SS Strassburg. Those military teams had the advantage of stable squads, whereas normal clubs suffered from sudden call-ups or travel orders. Not that the military sides were completely immune to such surprises. In May 1942 the NCO candidates from Marienwerder were preparing for their play-off match with the East Prussian club VfB Königsberg to get to the knockout rounds, when all of a sudden everybody was dispatched into combat. The teenage reserve team lost 7-1, and Königsberg next beat a police XI 8-1 to reach the quarter-finals.

The 1942 championship was won by Schalke, of course, who beat First Vienna 2-0 in the final. Schalke's line-up gave no indication that Germany was a country at war with the world. Szepan and Kuzorra played, as did Tibulski, Kalwitzki and Urban, who thus kept his promise of coming back to help his club erase the memory of the previous year's drama. Urban also played in the Cup final four months later, which Schalke lost 2-0 to 1860 Munich. However, this was the last big game he ever took part in. Urban's next stop was Stalingrad and he did not return. News of his death first reached many Germans via the BBC's German-language broadcasts.

In 1943, things became farcical in the early rounds. In some *Gaue*, teams scored well over 100 goals in 18 games. Nuremberg won one match 20-1. Even in the last 16, there were results of 8-0 and 8-1. In many cases, games had to be abandoned if the ball was damaged, because no replacement could be found. What the press pointed out, however, was that only seven of the 300 highest-ranking clubs had to deregister their teams. Yet Hans von Tschammer und Osten could not take credit for this 'proof of morale', as one paper put it. He died on March 25, 1943 from pneumonia.

The title that year was at last won by SC Dresden, 3-0 winners over FV Saarbrücken. Helmut Schön recalled that some of his team-mates were anxious about playing in this game, saying to him: 'The British will know that the final is on. Now what if they drop a bomb on the stadium?' (What Schön didn't mention in his memoir was that the 70,000-strong crowd booed him every time he touched the ball because he still hadn't seen the front.) But the RAF didn't attack then, nor a year later, in the summer of 1944, when Dresden defended their trophy against the Air Force Sports Club of Hamburg. 'But what did that mean during those days?' wrote Schön. 'The Allied forces had landed in France, in Belarus the Russians began their largest offensive. Didn't we feel fear? This question, people tend to forget, didn't present itself to Germans. The map of Europe still led us to believe in strength. Norway and Denmark, Italy, Greece, Bulgaria, Romania, Hungary – they all were "firmly in German hands". No one realised how quickly it could all tumble down.'

Six weeks after the 1944 final and two weeks after Major Claus von Stauffenberg's failed attempt to assassinate Hitler, the scheduled qualifying games for the first round of the Tschammer Cup were suspended, which made First Vienna, 3-2 victors over Air Force Hamburg in 1943, the last pan-German Cup winners. League matches in various parts of the country would in some cases continue into October, and selected places like Hamburg managed to have official competitions right up until the following April. But by and large German football surrendered to war in August 1944. The press, however, still found time for misleading boosterism: 'England will be able to restart league football at the earliest two years after the end of war, while Germany plans to create a *Reichsliga* immediately following final victory.' The reality was this – a coffin carrying the mortal remains of Fritz Unkel, the revered long-time president of Schalke 04, stood in a cemetery in almost completely destroyed Gelsenkirchen for eight days and nights, until members of the family finally buried it themselves.

In September, all males between the ages of 16 and 60 were drafted into the *Volkssturm*, a militia meant to defend the country against the Soviets coming from the east and the British and Americans advancing from the west and south. Now even Helmut Schön was called up and trained as a grenadier. 'I learned useful things such as driving a car and giving the Nazi salute to superiors,' he sarcastically recorded, adding: 'I didn't have what it took to be a hero, what was needed for the hero's death, which is how dying was then described.'

On February 13, 1945, Helmut Schön spent the night as an air-raid warden in a factory nine miles outside Dresden. American and British bombers were approaching Leipzig, he had been told, and it was his task to start the air-raid alarm in case of an attack from above. 'The English will never bomb Dresden,' his father had assured him. 'I know them, they are a civilised people. They love Dresden.' At 10.15, Schön's colleague yelled incredulously: 'Look! Christmas trees!' They stared at the sky above Dresden and saw thousands of glittering stars raining down on the city. It was completely silent. 'This is the death of Dresden,' someone said. The stars were firebombs.

Schön jumped into a lorry and headed towards the city to find his wife. 'The inner city, more than four miles in length and two and a half miles wide, was just one inferno,' he wrote. 'Hardly a soul got out of it alive.' But his wife had managed to reach an air-raid shelter in time, and five days later, while Dresden was still burning, Schön also found his father, a man of 87. He was not physically hurt but badly shaken. He had spent hours sitting on the ground and praying while all around him people burned to death. 'Negroes were everywhere,' he told his son in his confusion, meaning the charred corpses.

'We had been saved,' Schön remembered, 'but at least 130,000 were lying dead in the streets of Dresden.' (The exact figure has been debated for decades. In 2010, a panel of historians published a report that said between 23,000 and 25,000 people lost their lives.) The city he had loved more than almost anything else, perhaps more than football, was destroyed beyond recognition. He did not blame the English or the Americans, just the hate and the blindness that had caused all this.

Around the same time, the Allies also bombed another great football city, Nuremberg. On February 2, Nuremberg and Fürth played their last derby for the time being (the Club won 2-1). Six weeks later, the site where the Nazis used to hold their gruesome party rallies was taken by American troops. Hans Kalb, who won five championship medals with Nuremberg, died from blood poisoning during the days leading up to its capture. By that time, Georg Köhl, heir to the great Heiner Stuhlfauth in the Club's goal, had long since perished. He had sustained an arm wound in the course of front-line duty, and when doctors told him only an amputation could save his life, Köhl sent them away. He knew he would never be able to play football again with only one arm. Köhl's fight for survival was long, and he lost it. Other men faced their fate less bravely. On April 30, 1945, Adolf Hitler shot himself. The day before, Hamburg had beaten Altona 4-2 in the last official football match played during wartime. A week later, Germany capitulated.

The story of war is that of nations, but the stories of war are those of individuals. There was, for instance, the young centre-forward of the small club TuRa Bremen. Before he was all of 21, he had marched through snowstorms in the Russian winter, had witnessed the massacre at the bridge near Arnhem in Holland first-hand and had twice been captured by enemy troops but managed to escape both times. In September 1944, he spent three days and two nights in complete silence and darkness under the wreckage of a school building destroyed by British bombers. Unable to move any part of his body save the right arm, surrounded by a hundred or so dead, he waited in delirium for the rescue squad. When it finally found him, he was given little respite but thrown into Germany's last, desperate attempt at turning things around, the bloody Ardennes offensive.

The young man was finally arrested by the British in Belgium and deported to a POW camp in England. There he took up playing football again, this time in goal. The English had a few problems in pronouncing his name, and so Bernhard Trautmann, 'Bernd' to Germans, became Bert – and would go on to be the country's first foreign Footballer of the Year in 1956.

Fritz Walter, meanwhile, had spent 1943 and 1944 in what, given the circumstances, must be called relative safety. Major Graf, the war hero and ex-goalie, had formed an air force football team at his base, now moved to East Friesland, known as the Red Fighter Pilots. This side did not participate in official matches, like some other military teams, but it was a very good one which lost only a few of the 30 or so games it played against local clubs or other military squads. With more than a little help from Herberger, Walter joined the Red Fighter Pilots in mid-1943.

In January 1945, however, the Russian offensive signalled the end of the team. Walter later remembered that he had almost expected Graf and the other high-ranking officers to flee, leaving the soldiers at the mercy of the onrushing Russians, as this was the custom at other bases. Instead Graf said: 'We will destroy the planes that are left, and we'll all be taken prisoner together.' Then the squad boarded lorries that were to take them west. Everybody preferred to be captured by US troops rather than the Russians.

The plan initially seemed to have worked, but after a few weeks in an American POW camp, the German soldiers were carried east to be handed over to the Russians. That meant Siberia and a near-certain agonising death. Walter was filled with just as much fear as his 40,000 fellow prisoners, but with true *Pfälzer* stoicism he reckoned that since there was nothing he could do about the situation he might as well keep his eyes open for some football. One day, in a Romanian reception centre, close to the Ukrainian border and more or less the last stop before Siberia, Fritz Walter noted members of the camp police preparing for a game. Unsure of what to do, he silently watched the proceedings from the sidelines, until a stray ball rolled into his path. With his heavy, tattered army boot he lobbed the ball back into play – and a few seconds later he had become part of the match.

In one of his many ghosted autobiographies, Walter calls this 'the most important game of my life' and describes it thus: 'Not for an instant do I think about the unusual company I play with or what strange ground I'm moving across. For me, the left-winger is just a left-winger. That he's also a Slovak doesn't occur to me. What do I care that the inside right is from Hungary? We're footballers and nothing else.' At half-time, one of the other players stepped forward. 'I know you,' he said. 'Hungary v Germany in Budapest, 1942. You won 5-3.' The next day, Fritz Walter's name was erased from the list of prisoners to be sent to Siberia. He trained the camp team and returned to his home town Kaiserslautern in October 1945. Being a famous footballer had saved his life.

Not many people were that lucky. Asbjörn Halvorsen, the Norwegian who had won the 1923 and 1928 finals with Hamburg and who coached Norway when they famously beat Germany at the 1936 Olympics, saw his country taken by the Nazis in 1940. In 1942, Halvorsen was put into a concentration camp near Oslo because he was involved in *Whispering Times*, an anti-German underground paper. A year after that he was sent to Alsace. Some accounts say that he was tortured because he was unwilling to work as a warden, which would have meant tormenting his fellow inmates. Others indicate he was treated rather well, given the circumstances, but fell ill with typhus. In any case, Halvorsen was in very bad physical shape when he was eventually brought to a concentration camp in Neuengamme – very close to his former home of choice, Hamburg. Following liberation, he went back to Norway, where he became general secretary of the country's Football Association. Yet his health, and very probably his soul, had suffered beyond hope. Less than ten years later, he died.

His former team-mate Otto 'Tull' Harder was also in a concentration camp, but not as a prisoner. He had joined the NSDAP as early as 1932. By 1939, when he became a guard at a concentration camp near Berlin, he was also a long-time member of the SS. Five years later he was made head of the guards at a camp in the Hanover area, and during his few months in charge there well over 200 captives lost their lives. Rumours to the contrary notwithstanding, Harder and Halvorsen never met in one of the many camps they saw from the inside, but even if they had, it is very doubtful Harder would have done anything to alleviate the Norwegian's suffering. After all, this was a man who later explained the deaths at the Hanover camp in court by saying: 'The inmates' inner organs were weakened through malnutrition in the Jewish ghetto, so that they couldn't take the good and plentiful food in the concentration camp.' Harder was sentenced to 15 years in jail, but was released prematurely in 1951. He lived a secluded life in Hamburg, embittered by what he considered his unfair treatment, until his death in March 1956.

As regards the men who led German football during the Nazi years, Otto Nerz and Felix Linnemann were both put into internment camps. Nerz would practically starve in Soviet captivity and passed away from meningitis in Sachsenhausen in 1949, although some of the other detainees later claimed he was dead as early as 1947. Linnemann was released in November 1945 and expired three years later. Guido von Mengden wormed his way through all tribunals and denazification tests, eventually becoming secretary of the powerful German Sports Association in 1954. His successor as Von Tschammer und Osten's poison pen, Carl Koppehel, managed to pull off an equally swift transition from tyranny to democracy. He would continue to serve as the DFB's secretary, clerk and main chronicler until the 1960s, writing the first substantial (though not necessarily entirely frank) history of German football in 1954.

And the little man with the crumpled face? Sepp Herberger was sitting in a tiny flat owned by his parents-in-law in Weinheim, not far from the sea of debris that was Mannheim, when Hitler's 'thousand-year Reich' came to an end. He wrote countless letters to learn the whereabouts and well-being of his charges, especially that of Fritz Walter, spent hours poring over the files he had accumulated, and carefully answered the 131 questions in the denazification form.

Herberger had joined the NSDAP in 1933, guided by Nerz and Linnemann, who had told him it would further his career, but the occupying forces correctly did not judge him to be a committed Nazi, which spared Herberger the internment camp. A survey, held in late 1945 in the American zone, found that only two in ten Germans were accepting personal responsibility for the war. We can thus presume that Herberger did not spend many sleepless nights trying to figure out what had gone wrong and who was to blame. Besides, he was preoccupied with something else. While few people had any idea what tomorrow would bring, provided there was a tomorrow at all, Sepp Herberger was creating a new national team in his mind. He had no idea when or whether it would ever make it on to a football pitch, but he knew one thing – he would be ready.

7

GRAVESTONES FOR TERRACES

REBUILDING IN THE OCCUPIED ZONES

AS WE HAVE SEEN, the story of German football goes back quite a long way and down a pretty winding road. However, that does not mean that German football as most people know it today is very old. In fact, it's barely an infant. The Football League kicked off in 1888 and basically that was that. League football in England changed the name of its top flight, added divisions and tinkered with the promotion system, but the main structure has been in place ever since. In Spain, whose league began in February 1929, Barcelona and Real Madrid won three of the first five titles, and that pretty much set a trend. Italy's Serie A started the same year with 18 clubs playing each other home and away. Inter, Juventus, Roma, Milan, Napoli, Genoa, Torino, Bologna and Lazio met on the pitch – just like today.

But German football as understood by a modern fan really only began in 1963 with the creation of the Bundesliga. Unless, of course, you define a country's football not only in terms of club and league organisation but also include its psychological and technical peculiarities: in other words, mentality and style.

In Germany even that is probably not much older, the defining year being 1954, when Sepp Herberger pulled off the 'Miracle of Berne'.

This, then, is the chapter that deals with how a country in complete disarray managed to reach the watershed that was the 1954 World Cup in the first place. Romantically inclined people will go even further and tell you that this is the story of how it came to be that a slight, small Nuremberg boy could transform a whole nation by means of his big toe. We will come to that. For the time being, let's just say this is the story of how a young man by the name of Max Morlock went from playing for pigs to playing for the Jules Rimet trophy in only nine years.

Morlock was the second of three sons born to a Nuremberg factory foreman in the mid-1920s. From an early age, it was clear that he was the archetype of somebody who overachieves through sheer will and determination. When Max was still at school, he talked three friends into taking a bath in an ice-cold pond with him. The predictable result was a quadruple case of pneumonia and parental advice along the lines of: 'You'd better stop seeing that Morlock kid!' Why did Max do it? 'Well, we wanted to become famous footballers,' he explained. 'And we reckoned we had to toughen ourselves up.'

Morlock was not yet 17 years old when he made his debut for Nuremberg's first team in late 1941. Despite his diminutive stature (as an adult, Morlock stood 5ft 7in), he was excellent in the air, and, coupled with his work-rate and unquenchable spirit, that made him a fearsome forward. 'He was the greatest fighter I've ever known,' Fritz Walter, the sensitive soul, said of Morlock. 'His domain stretched from goal-line to goal-line.'

Shortly after his debut, Morlock scored twice against Schwaben Augsburg and was so elated he couldn't wait to see his name in print in the local paper. With trembling hands he flicked through the pages until he came to the Nuremberg match report. Search as he might, however, his name was nowhere to be found, not even in the line-up. It turned out that the veteran stopper Georg Kennemann, a detective constable by occupation, had misinformed the reporters, 'just to make sure Morlock doesn't get a swollen head'. He needn't have worried. Morlock may have shared his name with the brute cave-dwellers hunting for slaves in HG Wells's novel *The Time Machine*, but the man behind that name was gentle to a fault. Many decades later, when he had long since become a national football icon and the biggest Nuremberg legend of them all, he was still modestly running a small stationery shop, fending off customers eager for anecdotes with the line: 'I'm not much of a talker. Ask the others.'

Morlock was called up to the army in August 1943 and found himself marching towards Scandinavia with a pair of football boots in his rucksack. He was taken prisoner by US troops but sent home soon after Germany's capitulation. There, his boots initially seemed of little use to him. Nuremberg's legendary ground, the 'Zabo', was seized by the Allies, and all clubs, sporting or otherwise, were prohibited – the occupying forces were determined to shatter the structures that had been in existence under the Nazi regime.

If and when young men like Max Morlock were able to play anything like proper football in the months and years immediately following the war largely depended on where they lived, or rather, who was in command in their city or area. The Yalta agreement between the four leading Allied powers determined that the Soviet Union would control the territory east of a line reaching roughly from Schwerin in the north to Erfurt in the south, with the exception of Berlin. The British were to govern the north-west of Germany, apart from Bremen, which was added to the American zone. That otherwise comprised most of what lay south of Kassel. France would administer the south-western tip of the country, meaning Pfalz, Württemberg and the Saarland, while each power got a piece of the city of Berlin.

As a general rule, life for the defeated was hard in the Russian and French zones, liberal in the American one and a bit of both where the British were in charge. That, of course, is a simplification, but it's a useful one that is reflected in how football got its breath back in those four regions. The Soviets went about getting their part of Germany to shape up a lot more rigorously than the Americans, the British or the French, mainly because they were prepared. Stalin already knew what he wanted. Walter Ulbricht, a skilled joiner from Leipzig who would shape the future German Democratic Republic, had been trained in Moscow during the war with the explicit intent of beginning political work as soon as the time was ripe, returning to Berlin even before Hitler's death was reported.

Like the other victorious powers, the Soviets forbade the resurrection of the old clubs and seized their property. They banned any large assembly of people and put forward the idea of creating new and larger sporting organisations. Unlike the others, however, they never reconsidered this stance. In conjunction with other socio-political measures – such as compulsory expropriation, secularisation, state control and agrarian reform – football went through a fundamental restructuring in the Soviet zone, one so stringent and politically oriented that it ultimately drove Helmut Schön, the son of Dresden, to an act of desperation.

The French, meanwhile, had no political masterplan or vision of world domination. Just an axe to grind. And with the nightmare memories of first Verdun and then German occupation within three decades, they can hardly be blamed for feeling virtually no sympathy for their now hungry, cold and helpless neighbour. Just as everywhere else, any football match or other sporting activity had to be approved by the military, but the French were more likely to turn down such applications than the English or the Americans.

The club which had been known as FV Saarbrücken since 1909 was allowed to reform only on the condition that it changed its name. Thus, in November 1945 – while regular league football on a larger scale was already being reintroduced in the American zone – 1. FC Saarbrücken came into being. The club got its ground back only during that winter, and even then the French authorities inflicted severe travel restrictions on the team. In nearby Völklingen, the old club SV Völklingen 06 was forced to become part of a new multi-sports association, bitterly denounced as 'a monstrosity' by the club archivist.

In the British zone, things were sometimes even harsher. Famous Westfalia Herne, up there with Schalke and Dortmund in the *Gauliga Westfalen* during much of the 1930s, kept the name but lost everything else – including, literally, the shirts on their backs. Their ground and all the equipment the club owned was confiscated, then an English officer even demanded they burn their kits. On the other hand, a historian from Hamm (a town 25 miles north-east of Dortmund) would later remember how a British soldier gave him and his friends the priceless treasure that was a shiny new ball in 1945, saying the reason for his generosity was that he used to play for Manchester United at home. And a representative team of the 53rd Division met Schalke 04 in November 1945, in front of 35,000 people in Wuppertal (the Germans won 2-1), while in Bonn, the 5th Guards Brigade even took part in a seven-team district league which kicked off that same month.

Still, it was the Americans, who in theory had the least accurate idea of what the game was all about, who really kick-started German football after the war. Many players and officials in the south had tears in their eyes when they found their old grounds not only full of craters but adorned with baseball pitching mounds or American football posts. But the new masters, who only kicked a ball when they could no longer carry or throw it, were less inclined towards revenge than the French and British and, after an initial phase of scepticism, they proved downright lenient when it came to allowing football to go ahead. On July 1, 1945, Schwaben Augsburg – led by the great Ernst Lehner – were permitted to play a game against prisoners of war at a US barracks. They lined up for more than half a dozen friendlies during the next two months and finally met an old, big-name club in mid-September, when Bayern Munich beat them 3-1.

During those weeks, a VfB Stuttgart official by the name of Gustav Sackmann was restlessly scouring the American zone, travelling mostly on foot or on open coal trains. He was trying to get in touch with whoever might still be alive of the people who used to represent the tradition-laden clubs of the south, to invite them to a general meeting to be held on October 13, 1945. On that day, with the blessing of the American military police, a new South German Football Association was formed. In indestructible German fashion, the first thing this nascent association did was announce the creation of a zone-wide league – the *Oberliga* – that was to begin its programme only three weeks later. Needless to say, Sackmann and his friends proved true to their word.

'Needless'? No, that's taking too much for granted. Even given the proverbial German standards of discipline and organisation, the fact that what later came to be known as the *Oberliga Süd* really kicked off on November 4, 1945 can only be called a marvel. Because despite harassments and hindrance on the part of the occupiers, what really should have made football impossible was that the country was in total ruin.

To begin with, there were hardly any material goods to be had, and that included football essentials such as leather and cloth. Food was a constant problem, too, and regular passenger transport was virtually non-existent. There was also a serious shortage of living space. Many cities had been virtually flattened and more than eight million Germans who had been driven out of their homeland in what was now Poland and Czechoslovakia were pouring into the western parts of the country. Two bitter winters, 1946-47 being particularly relentless, made the situation even more hopeless, and the western Allies began to fear a complete breakdown that would drive people into the hands of the Soviets, who were now viewed as the new threat to peace and democracy. That was one reason why denazification, especially in the French and British zones, was never carried out as thoroughly as planned. In many parts of the country, the authorities simply felt they had more important things to do, such as helping people survive.

Under these circumstances, the footballers who had been prohibited from turning professional for so long suddenly made a living out of playing the game in a very literal sense. The bigger teams with better known players went on tour, meeting small clubs in return for meat and vegetables. Max Morlock's legendary 1. FC Nürnberg travelled to tiny Altötting because they had been promised a butchered sow. The pig made the bus journey back to Nuremberg packed in towels and lying between the feet of the players, who later carved it up themselves. The result, said the writer Hans Dieter Baroth, 'looked as if the animal had been hauled to kingdom come by a tractor'.

Fuel, however, was not to be had in the countryside – for that it took a trip to the Ruhr. Nuremberg played Schwarz-Weiss Essen as soon as the Allies lifted the ban on travelling from one occupation zone to the next. The reward was two tons of coal per head. Those games were not necessarily as lopsided as one might think. The country bumpkins were usually better fed and more healthy than the famous big-city players, who also tended to have a nightmarish journey behind them before they got to the ground. In fact, the home club often had a substitute team in waiting, in case the invited guests got lost, became stranded on the road or were stopped by the military police.

Equipment also proved a huge problem. Most teams only had one ball, and any uncontrolled goalmouth clearance could put an untimely end to matches played next to a river or wood. Unless, of course, the other side could produce a replacement. When Nuremberg played away at FV Karlsruhe on the sixth matchday of the *Oberliga Süd*, the Franconians couldn't get to grips with the small, light ball used by Karlsruhe. And so defender Willi Billmann secretly took out the safety pin that kept his shirt together and punctured the ball. However, the heavier ball from Nuremberg entered play too late. Karlsruhe won 4-1, one of only three victories they would collect in this first *Oberliga* season. The lowest of their many low points was a 13-0 drubbing at Munich 1860, after the Karlsruhe players had been travelling all through the December night without heating, sleep or food.

Many grounds were in deplorable shape and could not easily be repaired as there were no building materials. At Hamm, the club used gravestones to shore up the stairs on the stands, carefully placing them so that the inscriptions faced away from people flocking to football to forget about matters of life and death. Kits were also scarce. That is why a large number of teams suddenly took to playing in red strips, often with the addition of neatly cut holes. Because while fabric and cloth were valuable possessions, there were flags and banners in abundance that nobody seemed to want any more. With a bit of dexterity, they could be made into football kits once you removed the swastikas.

In spite of these and other travails, the 1945-46 season of the *Oberliga Süd* was carried through in full, even though line-ups were changing from week to week as soldiers returned from captivity, a process that would not be completed until well into the 1950s. Max Morlock's Nuremberg finished the 16-team league in second place, one point behind VfB Stuttgart. (A win at Karlsruhe would have made all the difference.)

Stuttgart had not played that big a role in German football up to this point. They had two notable showings in the national championship during the 1930s (one second- and one third-place finish), but VfB had usually been preoccupied with chasing local rivals Kickers Stuttgart. Now, after the war, the club was on the rise, challenging the established forces, a subversive development that was also taking place, as we shall see, in the west and south-west.

Almost half of Stuttgart's 91 goals were scored by Robert Schlienz, of whom the German football writer Hans Blickensdörfer once said: 'He was a greater threat in the penalty area than Uwe Seeler or Gerd Müller.' That might even have been true. During the next two seasons, Schlienz scored almost 50 more goals and even a decade later, after Stuttgart had played a friendly against Real Madrid, Alfredo Di Stefano remarked: 'He was the best man on the pitch. I would never have thought it possible that anyone could do what I saw him do.' The reason you have probably never heard of Schlienz was precisely what impressed Di Stefano so much. He was a star against all odds, because after a car accident in August 1948 Schlienz was left with only one arm. He was still good enough to play for Germany, but Sepp Herberger only picked him during the years between the 1954 and 1958 World Cups. The reason, many people say, was that Herberger thought opponents would be inhibited in the face of a disabled player and he didn't like that idea.

Robert Schlienz and his VfB Stuttgart had no chance to challenge for a more significant trophy than the Oberliga Süd title in 1946. The British and French zones could not really get their leagues off the ground. In the area around Hanover and Braunschweig, competitive matches were even stopped after the first half of the season. Moreover, it was still not easy to get passes to cross the borders between the zones. There was no national championship in 1947 either, but at least regular leagues had now been created in most parts of the country and plans were ripe for installing *Oberligen* everywhere, with a view to the winners playing each other for the national title. The 1946-47 season was an intermediate stage in most parts of western Germany, meant to determine who would qualify for the following year's *Oberliga* through smaller, regional leagues. Still, that season was not without dramatic footballing moments of national interest.

In Westphalia, 20 teams were split into two leagues, from which the five best teams were to join next year's *Oberliga West* together with eight sides from the Rhine regions. League One was won, of course, by Schalke 04, while Borussia Dortmund came out first in League Two. On May 18, 1947, the two clubs met in what was called the final for the championship of Westphalia. It was a terribly rainy day, yet 30,000 came to Herne to watch. Schalke still fielded the Klodt brothers, Tibulski, Kuzorra, Hinz and two other champions of 1942, though Szepan missed this game. He was now almost 40 and would play only six more games in the coming season before taking up managerial duties.

Still, Schalke were considered hot favourites. But five minutes from time, with the score 2-2, Dortmund's wartime international August Lenz set up defender Herbert Sandmann, whose shot beat Hans Klodt and ended a 21-year reign for Schalke as the top club in the Ruhr, Westphalia and even the whole of the country. The Spinning Top had lost momentum, and the ageing team would finish the first season of the *Oberliga West* in a disastrous sixth place, soon to drop even further.

A similar upheaval took place in the French zone, the south-west. That region had never been brimming with top-class clubs, but it was still surprising to many how easily 1. FC Kaiserslautern suddenly dominated. The set-up was similar to that in Westphalia, and Kaiserslautern won what was called the

Northern League with ease. Fritz Walter and his brother Ottmar finished as top scorers with 46 goals between them – more than any other entire team. Then they played two games against VfL Konstanz, winners of the Southern League, for the championship of the French Zone. The aggregate result was 16-5.

Maybe it helped that Sepp Herberger, still without a national team and denied a work permit as a former high-ranking Nazi employee, gave the club of his protégé Fritz Walter a few hints and tips. 'But I'm not training them!' he said. Few believed him, but figured there was no reason to worry unduly about the upstarts from Pfalz. They would certainly be put in their place the following season, 1947-48, when the *Oberligen* really began.

And so real nationwide football returned to Germany in September 1947. There were four *Oberligen* – Berlin, North, West and South. The south-west had to wait another year, due to problems with the French authorities, but made do for the time being with two divisions and a play-off to see who would join the other winners in the knockout rounds for the national title. There was also the return of something else – hot-blooded 1920s-style hooliganism.

When the famous SpVgg Fürth played at Mühlburg (Karlsruhe), there was constant crowd trouble, with spectators repeatedly running on to the pitch. After the final whistle, fans attacked Fürth players and even the referee, who had to be taken to hospital under the protection of the military police. And Nuremberg's Willi Billmann later remembered: 'Looking back on the *Oberliga Süd* days, I recall all games against Waldhof Mannheim as being particularly vile. After one of these matches, there was a terrible punch-up involving players and spectators. Former Estonian soldiers, who couldn't get home after the war, had to save us from the Waldhof supporters.'

Billmann consoled himself with the first postwar German title, or the 'Championship of the Western Zones', as it was dubbed (it did not include any teams from the Soviet area of occupation). Nuremberg won the *Oberliga Süd* and met St Pauli in the semis. The Club went ahead 2-0 and even missed a penalty, but then St Pauli got back into the game and scored twice. The match went into extra time and was decided through a Golden Goal by Nuremberg's Hans Pöschl.

The other team in the final was 1. FC Kaiserslautern, featuring that quintet of boyhood friends, Werner Kohlmeyer plus the Liebrich and Walter brothers. They had again dominated the south-west and then defied predictions by not only holding their own against tougher opposition but practically walking all over them, having scored ten goals in the two knockout games prior to the final. But Nuremberg overcame them in a closely fought encounter. 'Few contests can claim to have offered the speed, skill and power of this dramatic match,' enthused a newspaper report. A crowd of 75,000 was on hand in Cologne to watch Nuremberg run out 2-1 winners and on June 21, 1948, (West) Germany had a new champion at last.

'Nuremberg was in ruins, many people were still living in cellars,' an eyewitness reported, 'but we were proud of the club. The team returned from Cologne by train. In front of the railway station there was a huge expanse of rubble, that's where people stood. I think there were 50,000 of them, standing on the debris as if it were a grandstand. However, I was shocked at the behaviour of the players. Some of them were visibly drunk.' A few of the new champions were still carrying bottles of wine, and one of them fell off the car as the team was paraded around town.

The final was not the only significant event of 1948. In mid-February, two Cologne clubs – Sülz 07 and BC Köln – merged to form 1. FC Köln. It was by no means the 'first football club' in the city, but the members' hubris proved not to be misplaced.

The new club would go from strength to strength, and its president Franz Kremer was to become known as the 'Father of the Bundesliga'.

On the last day of March, another event of lasting significance to German football, and indeed the whole of world sport, took place. The escalation of a mysterious family row in the small town of Herzogenaurach, some 16 miles north of Nuremberg, hardly seemed that important at the time, but its repercussions are felt to this day. The brothers Rudolf and Adolf Dassler came from a working-class family. Their father worked in a shoe factory, their mother ran a small laundry. Adolf was a solitary but practical boy, inventive and adroit, a born craftsman. His older brother Rudolf leaned towards business matters, while enjoying parties and the good side of life. Adolf dreamed of becoming a baker, but at the tail end of the First World War there were no jobs to be had and so the family decided to make the best out of nothing. They started producing shoes themselves from whatever material they could find, including surplus military helmets.

During the 1920s, the small company began to grow as Adolf, who loved boxing, football and winter sports, had found his niche market: sports shoes. In 1926, Adolf made the first running shoes with spikes (back then, actually nails). Two years later, athletes at the Amsterdam Olympics began wearing his designs, and in 1936 Jesse Owens would win four gold medals in Berlin running in Dassler shoes.

It is often said that Adolf Dassler rose to the very top making shoes for Hitler's soldiers. This is a tempting reduction, but it is also unfair. By 1943, when the office for arms production forcibly took over his company, Adolf was obsessed with special-interest shoes to the point of fanaticism, and it probably broke his heart to have to concentrate on military gear.

Both brothers had joined the NSDAP in May 1933 and both were drafted into the army. However, their experiences during the war were very different. Adolf was sent home to run the company after just one year as a soldier, while his older sibling returned to Herzogenaurach only in the summer of 1946, having spent one year in a prison camp after the Americans had somehow gotten it into their heads that he had worked in counterintelligence. At home, Rudolf found his younger brother healthy, content and on excellent terms with the American occupiers. It is sometimes suspected that the seeds for the later drama were sown here. A theory says that Rudolf suspected his imprisonment was the work of his brother, who was trying to seize sole control of the company. Other people think the quarrels began over a woman, Käthe Dassler, Adolf's wife. Nobody knows for sure, as the brothers never really explained exactly what happened during the first months of 1948. Frank Dassler, Rudolf's grandson, once said: 'No one knows how it started. They took it to their graves. Some older family members simply talk of a big misunderstanding that was never solved.'

What we do know is that Rudolf Dassler moved out of the family home in the middle of the night. He crossed the river Aurach and set up his own company on the other side of town. It sounds like a story straight out of a Biblical parable, but on that day Herzogenaurach became a divided town, with an innocent stream serving as a natural barrier between the two factions. There were soon bars, shops, hotels and whole streets that practically belonged to one of the hostile camps, and somebody who worked for Adolf risked a shiner when walking into pubs run by Rudolf's men. Soon, Herzogenaurach was called 'the City of the Lowered Eyes', because when people met on the street the first thing they did was look at each other's shoes. This situation never really changed. Over 30 years later, the son of a watchman at Rudolf's factory became a professional footballer. During a career that spanned three decades, the boy by the name of Lothar Matthäus would only wear Adolf's shoes when there was absolutely no way around it.

For all we know, Adolf and Rudolf never spoke to each other again after April 1, 1948. However, before going their separate ways they agreed on one thing: neither of the brothers would use the family name for his company. Rudi settled on 'Ruda', until an advertising expert told him that sounded a bit like 'Puma', which would be a much better name anyway. Adolf, whose first name now had some uncomfortable connotations, started calling himself 'Adi' and attempted to save part of his surname by christening his business 'addas'. Ten months later, that was changed to adidas (always written by the company with a small 'a').

While hitherto unknown Herzogenaurach thus became a city of two halves, the same happened more famously to Berlin. In June 1948, the western Allies brought in a monetary reform, distributing the Deutsche Mark (German mark) across their three zones. The reform also became effective in the American, British and French sectors of Berlin. That naturally disturbed the Soviets, who feared Berlin would turn into a foothold of capitalism on communist territory. They blocked all access roads and railways to West Berlin, trying in effect to lay siege to the city until hunger forced the western sectors to surrender. The Cold War had begun. One of its immediate consequences was that SG Planitz, the team that had won the championship of the Soviet zone, were not allowed to travel to Stuttgart to meet Nuremberg in the quarter-finals of the 1948 championship, scheduled for July 18.

The blockade lasted for 321 days, and during that time two German mayors were installed, one by the Allies, one by the Soviets. Politically, a rift was developing fast, but as far as football was concerned, the lines were blurred and the frontiers still permeable. While West and East faced off in their tug-of-war over the metropolis, the 12 best Berlin football clubs, three of them resident in the Soviet sector, competed for the city championship in a joint league.

These clubs bore strange names, as the occupiers had created 36 'sporting unions' (the German abbreviation was 'SG' – *Sportgruppe*), each representing a city district. Thus Hertha Berlin became SG Gesundbrunnen and Tennis Borussia Berlin were known as SG Charlottenburg, the parts of Berlin these clubs traditionally represented. Union 06 Berlin, from the eastern half of the city, was now SG Oberschöneweide. It wasn't until late 1948 that the clubs based in West Berlin began to get their old names back. The officials of SG Gesundbrunnen had to fill in 29 application forms in four languages, until, in August 1949, they were allowed to call their team Hertha BSC again. The following season was the last one for two generations in which western and eastern clubs competed for the same city championship.

In May 1949, the blockade was abandoned. That same month, the constitution of the Federal Republic of Germany was proclaimed, and in October the German Democratic Republic came into being. And so, after the end of the 1949-50 season, the clubs from the east were withdrawn from the Berlin league. Most of the players from Oberschöneweide fled west to set up SC Union 06 Berlin again. The remnants of the club joined the GDR's own *Oberliga* as Union Oberschöneweide. Talk about crazy times – there were now two Germanys, two Berlins, and two Berlin clubs called, of all things, Union.

These chaotic events did not bode well for Helmut Schön. His club, SC Dresden, had been dissolved by the Soviet occupiers and turned into SG Dresden-Friedrichstadt, soon to be completely done away with by the authorities. It was still possible, though not easy, to commute between east and west, and Schön did so, playing now and then for FC St Pauli but living in Dresden. In mid-1949 he first got into serious trouble when a mysterious man who had introduced himself to Schön as 'the press officer of Borussia Dortmund' attempted to talk Schön and other former Dresden players into giving him the Victoria, the old championship trophy which had been gathering dust in the city since 1944. 'This plan failed,' Schön noted, 'and I received a severe telling-off from East Berlin. The chairman of the sports committee threatened me with dire consequences, a certain Erich Honecker.' Schön compounded his difficulties by arguing that he thought the trophy should be given to the west, as the old clubs still lived on there.

Next he crossed the sports official Manfred Ewald, who was to become infamous as the man responsible for mass doping within the GDR's sporting system, and realised his time was running out. He would soon lose the right to play or coach, that was for sure. Secretly he contacted Sepp Herberger, who told him he would see to it that Schön would be admitted to a coaching course at the Sports College in Cologne. Then he got in touch with Hertha BSC in west Berlin to find out if the club was interested in a former international as player-manager. In May 1950, Schön, his wife and their young son packed all their belongings and left their cherished Dresden at the break of dawn, like criminals. He would never forget being forced to creep away from his home and, in spite of his meek disposition, he would never forgive.

Schön stayed in west Berlin for only one year, then he moved on southwards, to Saarbrücken. He had been offered the job of coaching a team in a small but prominent part of the French zone, and it was a national team at that, albeit a bizarre one. The Saarland had always been a special case, seemingly forever doomed to being the subject of squabbles between Germany and France. The region was French between 1801 and 1815, then German, then neither, then part of the French customs territory again, before rejoining Germany in 1935. After the war, the

Saarland was in limbo, and its clubs went through tumultous times under the often bullying French administration.

The biggest one, 1. FC Saarbrücken, even became part of the French Second Division in 1948 under the name FC Sarrebruck, because the military police forbade games against clubs from other occupied zones. A year later, the Saarland Football Association held a vote on whether to join the French Football Federation, but the idea was summarily rejected. In April 1950, the Saarland applied for official membership of FIFA, having come to the conclusion that they counted as neither French nor German. A year later, they were playing international matches, had a president by the name of Hermann Neuberger who was destined for greater things, and finally also a full-time coach – Helmut Schön.

The proudest moments in the five-year history of the Saarland national team came during the qualifying matches for the 1954 World Cup. Drawn into a three-team group, Schön's team (featuring nine players from 1. FC Saarbrücken) opened the campaign in Oslo against Norway. The home side went into an early 2-0 lead, but at half-time it was 2-2, and when Norway got a bad case of the shakes, Gerhard Siedl scored a surprise winner. The makeshift country of only 990,000 people suddenly topped the table. Were they on their way to Switzerland to challenge Brazil? No. Football history has that fine sense of irony, and so the third team in the Saarland's group were – West Germany.

The truths, or truisms, of sport are often expressed in long-winded stock phrases. It's not over until the fat lady sings. You have to approach every game as if it were a final. Sepp Herberger never wasted so much breath. 'Games last for 90 minutes,' he would say. 'The next opponent is always the hardest.' His most famous line consisted of only four words, and it was used to remind journalists, fans and players that in football you never know what is going to happen. 'The ball is round,' Herberger would state with calculated simplicity.

'*Der Ball ist rund*' is an expression often parodied and sometimes ridiculed in Germany (the idiosyncratic coach Max Merkel called one of his books *Das Runde ist der Ball* – That round thing is the ball), but its meaning is simple. What Herberger meant was that in football, anything can happen. Round objects have the disturbing characteristic that they are not easy to control, rolling sometimes this way, sometimes that. Therefore you need to prepare for the unexpected, but you must also believe you can do extraordinary things yourself.

And so Herberger spent the first four years after the end of the war waiting to see where the ball would happen to roll. That is not to say that he didn't nudge the little devil as best he could to force it in his direction. He had stayed in touch with his former players and meticulously judged and analysed young prospects. He now lived in Cologne and schooled future coaches or, as they were termed, 'teachers of football' – among them men who would one day feature prominently in German and European sport, such as Hennes Weisweiler and Dettmar Cramer. They all respected, loved and feared him, and any one of them would have confirmed that there was no person better suited to build a new (West) Germany team. When the members of a provisional football committee met in March 1949 to pave the way for the DFB to be re-formed and the national side re-established, Herberger had good reason to hope no official could look past him when searching for a national coach.

But Peter Joseph Bauwens (known as 'Peco') had other ideas. The former player and referee was a respected man in world football. He had been a member of FIFA's executive committee and his name was as yet untarnished by the Nazi years because he and his Jewish wife Elisabeth had been bullied so much that she was driven to suicide in 1940. Bauwens would become the DFB's first postwar president when the association was resurrected, effectively in July 1949, officially on January 21, 1950. He wanted to start with a clean slate and do the normal thing: advertise the job of national coach and then examine the applicants.

Herberger was horrified. He was the born national coach, he felt, the only man in the country who could begin work today and have a team ready tomorrow. He wrote angry letters to various officials and asked the journalists he used to supply with snappy one-liners to repay the favour by lobbying for him. When he wasn't invited to the 1949 championship final (somewhat surprisingly won by VfR Mannheim over Borussia Dortmund), one newspaper stressed his absence and pointed out: 'There is one man in German football who could spin the threads anew, because he never let them out of his hands during the long intermission – Sepp Herberger.' Finally, Bauwens relented. He even changed the contract at Herberger's insistence to state unequivocally that the DFB's playing committee would have no say in how the national team was run or any control over who was selected. By February 1950, Sepp Herberger had won – again. When a reporter asked him how he felt, he replied: 'Like nobody else.'

West Germany could now lay claim to a proper football association again, a national coach and the first signs of a new representative team. All that was lacking were opponents. In 1949, FIFA had partly lifted the ban on German football by consenting to clubs playing friendlies against foreign sides. In May 1950, Hamburg even travelled to the US on an invitation from German expatriates living in America, who were publishing German-language newspapers and running something called the German-American Football Association. The tour was marred by a small but well-publicised anti-German demonstration in New York City, where some 20 young Zionists showered the team with rotten fruit. Otherwise, the club was received astonishingly warmly, and a few Jewish sporting organisations even urged their members to watch the football. Hamburg won six games out of six, one of them being the first floodlit match the players had ever experienced.

However, such cosmopolitan adventures were only possible for club sides, and then only against teams from a few selected countries such as Italy, Turkey, Austria or the US, where feelings of resentment did not run as deep. Belgium, for instance, had just vetoed a motion to allow West Germany membership of FIFA, while accepting the Saarland. As in 1908 and 1920, Switzerland came to the rescue. With a nobility bordering on obstinacy, the Swiss had organised city matches between, for instance, Stuttgart and Zürich in October 1948, when FIFA still sternly opposed such fraternisation. 'That was wrong, that was tasteless,' scolded a Dutch paper, and FIFA fined the Swiss FA 500 francs. The small country was undaunted. The money was raised by the readers of a Swiss sports paper and Gustav Wiederkehr, future president of Switzerland's FA, tirelessly brought up the topic of 'the unifying mission of sport' until FIFA finally relented. On September 22, 1950, the DFB rejoined world football, and three weeks later the West German national team played its first postwar international against, of course, Switzerland.

November 22 was rather unpleasant and rainy, but more than 115,000 people filled the Neckarstadion in Stuttgart, whose name only a few years ago had been 'Adolf-Hitler-Arena'. To match the oddness of the situation, Sepp Herberger sent a strange line-up on to the pitch. First of all, his best player was missing. Fritz Walter had hurt his knee in a friendly and was unable to play. Herberger phoned his favourite footballer almost daily during the weeks leading up to the game and at one point the following conversation ensued. 'Please kick your desk rather hard, Fritz!' Herberger said, and then: 'I didn't hear anything.

Kick harder!' Walter did as he was told, later saying his desk suffered not a few scratches. 'Are you having trouble with the knee now?' Herberger inquired. 'You bet,' the wincing Walter replied, whereupon his coach stated: 'Then you won't be able to play against Switzerland.'

There was only one player from the newly crowned national champions VfB Stuttgart, who had beaten Kickers Offenbach 2-1 in the 1950 final five months earlier. What's more, the 16 teams that had reached the finals of the championship were represented by only two players: Stuttgart's Karl Barufka and Kaiserslautern's Ottmar Walter. Three members of the team had already been internationals during the war, three others would hardly figure in Herberger's plans during the years to come, while the great Andreas Kupfer, the last survivor of the *Breslau-Elf*, wore the white shirt with the black eagle for the last time.

Three minutes before the interval, the English referee Arthur Ellis awarded West Germany an undisputed penalty for handball. Herbert Burdenski of Werder Bremen stepped up and calmly scored his country's first postwar goal. At half-time, the 36-year-old captain Kupfer trotted off the pitch covered in sweat, his hair a tousled mess. Walking next to him was a young man with rolled-up sleeves. His shirt and shorts were adorned with huge blotches of mud, but his hair was perfectly slicked back and he wasn't even breathing hard. Kupfer panted a few words of encouragement, but Max Morlock was so focused he only nodded silently. There were no more goals in the second half.

In late 1952, less than eight months before the qualifying games for the 1954 World Cup were due to begin, West German football fans regarded the domestic game and the *Oberligen* as an unqualified, wonderful success. There were regional derbies aplenty – to win the 1951 *Oberliga West*, Schalke 04 had

143

naturally played Borussia Dortmund and Rot-Weiss Essen, but then also Horst-Emscher (another district of Gelsenkirchen) and Katernberg (a district of Essen) home and away – and the new group system of the finals (two groups with four teams each, the winners of which contested the final) softened the potential injustice of pure knockout matches.

Kaiserslautern, hitherto often defeated by their own wobbly nerves rather than their opponents' strength, promptly won their first national title in 1951, beating Preussen Münster in front of 85,000 fans, with two goals from Ottmar Walter. A year later, 84,000 saw VfB Stuttgart triumph over 1. FC Saarbrücken, the two biggest Saar clubs finally having been allowed to join the *Oberliga Südwest*. Last but not least, in August 1952, the Cup competition had been resurrected. After a nine-year hiatus, the *DFB-Pokal* offered the spectacle of giant-killing minnows on the rampage again. When tiny Concordia Hamburg beat Borussia Dortmund 4-3 in the first round, there were knowing smiles everywhere. The ball was round indeed.

The man who had originally said so was not at all happy, though. For Sepp Herberger, the *Oberligen* were a problem. His Kaiserslautern players, for instance, spent the best part of a typical football season beating clubs like Kirn or Engers by scores of 8-0, while putting nine past Hassia Bingen (actual results from the 1952-53 campaign). The situation was even more drastic in the north, where Hamburg's only challenge in the *Oberliga Nord* was to score 100 goals (they would reach this mark seven times between 1946 and 1963). For all the best players, real competitive matches started only in late April, when the nationwide finals began. (The exception was the intensely fought *Oberliga West*, where at least six clubs of national calibre were to be found in any given year.)

However, few wanted to listen to Herberger's complaints, judging them cheap excuses. By 1952, even the newspaper men who had clamoured for him two years ago were getting restless. Where was the decent national team they had been promised? Since the historic match with Switzerland, West Germany had lost to Turkey, Ireland and, an especially painful debacle, to France. Almost 10,000 German fans had made the trip to Paris to see the two arch enemies play in peace for the first time in 15 years. They returned home disillusioned, as West Germany never stood a chance. Herberger's men were outplayed so thoroughly that Fritz Walter, always the self-doubter, locked himself in his hotel room and later offered to stand down from the team. A French journalist concluded: 'Fritz Walter went under because he couldn't handle the expectations. Revenge was in the air at this match, and to somebody like him that simply didn't mean a thing, as it went beyond football. For me, he is still an artist of the game.'

Those kind words did nothing to help Herberger's situation. People began calling for his head – in pubs and in print. A Munich newspaper informed the master tactician: 'If we depend on tactics, we're lost.' It took a marvellous 2-2 draw in Madrid, in December 1952, to save Herberger's job. Spain's equaliser came through a very doubtful penalty, and seconds before the end a lob from Rot-Weiss Essen's Bernhard Termath just missed an empty goal. West Germany's coach had some breathing space again.

The following qualifying campaign was no glittering affair, either. West Germany's first result was a draw in Oslo, where Fritz Walter's equaliser seconds before half-time secured what was considered a meagre point (after all, the Saarland had won there). The public grew restless. Hadn't all those Kaiserslautern players in Herberger's team lifted the 1953 championship only two months earlier in great style, beating Stuttgart 4-1? Hadn't one paper called their play 'perfect'? How come they had feet of clay when playing for their country?

The national team then squeezed past Helmut Schön's Saarland side in Stuttgart, the 3-0 scoreline disguising yet another middling performance. A month later, in November 1953, the return match against Norway was won 5-1, yet the crowd had to wait over an hour until Max Morlock's second goal made it 2-1 and eased everyone's nerves. Helmut Rahn, the beefy and beer-loving right winger from Rot-Weiss Essen was constantly booed, so sick were the spectators of his aimless dribbling.

Finally, in March 1954, West Germany travelled – as it were – to Saarbrücken for the deciding game with the Saarland. On Herberger's 57th birthday, Morlock scored twice and Cologne's Hans Schäfer added a third, as West Germany won 3-1. 'This was a shrill SOS as far as the World Cup is concerned,' wrote *kicker* about an ugly game. As Herberger and Schön shook hands, the older man said: 'We should be glad that this is over. I, for one, am.' Schön genially replied: 'Now that the Saarland can no longer win the World Cup, please do it with the West German team.' Herberger laughed. 'We'll see what we can do,' he said.

After many disappointments and setbacks, West Germany had fulfilled the minimum demand: they were on their way to Switzerland to compete in the 1954 World Cup. Competing in it, yes, but challenging for it was another matter. Hungary were about to dismantle England 7-1 in Budapest, further extending an unbeaten streak that now covered four years. Everybody knew there was no way any other team could lift the Jules Rimet trophy.

8

'CALL ME MAD, CALL ME CRAZY'

THE MIRACLE OF BERNE

ONE OF THE MOST baffling accusations that used to be levelled against German national teams was that of arrogance. While Germans do tend to think of certain sides as sometimes leaning towards an arrogant attitude – the Dutch, for instance, or the Brazilians – we would never allow one of our teams even the slightest air of complacency. Arrogance is the beginning of the end, every German football fan has internalised that, and it is the one thing that can never be excused. After all, this is the first of roughly a dozen eternal football verities established by the patron saint Sepp Herberger. 'Games last for 90 minutes', 'The ball is round', 'The next opponent is always the hardest' – they all mean the same thing: you have no laurels to rest upon. And every German knows this theory was proved beyond reasonable doubt on a rainy summer day in 1954.

There have certainly been players strutting the international stage decked out in black and white who have, shall we say, tested people's tolerance. Franz Beckenbauer appeared to float around with regal grace, that's true. Stefan Effenberg made most people's top ten list of snotty brats. Harald Schumacher has entered the history books as the goalie who almost killed an opponent and didn't even say sorry. Lothar Matthäus was an annoying chatterbox. As regards coaches, former national manager Jupp Derwall is mainly remembered in Germany as the man who was responsible for our most shameful international match of all time and then stubbornly refused to admit what he had done wrong. (He was also the man who substituted Gerd Müller against his will – in Müller's testimonial.)

But these are individuals, isolated exceptions who have stuck in German minds precisely because they are unusual. Beckenbauer was not exactly loved. (When he returned to Germany after three and a half years at New York Cosmos, he said: 'As soon as I heard the catcalls, I knew I was home.') Effenberg was booed wherever he played. Derwall went into Turkish exile and Schumacher followed him. As for Matthäus, Rudi Völler spoke for the eye-rolling majority when he once told him: 'Why don't you go and talk to a toilet seat?' Still, even these controversial and not particularly revered personalities were either over-confident, too focused, narrow-minded or simply stupid. Not, however, truly arrogant, at least not during their working hours. That would have been a no-no even for Matthäus (although he did like to talk of himself in the third person).

Until their 5-1 defeat by England in 2001, (West) Germany had lost only one World Cup qualifier (against Portugal in 1985). You cannot build such an improbable record without taking even the supposedly weakest opponents seriously, without repeatedly resisting an urge familiar to every successful sportsperson, that of becoming complacent. The fine line every German team attempts to first locate, then carefully tread, is that between nurturing doubts and being stuck-up. Any step into the swamp waiting on either side of that line invites disaster. If you lack belief in what you can do, you will always fall short. But if that belief becomes arrogance, you will overreach and stumble. In other words: if you are ahead, don't showboat; if behind, don't whine.

In order to illustrate this frame of mind, let's create a hypothetical situation. You are playing against the best team in the world. Two weeks ago, this team has put eight goals past your keeper. The game is now less than ten minutes old, and you are already two down again. What do you do? You walk to the centre circle with your head held high and tell your distraught captain: 'Now let's show them!' Well, you might say, that's easy in theory, tricky in practice. A German will reply: if Max Morlock could do it, why not everybody else?

Sometimes the small man wished he was even smaller. 'Her-ber-ger! Her-ber-ger!' many of the 76,000 football fans in Hamburg were yelling. It was not a cheer, however, it was sneering abuse. The national coach wished he was invisible. Down on the pitch, half of his World Cup team was being taken to pieces by unfancied nobodies. Werner Kohlmeyer, Horst Eckel, Werner Liebrich, Ottmar and Fritz Walter were playing for Kaiserslautern against Hannover 96 for the 1954 championship, and with a few minutes to go on this day in late May, they trailed the underdogs 5-1. The crowd chanted Herberger's name until he rose from his seat to receive the inevitable hail of whistles. 'They were telling me: look at your Kaiserslautern darlings,' Herberger noted after the match. 'It was criticism of my team selection.'

There were only three weeks left before the World Cup was to begin, and Herberger knew what the papers would say: 'What does he expect in Switzerland with those dead losses?' Still, some part of him clung to the hope that this terrible defeat against Hannover 96 would maybe make the Kaiserslautern players hungry for vindication. Perhaps it would turn out to be a blessing in disguise? For the time being, however, he could only listen stoically to the catcalls and wish he was somewhere else, far away. As far away as South America, for instance. Because that's where Helmut Rahn had been in the weeks before Hanover humiliated the Walters. The man who had spent a great part of his youth working in a coalmine some 800 metres beneath the surface of the earth was touring sunny Argentina, Uruguay, Chile and Bolivia with his club Rot-Weiss Essen. Essen had lifted the Cup in 1953, whereupon they received an invitation to take on the big clubs of South America.

Independiente of Buenos Aires were beaten 3-1, Peñarol 3-0 in Montevideo. The whole trip was almost unreal to somebody like Rahn, but he enjoyed it a great deal. Even when he was kicked by an opponent after opening the scoring against Independiente, even after fans attacked the referee for allowing that goal, even when the unfamilar climate began to take its toll. Essen lost to Uruguay's national team, who were preparing for the World Cup, then drew with Bolivar in La Paz, where the Germans needed oxygen tanks on account of the altitude. In all, Rahn had spent four weeks in the heat and humidity and was preparing to travel to Peru and then Ecuador with his club when he received a call from Sepp Herberger. 'Please come back as soon as possible,' the national coach said. 'I need you for the World Cup.' Rahn was delighted because he hadn't played well in the qualifiers and thus didn't expect to be called up to the German squad. He boarded the next flight to Lima, from where he went to Panama, then Miami, London, Brussels and finally Frankfurt. 'The Boss', as he was known in Germany, had seen the world; now he would play against it in Switzerland.

Germany set up camp in Spiez on Lake Thun. Spiez was a quiet, scenic town of some 10,000 people, 607 metres above sea level. The next weeks would produce so many legends, myths and pithy slogans that even this village wasn't spared. 'The Spirit of Spiez' entered German football parlance as a synonym for comradeship. Helmut Rahn and Fritz Walter shared a room. That was no coincidence, as Sepp Herberger thought it important that the players supported each other. Max Morlock and Schalke's Bernhard Klodt, for instance, roomed together because they were supposed to form the team's right wing and should get to know each other as well as possible. Rahn, on the other hand, went to Switzerland only as a substitute, but he was the squad's life and soul, a boisterous, humorous man who never worried about tomorrow. Herberger tolerated his escapades, to the astonishment of many observers, because he felt a well-rounded team needed that sort of character.

The man who needed Rahn most of all was Fritz Walter. Moody, sensitive, prone to excruciating self-doubt – Germany's greatest player was a man constantly in search of a moral prop. Anything could and would throw Walter off-balance: a bad refereeing decision, a critical remark, and especially the weather. Ever since he caught malaria during his wartime marches through southern Europe, Walter was ineffective on hot, sunny days. He loved rain, though, and a steady downpour is still called 'Fritz Walter weather' in Germany.

The team Walter captained was drawn in a group with Turkey, South Korea and Hungary. Under the bizarre rules of the tournament, West Germany were to play only the two seeded teams, Turkey and Hungary, and a play-off would decide between sides level on points. Turkey were seeded because FIFA had expected the strong Spanish to do away with them in the qualifiers. Since the ball was still round, however, Turkey had gone through by drawing lots, after each side had won one match (goal difference, which favoured Spain 4-2, did not count) and a play-off had ended 2-2. If Turkey beat South Korea, which was very likely, and if Hungary beat West Germany, which was dead certain, then Herberger's men would need a victory over the Turks in their opening match on June 17 to stay in contention.

With less than three minutes of the game gone, goalkeeper Toni Turek was late going down for a swerving shot, and it was 1-0. Instantly, Fritz Walter could hear a nagging voice in the back of his head reminding him that the Turks only needed a draw, and that the Germans now had to... 'Never mind, let's go!' Max Morlock yelled for the first but not the last time in this tournament, making Walter snap out of his misery. Just 12 minutes later, Hans Schäfer equalised. West Germany won 4-1.

Hungary were next. In the months to come, German football's most brilliant analysts would construct the theory that Herberger decided to field what amounted to a reserve team against the Magyars because he could see ahead to a possible final and wanted to lull Ferenc Puskas and the others into a false sense of security. Herberger, ever the fox, would later answer evasively when the question was put to him. If people wanted to call him a clairvoyant, he certainly wouldn't object, probably calculating that a casually dropped reminder of this supposed long-sightedness might come in handy the next time a crowd chanted his name in anger. The truth, of course, was that the coach only saw as far ahead as the play-off match with Turkey and decided to rest eight players of what he still thought was his first XI. And so even Helmut Rahn came on against Hungary in place of Klodt.

On a very hot day, West Germany lost 8-3. That was a bit steep, reserve team or not, but the main thing of interest to Herberger was that Rahn had done well, scoring a goal when he lobbed three defenders plus the goalkeeper after cutting inside, as was his wont. Among the German fans at the ground and back at home, however, the atmosphere was saturated with vitriol. *Der Spiegel* summed up the tenor of the coverage: 'It seemed the time had come to hang the treacherous coach Herberger from an apple tree.' And there was another thing: 20 minutes from time, Liebrich had injured Puskas's ankle. The damage kept Puskas out of the next two games and it was later claimed not only that he wasn't fit in the final but even that Liebrich had deliberately set out to crock him.

There are no conclusive images of the foul. What seems certain is that Liebrich did not 'kick' Puskas, as is sometimes said, at least not in this instance. Judging from the grainy TV footage, it would seem that Liebrich tripped his opponent. Maybe he was attempting to play the ball, maybe we would use the term professional foul today, as the Hungarians were mounting a dangerous counter attack and Puskas was running away from his marker. Puskas himself said that Liebrich 'caught me from behind', which is not quite correct but must have felt like that to the Hungarian.

In any case, it's certainly excessive to claim that the foul 'won the World Cup', as Brian Glanville wrote. Puskas's fame sometimes makes us forget that he was not the playmaker of Hungary's team – that was Hidegkuti. Also, Puskas certainly didn't look as though he was much troubled by the injury during the final. He scored the first goal, and his legs were still fresh enough a few minutes from time to carry him away from his opponents and score another which was disallowed for offside. He himself admitted: 'My fitness never wavered, even in the mud.'

But what is also true is that many contemporary observers felt Liebrich had no business fouling Puskas so recklessly at a point when Hungary were already leading 5-1. In fact, many of those observers were German. 'We did not behave well,' said *Die Welt*. 'The meanest deed was done by the rough Liebrich. He took revenge on this wonderful player only because Puskas was the better man. Liebrich should never again be selected for the national team. He harms us more than ten defeats.' (After that, Liebrich's clandestine but commonly known trips to the toilet became more frequent. He didn't go there to sulk in silence or empty his stomach, though. Liebrich, like quite a few other members of the team, was a smoker.)

West Germany then won the play-off against Turkey 7-2, with Morlock and Schäfer scoring five between them. That brought up Yugoslavia in the quarter-finals. Before the kick-off, some of their players were due to receive bouquets of flowers for having earned a certain number of caps, including the future Bundesliga coach Ivica Horvat, who might have made his 50th appearance. (Reliable and complete statistics are hard to come by today.) Seeing an official carrying the flowers, Herberger spread the rumour among his players that the Yugoslavs were so certain of victory that they had already begun to prepare the post-match festivities. This particularly incensed Morlock, who went on to play what may have been the best 90 minutes of his career, and West Germany won 2-0, thanks to an own goal from Horvat and a late strike from Rahn.

Despite the good results and the now euphoric, if slightly disbelieving, press at home, Herberger was not entirely happy. He had come close to finding a team that could really go far, he sensed, but the defence still worried him. He had made changes after each match and he now made one more – his last at this World Cup. Hamburg's Fritz Laband made room for his club-mate Josef Posipal, whom Herberger had previously tried at centre-half and left-half. And on the strength of the Yugoslavia match, Rahn, not Klodt, was now the regular right winger. This was the team that would line up for only two matches in their country's football history, the second of which is to this day the greatest and most famous one ever played by a German team:

Goalkeeper   Toni Turek (Düsseldorf)
Right back   Jupp Posipal (Hamburg)
Left back   Werner Kohlmeyer (Kaiserslautern)

Right half	Horst Eckel (Kaiserslautern)
Centre half	Werner Liebrich (Kaiserslautern)
Left half	Karl Mai (Fürth)
Right wing	Helmut Rahn (Essen)
Inside right	Max Morlock (Nuremberg)
Centre forward	Ottmar Walter (Kaiserslautern)
Inside left	Fritz Walter (Kaiserslautern)
Left wing	Hans Schäfer (Cologne)

In the semi-final they met Austria. The heirs to the *Wunderteam* legacy had beaten Switzerland 7-5 in one of the most incredible games in World Cup history and were now eager to show their larger neighbours who played the better football. But on June 30, a rainy day, that proved to be West Germany. Four of their goals in the spectacular 6-1 thrashing of a good team came from set pieces, but that should not cloud the fact that Herberger's men did not prevail due to proverbial German virtues. 'The Germans did not overcome their opponents through fighting,' an almost perplexed *kicker* reporter noted. 'They outplayed them.' The Austrians played in black and white in this match, while West Germany wore the green away kit which had replaced the old, red one after the war. (Until 1945, the DFB's colours had been black, white and red – the colours of the Reich. When the DFB was reformed in 1950, it settled on the untarnished combination green-white.)

Schäfer delivers a cross into the box. Header. Cleared. Such innocuous words, but with such profound meaning if all you do is change the language. '*Schäfer nach innen geflankt . . .*' On the early evening of Sunday, July 4, 1954, a breathless, cracking voice rang through hundreds of thousands of German households. '*Kopfball . . . abgewehrt . . .*' Half a century later, every true football fan beyond school age can still recite the words as if they were a poem, knowing that what follows is the voice urging Rahn to try a shot from deep, then realising the player does exactly that. '*Aus dem Hintergrund müsste Rahn schiessen . . . Rahn schiesst!*'

The reporter Herbert Zimmermann, born near Aachen but living in Hamburg, was in his mid-thirties when he covered the final for German radio. That he was clutching the microphone on this day happened by pure chance. There were four German broadcasters at the tournament, and they had decided to take turns. Zimmermann was chosen for the group game with Hungary, and at the time no one had enough faith in the German team to believe that this would mean the same reporter would be on duty for the final.

Like many other men, Zimmermann became a national legend on this Sunday. It is hard to describe the impact of his broadcast to non-Germans, let alone transport its content into another language. 'They think it's all over' does not even come close. For one, television was a luxury in 1954. Second, the TV broadcast could not be recorded back then and is thus lost forever. And so Zimmermann's high-pitched shriek has become the sole voice of the game, and it's not stretching it too far to say, the voice of a generation. In an autobiographical novel, the German writer Friedrich Christian Delius has described how he, a sickly, weak, nerdy boy trapped in an ultra-religious family, listened to the broadcast and felt a sudden surge of freedom: 'I was in a state of happiness that made me forget my stuttering, the psoriasis and the nose-bleed, where my conscience and God's pincers fell away from me. I had never felt that light before.'

Naturally, a writer like Delius uses his individual predicament as a metaphor for the state of postwar West Germany. A guilt-ridden, inhibited nation was suddenly reborn, feeling the World Cup to be a liberating godsend. *Wir sind wieder wer* (We are somebody again) is the catchphrase commonly used to summarise this reaction to the 'Miracle of Berne', and its effects can hardly be overestimated. The young West Germany had been dubbed the Bonn Republic to differentiate it from the Weimar Republic, but as one of Herberger's biographers, Mikos Nutt, put it: 'Not a few people consider winning the World Cup in Berne the true founding day of the Federal Republic – the Berne Republic.'

Zimmermann's report carried undertones of all this: the doubt, the need to be reserved, the lack of identity and then the sudden outbreaks of emotionalism, the sense of once again having the right to feel good about belonging to a wider entity – a nation. In so doing, it was also refreshingly un-German.

Three decades earlier, when radio began, the reporter Alfred Braun divided the pitch into ten grid squares and 22 zones, then asked a magazine to print the diagram. The idea was that people would learn his calibration by heart and visualise the field while Braun said things like 'the left half dribbles from A5 through A4 to B1'. It was a very rational, clever idea. It was also very loony. Zimmermann just described what he saw, and then – grippingly – what he felt.

'This is a proud day,' he began cautiously. 'Let's not be so presumptuous to expect it has to end successfully.' When West Germany scored their first, he sighed 'Thank God, it's no longer 2-0', as if the thing he hoped for was not victory but merely a decent showing. He had spent large parts of the previous night with his friend and colleague Rudi Michel preparing his live commentary. Preparing for disaster, that is. 'He was still suffering from the 8-3 game,' Michel said later, 'and I was to suggest things he could tell the audience to explain that we should be glad to have reached the final at all.'

Then, however, Zimmermann slowly began to fall under the spell of the match. When Toni Turek punched away a volley from Hidegkuti with 23 minutes gone in the first half, he waveringly intoned: 'Toni, you're a football god!' Delius noted: 'More and more often, there were words uttered that had nothing to do with football. "Miracle!" "Thank God!" And I was stunned how the reporter could use the word "believe" with more fervency than a preacher.' Finally, Zimmermann lost control of his voice and began to resemble one of his South American colleagues, who had long since taken up the habit of going nuts when covering football. '*Rahn schiesst . . . Tor! Tor! Tor! Tor!*' Then eight seconds of silence for Zimmermann to catch his breath and make sure he can trust his eyes. Then: '*Tor für Deutschland!*' (Rahn shoots . . . A goal! Goal for Germany!) And, even more famously: '*Drei zu zwei führt Deutschland. Halten Sie mich für verrückt, halten Sie mich für übergeschnappt!*' (Germany lead 3-2. Call me mad, call me crazy!)

Zimmermann could not believe what he was seeing, just as a nation could not believe what it was hearing. The broadcast was later made into a record and sold in astounding quantities, as if one needed aural proof again and again that the impossible had indeed taken place. Even the GDR's reporter, caught in a desperately uncomfortable situation, fell back upon superlatives: 'The unimaginable has happened!'

How, then, did West Germany cause Zimmermann to throw reason and rationality overboard? How did they beat the unbeatables? According to Mikos Nutt, Herberger once defined success as 'one third skill, one third togetherness, one third luck'. There was certainly enough of all that on this day. Turek, normally just an average keeper, played the game of his life; Rahn tore through the Hungarian defence almost at will; Liebrich read the game admirably. That's the skill, and the togetherness was never in question. Luck was there, too – the Magyars hit the post and the crossbar and had a late goal controversially disallowed. Still, that can't be all. And I do have my doubts about the authenticity of Nutt's quote, because Herberger doesn't mention himself, the coach.

Two weeks before the tournament, Herberger made his team watch a film of the England v Hungary match at Wembley in 1953 (a game Herberger had attended), not once but twice. When the pictures flickered across the screen for the first time, the players were in awe. The second time around, however, they began to see the flaws in the Hungarian game – and make no mistake, there were flaws. No team is unbeatable, says the gospel according to Herberger.

The Hungarians, meanwhile, apparently had no interest in the opposition they were to face, otherwise they would have known that Rahn roamed more freely than even Hidegkuti and that his favourite ploy was to fake a cross or shot and then cut inside – which was a formidable threat because, unlike most other right wingers, Rahn possessed a ferocious left-foot shot. Bizarrely, the Hungarians did not even learn about Rahn from their group game, or so it seems, considering how the match developed. Rahn set up West Germany's first from the left, completely unmarked, and during the second half he let go with three dangerous strikes after wrong-footing defenders, the last of which decided the World Cup.

West Germany were prepared not only for the opposition but also the weather. Sitting on the bench next to Herberger was Adi Dassler. He had been supplying Adidas boots to the squad for a few years, and at this World Cup he trusted a secret weapon that had been around for some time but wasn't yet widespread: removable studs. When the Berne pitch began to turn muddy on account of the 'Fritz Walter weather', Dassler simply put longer studs on to the players' boots. He was able to plan ahead because he and Herberger had adopted the habit of closely inspecting any pitch West Germany would play on, often weeks ahead of the game in question.

Yet all these things – the planning, the equipment, even Puskas's injury – are just details. Because there was still a game to be played, and the main reason why West Germany beat Hungary is that they played a much better game than some history books give them credit for. West Germany trailed the favourites by two goals after eight minutes. Yet this was not only against the run of play, it was also partly down to bad luck. Schäfer and Morlock had already threatened the Hungarian goal and the Germans had won the first corner of the game before a shot from Czibor hit Horst Eckel's back and rebounded into the path of Puskas, who finished coolly. Then Kohlmeyer, under no great pressure, played an awful back pass to Turek, who could only get one hand to it. Czibor nicked the ball, and it was 2-0.

Fritz Walter stood on the halfway line, staring at the ground. How could you gift the giants of the game two goals without inviting disaster? 'Now let's show them!' Morlock yelled, loud enough for every team-mate to hear. And suddenly Walter thought back to the game in May 1942, when his team had come back from 3-1 down against the same opponents. Crucially, Germany struck back immediately. Only two minutes later, Gyula Lorant, another future Bundesliga coach, lost possession to Eckel. The ball reached Fritz Walter, who played it first-time into the path of Rahn. The right winger had suddenly materialised on the left and now tried a shot at goal that became a cross. Jozsef Bozsik attempted to clear the ball, but instead deflected it goalwards and, with a last-gasp effort, Morlock stretched his small body and poked the ball past Gyula Grosics with the tip of his boot. Or, as it was put then, with his big toe.

Now the Germans were in the game and held their own, maybe more. There was a telling moment when Eckel, challenged by an opponent, passed the ball to Fritz Walter, who laid it off for Rahn. However, he did so by first stepping across the ball with his left leg, then giving it a brief flick with the right foot. It was a totally unnecessary gimmick, as Walter had time and space enough to pass the ball properly. Germans are and were not supposed to add flourishes like that to their game, and certainly not when trailing a team like Hungary. It might have been just Walter's style (two years later, he scored a famous goal with a variation of Rene Higuita's 'scorpion kick'), but a better explanation seems to be that the pensive playmaker was beginning to have fun. Later, Kohlmeyer – a true defender – got Germany out of trouble by back-heeling the ball out of the danger zone.

With still only a quarter of an hour gone, Morlock ran past three defenders, but Mihaly Lantos blocked his shot. The ensuing corner was cleared at the near post for another corner. It reached Rahn at the far post who side-footed the ball into the net. It was 2-2. After the game, Rahn would tell Eckel: 'Now, who said I can only bang them in?' The equaliser woke up the Hungarians, who so far had played like men either in shock or suffering from nerves. (Before the kick-off, goalkeeper Grosics had visited the gents to vomit.) Hidegkuti was very unlucky to hit the inside of the post from 12 yards out, as Turek was rooted to the spot. When the English referee William Ling ended the first half, there had been no further score.

The first 15 minutes after the break marked the Hungarians' best phase. Whatever it was that had stifled them, perhaps astonishment at how good and confident the opposition was, the Magyars must have managed to leave it in the dressing room. Temporarily. Because after they had been denied five times – by Turek twice, Kohlmeyer and Posipal with goal-line clearances and then the crossbar – they appeared to lose faith again. The match was open once more, and Rahn forced a good save from Grosics.

And then there were six minutes left to play. 'Schäfer delivers a cross into the box,' Herbert Zimmerman reported. Lantos and Ottmar Walter rise for it, and the Hungarian gets to the ball first. 'Header, cleared.' The ball falls to Rahn, who fakes to shoot with the right foot, turns and strikes with the left. While the ball is still travelling, Rahn knows that Grosics is not going to reach it. *'Tor! Tor! Tor! Tor!'*

'Helpless, I felt a mountain of bodies on top of me,' was all Rahn could recall of the next moments. 'I almost suffocated. "Let me live," I wailed, "let me live."' The next thing Rahn noticed was that Puskas had scored. He angrily plodded over to Fritz Walter and mumbled: 'It was all in vain.' His captain stared back in disbelief. 'You idiot!' Walter said. 'It was given offside.' On film, the decision looks dubious, but Eckel always swore that the linesman, the Welshman Mervyn Griffiths, 'waved his flag instantly'. Which, granted, doesn't mean a thing. More remarkable is that Zimmermann said 'Kocsis crosses – offside!' even before Puskas had got the ball and before the reporter had time to glance over to the linesman. In any case, Zoltan Czibor had one last chance to ward off the unthinkable. But Turek parried his shot from only eight yards, and at long last Zimmermann could succumb to his impulses and go into overdrive. *'Aus! Aus! Aus! Aus! Das Spiel ist aus!'* he cried (It's over! The game is over!).

Germans can organise a party, but they can't have one. In the wake of 'The Miracle', this saying was first proved wrong, then validated. That would turn out to be another of the many, many precedents the 1954 World Cup set for postwar German football.

In the first few days after the game, the country celebrated like seldom before and rarely since. 'There was no controlling oneself,' said the journalist Arthur Heinrich of the reaction at home, 'and the return of the World Cup winners roused the masses.' A newspaper from Rahn's home town of Essen called the recurrent scenes 'a joyous inferno', as the players were paraded from city to city, from town hall to town hall, thousands of cheering men, women and children wherever they went, no matter how tiny the locale. Schools and shops closed, and a Munich paper said: 'No king was ever given a more tumultuous reception.'

The team's first planned stop back on German territory was the small railway station at Singen, though the people of the village Jestetten had stopped the train earlier by simply pouring out on to the rails. Almost 6,000 people flooded a platform that could hold only a fraction of that. However, each and every one of these delirious fans had had the decency and discipline to buy a platform ticket before there was 'no controlling oneself'.

Decency and discipline won the upper hand and the backlash soon set in. Not as regards the team and the coach, that would not come until the 1970s, when political writers discovered football as a topic and argued that Herberger mirrored Chancellor Konrad Adenauer in his paternal conservatism and that the players were subservient yes-men. (Werner Liebrich, for one, would not have appreciated this characterisation, since his family was considered politically untrustworthy by the Nazis and his father, a communist, had twice been imprisoned in a concentration camp.) Besides, they claimed, Germany had only won the match with a lot of luck. All of which was somehow true, and yet not really and anyway completely beside the point.

No, the backlash in 1954 concerned the public reaction to the unlikely triumph. 'Well now, celebrate the players,' wrote the *Süddeutsche Zeitung*, the largest south German paper, only days after the triumph. 'But let's become sober again: the game is over, and it was just a game.' It soon added: 'What kind of enthusiasm will we have left in store when the reunification of Germany occurs, or world peace breaks out?' The motivation behind this and a dozen other warning pieces was fear. Fear of sounding chauvinistic a decade after the war, fear of stepping out of line, fear of arrogance.

The fear had crept in only minutes after the presentation ceremony. As the West German national anthem rang out, large parts of the crowd sang the now taboo, deeply nationalistic first verse instead of the third, which had officially replaced it in the new Federal Republic. Swiss and East German radio immediately stopped their transmissions in horror. It was an embarrassing moment that gave the World Cup winners a lot of bad press in Europe, which in turn led German journalists to bemoan the incident in print.

The really sad aspect of the row was that, typically, it had been home-made and predictable. For years, there had been discussions about the Republic's anthem (before the first postwar international, in 1950, no music at all was played for the West German team). In May 1952, Adenauer, after much mud-slinging, got his way, and the old anthem, despite its adoption by the Nazis, was allowed to stay in use. However, to lessen the unpleasant memories many people connected with the music, it was recommended that the inoffensive and largely unknown third verse be sung. It says something about the confusion created by this half-baked compromise that many commentators to this day call the first verse 'forbidden' or 'unlawful', which it is not (though perhaps it should be). And so the singing after the match can to some extent be excused by ignorance, as people were supposed to sing words they didn't know. But – also typically – it was still tactless.

Which leads us swiftly to Peco Bauwens, president of the DFB, who caused the next stir two days after the final with a speech that gained him instant anti-stardom. His words were so badly chosen that a Bavarian radio station stopped its broadcast halfway through the speech. No transcripts and no recordings have survived, but we know that Bauwens called the team's performance 'representative of perfect Germanness' and he seems to have used the Nazi-era word '*Führerprinzip*' (the principle of having one man lead all others), which led the *Süddeutsche Zeitung* to angrily denounce the toast as 'a Sieg-Heil speech'. Even the president of the Republic, Theodor Heuss, reprimanded the official: 'Bauwens seems to think good football is good politics. That's not necessarily so.'

Another quarrel with a considerable shelf life was started in 1957 by Ferenc Puskas in an interview for *France Football*. Some two months after the final, Helmut Rahn was diagnosed with jaundice. The Walter brothers followed, then Morlock and third-choice goalkeeper Heinz Kubsch. Puskas intimated this was proof the players had been doped, 'provoking a bitter and harsh war of words in the press', according to Herberger's biographer Jürgen Leinemann. Rahn himself suspected he and his team-mates had become infected through a dirty syringe, used for injecting vitamins and glucose.

Whether anything else was injected has never been proven or disproven, although the subject makes headlines and enters the public debate roughly once a decade. The historian Erik Eggers suspects that the players might have been given Pervatin, an amphetamine that was common at the time among endurance athletes. The cardiologist Franz Loogen, then the team physio, always denied such claims. Although the world of sports was still many years away from drawing up a list of forbidden substances, the DFB was so infuriated by Puskas's claims that it forbade all German clubs to meet a team he coached or played in. Puskas later took his charges back, but some people's feelings had been hurt beyond forgiveness.

Finally, even Herbert Zimmermann wasn't spared his moment of humiliation. A powerful banker, who was now a close friend of Adenauer's, objected to the reporter's use of the term 'football god'. Zimmermann was ticked off by the director of his station, and it is widely believed that the blasphemic expression was replaced with 'Toni, you're worth your weight in gold' on the record sold to the public. (In fact Zimmermann also used this phrase in the live commentary, but the precise chain of events remains unclear.) 'For the rest of his life, he suffered under this censure,' says the lecturer Horst Seifart, then a trainee reporter under Zimmermann. That wasn't very long. Zimmermann died in 1966 in a car accident, less than five months after celebrating another highlight of his broadcasting career, the second World Cup final reached by a West German team. In stark contrast to 1954, this second final would be contested by German footballers who at long last played in a nationwide league and were termed 'professionals'.

However, no matter what these coming generations of players – from Seeler to Beckenbauer to Matthäus – would achieve (and they achieved quite a lot), they never managed to rival the 11 simple men who beat Hungary in terms of popularity and adulation. Gerd Müller's winner against Holland in 1974 is basically just a goal, as is Andreas Brehme's penalty against Argentina in 1990. But Rahn's left-footed shot on that rainy summer day in Switzerland is something else entirely, something for which even the word 'legend' seeems strangely insufficient. When the German film-maker Sönke Wortmann brought the game to the silver screen in 2003, more than three million Germans flocked to cinemas, an astonishing figure for such a film. And when those three million people saw Rahn, portrayed by a young actor from Essen, come from deep to feign a shot with his right foot and heard Zimmermann's words, they felt a lump in their throat and a tingling down their spine. Even those born in, say, 1966.

9

THE BUNDESLIGA

. . . AND THE BUNGSLIGA

JOSEF DERWALL WAS A bit of an oddity. The inside-left first saw the light of day in Würselen in 1927, and as this town lies in the Rhineland people called him 'Jupp'. (Further south, Josef will turn into Sepp, as happened to Herberger.) He started out with Rhenania Würselen, then moved to Alemannia Aachen in 1949. Four years later he joined Fortuna Düsseldorf and played in two internationals. In 1959, Derwall became player-manager at FC Biel in Switzerland before he hung up his boots to concentrate on coaching. In 1963, he would become a coach with the Saarland FA, by then part of West Germany, but obviously still churning out future national managers.

What makes Derwall's playing career odd is that he changed teams quite often at a time when that was still unusual. Under the *Oberliga* set-up, you could play top-flight football and expect to be called up for higher honours even if you came from a small club. Like Würselen, for instance. The side had been promoted to the *Oberliga West* in 1948, after two memorable play-offs against Cologne, decided by a lone Derwall goal, and would not do much worse than their bigger local rivals Alemannia Aachen for the next couple of years.

Yet Derwall joined Alemannia, and that did not go down well with his former friends and neighbours. Würselen fans drove into Aachen at dead of night and placed coffins on various players' doorsteps. Inside the coffins were life-sized figures in Alemannia kits. Still, Derwall could probably consider himself lucky that the anger didn't amount to more, because until roughly the mid-1950s, changing clubs could easily result in a broken nose. Felix Gerritzen, a forward with VfB Oldenburg, his home town club, was well aware of this. When he decided to join Preussen Münster in 1950, he hired a removal company from that city and told the furniture packers to empty his Oldenburg home late at night and as quietly as possible. However, a neighbour got wind that something was happening, and the packers told him they were delivering furniture, not collecting it. When the man expressed doubt, considering the unusual time of day for a delivery, the removers had to keep the sham alive by carrying some of the chairs and desks they had already heaved on to the truck back into the house.

Derwall's reason for making the three-mile trip from Würselen to Aachen was that he had fallen out with a team-mate. At least that's what he always said, and who are we to doubt him? In Gerritzen's case, however, the motive was clear, unchallenged and slowly beginning to dominate much of what was happening in German football: money.

When the *Oberliga Süd* was formed, in October 1945, paying the players was legalised – as long as their wages did not exceed the princely sum of 30 Reichsmarks per game. Following the monetary reform, the *Oberliga Süd* went one step further and created the *Vertragsspieler* (player under contract) on August 1, 1948. This term did not exactly denote a professional, but it came close. A 'player under contract' was precisely that – a footballer who had signed a contract. That was not how German football had worked until that time: a club's players were members who had signed an application form. A 'player under contract', on the other hand, was something akin to an employee, but he was not a full professional. Calling him that would have put the charitable status of the clubs in jeopardy and with it their tax benefits and many other advantages.

The 'player under contract' was meant to prevent the shamateurism rampant before the war, but in the long run it would prove to be yet another neither-fish-nor-fowl affair, since not even the most progressive of club officials could find it in them to bury their Corinthian ideals for good. A salary cap was set that would by and large survive the next 15 years. The basic wage could not exceed DM320, the maximum match bonus was DM80, all per month. (Throughout the 1950s and most of the 1960s, the Mark was held at just over 11 to the pound. In England, the maximum wage had risen to £20 a week by the time it was abolished in 1961.) Also, the 'player under contract' had to have a regular job and prove he was actually practising it. In 1949, the *Oberliga West* and *Oberliga Nord* adopted this set-up, and the others soon followed suit.

That's when Preussen Münster acted. The fiercely ambitious club lured Siegfried Rachuba from Erkenschwick in 1949, and a year later they got Adolf Preissler, Rudolf Schulz (both from Dortmund) and the above-mentioned Felix Gerritzen. Together with Josef Lammers, they were dubbed the 'Hundred-Thousand-Mark forward line' by a national magazine, so stunned was the country that, for the first time in history, a club had actually begun to build a team by signing new players. Not only that, but by buying them.

It goes without saying that that incredible sum never actually changed hands – it was just a catchphrase. Yet it is equally obvious that Münster did not get the players by extolling the delights of the Westphalian countryside. Lammers was a 'player under contract' while studying at Münster University, receiving DM400 before tax. When he finished his studies, he took a job and played as an amateur again. 'Of course I still got the 400 marks,' he later chuckled. 'Under the table and tax-free.' With this squad, Münster reached the 1951 championship final, which they narrowly lost to Kaiserslautern, having led through a goal by Gerritzen.

The *Vertragsspieler* system, noble as the concept was, did not prevent footballers from seeking greener pastures. It was nice to be able to pocket money legally for being good at the game at last, but places existed where, well, it was even nicer. Hans Pöschl, whose golden goal against St Pauli had taken Nuremberg into the 1948 final, became the first postwar player to move abroad when he joined Grasshoppers Zürich in March 1949. Yes, even Switzerland was, in Pöschl's words, a 'land of milk and honey' compared to West Germany. Or it would have been if FIFA had allowed Pöschl's transfer to go through. But that didn't happen, because the DFB had not yet rejoined the international governing body. So Pöschl returned home after only six months, joining Bremen, but was blacklisted in the corridors of power nonetheless and was never seriously considered for the new national team despite impressive performances.

In November 1949, 1860 Munich's Ludwig Janda signed for Fiorentina, the first German to move to Italy. The club received a transfer fee of at least DM30,000 and Janda got an astronomical wage rise. As he told disbelieving journalists: 'If we win, I get more just for one game than I earned in a month at Munich.' Needless to say, Janda thus joined the fraternity of players, spearheaded by Pöschl and Bernd Trautmann, who, as filthy full-blooded professionals, would never collect an international cap.

Soon, the issue of money and foreign clubs with deep pockets became a problem of national concern. Only hours after West

Germany's first postwar game, against Switzerland in 1950, representatives of a French club secretly met Ottmar Walter and offered the man who ran a petrol station in Kaiserslautern DM100,000 for his signature. A year later, following West Germany's 2-2 with Spain in Madrid, Helenio Herrera, then in charge of Atlético, negotiated with Fritz Walter. The breathtaking sum of DM225,000 could be Walter's, the soon-to-be famous coach said, and he was also offering a further DM150,000 if Fritz could talk his brother Ottmar into joining Atlético as well. In 1954, during Rot-Weiss Essen's tour of South America, Racing Club of Buenos Aires promised Helmut Rahn and his team-mate Franz Islacker DM150,000 each in cash, plus a business in the Argentinian capital.

In all these cases, the players declined the offers. That was partly because their clubs, and especially Sepp Herberger, moved heaven and earth to find ways of giving them at least a modicum of financial security. Fritz Walter, for instance, was granted a loan of DM45,000 so that he could start a cinema and a laundry. That guaranteed him a good life in 1950s West Germany, but it didn't make him a rich man – and he had to pay back the loan. Yet the DFB, looking into the affair with clear eyes and a cold heart, eventually fined the club. It might have been worse – the DFB's control commission (a committee that looks into possible breaches of the rules and regulations) had demanded that Walter be suspended for three months and Kaiserslautern deducted four points.

Another reason for the players' reluctance to follow the trail of money was that they knew they would never again play for their country if they let themselves be bought. And last but by no means least, they were regular, average Germans moulded by almost 100 years of glorifying the amateur spirit and condemning the professional. They also lived in *Wirtschaftswunder* ('economic miracle') West Germany, a country that was beginning to prosper against all the odds thanks to a dogged work ethic, communal spirit and a bit of help from the Marshall Plan. Clearing off for some sunny country to make lots of money by playing a game was very much against the *Zeitgeist*.

But for how much longer? That question was of particular importance to Sepp Herberger. In the years following the 1954 triumph, the names of quite a few young prospects made it into his famous notebook. There was, of course, the chunky striker from Hamburg, Uwe Seeler, who had been one of the stars of the 1953 FIFA Junior Tournament and was first tried out by Herberger three months after Berne, when the kid was barely 18. Others were the left-half Horst Szymaniak, who had started out with Erkenschwick, the defender Karl-Heinz Schnellinger, from near Cologne, and Augsburg's Helmut Haller, useful in any attacking role. They needed a few more years to mature, but wasn't it becoming increasingly likely they would leave their country for Italy as soon as they reached their prime?

Herberger was no friend of professionalism, but he was also a pragmatist and a man whose job was to produce a strong national team. That is why he lobbied for the creation of a nationwide league that would earn the players more money and certainly raise the standard of play compared to this cumbersome *Oberliga* mess. Few people listened. The DFB had the World Cup to cite as proof that standards were excellent, and so the Saarland's Hermann Neuberger was the only high-ranking functionary on Herberger's side. The clubs were happy as well, because the crowds loved the league structure. One crucial exception here was Cologne's cigar-munching Franz Kremer, who had visions of greater things exemplified by the fact his team would soon start playing in an all-white kit, just like Real Madrid.

From 1955 to 1958, the title races were dominated by clubs from the *Oberliga West*. Helmut Rahn's Rot-Weiss Essen, coached by Fritz Szepan, beat Kaiserslautern 4-3 in 1955 (thanks to an

Islacker goal five minutes from time), then Borussia Dortmund triumphed in 1956 and 1957, before Schalke 04 won their last championship to date by crushing Hamburg 3-0 in 1958. This was no coincidence. The *Oberliga West* was the most competitive league by far, so much so that in 1957 Borussia Dortmund could afford to leave out their rising star Alfred Schmidt for the final, and in doing so set a unique record: the same 11 players that had beaten Karlsruhe the year before now defended the title against Uwe Seeler's team. Which also led critics to point out that Herberger's fear of footballers leaving the country was unfounded – at Dortmund, they didn't even leave their club.

And there was another reason why Herberger's complaints fell on deaf ears. They were considered cheap excuses from a man badly under pressure. There were some terrible results for West Germany in the wake of Berne, such as defeats against minnows Belgium and rivals France in late 1954. England beat the world champions 3-1, twice, and in late 1956 Herberger's team was even humiliated by Switzerland.

Those were black years for the little man who seemed to have lost his Midas touch. The heroes of Berne were ageing, hampered by injuries, or both, and the newcomers were too erratic. One of the few highlights was a game in Moscow against the Soviet Union, but only for political reasons – once the deeper implications of this first postwar match between the two countries had been explored, it was back to football and another defeat, 3-2.

A hiding in Dublin, where the Republic of Ireland scored three against the defenders of the Jules Rimet trophy and conceded none, marked the end of that poor run. By late 1956, the results slowly began to improve, and West Germany won seven of their next nine games, albeit not against strong opposition. Had the coach again managed to turn things around just in time for a World Cup? Few thought so.

'Nowhere in the world were Germany mentioned as favourites,' wrote Gerhard Bahr in a contemporary book on Sweden 1958. 'The country was right at the bottom of the list of fancied nations.' At home the pundits were no less pessimistic. The common verdict was that the old players were too old, the young too young. Fritz Walter made a comeback less than three months before the World Cup, as Herberger felt he desperately needed a player who could feed Uwe Seeler up front. Walter was now 37 and hadn't played for the national team between November 1956 and March 1958, being a master at the art of officially retiring whenever a writer claimed he was over the hill. 'Herberger used all his powers of persuasion,' Walter later said, to explain why he relented.

Also back was Helmut Rahn. His drinking habit had, some said, developed into a problem, and in late 1957 the living legend had been sentenced to two weeks in prison for drunk driving and resisting arrest. The DFB banned him from the national team, and it took another mammoth diplomatic effort from Herberger to have Rahn eligible for the World Cup. He arrived at the German camp overweight but grateful.

Two foster sons, one geriatric, the other a drunk, moaned the press, while asking why Herberger had not picked Eintracht Frankfurt's Richard Kress. The winger, who had just turned 33, was a reasonably consistent goalscorer in the *Oberliga Süd* (he finished his career with 68 in 274 matches) and, more importantly, a great team player. He would set up three goals when Eintracht Frankfurt beat Kickers Offenbach 5-3 in the wonderful 1959 final to claim the club's only national championship to date. But Herberger was as stubborn as ever and – as so often – was proved right.

West Germany started the World Cup in traditional fashion by making things hard for themselves. With barely two minutes gone in their opening game, they trailed the huge favourites Argentina. But two goals from Rahn and one from Uwe Seeler turned the game around and set the stage for the first but not last controversy of this tournament. In the second match, against Czechoslovakia (and this was becoming boring), West Germany fell two goals behind before half-time and yet came back. The result was 2-2, but the Czechs were at odds with referee Arthur Ellis, who had allowed the Germans' first to stand even though it appeared Hans Schäfer had pushed the goalkeeper across the line with the ball. However, Ellis had a perfect view of the incident and later sent a hand-written note to the press that said: 'Goalkeeper Dolejsi caught the ball in the air and, falling backwards, he carried the ball over the line as he turned round.' No mention of Schäfer's nudge.

Herberger's team needed only a draw in their last group match, against Northern Ireland. Almost inevitably, Peter McParland twice put the Irish ahead but, equally predictably, West Germany got their point regardless. The goals were scored by – guess – Rahn and Seeler, the latter beginning to intrigue crowds with the speciality he was known for at home, bicycle kicks.

In the quarter-finals, Helmut Rahn's strike from an impossible angle beat Yugoslavia, and now it was West Germany against the hosts Sweden in the semis. What is certain is that this clash turned out to be one of the most scandalous games in West Germany's chequered World Cup history, but what is less certain is who was to blame. The Swedes had not warmed to the German supporters who had travelled in great numbers to the tournament, considering them loud, unfriendly and a bit too proud of their powerful Deutsche Mark.

The team, meanwhile, was regarded as pretty rough around the edges, mainly because of Schäfer's barge on Bretislav Dolejsi. The West German players, on the other hand, professed themselves shocked by the hostile atmosphere at the stadium in Gothenburg. There were cheerleaders with megaphones who whipped the crowd into incessant cries of 'Heja Heja', while others waved flags right next to the sidelines. And that was only the beginning.

Sweden won six corners inside 20 minutes, but for once West Germany scored first. Schäfer was set up by Seeler and volleyed the ball past keeper Kalle Svensson from 12 yards. With half an hour gone, Sweden's Nils Liedholm appeared to handle the ball, but the referee Istvan Zsolt waved play on, and Lennart Skoglund equalised. (The referee was Hungarian, as no German observer failed to point out.) Shortly before the interval, Seeler had a golden opportunity but was obstructed, perhaps illegally, in the box. Then came the deciding moment. Kurt Hamrin fouled Erich Juskowiak, who retaliated and was sent off. Then the Swedish left-half Sigvard Parling committed a bad foul on Fritz Walter that went unpunished and had Walter limping for the rest of the game, if that's what it was. Sweden won 3-1.

That West Germany lost the third-place play-off to the brilliant French (6-3) was of no interest at all. At home, the nation was enraged to the point of mindlessness. One magazine spoke of 'the lunatic asylum of Gothenburg' and asked: 'What have we done to the Swedes? In both wars, no German soldier even set foot on Swedish soil.' (It's always the war, right?) It was also pointed out that Sweden had fielded four professionals playing with Italian clubs, who, it went without saying, had picked up habits like play-acting and diving. Swedish tourists travelling through West Germany had their tyres slashed and were refused service at petrol stations and restaurants.

The only person not to lose his common sense amid this madness was Germany's best player at the World Cup, Helmut Rahn. In his autobiography, he wrote: 'When the Swedes made it 2-1 and then 3-1, the only surprise was that it took them so long.' He also called the foul on Walter 'a collision' and shrugged away Liedholm's handball with a typically throwaway: 'What the hell?' About the sending-off he noted: 'Even if Juskowiak had remained on the pitch, Hamrin would have found ways to get past him.' Level-headed words, but from a lone voice in the wilderness. Juskowiak couldn't forgive himself for losing his cool and was never the same player again, perhaps not the same man. Four years later, he was charged with indecent exposure in front of minors and had to pay a fine. In 1964, he was put on probation for an act of exhibitionism. He died of a heart attack in 1983, aged only 56.

The true winner of the World Cup campaign was Sepp Herberger. Or was he? West Germans treated their team's fourth-place finish as a wonderful achievement, especially given that they had been denied, supposedly, through no fault of their own. Herberger was now, once and for all, a cunning, wise genius who could make anything happen. The coach liked this adulation. But he was less keen on the conclusions drawn by the public. Who needed a nationwide league when the national team was still among the best in the world? And who needed professionalism, which would only make Germans sink to the level of that despised mercenary, Hamrin?

Maybe the guardians of amateurism did have a point. The *Oberliga* clubs were even beginning to do well in the European Cup. When the new competition began in 1955-56, Essen lost badly to Hibernian at the first attempt, and the following year Dortmund needed a play-off to get past Spora Luxembourg before losing narrowly to Manchester United. In the next two seasons Dortmund and Schalke both made it to the quarter-finals without impressing anyone too much (though Schalke put out Wolves), but in 1960 Eintracht Frankfurt reached the final against Real Madrid.

In the semis, the team had been drawn against Rangers. Upon landing in Germany, their coach Scott Symon said: 'Eintracht? Who are they?' Asked if he would like to inspect the pitch, Symon replied: 'Why? One pitch is like the next. We'll have time to inspect the pitch during the match.' Kress missed a penalty after eight minutes and at half-time it was 1-1. But then the roof fell in on Rangers, the team conceding five without reply. Adding insult to injury, the Germans scored six again in the second leg, going through 12-4 on aggregate. (The Frankfurt journalist Ulrich Matheja remembered how, when he visited Scotland, people in Glasgow sadly nodded their heads on hearing where he was from, saying: 'Yeah, Eintracht.' That was 16 years later.)

The final wasn't bad either. What is often forgotten is that it required a diplomatic climbdown even to ensure that it took place. There was still that ban on Puskas issued by the DFB three years earlier. Luckily for all involved, the Hungarian sent a formal letter of apology and on May 9, the newspaper *Der neue Sport* reported that 'the ban on playing against Puskas has been lifted'. It meant that Frankfurt were allowed to meet Real Madrid at Hampden Park nine days later. Kress scored the first goal of the game, and Eintracht were a bit unlucky not to get a second. Then Di Stefano made it 2-1 inside two minutes, Puskas added a third, and it was over. After the final whistle the Frankfurt players formed a guard of honour for the Spanish giants, whose 7-3 victory has gone down in football history as their signature performance.

If Schalke 04 once considered themselves a family club, the same can be said for SV Hamburg (generally known as HSV, because Germans call the club Hamburger SV, 'the sports club from Hamburg'). In the four decades between 1933 and 1972, four Dörfels and three Seelers played for the first team, wearing the famous red shorts and the shirts carrying the club's unique rhombus insignia. The Dörfels were Richard (in the squad from 1931-39 and 1945-48), his brother Friedo (1933-48), plus the latter's sons Gert (1959-71) and Bernd (1960-68). The Seelers were 'Old' Erwin (1938-49) and his sons Dieter (1955-65) and Uwe (1953-72).

Erwin Seeler once scored seven goals for Germany in a 9-0 rout of Hungary – yet you won't find his name in the published lists of internationals. That's because the son of a barkeeper who worked in the Hamburg docks played for a team affiliated with the *Arbeiter-Turn- und Sportbund* (Workers' Gymnastics and Sports Association). This leftist organisation was formed in 1893 as a counter-movement to the regular clubs, which it regarded as nationalistic and conservative. The association held its own championships and even fielded a national team that competed in the Workers' Olympics. Any hint of a budding star cult was frowned upon, to the extent that official line-ups and match reports often mentioned only the positions, not the names of the players. The workers' clubs were crushed when Hitler came to power, but by that time Erwin Seeler had already moved to a mainstream club, Victoria Hamburg, from where he joined HSV.

Uwe was born in November of 1936, five years after his brother Dieter. A man deeply in love with sport, Erwin Seeler enrolled his children at Hamburg when they were ten, Dieter and Uwe with the football division, their sister Gertrud with the handball team. There are pictures of Uwe Seeler in an HSV kit when he was not yet 12, and he already looks like the strongest boy for miles around. (His team-mates would soon start calling him 'Fatty'.)

In 1949, Sepp Herberger noticed Dieter Seeler, then 18, playing in a youth match and struck up a conversation with his parents. When Herberger said he thought Dieter looked like a promising player, Erwin's wife Anni told him: 'Wait until you've seen our little one!' Three years later, the 'little one' was in West Germany's squad for the 1953 FIFA Junior Tournament in Belgium – and already as muscular as most grown-ups. Uwe Seeler was deceptive. One look at him, and you knew he was probably good in the air, difficult to separate from the ball and possessive of a fearsome fighting spirit. Yet you would also maybe think he was pretty slow and lacked intricate ball skills. Well, you would quickly find out that he could explode over the crucial first yards and perform scissors and bicycle kicks without batting an eyelid. But then it would be too late.

Uwe Seeler scored 28 goals in 30 games in his first *Oberliga Nord* season, 1954-55. The tally rose to 32 the next year, then it was 31. Hamburg had a great team, featuring 'Hero of Berne' Jupp Posipal, the great inside-right Klaus Stürmer, the clever right-half Jürgen Werner, and soon Gert Dörfel on the left wing. Yet after waltzing through their weak *Oberliga* they often struggled when meeting the country's other top clubs, by and by becoming the nation's perennial hard-luck story. In 1956, they were denied a place in the final on goal average. (Goal difference wasn't used until 1968, though Hamburg would have been eliminated under that system as well.) In 1955 and 1959 it was because they fell one point short in their group. In 1957 and 1958, they reached the final but lost.

On a hot day in June 1960, they were given the chance to prove it could be third time lucky. Over 70,000 came to Frankfurt to see a Cologne team that now featured two World Cup winners (Hans Schäfer and the recent arrival, Helmut Rahn) plus four other internationals, among them Karl-Heinz Schnellinger, take on Uwe Seeler's team. Cologne's president Franz Kremer would now get the title he'd been working for ever since the 1948 merger created his club, pundits agreed. Cologne were easily the most efficiently run and modern club in the country, as Kremer was already making preparations for the nationwide league he knew had to come. What he didn't have was Uwe Seeler.

Cologne went ahead, but Seeler equalised before spirits could sag – in the same minute. Dörfel made it 2-1, then Christian Müller equalised five minutes from time for the favourites. But seconds later Hamburg were awarded a free-kick. Dörfel chipped the ball over the wall to Stürmer, who put it past the goalkeeper and into the path of Seeler. A gentle push was enough to finally capture the long-awaited title for HSV.

A year later, Hamburg again finished a single point behind the group winners, Dortmund. In the other group, Cologne stood no chance against a possessed Nuremberg side, who then won the final 3-0 against Dortmund. When Max Morlock lifted the trophy (a dish-like thing, manufactured in 1949 to replace the Victoria that was still on the other side of the Berlin Wall, and affectionately dubbed 'the world's ugliest salad bowl'), Nuremberg celebrated their eighth title – and yet the season had somehow belonged to Hamburg and Seeler nonetheless.

For one thing, that was because HSV had done brilliantly in the European Cup. Young Boys of Berne weren't a problem (8-3 on aggregate) and in the quarter-finals Hamburg eliminated Burnley. The away leg at Turf Moor was lost 3-1, but goals from Seeler (2), Dörfel and Stürmer won the second leg 4-1. The press began calling Seeler '*Uns Uwe*', an intentionally ungrammatical version of 'Our Uwe'.

In the semis, Barcelona were waiting. The Catalan squad included Czibor and Kocsis, veterans of Hungary's 1954 team. It was certainly just a coincidence, but following Hamburg's 1-0 defeat at Camp Nou, a Spanish newspaper spread the rumour that the Germans had been doped, citing 'white powder' in the Hamburg dressing room as evidence. The 'white powder' turned out to be glucose and the Germans approached the second leg not a little miffed. Peter Wulf and, naturally, Uwe Seeler made it 2-0, which would have been enough to see Hamburg through. Then, in injury time and nine seconds from the final whistle, a terrible pass from Seeler was intercepted and the ball reached Kocsis, who scored the vital goal that guaranteed Barcelona a play-off (this was before the away goals rule). The Spanish side won that third match deservedly but by the narrowest of margins.

Still, there was more. Hamburg, the city, was not only shaken by dramatic games and glorious goals, there were also foreign-sounding names and unheard-of sums of money. Hours after the second Barcelona game, Uwe Seeler met Helenio Herrera, now with Inter. The manager offered the striker a signing-on bonus of DM500,000 and an annual salary of DM155,000. (You normally read even bigger figures today, but these are the sums Herberger jotted into his famous notebook after Seeler had informed him of the offer.) His head reeling, Seeler asked for time to think it over.

The dean of Hamburg university wrote Seeler an open letter that said: 'If you manage to withstand this temptation, that would be a radiant signal, giving people cause to reflect on their ways.' And Herberger growled: 'They'll get me before Uwe!' Then the national coach pulled a few strings again and landed Seeler a well paid job as a representative for Adidas. 'Well paid', of course, is a relative term. But knowing Seeler, it seems certain he would have stayed anyway, as there has seldom been a more down-to-earth and straightforward football star in this country. Others, however, didn't give a damn about radiant signals and didn't much like the idea of driving around the countryside with a car full of Adidas boots.

Six months after Seeler had stood firm, his team-mate Stürmer signed for Zurich FC. Helmut Rahn had already joined the Dutch club Enschede for DM100,000. Horst Szymaniak went from Karlsruhe to Catania in Italy. Helmut Haller was in talks with Bologna and would soon sign. Roma put out feelers for Karl-Heinz Schnellinger, landing him after the 1962 World Cup. 'The rich clubs from countries that have professional football are courting our players more intensely than I and the German fans would prefer,' Herberger cautiously told a newspaper. Inside, he was seething, and not necessarily at the 'rich clubs' or the players eager to earn some real money.

That the Bundesliga came into being at all was due to furious lobbying by Herberger, Kremer and Neuberger, and the threat of players moving southwards. But what really tilted the scale may have been the one thing that convinces even the most reactionary funtionary – a disgrace. This one was known as the 1962 World Cup. Herberger had opted not to participate in the inaugural European Nations Cup in 1960, and so his team had played only four competitive matches in as many years (the qualifiers against Greece and Northern Ireland, all of them won) when the West German delegation boarded a plane to Chile. Lack of practice, however, did not bother the coach as much as lack of quality.

So desperate was Herberger that he even paid a visit to Fritz Walter in mid-1961. Walter, now 40 years old, hadn't played serious football in two years, yet Herberger gave him a piece of paper that read: 'Centre-forward: Uwe Seeler (FW).' Fritz Walter recognised his initials and immediately knew what was coming. 'You can't be serious,' he said. But Herberger was, and he would forever regret not having being able to convince Walter to join the squad in Chile. In fact, the idea may not have been entirely fanciful, for Walter did travel to South America and played impressively as a guest in a match between Germany's reserves and Switzerland's reserves.

West Germany's opening game was a scoreless draw against Italy that befitted the depressing atmosphere of this tournament. Seeler came closest, hitting the crossbar in the opening stages. Then Switzerland were beaten 2-1, but the game was no beauty either, and the Swiss had to play the second half with ten men. For the final group match with the hosts Chile, Herberger fielded only three forwards (four being the norm then). Still the team scored and held on to the lead until the last ten minutes. Then Chile's centre-forward Honorino Landa hit the woodwork, and two minutes later Seeler decided the game with a brave flying header.

For the third time in as many World Cups, the quarter-finals pitted West Germany against Yugoslavia. After three minutes, Seeler made the post quiver. Seven minutes from time, defender Schnellinger forced a fine save from Milutin Soskic. These were the highlights – until the 86th minute. 'I'm getting sick even thinking of having to play Germany again,' Yugoslavia's coach Ljubomir Lovric had said before the game, but there was no reason to fear fate's cruelty on this afternoon. Petar Radakovic's strike from a few steps inside the area bulged the back of the net and sent West Germany home to complaints that they had played too defensively. (The man who refereed this game was lauded in many German papers. He was a Peruvian called Arturo Maldonado Yamasaki, and Germany would meet him again.)

West Germany's listless, cautious performance at the World Cup had a positive side-effect. The regional FA of the Saarland (led by Hermann Neuberger) had introduced an official motion in 1960 that innocently asked the DFB to 'reduce the number of clubs with *Vertragsspieler* teams'. It was a cunning move. In 1960, there were no less than 74 clubs that were playing top-level football and they all needed squads with salaried players. That was a massive problem for many smaller, poorer clubs. And so the DFB agreed to form a commission that would examine the motion and offer solutions to the problem. The commission found the one solution Neuberger had aimed at all along. Its report led the DFB's advisory council to propose that the FA's *Bundestag* (ruling council) should vote in favour of creating a nationwide, professional league during a general meeting scheduled for July 1962.

Many of the 129 representatives who attended still harboured doubts. But events in the first half of the year practically forced their decision. First, Nuremberg met Benfica in the European Cup. Morlock's men beat the Portuguese pros 3-1 in the first leg (each receiving the grand sum of DM50 for this sensational result), but smug smiles vanished fast. In Lisbon, Eusebio and his fellow wizards won 6-0, sending Morlock back to his pools agency pronto. Three months later, Nuremberg were again beaten soundly, this time in the championship final. Franz Kremer's Cologne team won 4-0, proving that a club run professionally had an edge. Then followed the World Cup in Chile, such a sobering affair that only 300 fans welcomed the team home at Frankfurt airport.

On July 28, 1962, the DFB council met in Dortmund to take a vote on the Bundesliga. At 5.45pm, the result was announced: 26 said no, 103 said yes. The new one-tiered nationwide league was to kick off on August 24, 1963 – 34 years after Italy's Serie A and Spain's Primera Liga, and 75 years after England's Football League. However, when the meeting ended some two hours later, Franz Kremer smiled but did not celebrate. Once again, the venerable DFB officials who caused him so many headaches had left a party without clearing away the dirty dishes. On the question of professionalism, the delegates had decided to defer a real decision. Another commission was created and given the task of coming up with statutes for the legalisation of a *Lizenspieler* – licensed player. Upon hearing that term, Kremer was sure that the problems had only just begun.

Like the old 'player under contract', the new 'licensed player' was not a full-blown professional. The main difference was that the licensed player no longer had to have a regular job and that he was allowed to earn more money. The new maximum basic salary was DM500 a month, but DM700 in bonus payments was sanctioned, so that a footballer could legally earn DM1,200. (In some isolated cases, the FA would even allow a salary of DM2,500. Players of national merit, such as Max Morlock and Hans Schäfer, were to benefit from this.) Further, the maximum transfer sum was fixed at DM50,000, 20 per cent of which could go into the players' pockets.

The Bundesliga was to be made up of 16 *Oberliga* clubs, chosen on the basis of current form, points accumulated over the past decade and economic stability. Moreover, the two 1963 finalists would be automatically admitted. That turned out to be the smallest bone of contention: Borussia Dortmund beat fancied 1. FC Köln 3-1 on June 29, 1963, collecting the last West German championship decided by a final. Both of these clubs would have been automatic choices for the Bundesliga anyway. It was some of the other 14 spots that caused unrest.

The five-man committee trusted with carefully selecting the 16 Bundesliga teams included Kremer and Neuberger. In January 1963, they announced that nine clubs were assured of a place in the new top flight. Six of these were publicly acccepted without dispute: Hamburg and Bremen from the north, Nuremberg from the south, Cologne, Dortmund and Schalke from the west. The trouble began with the seventh club, Frankfurt. Their local rivals Offenbach suspected nepotism here, as they had the better ten-year record. The eighth name was that of 1. FC Saarbrücken, playing in the *Oberliga Südwest*. That was as bold a choice as can be imagined. Neunkirchen, Pirmasens and Worms were all doing better than Saarbrücken – not to mention two-time national champions Kaiserslautern. So why were Saarbrücken chosen ahead of the pack? Obvious, said the conspiracy theorists – they were Hermann Neuberger's club.

The ninth name belonged to Hertha Berlin. The first problem here was that Hertha had won the *Oberliga Berlin* only once in the past five years, while Tasmania Berlin had triumphed three times. The second was that the other Berlin teams felt Hertha had paraded their living legend Hanne Sobek around the corridors of power in Frankfurt to butter up the DFB in a quite shameless manner. The third was that there were many clubs in the rest of the country who secretly felt Berlin didn't deserve a place in the Bundesliga at all – no club from the city had reached a final since 1931, had in fact never even come close since the war.

However, there was grudging consensus that the Bundesliga needed a Berlin team for political reasons. In June 1953, three months after Stalin's death, extensive strikes and demonstrations in the GDR had evolved into the *Volksaufstand* (people's uprising), aimed at a loosening of the planned economy's rigorous targets and then also at a general liberalisation. The revolt was quelled by Soviet tanks. Some sources say as many as 75 people were killed and more than 1,500 were imprisoned. Relations between West and East Germany deteriorated fast, and more and more people fled the GDR for the west. In the first half of 1961 alone, 155,000 East Germans crossed the border. On August 13, the GDR began building the Berlin Wall, practically cutting off West Berlin from the rest of the world. An isolated but not lonely island, West Berlin would now take on a symbolic meaning in the struggle between East and West and was granted a special position in all walks of life. And that included football.

In May 1963, the Kremer/Neuberger committee announced the names of the remaining seven clubs that would make up the new league. MSV Duisburg (then called SV Meiderich, after the part of Duisburg the club was from) and Preussen Münster (West), Eintracht Braunschweig (North), 1860 Munich, VfB Stuttgart and SC Karlsruhe (South), Kaiserslautern (South-west).

Thirteen clubs not admitted immediately filed a protest with the DFB, among them Bayern Munich, but not Borussia Mönchengladbach. Bayern had slowly started to rise again after the war. In 1957 the club even won the Cup, but at that time the competition was nowhere near as popular as it would become during the 1960s. The *Oberliga* system itself offered too many giants v minnows match-ups and knockout games for the Cup to be special. Bayern loitered in the middle ranks during most of the 1950s, and two third-place finishes in 1962 and 1963 were too little too late. Who could have known that the young reserve goalie, Sepp Maier, was quite good, that a 17-year-old Franz Beckenbauer was waiting in the wings, and that Bayern would soon find a chunky striker even younger than Beckenbauer, Gerd Müller?

Borussia Mönchengladbach (usually simply called Gladbach), meanwhile, had taken a different route. Formed in 1900, the team had initially played second fiddle to local rivals FC Mönchengladbach, who were founded in 1894, which makes them the oldest still existing club in all of western Germany. Also, Mönchengladbach was not exactly the largest and most fashionable of towns, as nearby Cologne and Düsseldorf would always overshadow it. Borussia had been a second-division team as recently as 1959 and had only once finished higher than 11th place in the *Oberliga West*. However, they weren't bad. The *Oberliga West* was quite simply an awfully tough league – and there were a few talented homegrown boys, 18, 19 or 20 years of age, at the club in 1963 who gave Borussia hope that better days were around the corner. There were Herbert Laumen and Horst-Dieter Höttges. Plus Jupp Heynckes and Günter Netzer.

Three 1954 World Cup winners were still in action when the brand-new league kicked off in 1963. Helmut Rahn was back from Enschede and playing for Duisburg, having been dragged out of a Dutch prison cell he was occupying on account of a car accident brought about by too many Heinekens. Hans Schäfer was captaining Cologne. And Max Morlock was still there with Nuremberg – which made him the only player who saw action in the *Gauliga*, *Oberliga* and Bundesliga eras.

The first Bundesliga goal was scored by Dortmund's Timo Konietzka, barely a minute into a game at Bremen that his club eventually lost. Rahn and Morlock scored, too, on this inaugural day. The first own goal befell Willi Schulz, playing for Schalke, a week later. On day four, the first 'licensed player' was sent off – Helmut Rahn (he headbutted an opponent). Uwe Seeler won the Golden Boot with 30 goals, Münster and Saarbrücken were relegated, Cologne won the title.

By and large, the mood was excellent. Crowds flocked to the games, having realised that while the number of derbies had decreased, they could now watch a top-level team every second Saturday. There were some crazy games, like Dortmund's 9-3 win over Kaiserslautern, at a time when only two points separated the teams. And there were mind-benders, like Cologne losing at home to Saarbrücken.

Yet some people still feared this more or less professional nationwide league would irreversibly shake up German football, would produce a few rich, big-city clubs destined to dominate everything, while the underdogs fell by the wayside. Developments in the rest of Europe appeared to bear this out. Between 1929 and 1963, only seven different clubs had won Italy's Serie A and eight teams had triumphed in Spain's Primera Liga. Even in England, which admittedly had lost six full seasons to the war, Arsenal's domination in the Thirties meant only 13 sides were crowned as League champions. In West Germany, however, no fewer than 17 different clubs had won finals for the national title during that span. Since the war, there had never been one team that dominated everything, like the 1920s Nuremberg or the 1930s Schalke sides. Now, it seemed, everything would change. Cologne had grabbed the first Bundesliga title, as expected, and that could only mean they and one or two other well-off, well-prepared big shots would have the say.

And indeed there were signs from different directions in 1963 and 1964 that an age was coming to a close. The eccentric ex-referee Peco Bauwens died, to be replaced at the DFB's helm by the lawyer Hermann Gösmann. Then Sepp Herberger announced he would step down in late 1964, somewhat piqued that his successor would not be Fritz Walter (who knew he was too tender a character to make a good coach at such a high level) but his long-time assistant Helmut Schön. Helmut Rahn tore his achilles tendon and finished his career. Morlock and Schäfer retired a year later.

But, as the doom-sayers would soon find out, even in the Bundesliga, the ball insisted on being round. Promotion was decided through group matches between the best-placed teams from the *Regionalligen* (regional leagues, the new name for the *Oberligen*), and one of the sides that got through to replace Münster and Saarbrücken was not ambitious Bayern Munich but little Borussia Neunkirchen, whose biggest claim to fame could be that they would one day produce Stefan Kuntz. The theory that the big dogs were about to divide the territory among themselves suffered more dents as the seasons passed: the first seven years of the shiny new league saw seven different champions.

First there was Werder Bremen, whose trophy cabinet had been depressingly empty save for a Cup victory in 1961. They fought off Cologne and Dortmund for the 1965 title thanks to a frustratingly solid defence organised by young Horst-Dieter Höttges, signed from Gladbach and destined to be nicknamed 'Iron Foot'. Bremen conceded only 29 goals, the next meanest team let in 38.

In 1966, 1860 Munich triumphed, also for the first time in their history. This time the surprise wasn't quite as big, because the Bavarians had a few well-known players, such as the ex-Dortmund striker Timo Konietzka, the Yugoslav goalkeeper Petar Radenkovic, who would quite often venture into the opponents' half to nutmeg somebody just for a laugh, and – perhaps above all – Rudi Brunnenmeier. A marvellously talented forward, Brunnenmeier knocked them in like there was no tomorrow (58 goals in the first three Bundesliga seasons), became an international at 23, captained West Germany four months later, and topped off that rise to fame with the usual offer from Italy (Torino).

Then there was 1860's coach, the idiosyncratic Austrian Max Merkel. When he first took charge of 1860, he called the club 'the most beautiful corpse in the league'; the second time around, he told the president, a politician: 'You know nothing about football, I know nothing about politics. Let's make a deal: you don't meddle in the team's affairs, and I won't enter parliament.' That might give you an idea why, despite his success, he never stayed too long at any one club.

In 1967, it was back to shock results. Eintracht Braunschweig won the championship – and guess how often they had done that before. Again it was good defending that brought success, as Braunschweig conceded a mere 27 goals. Away from home, they shut up shop completely; at home it was down to Lothar Ulsass to do what was needed. (Ulsass found the net 14 times, the squad as a whole scored only 49.)

A year later, Max Merkel was on top again, this time with Nuremberg. He had spectacularly overhauled the team, selling no fewer than 11 players before the start of the campaign. Also noteworthy were some of his training methods, usually aimed at loafers or prima donnas. Winger Georg Volkert, notoriously averse to tackles, was forced to practise challenges twice daily with Fritz Popp, Nuremberg's answer to Nobby Stiles. Popp was given boots with extra long studs for those sessions.

It paid off. On December 2, 1967, Nuremberg, topping the table, played second-placed Bayern Munich at home. Some 65,000 were on hand to see Heinz Strehl and Volkert make it 2-0 with less than half an hour gone. Then Franz Brungs acquired a taste for it and added five more for the Club. The result was 7-3, and Nuremberg never looked back, sealing the

1968 championship on the penultimate day with a 2-0 victory in the return match at Bayern.

The Bundesliga began to look like a league no one wanted to win more than once. Cologne, who could and should have become West Germany's Real Madrid, were always there or thereabouts, but never near enough. When Franz Kremer died of a pulmonary embolism in November 1967 (while listening to a radio broadcast of his team's 2-1 win at Frankfurt), no one suspected his club would have to wait more than a decade for their next moment of glory. Or what about perennial favourites like Borussia Dortmund? In 1966, the title was as good as theirs, until they suddenly faded on the stretch, losing four of their last five games.

While it seemed few were willing to rise to the top, those who got there just couldn't stay. Rudi Brunnenmeier lived a life that may have inspired George Best, only – if that's possible – a bit sadder. He spent whatever he earned on women and cars and gambled away most of the rest. Drinking was also one of his hobbies, but neither an expensive one, as Brunnenmeier later conveniently owned a nightclub, nor one that was detrimental to his performance, it seems.

In the early hours of September 1, 1965, for instance, Brunnenmeier was trying to find his way home from a watering hole without hitting the concrete, when he almost literally ran into a postman trying to deliver an emergency telegram. Germany's B team (the reserve side where hopefuls were tested) was to meet the Soviet Union in Cologne later that day, and Brunnenmeier had been called up at the last minute due to an injury to another player. Brunnenmeier was too drunk to know exactly what he was doing, but he went to the airport anyway and boarded a plane to Cologne. He spent the afternoon in a hotel bed, trying to sleep off his hangover. Then he scored two goals against the Soviets and flew back to Munich to hit the nightlife again.

Part of Brunnenmeier's problem may have been that his father and both his brothers died of cancer, and he was subconsciously convinced he too was doomed. He lost everything he owned in a tawdry divorce and spent the rest of his life living with his mother and doing manual work, interrupted by convictions for drink-driving and robbery. He did indeed die of cancer, although not until 2003, aged 62.

As for Nuremberg, a year after winning the league they managed to get themselves relegated, the first and so far only time this has happened to a reigning champion. But perhaps the most bizarre development of all was that suddenly the Cup appeared to be the indicator of true quality. Between 1965 and 1968, four West German teams reached the final of the Cup-Winners' Cup, while no Bundesliga champion progressed even to the semis in the European Cup. Admittedly, Cologne and Braunschweig were unlucky to be eliminated. In 1965, Cologne came back from two goals down against Liverpool and had their winner wrongly ruled out, even though Wolfgang Weber played all through the second half and extra time with a broken fibula. Then they lost the coin-toss necessitated by three draws between the two sides. Braunschweig were beaten 1-0 in a play-off with Juventus in 1968.

Munich 1860 became the first German club since Frankfurt to reach a European final, the Cup-Winners' Cup in 1965, but lost to West Ham at Wembley. Twelve months later, on May 5, 1966, Borussia Dortmund met Liverpool at Glasgow's Hampden Park. The Reds had eliminated Celtic, somewhat controversially, and so the Dortmund players hoped the neutral spectators would lean towards them. The Germans certainly welcomed any support they could get, as Liverpool were the huge favourites. Bill Shankly had given the reporters the 'Victory' sign upon landing at Glasgow airport, before telling them: 'Tomorrow we will win this Cup-Winners' Cup, next year the European Cup!'

Borussia had a good team, though. They had twice beaten West Ham in the previous round, and the squad included four players who would go to England for the World Cup: keeper Hans Tilkowski, stopper Wolfgang Paul and forwards Sigfried Held and Lothar Emmerich. Still, they were the underdogs against a Liverpool team that was about to win the league title by six points from Leeds.

The match has been somewhat mythologised in Germany because it produced the country's first victory in Europe. If the truth be told, it was a drab affair. The weather was terrible, and only 42,000 had come to Hampden Park (capacity 130,000). Dortmund went ahead after an hour following a nice one-two between Emmerich and Held. Seven minutes later, Liverpool equalised, though it seemed a dubious goal. Extra time it was, and in the 107th minute the nimble Held was clean through on goal. Tommy Lawrence saved, and the ball fell to winger Reinhard Libuda (another tragic drunk in the making), who lobbed it in from some 33 yards. 'German football is now established in Europe,' rejoiced the breathless radio commentator. 'It has earned the right to be mentioned in the same breath with Real Madrid, Benfica, Inter.'

That wasn't too far-fetched. In 1967, West Germany successfully defended the Cup-Winners' Cup, when Bayern Munich beat Glasgow Rangers through a 109th-minute goal by Franz 'The Bull' Roth. A year later, Hamburg reached the final but were defeated by Milan – both goals for the Italians were netted by Kurt Hamrin, still unloved in Germany but no longer called a vile professional.

It is tempting to argue that the competitiveness of the league was down to the salary cap, ensuring talent was evenly spread among the clubs. Yet this theory will not do, because the practice had nothing to do with the theory. The figures indicating the maximum wage and the upper limit for transfer sums were just that – figures. In the 1960s Bundesliga, there were probably more hidden accounts and suitcases stuffed with cash than in all the world's dubious offshore tax havens put together.

Behind the scenes, unappetising agents wheeled and dealed their way around the league. There was Raymond Schwab, a former circus artist who used to pull oxcarts with his teeth. Now he pulled strings. Münster's striker Manfred Rummel claimed that in early 1964 Schwab offered him money and a contract with Hertha Berlin if he took it easy in a game against Stuttgart that was of relevance to relegation-threatened Hertha. Then there was the Hungarian lawyer Otto Ratz, who once said: 'In football, words like "slave trader" and "trafficker" are terms of affection.' Ratz signed Rudi Brunnenmeier to his stable of clients the day the player turned 18 and became an adult under German law.

The unholy alliance of ambitious clubs, ruthless agents and players eager to pocket what they were worth led to a secret, yet well-known, circumvention of the rules. Kaiserslautern probably gave Ajax Amsterdam DM120,000 for Jacobus Prins, more than twice what they were allowed to, and simply added these expenses to a bill for new floodlights. When Willi Schulz moved from Schalke to Hamburg, he allegedly pocketed DM80,000, eight times the maximum. Schalke bought two players from Karlsruhe for the permitted sum of DM50,000 each. Yet one, Günter Herrmann, was an international; the other, Hans-Georg Lambert, had never played a Bundesliga game (and would play only one). In other words, Herrmann had cost DM100,000. Nuremberg, who were allowed to pay Morlock DM2,500 a month, later disclosed that almost their whole squad was on a comparable salary. And so on.

The club hit hardest by this chicanery were Hertha. There were very few sane, healthy and talented footballers willing to ply their trade in some godforsaken place encircled by a wall, right smack in the middle of the GDR, that you could reach only by plane or over heavily guarded special roads. This situation practically forced Berlin to offer something on the side, and even that was seldom enough. When Hertha's official Wolfgang Holst travelled to Munich to talk contracts with Bayern's Willi Giesemann in 1963, Holst felt very cunning while explaining how the player would receive more money than he was allowed to. Giesemann stared at Holst in disbelief. 'I knew that Berlin is quite removed from the rest of the country,' he said slowly. 'But I didn't know it was in the Stone Age.' That's when Holst realised his illegal offer was well below the going rate in the nascent Bundesliga.

And so Hertha began emptying the coffers. The team's star, Helmut Faeder, was given DM10,000, just to stay. Goalkeeper Wolfgang Fahrian received DM80,000 for his signature. The treasurer Günter Herzog, the owner of a funeral parlour, later admitted that Hertha even bribed 1860 Munich's Alfons Stemmer to take it easy against them in April 1964 and recalled how he once hid 55,000 tickets in coffins on his premises, illegally printed to avoid having to pay tax on them.

The bust came early. In February 1965, the DFB's auditor examined Hertha's books and found a deficit of DM192,000. It soon became obvious where that money had gone. The DFB's control commission stated that 'while Berlin has a special position, Hertha cannot expect special treatment'. On May 18, it was decided that the club was to be expelled from the league and demoted to the *Regionalliga*.

Whoever said that Germans are organised and efficient must have taken a long holiday in the summer of 1965. All hell broke loose when the verdict against Hertha was announced, and the wholesale mud-slinging was more intriguing than the title race that had just finished. Hertha's officials dug up confessions, private memos and bank statements to prove they had only done what everybody did. Holst charged 13 other clubs with having broken the rules, only sparing Schalke and Karlsruhe because they had been relegated anyway (or so he thought). It was all to no avail, as the authorities were adamant: Hertha had to go.

That would have left the Bundesliga Berlin-less, because Tennis Borussia had only managed to collect three points from six games in their promotion group. Political niceties, however, demanded that the divided city be represented in the Bundesliga, and so the farce entered its next act. The DFB would have been unable to explain to Saarbrücken and Aachen why Tennis Borussia could go up despite finishing behind them during the promotion play-offs. And so it had to be somebody else. Spandau were the team placed behind Tennis Borussia in the *Regionalliga Berlin*, but the club had the common sense to refuse what was surely a suicide mission. Tasmania were next on the list, however, and they agreed to take Hertha's place.

Meanwhile, Schalke and Karlsruhe both demanded that the free spot in the league should be granted to them and not some no-hopers from Berlin. Also, there were the two teams who had won promotion fair and square. There was only one way out of this chaos bordering on the absurd: the DFB enlarged the Bundesliga to 18 clubs. Suddenly everybody was in and everybody (except Hertha) was happy.

But not for long. The teenaged founders of Tasmania Berlin had chosen that peculiar name in 1900 because some sailors had told them exciting stories about this far-away island. Such blue-eyed awe made a major comeback in 1964-65, as the club was spectacularly unprepared for the Bundesliga. Most players only learned of their promotion during their holidays and hurried back home.

In order to have at least one player of some stature, the agent Raymond Schwab brought the international midfielder and somnambulist (which is not a metaphor) Horst Szymaniak to

Berlin. Szymaniak had gone from Catania to Inter to Varese in Italy, and he thought he had seen enough of the world to negotiate his bonus payments himself. One problematic aspect of the contract was that Szymaniak demanded a share of the gate receipts. He later told his team-mate Hans-Günter Becker: 'They wanted to fob me off with a third, but I demanded at least a quarter!' (And yes, this famous story is apocryphal.)

And so it happened that Tasmania embarrassed the DFB by setting a multitude of records during their Bundesliga season, all of them negative. They collected only eight points from 34 games, scored only 15 goals and conceded 108. One of their home matches was watched by 856 people; another resulted in a 9-0 defeat. They won only two games, one of them on the very first day of the season. It was so awful that the club never recovered: in 1973, Tasmania 1900 went bankrupt and reformed as Tasmania Neukölln Berlin 1973.

As a result of the scandal, the DFB did – hardly anything. The maximum transfer fee was raised from DM50,000 to DM100,000, the player's share in this from DM10,000 to DM20,000. New Bundesliga clubs had to put up DM200,000 as a bond, and no footballer could change teams without having appeared on the DFB's list of transfer-seeking players, which would enable the governing body to look more closely into deals. At least that was the idea. There was still no full-blown, open professionalism in West Germany. It would take another, much bigger, scandal only six years later to achieve that.

Despite his unusual name, Horst Gregoria Canellas, the son of a Spanish father and a German mother, was not a *Cosa Nostra* don but an importer of bananas. Legend has it that he supplied the DFB headquarters. What is certain is that he had a raspy voice worthy of Al Pacino and was a chain-smoker, despite persistent asthma problems. He had also been the president of Kickers Offenbach since 1964.

On June 6, 1971, Canellas celebrated his 50th birthday with a party in his garden. The shiniest array of new cars this side of Monte Carlo was parked outside, as Canellas had invited many well-known football people, among them national coach Helmut Schön and the DFB's general secretary Wilfried Straub, plus a few hand-picked journalists. When they arrived, the main surprise on display was not the lavish buffet, but a tape recorder sitting on a table in the middle of the patio.

There was a smile frozen on Canellas's face that made a few of the well-wishers uneasy. Offenbach had been relegated from the Bundesliga the day before, but the club's president looked almost, well, pleased. He said something about having 'interesting news', and then one Werner Hix, a sound technician sporting spectacular sideburns, pressed the Play button. The Bundesliga scandal was under way.

The party guests were first treated to taped phone conversations between Canellas and two Hertha Berlin players – Tasso Wild and Bernd Patzke, the latter an international. Then there was a recording of a talk with Cologne and West Germany goalkeeper Manfred Manglitz. The gist of the discussions was that Wild and Patzke wanted DM140,000 from Canellas for beating Bielefeld, Offenbach's rivals in the fight against relegation. Wild said that Bielefeld had already offered DM220,000 for Hertha to lose ('For heaven's sake!' Canellas groaned on tape at this point), but that he had a soft spot for Kickers and would be happy with DM140,000. Manglitz, meanwhile, demanded DM100,000 from Canellas for Cologne to lose to Offenbach, saying: 'There are five players on my side, but they don't know of each other.'

It has never become clear whether Canellas had really been doing what he later claimed, namely playing along with the cheats once he had got wind that something was up, merely to collect evidence. We know that Canellas first got in touch with the DFB in early May, after he received a call from Manglitz who wanted DM25,000 for beating Essen, hinting he might otherwise have a bad day. The DFB official Horst Schmidt had to admit there was nothing in the rules that forbade such a third-party 'win bonus'. From then on, Canellas tried to find out who was paying whom, his suspicion aroused by the fact that relegation fodder like Oberhausen and Bielefeld were suddenly regularly collecting points. However, whenever he asked Schmidt or Straub to look into the matter he was rebuffed. Still, it's also possible that Canellas was cunning enough to play it safe: if some other club bid more money than he did, he could always blow the whistle, as he finally did, and still appear honest.

Canellas did not pay Manglitz for the Cologne v Offenbach match, the last game of the season. Instead he took his five-year-old son and drove to the house of Cologne's captain Wolfgang Overath, whom Canellas knew to be clean. There he spilled the beans. (The boy's presence was meant to prove that Canellas wasn't playing tricks. He also provided the cue for his heart-rending statement that: 'My son is the only person I can still look in the eye without suspicion.') Manglitz was left out of the Cologne side and Offenbach lost 4-2 (Overath was among the scorers). A draw would have been enough for Kickers to be safe and indeed they held on to a point until 12 minutes from time. But Oberhausen drew away at Braunschweig and Bielefeld incredibly managed to win 1-0 in Berlin against Patzke and Wild.

Offenbach were relegated, but only temporarily – at least that's what Canellas figured. Once he produced the pieces of information he had gathered, the DFB would have no choice but to demote Bielefeld and keep Kickers in the league. As it turned out, he had underestimated the discretion of the conspirators as well as the ignorance of the DFB. In July, Patzke was suspended for ten years, while life bans were imposed on Wild, Manglitz

– and Canellas. After all, the Offenbach president had admitted to attempted bribery, the investigators argued, among them representatives of Bielefeld and Berlin.

For the umpteenth time in its history, the DFB managed to make a bad situation worse by turning a blind eye and hoping the storm would pass if they paid no attention. Because now an outraged Canellas went on a solitary, Philip Marlowe-style trip into the netherworld of bungs and bribes. Tipped off by journalists sensing the story of their lives, bit players seeking publicity, and even wives looking for revenge, he came up with more dirt than even professional cynics had thought possible. Dirt that would keep the DFB and law courts busy for months, in some cases years.

Bielefeld had indeed paid Hertha to lose, Canellas found out, handing out roughly DM15,000 per member of the Berlin squad. The Offenbach president then learned that Max Lorenz, an international with Braunschweig, had been given DM40,000 because his team had drawn with Oberhausen on the last day of the season, the implication being that Braunschweig may have accidentally lost otherwise. Oberhausen, Canellas uncovered next, were less than innocent themselves: their chairman Peter Maassen had shelled out DM30,000 for a much needed victory in Cologne, and had possibly also paid for a win at Bremen. Schalke had been bought too, Canellas discovered. The sum of DM40,000 had obtained two points for Bielefeld against them. Eight Schalke players immediately sued for libel, swearing under oath they had not been bought. Among these eight were Rolf Rüssmann and Klaus Fischer, future internationals, and Reinhard Libuda and Klaus Fichtel, members of West Germany's 1970 World Cup squad (as were Manfred Manglitz, Bernd Patzke and Max Lorenz).

The extent of the accusations based on Canellas's investigation was enormous. Two-thirds of all Bundesliga clubs found themselves drawn into the quagmire, and who was to say the remaining six were really lily-white? VfB Stuttgart admitted members of their team had conspired to lose at Bielefeld. It was also established that Eintracht Frankfurt were at the very least approached with an offer to throw games of which they did not inform the DFB. Furthermore, an Offenbach player claimed Jürgen Grabowski had promised him DM5,000 for not performing well. (Grabowski defended himself by saying: 'I was only kidding.' Three years later he won the World Cup.) It was then proved that Bielefeld officials had met the coach of MSV Duisburg to negotiate a deal. Finally, even the name of Bayern Munich was mentioned. Duisburg's goalkeeper said he was to receive DM12,000 for letting in a few more than necessary against a Bayern side in need of a better goal difference.

When it was all over, more than 50 players from seven clubs (Cologne, Hertha, Stuttgart, Schalke, Bielefeld, Duisburg, Braunschweig), two coaches and six officials were found guilty by the DFB, based on the evidence accumulated by Canellas. All of them were fined and suspended, in many cases for life – even though most were pardoned as early as 1974 and went on to have decent careers. Not Schalke's Reinhard Libuda, though. He was approaching the age of 30 when he was suspended and had to move to Strasbourg to still be able to earn money from football. In France, the home-loving, painfully introverted Libuda grew increasingly unhappy. When he and his seven Schalke team-mates were found guilty of perjury in court in 1976, Libuda never recovered from this additional blow. Tormented by guilt or feeling misunderstood (maybe both), he began to drink. After he finished his career, he went through a divorce, his health deteriorated and for a while he lived on the dole before landing a job at a printer's. Libuda died from a stroke in 1996, aged 52. Even then, his club were still greeted with chants of 'FC Perjury' when visiting places like Dortmund.

Arminia Bielefeld were demoted into the *Regionalliga*, but, incredibly, Offenbach's relegation stood – as well as Canellas's conviction. Consumed with bitterness, he left Germany for Mallorca to join his brother. The DFB pardoned him in 1976, but that was scant consolation for the man who had exposed the biggest scandal in German football. Canellas died of lung cancer on July 23, 1999 – a few weeks after once-proud Kickers Offenbach had at long last won promotion back to the Second Bundesliga.

The creation of this new division was one of the results of the scandal. Back in the early 1970s, dropping from the Bundesliga to the regional leagues meant that a footballer was no longer a 'licensed player'. He would have to find a proper job again and see his wages cut back to the DM500 a month allowed in the lower league. The fear of dropping into what was almost amateur football, observers said, had driven the sentenced players to their acts of desperation. Thus a second league for licensed players was formed, though it was played in two regional divisions until 1981. However, this sympathetic view couldn't quite explain why somebody like Manglitz, who had no drop to fear, let himself be bought.

And so the DFB grudgingly admitted that a maximum wage system caused more problems than it solved. From 1972 on, players were finally allowed to earn whatever clubs were willing to pay them. Full-blown, open professionalism was no longer considered an impending disaster for the league. Because when Canellas gave his birthday party, the Bundesliga champions had just successfully defended their title for the first time. And there were sure signs that West Germany, maximum wage or not, was following in the footsteps of Spain and Italy in that it was about to produce dominant teams.

It had all somehow started in 1965. The two clubs promoted along with ill-fated Tasmania Berlin during that summer were Bayern Munich and Borussia Mönchengladbach.

10

BLACK AND WHITE WORLD

THE POLITICS OF BAYERN V GLADBACH

IT'S A WELL-ESTABLISHED fact that you should not slap people in the face at football matches. It's a mark of impolite behaviour and will get you a bad reputation. When, for instance, the Uruguayan Horacio Troche signed a contract with Alemannia Aachen in 1967, the press hurried to point out that this was the player who had given Uwe Seeler a clip round the ear during the quarter-final of the 1966 World Cup. When Aachen met Hamburg a few weeks into the season, the South American presented Seeler with a large bouquet of flowers to pacify the public.

However, Troche's is not the most famous slap in German football history. That honour belongs to a youth team player who hid his identity for more than half a century after his deed. When he finally stepped forth, in mid-2010, he said he'd been afraid of 'fanatics who might take it out on my property or whatever'. It wasn't a far-fetched fear. There are people, and I'm not making this up, who are convinced he was solely responsible for letting the Forces of Evil loose on the world. That's a lot of guilt for one person to carry, so let's ease the conscience of Gerhard König from Munich by viewing things a bit differently. We could also say that he made possible the 1970s, the glory decade of the West German game, marked by not only successful but also beautiful football, both domestically and internationally.

The 1970s, as far as football is concerned, lasted from the summer of 1968, when Branko Zebec became head coach of Bayern Munich, to the first half of 1978, when quite a few noteworthy things happened, many of which will be dealt with in the next chapter. For instance, *Star Wars* opened in cinemas around the country. The basic idea of the film had been played out on the Bundesliga's pitches in the preceding ten years. Bayern Munich, the Forces of Evil, had taken over the universe, and the only hope rested with the brave Jedi knights, known as Borussia Mönchengladbach. I know the analogy is a bit dubious (not least because, in football, the Empire won), but you really had to be there.

I take it for granted that most non-German football fans at the very least sense that Bayern are not greatly loved in this country. It's true, they have more supporters than anybody else according to polls, but since they are also the one team everybody has an opinion about, almost everyone who doesn't support them hates Bayern with a vengeance. It is tempting to argue this has to do with envy of their money and over-flowing trophy cabinet – the Real Madrid effect. But with Bayern, things are a bit more complicated. From 1968 to 1978 the Bavarians won four championships. Mönchengladbach, on the other hand, won five – but still Gladbach remained the popular favourites, the second team of most fans.

It's hard to pinpoint when people began viewing Bayern as evil incarnate, but what's certain is that it happened a lot earlier than is generally believed today. Take the last day of that memorable 1970-71 season. Bayern travelled to Duisburg, level on points with Gladbach. The Bavarians were not yet a superpower, having won just two championships (one of which was covered with 40 years' worth of dust). When the players ran out, Franz Beckenbauer was, according to an opponent, 'shocked at the hate' confronting his team. It seemed as if the whole of Duisburg had crammed into the ground just to see Bayern lose. Their team had nothing to gain from the match, yet pushed on by a fanatical crowd, the players fought for every 50/50 ball like men on amphetamines. When Duisburg won, the Munich side was jeered off, regardless of the fact that it included the nation's World Cup heroes Sepp Maier and Franz Beckenbauer (Gerd Müller was suspended).

Two years later, in December 1973, Bayern won a Cup match away at Bremen, 2-1. The players were sitting in their bus, ready to leave for the airport, when, as Beckenbauer recalled: 'Shouts outside. About 20 young boys have blocked the exit. "Bayern rabble!" they bawl. Fists drum against the window. "Maier-manure, Müller-shit, Beckenbauer-piss!"' The scene ended with the players getting off the bus. Sepp Maier floored a fan, Franz Roth kicked another. The people insulted by the Bremen fans weren't public enemies but the celebrated 1972 European Championship winners Maier, Beckenbauer, Müller, Paul Breitner, Georg Schwarzenbeck and Uli Hoeness.

These were no isolated incidents. Sepp Maier remembered a game in late 1970 that Bayern won at Oberhausen. Afterwards, a few hundred people encircled the team as they headed for the coach. 'It was an eerie feeling,' Maier said. 'Like lynch justice in the Wild West.' The players had things hurled at them, and Franz Roth (again) even threw a few punches. A couple of years earlier, Maier had been attacked by a Hanover fan while leaving the pitch. 'I'm going to kill you, you Bayern pig!' the man cried, and lifted his umbrella. Maier was faster, and his uppercut put the assailant on the floor. That was in December 1968. In the same match, Gerd Müller was sent off for hitting Jupp Heynckes and Beckenbauer was fined DM1,000 by the DFB because he had, the officials claimed, 'provoked the crowd'. (As he left the field, Beckenbauer had pretended to urinate at the supporters.)

These were not cases of budding hooliganism, though this was something which would plague the league in the 1980s. While the first reports about growing aggression among fans did reach the public in 1971 and 1972, such early accounts centred around derbies (most notably Dortmund v Schalke). Only Bayern could cross the whole country and still find themselves physically attacked.

How all this came about, and how the 1970s saw foundations laid for the Evil Bayern Empire, is really somehow the story of that slap in the face. It happened in the summer of 1958, at a youth tournament in Neubiberg, near Munich. The final of the Under-14 event was contested by Munich 1860 and little SC 1906 Munich. The latter team's centre-forward, a small but crafty boy by the name of Franz Beckenbauer, had scored in the semi-final against Bayern Munich, and 1860's centre-half knew he had to watch him very closely. He figured it made sense to show this Beckenbauer who was boss and tripped him up a few minutes into the match. Beckenbauer retaliated with a late tackle, and from then on the two kids had a go at each other with increasing frequency.

Franz Beckenbauer wasn't, and never would be, the sort of player who enjoys the physical side of football. But he was fired up for this game, because 1860 Munich were his favourite club, and he was about to join their youth squad. 'I supported 1860 even when they were relegated from the *Oberliga*,' Beckenbauer later said. 'And it was always my dream to play for them.' That was because Franz Beckenbauer hailed from Giesing, a working-class district of Munich that traditionally bred Blues (1860 fans or players), whereas Reds (Bayern) normally came from wealthier districts, such as Schwabing. Beckenbauer's father worked at the post office and had neither time nor sympathy for football, especially as a profession. 'Look at your idol, this Fritz Walter,' he would tell young Franz. 'What's he going to do once he's too old for football and hasn't learned a proper job?' When the son replied that the player would live on the money he had saved, his father let out a laugh. 'Footballers are too stupid to save money,' he declared.

At the age of eight, Beckenbauer joined SC 1906, and he played there for five years, until he learned that the club lacked the funds to keep its schoolboy squads going. He talked to his team-mates, and they decided to move to 1860 as a group. Then came the Neubiberg tournament. There are two versions about how exactly it came to pass that Gerhard König, the 1860 centre-half, hit Beckenbauer in the face. The older, and thus more trustworthy, account says that Beckenbauer fouled his marker, who jumped up and gave Franz a slap. The second version has it that the 1860 boy called Beckenbauer 'a dolt' and advised him to play with marbles instead of footballs. A few minutes later, Franz scored a goal and used the occasion to explain in detail who was and who wasn't mentally up to scratch. Whereupon the boy in blue saw red and ruined everything.

On the spot, Beckenbauer decided he would never join a club whose players behaved like that. Instead, he and his pals applied for membership at FC Bayern. At that time, Bayern had a decent first team, but they were no real match for Offenbach, Frankfurt, Nuremberg or Karlsruhe. However, they were only a few years away from signing a new coach, the Yugoslav Zlatko Cajkovski, whom everybody called 'Tschik'. (In his native Zagreb, they had nicknamed the small, compact Cajkovski 'Čik', or cigarette stub.)

Cajkovski had been the playmaker of the Yugoslavia side that lost the 1954 World Cup quarter-final to West Germany, but life had been good to him since, and so he was pretty portly by the time he coached Cologne to the 1962 championship. Twelve

months after this triumph, Cajkovski received a phone call from
the agent Otto Ratz, who told him Bayern were looking for a
coach. A move to Munich meant a step down the ladder for
Tschik, as the Bavarians had not been admitted to the new
Bundesliga, but club president Wilhelm Neudecker gave the
impression of a man aiming for the stars.

'We have a lot of talent in our youth set-up,' he told
Cajkovski, and it took the Yugoslav only a few days to realise
this was an understatement. That Beckenbauer kid was priceless,
the goalie Sepp Maier a great prospect, a tall defender, Georg
Schwarzenbeck, improving fast. Cajkovski took the job,
optimistic those teenagers would one day form the nucleus of
a really good side. He couldn't know it at the time, but a few of
the other young players he would find during the next two years
turned out to be half-decent as well: the strong midfielder Franz
Roth, or that shy boy who was such a devoted Nuremberg fan,
Gerd Müller.

While Cajkovski was laying the foundations for the Bayern team
that would dominate the country and the continent, Hennes
Weisweiler was doing a similar thing at Mönchengladbach.
Weisweiler had been a no-nonsense defender at Cologne. He
once suffered a fractured skull during a promotion game against
Würselen and played the whole 90 minutes nonetheless (the
same match that was decided by Jupp Derwall's goal). Like many
hard men, he favoured an altogether different kind of football
when he became a coach. Many years later, Günter Netzer
would say: 'About once a year we stop talking to each other.
He wants no-holds-barred attacking football for 90 minutes.
I think you should take the pace out of a match when that's
called for.' Weisweiler's devotion to moving forward at all costs
stemmed from (who would have guessed it?) a fascination with

English football. 'That up-and-down-the-pitch game,' as Netzer scornfully called it.

Weisweiler worked as Herberger's assistant in 1954-55, but his place was taken by Helmut Schön when Weisweiler opted for club football and his old team, Cologne. And it is here that the stories of Bayern and Gladbach start to become closely entwined. After all, every decent story about the struggle between the forces of Good and Evil works on the premise that both come from one source, that they were the same until their paths began to diverge. (Darth Vader was once a Jedi, remember?)

At Cologne, Weisweiler had a player who hated to track back when he lost the ball. 'Tschik!' the coach would yell at such moments before adding a heartfelt: 'You arsehole!' Cajkovski just shrugged his shoulders. A few years later, the two met again when Cajkovski was taking an exam to earn his coaching badge. His teacher was none other than Weisweiler, and legend has it that this dialogue took place:

> Weisweiler: 'Name a famous educationalist.'
> Cajkovski: 'Herberger.'
> Weisweiler: 'Well, that's not what I mean. Think of Switzerland.'
> Cajkovski: 'I don't know.'
> Weisweiler: 'His name is Pestalozzi.'
> Cajkovski: 'There was no player of that name in Switzerland.'

One player who was in Switzerland in 1954 was Branko Zebec, a Yugoslav team-mate of Cajkovski's. He would later take over the Bayern side that Tschik had built, before making way for Udo Lattek in 1970. Lattek, meanwhile, had also received his coaching badge from Weisweiler – and would replace him at Gladbach in 1975.

But it's not just the names or people that linked the two clubs. It's also how they rose to prominence in the first place. When

Weisweiler became Gladbach's coach in 1964, barely a year after Cajkovski had taken over at Bayern, he found himself in the same situation as the easy-going Yugoslav. Borussia were doing all right, but not much more. However, there were some talented youngsters just waiting to be given a chance, such as Günter Netzer, signed the year before from 1. FC Mönchengladbach, Herbert Laumen and Josef Heynckes.

What Weisweiler did over the next months basically followed the same method of Cajkovski at Bayern. He did not sign established players but started building on what he had and then added a few very young prospects. First he promoted Heynckes to the first team and found a fleet-footed attacker called Bernd Rupp. Later, he would lure the limited but very willing Berti Vogts, an orphan since boyhood, and the tireless runner Herbert Wimmer to Gladbach, both from obscure neighbouring clubs. (Some people say the most important thing was that Weisweiler's wife Lilo suggested the team should play in white instead of their then customary black, but this is really overdoing the symbolism.)

The team that won promotion for Gladbach in 1964-65 was the youngest among the close to 100 competing in the Bundesliga and the *Regionalligen*. On average, a player in Weisweiler's squad was 21.5 years old. The local journalist Wilhelm August Hurtmanns began to refer to the team as the Foals, a nickname destined to survive the decades. However, it might just as well have been applied to Bayern, since the average age of Cajkovski's squad was only 21.8. Gladbach scored 92 goals in 34 games during that *Regionalliga* season and then added 17 more in their promotion group to make it to the Bundesliga. Bayern netted a phenomenal 146 in 36 league matches, scored 18 in their own promotion group and were also finally in the top flight.

Bayern acclimatised themselves somewhat quicker in the Bundesliga, finishing third in their first year, while Gladbach ended the campaign in 13th place. Soon, however, the two marched side by side and were loved by the public in equal measure. Both clubs had young, exciting teams that didn't seem to care how many they conceded because they hoped to score more. Netzer and Beckenbauer were ball players, the antithesis of rugged enforcers such as Otto Rehhagel (Kaiserslautern), Klaus-Dieter Sieloff (Stuttgart) or Ludwig Müller (Nuremberg) who were an essential part of some of the other Bundesliga teams. By 1974, Netzer and Beckenbauer had scooped up five of the nine Footballer of the Year awards handed out since 1966. Between 1966 and 1972 there would never be more than two places separating the clubs in the final standings and they both finished each of these seasons among the four highest-scoring teams.

The main difference between the sides was one of style. Gladbach's game, despite Weisweiler's positive inclinations, was built around counter-attacks, often initiated by Netzer, whose legendary 50-yard passes split defences and invariably found their target. They also spread their goals more evenly among a strikeforce that included three quick, dangerous forwards. Bayern, on the other hand, preferred to take matters into their own hands by keeping possession of the ball. Beckenbauer built from the rear, and the midfield – often without a really defensive player – applied the pressure that would eventually crack even the most solid defence. Bayern could do this because they had 'the Phantom' up front, 'the Ghost of the Penalty Box', 'the Bomber', or 'the Executioner' as a Spanish paper called him, a player who was probably the most inexplicable and unlikely superstar since Garrincha.

Gerd Müller scored with his shin, his knee and his backside, and sometimes even with his feet. He scored when he got into the league and when he left it. He scored in cup games against lowly opposition and on the world stage marked by the best defenders there were. Basically, the only two things he did not do were score meaningless goals – and 'bomb' them in. (The much-criticised nickname, by the way, probably stemmed from an article in a Glasgow newspaper that compared Müller to a Stuka.) Why he did all those things has never been conclusively explained. Some people argue that his stubby build meant he had a low centre of gravity which gave him that tenth-of-a-second edge, guaranteeing he would get to loose balls first. Others claim he 'sensed' what was going to happen, as if he were an animal.

All of which sadly ignores the hours of practice Müller put into honing his skills, especially perfecting the lightning-quick one-twos he would play with Beckenbauer. At the 1974 World Cup, Müller was chosen as the outfield player to go in goal should something happen to both regular keepers during a match. It didn't come to that, but Müller was such a professional that he felt it was his duty to work on his goalkeeping skills during training. He promptly damaged a finger on his right hand and played in the ill-fated GDR game with a bandage.

Müller scored an astounding 365 goals in 427 Bundesliga games and found the net 68 times in 62 internationals. When the striker celebrated his 50th birthday, Beckenbauer stood up and said: 'Without Gerd Müller, we'd probably still be in the wooden hut that was once our clubhouse.' Uli Hoeness, Karl-Heinz Rummenigge, Paul Breitner and all the others who had become rich and famous with Bayern, rose to their feet and applauded the former 'Bomber'. Gerd Müller squinted through his spectacles and mumbled something into his salt-and-pepper beard as if he wished the ground would swallow him up. A period of alcoholism that had almost destroyed his marriage behind him, he was as grateful to the club for picking him up from the gutter in the early 1990s as Beckenbauer was to him for making Bayern the world's best team in the early 1970s.

With hindsight, it was in 1968 that Bayern and Gladbach stopped being brothers-in-arms fighting for a better, more beautiful football world and instead became rivals with different agendas. That was the year Tschik Cajkovski was replaced by Branko Zebec. Zebec favoured a more disciplined approach and he made that clear by cementing an idea that had originated with Cajkovski: Zebec permanently pulled Beckenbauer from midfield back into defence. Bayern promptly won their first Bundesliga title, a stunning eight points ahead of Aachen.

Equally importantly, 1968 was also the year West Germany's youth became politicised to a degree hitherto thought impossible, so much so that soon even 'Bayern or Gladbach' would become a question of ideology. In the wake of the maelstrom in America over the Vietnam war, Marxist student groups formed at every major university and took to the streets. Demonstrations, violent blockades and arson attacks on conservative publishing houses rocked the Republic in 1968. At times, it seemed as if the country was on the verge of engaging in a civil war against its own young people, who were disillusioned by the grand coalition between the Christian Democrats and Social Democrats that seemed to signal the end of a functional opposition and thus all democratic foundations. The lasting results of the uprising were a general liberalisation of German society's set of values and the long-overdue first steps towards a thorough analysis of its fascist past.

However, it also led to the creation of militant, violent splinter groups and a general tendency to view events in every walk of life according to black-and-white patterns. 'Every walk of life' includes football. Soon, Germany's writers, journalists, authors and fans would use the evolving struggle between Gladbach and Bayern as a symbol. Politics, philosophy, art and sometimes even sport – whatever there was that needed classification, you could bet somebody was there who would argue it all boiled down to Gladbach v Bayern, Netzer v Beckenbauer, Good v Evil.

Now that Bayern had made it to the top, Gladbach wasted little time in drawing level. They won the league in 1969-70, and a year later they became the first club to win two Bundesliga titles in a row. That was the campaign which went down to the wire and was decided by Duisburg's courageous performance against Bayern on the last day. Gladbach had set a record, and, sure enough, Bayern immediately set about improving on it. They became the first West German club to win three championships in a row when they triumphed in 1972, 1973 and 1974. Even the powerful Nuremberg or Schalke teams hadn't managed to do that all those decades ago.

That was a formidable challenge to Gladbach, but the club did not succumb. The team had lost Günter Netzer to Real Madrid in 1973 after one too many rows with Weisweiler. (It seemed the two could live neither with nor without each other, but when Netzer was even pencilled in as sweeper, he'd had enough.) Yet the coach managed to compensate for even that grievous loss by unearthing new talent. Rainer Bonhof, the son of Dutch parents, had broken into the team, Ulrich Stielike was coming through and the Dane Allan Simonsen emerged from a two-year slump in form.

Gladbach instantly equalled Bayern's achievement by winning the league titles of 1975, 1976 and 1977, the third of which was secured on the last day with a 2-2 draw at Bayern, who were having the second of three off-years during which they regrouped. The year after that, Borussia missed out on a new record by the narrowest margin in Bundesliga history – there were only three goals separating them from Cologne at the very top.

And then it was all over. The Foals had begun to limp and would soon slow to a trot. The club came close to another title in 1984, when they finished as one of the top three teams, all level on points. However, that outcome was not quite as frustrating as it appears from the final standings (Gladbach went into the last matchday two points and 17 goals behind the league leaders), and it was only the last hurrah, a farewell fanfare.

Eras came to an end in 1978 wherever you looked. It was Bayern's first year without Franz Beckenbauer, who had joined New York Cosmos, and their last with Uli Hoeness on the pitch. It was Gladbach's first season with a young midfielder called Lothar Matthäus, who would get the club's 'rebel' image badly wrong, and their last with the iconic Jupp Heynckes as a player. As it turned out, there was no one to replace the man who had scored 195 goals in 283 games for the Foals. The spring that had poured out talent after talent for Gladbach had abruptly run dry.

There are still many people who claim this was the fault of Udo Lattek, who had replaced Weisweiler in 1975. The new coach did win with Gladbach, as he had done with Bayern, but he failed to rebuild the squad when it became apparent new blood would soon be needed. That was exactly what had happened at Bayern, where it was, in addition, secretly whispered that any fool would have lifted silverware with a squad that included Maier, Beckenbauer and Müller. However, midfielder Horst Wohlers once told me: 'I think it's an unfair charge. Perhaps Lattek failed to bring in young blood, but it was an almost impossible task. It's a miracle that we dominated for as long as we did in the first place.'

Mönchengladbach were the epitome of an era in which some people cared about things other than wins and losses. Beauty, for instance. Taking risks. Going for goals, not results. Bayern, on the other hand, soon caught a whiff of the approaching age of technocratic football. They loved the taste of champagne and the feel of banknotes more than the adulation of fans and the self-sufficiency of the game. That is why the public hated their guts and cheered on the tomorrow-be-damned attitude of Gladbach. So says the myth.

'Gladbach and Bayern: radicalism or rationality, reform or pragmatism,' wrote the football essayist Helmut Böttiger. 'If need be, Bayern won 1-0. Bayern never played themselves into rapture, they won in a calculating manner.' Contrast this with 'the young foals who played free of all restraints, irresistibly moving forward'.

Or let's hear some other voices. 'All the reformers, the progressives,' wrote Holger Jenrich, 'sided with Borussia instead of Bayern. They considered the team's risky "look-out-here-I-come" football a continuation of political change through footballing means.' The sociologist Norbert Seitz said: 'Since the days of promotion to the Bundesliga, the Foals cultivated a reckless style that brought record victories – 11-0 against Schalke, 10-0 over Neunkirchen, but on the other hand also a 7-0 defeat at home against Bremen. When Gladbach lost 6-5 to Dortmund, Weisweiler stood up against the charge that his team had played naively: "Better to lose 6-5 than 1-0!"' Such obvious disdain for playing it safe led Bernd Rupp (no radical, it seems) to move to Bremen, saying: 'I want to be with a team that can hold a lead.'

The problem with all this transfigured romanticism is that the naked facts don't bear it out. The contradictions start with details such as the line above that Seitz attributes to Weisweiler. Dortmund did not win 6-5, it was 5-4. One could argue that adding the flourish of two extra goals harms nobody and just makes it sound more 'Gladbach' somehow. However, another fact is that while the match was certainly stirring, it had little to do with 'look-out-here-I-come' football: four of the nine goals came from the penalty spot. And it didn't even prove that Gladbach couldn't or didn't want to hold a lead, as Dortmund were in front three times and Gladbach only once.

But perhaps Seitz and/or Weisweiler meant a different game, Gladbach's 6-5 defeat at Bremen on the last day of the 1968-69 season? Well, no giving away a lead here, either. Bremen were ahead 2-0, 3-1 and 6-3. (Former Gladbach player Rupp scored a hat-trick for Werder.) A few weeks later, Weisweiler held a team meeting and said: 'If we don't win the championship this year, I'm leaving.' So much for not caring about results.

The myth crumbles further when you look at the bigger picture. The writer Dietrich Schulze-Marmeling has pointed out that between 1969 (Bayern's first Bundesliga title) and 1977 (Gladbach's last), the 'pragmatists' from Munich actually scored more goals than the 'reformers' from the Rhineland. They also conceded more, which means that over these nine seasons, attending a Bayern game was the safer bet if you wanted to see goals (3.65 per Bayern game, 3.4 at Gladbach).

And there is another thing. Most of the truly rousing Bundesliga games from this era involved Bayern, not Gladbach. True, the Foals were responsible for the most crushing victories: 12-0 against Dortmund (1978) and 11-0 against Schalke (1969). But these are spectacles, not exciting games. Compare that to Bayern's legendary match at Kaiserslautern in late 1973. They led 4-1 after 57 minutes, yet lost 7-4. That same year, Bayern fell behind 3-0 and then 5-2 at Schalke, but still came back to earn a point. Flukes from one particular season? We can extend the list. On the penultimate day of the 1974-75 season, Gerd Müller scored four goals at Düsseldorf, Bayern were ahead 3-1 and then 4-2, but they still lost 6-5. There was also a day in September 1976, when Bayern were trailing hosts Bochum 4-0 eight minutes into the second half. Twenty minutes later, they led 5-4, then conceded an equaliser, but won 6-5 in the final minute.

That's not in keeping with the '1-0' philosophy held against Beckenbauer's team. Instead, one could claim that it was Gladbach who rose to the top by shutting up shop. They won their first title by keeping a clean sheet in 13 games. And it was they who signed Ludwig Müller and Klaus-Dieter Sieloff in

1969. To imagine such ruffians partnering Berti Vogts – known as 'the guard dog' or 'the terrier' – hardly smacks of 'the spirit of utopia' Böttiger sees in Netzer's style of play. Granted, Bayern's stopper 'Katsche' Schwarzenbeck hardly wore ballet shoes either, but the Bavarian backline also featured skilled men like Paul Breitner (a defender from 1971 to 1974) and of course Franz Beckenbauer, who sometimes strutted around as if he was saying: 'Hold on, there's no need for violence. Nobody tackles anybody on my pitch!'

And so the truth is that the great Bayern v Gladbach debate had nothing to do with football. Both teams often played pleasingly and entertained crowds, and sometimes they didn't. The Bavarians were probably, even at this early point, a bit more adept at conserving energy and had a better sense of timing, but the explanation for this has to be that they simply had more individually talented footballers in their squad, not that they set out to play 'rationally' or 'pragmatically'.

The Beckenbauer v Netzer dichotomy was often said to exemplify the Bayern v Gladbach argument. But these cliches do not bear much close scrutiny either. 'Beckenbauer was encumbered with the attribute of being vain and arrogant, at best he became a star, while Netzer turned into a myth,' Jenrich argued, calling the latter 'a football rebel', which has been an overused term for Netzer since his first biography, *Rebell am Ball* (Rebel on the ball). It goes without saying that Beckenbauer's nickname didn't help. 'The Kaiser' suggested aloofness and conservatism. The journalist Jupp Suttner wrote: 'Somehow Germans were never proud of Beckenbauer. When something comes easily to someone, that person is viewed with suspicion.' Thus Gladbach became the mythic rebels, Bayern the vain stars.

In truth, there were probably more 'rebels' at Bayern than at Gladbach. It's hard to imagine a more mainstream person than Berti Vogts, while Paul Breitner paraded his Afro, teasingly toyed with Maoist chic and refused to sing the national anthem. Even Beckenbauer may have been more of a rabble-rouser at heart than Netzer. He got his girlfriend pregnant when he was barely 18 – and then shockingly refused to marry her. This was 1963, and the DFB immediately banned Beckenbauer from the national youth team. Dettmar Cramer, then coaching the West German prospects, even phoned Sepp Herberger to have him exert some influence and help the kid. Beckenbauer was pardoned on the condition that on away trips he shared a double room with Cramer.

Günter Netzer, meanwhile, was more of a self-centred loner than a rebel. He came from a background much more middle-class than Beckenbauer's, not to mention a more provincial city. His father Christian supplied seeds to the many horticulturists and farmers around Mönchengladbach, his mother Barbara ran a corner shop. Christian Netzer even entrusted Günter and his friends with a small piece of land they could turn into a football pitch. 'I guess I really was a bit spoiled,' Netzer later said about his genesis as a footballer. 'Many things had come too easily to me, my self-confidence was astonishingly great.'

As an adult, Netzer was that rare mixture of aestheticism and, yes, pragmatism. It was he who said: 'I love football, but I want to control this passion so that it doesn't devour me.' He could also be shockingly calculating and rational. 'There are 11 businessmen on a pitch,' Netzer coolly said, 'each looking after his own interests.'

But there was also the Netzer who excited anyone who ever saw him play because he was so different. 'I regarded headers as something akin to handballs: against the rules,' he says today. 'And I immediately found myself somebody to do the running for me.' Still, he did use his head and his feet, only unlike most of the players around him. He delivered the longest passes ever seen in the league, his free-kicks bent wickedly, and he could switch suddenly from complete inertia into an irresistible run through midfield that caught the opposition flat-footed.

All these elements of a complex personality came together in his last match for Gladbach, the 1973 Cup final against local rivals Cologne. Netzer had told Weisweiler he had signed for Real Madrid and that, coupled with the fact that Netzer's mother had just died, made the coach do the unthinkable: he left out the team's star for the final. It was one of the most brilliant games ever played on German soil. The half-time score was 1-1, but it might as well have been 3-3. The crowd chanted Netzer's name and during the interval Weisweiler approached the brooding genius. 'I'll bring you on if you want me to,' he said. 'They're doing OK,' Netzer sulked, 'they don't need me.'

With 90 minutes up, it was still 1-1. Netzer's heir apparent, young Christian Kulik, went down with cramp, and while everybody was preparing for extra time, Netzer approached him. 'Can you carry on?' he asked. 'I'm afraid not,' Kulik groaned. Netzer turned around and walked to the bench. Passing Weisweiler, he casually said: 'Now I am playing.' Then he took off his tracksuit top and joined the team on the pitch.

Three minutes into extra time, Netzer got hold of the ball for the first time, ten steps or so into the Cologne half, close to the centre circle. He half-ran, half-jogged some 15 yards into the inside-right position, an opponent close to his side. Then he played a short pass to Bonhof and abruptly turned left. There were five defenders gathered on the edge of the penalty area, but none of them was prepared for the maestro's sudden acceleration. Bonhof relayed the ball immediately into the open space created by Netzer's move ('the first time he ever played a proper one-two,' Netzer quips today). By the time the Cologne players realised what was happening, they had lost a step on Netzer. He could have taken a touch to get the ball on to his stronger right foot. But he was in full stride – and not one to shy away from risks. Two yards inside the box, his left foot met the ball and it whistled into the roof of the net.

It's this image of Netzer that has stayed with us. The long, blond mane flowing as he jumps into the air to celebrate, knowing exactly what he has just done. Other images, stuff that has nothing directly to do with football, supplement this picture stored in the back of people's minds. Netzer at the wheel of his Ferrari, his Porsche or his Jaguar. Netzer in front of his pub-cum-disco, called Lovers Lane. Netzer arm-in-arm with his beautiful black-haired and black-clad girlfriend Hannelore Girrulat, a goldsmith by trade. It should be no surprise, then, that he captured the imagination.

In Hanau (just east of Frankfurt), a ten-year-old kid became so obsessed with Netzer in 1970 that he begged his parents to buy each issue of *kicker* to collect coupons that would earn him the Netzer *Starschnitt* (a series of posters that, if put together, would form a life-sized picture). No sooner was he done with the job, lovingly staring at the giant poster, than his uncle told him to take it down because 'that man's hair is way too long'. The boy refused and got his way. He had won a fight with a grown-up, all because of Netzer – and young Rudolf Völler loved him the more for that.

Beckenbauer just could not compete with Netzer in that arena. First, he played in a different position and was never asked to score glorious goals that won a Cup. Second, he also lacked the means to challenge Netzer's image. Being known as 'the Kaiser' had nothing to do with football. The name was first attached to him by a magazine that said he looked like the eccentric Bavarian sovereign Ludwig II, known as the Fairytale King (or, in England, more often as Mad King Ludwig) and he did indeed have that rapt, altar-boy look. In August 1971, Bayern played a friendly in Vienna. During the post-match banquet, Beckenbauer was photographed standing next to a bust of the former Austrian emperor Franz-Joseph, Kaiser from 1848 to 1916. As soon as the picture was published, Beckenbauer was 'the Kaiser' for good.

And so the whole Beckenbauer v Netzer question had little to do with football either, with who played better or more beautifully. It also had nothing to do with 'pragmatism' or 'arrogance', let alone 'the spirit of utopia'. That's the sort of thing sociologists and political scientists come up with when asked to explain popular culture, while reality is usually a lot simpler. There were two players, and Netzer was the sexier.

And that's also the main difference between Gladbach and Bayern. Borussia, as a team, were more sexy. Apart from Netzer, this aura didn't really have to do with the players themselves. After all, there were people like Horst Köppel at Gladbach, who played with a toupee for almost five years, and – but let's not drag Berti Vogts into this again. What made Gladbach sexy in a James Dean sort of way was an element of tragedy counterbalancing all that gung-ho football and juvenile swagger. These players, one sensed, were somehow doomed, jinxed. As always, Netzer comes to mind first. The most exciting German footballer of all time played only 20 minutes in a World Cup. And that was in the defeat against the GDR in 1974.

The things most people remember first about Gladbach are not their record victories, which never meant a thing anyway. Even the 12-0 win against Dortmund on the last day of the 1977-78 season was not enough: it would have taken another three goals to win the league. It's the defeats. Gladbach's two UEFA Cup triumphs (in 1975 and 1979) pale in comparison to their epic clashes with Liverpool in 1973 (UEFA Cup final), 1977 (European Cup final) and 1978 (European Cup semi-final), all of which were lost. Then there was the ill-fated penalty shoot-out against Everton in the 1970-71 European Cup, which could have been avoided but for a mistimed display of stereotypical German cleanliness. Gladbach were leading 1-0 in the first leg when goalkeeper Wolfgang Kleff decided to remove a roll of toilet paper from the box. Howard Kendall seized the opportunity and equalised from a distance.

Or how about the scandalous European Cup quarter-final against Real Madrid in March 1976? The first leg finished 2-2, at the Bernabeu it was 1-1. That second match was refereed by the Dutchman Leonardus van der Kroft. 'The team played a great game,' Wohlers remembers, 'but scored two perfectly legal goals which were disallowed.' Netzer, then playing for Real, said even his Spanish team-mates had no idea why the goals weren't given. UEFA rejected Gladbach's protest, but FIFA barred Van der Kroft from officiating at the 1976 Olympics, which should have been the referee's farewell tournament.

It was all strangely reminiscent of Gladbach's semi-final tie with Milan in the Cup-Winners' Cup two years earlier. The Germans needed three goals to win the tie, and they got one early. Then the Spanish referee denied them a penalty for handball, refused to send off Karl-Heinz Schnellinger (playing for Milan), who broke Christian Kulik's ankle with an awful tackle, and crowned his performance three minutes from time by looking the other way when Bernd Rupp was scythed down in Milan's penalty area. However, these outrages and hard-luck stories paled into insignificance compared to the pinnacle of the Borussia drama. That was a game hardly anyone saw, but everyone recalls.

On October 20, 1971, Gladbach played Internazionale at home. It was the first leg of the European Cup second round, and Inter's team featured four men who had played for Italy against West Germany in the unforgettable 1970 World Cup semi-final (marred, according to Germans, by disgusting Italian play-acting). Gladbach's ground, the *Bökelberg*, was small to begin with, but because the east stand was being rebuilt, merely 27,500 fans could be crammed into the stadium. They were the only people who really saw what happened that night. German TV had struck a deal with Borussia for a live broadcast, but hours before kick-off, a squabble arose over who would have to cover the sales tax, DM6,600. The two parties found no agreement, and the most legendary match featuring a Bundesliga club was not shown live on television. (Only a painfully short highlight reel exists.)

It was 1-1 after 20 minutes, Roberto Boninsegna having equalised after Jupp Heynckes's early goal. Led by an awesome Netzer, who had had his leg in plaster until a few days before the match, the Foals then stampeded across the pitch for 30 minutes that produced five goals against the fabled Inter defence. Netzer himself scored twice, first from a long-range free-kick, then a breath-taking chip with the outside of his right foot. The Italians were able to stem the tide until eight minutes from time, when even muscle-man Sieloff was allowed to score from the spot to make it 7-1.

'In the spring of 1971, the Bundesliga scandal had covered the game with its dark, deep shadows,' wrote Karl-Heinz Huba, 'but then, right in the middle of the darkness, there came deliverance. Only once in a blue moon can a team somewhere on this planet manage a game like that.' Matt Busby, watching the match for UEFA, said: 'What a fanatastic team! Such pace, power and invention!'

The second leg was won 4-2 by Inter, a rough affair that left four Gladbach players injured. And yet it was Inter who reached the next round and, eventually, the final against Ajax. That's because after 27 minutes of the first leg, an empty can thrown from the stands had hit Boninsegna in the throat. He was carried off the pitch and substituted, whereupon Inter filed a protest with UEFA. The match was replayed in Berlin and finished scoreless.

Most people who witnessed the incident swear that Boninsegna was acting, and the report of the Red Cross attendants stated there was no mark to be found on the player's body. Max Merkel, the Austrian coach, later wrote: 'He was having a natter with his mates while lying on the ground, telling them to complain to the referee. Since that day I know that, in football, an Italian lying down is often more dangerous than one standing up.' Why Boninsegna should have done such a thing, at a time when it was only 2-1, is unclear. The investigating UEFA commission claimed that Busby visited Inter's dressing room and found Boninsegna unconscious.

Whatever the truth, this match remains the best example of the mishaps that seemed to befall Gladbach with regularity when the stakes were highest, sometimes even in the league. In 1971, with seven games to go, Borussia led Bayern by a point and were playing Bremen at home. Some 15 minutes from time, with the scores level at 1-1, a cross sailed into Bremen's box and Herbert Laumen rose to head it in. He missed the ball, fell into the net, and the sudden tug caused the left goalpost to break at the base. There was no spare goal available and no one connected with Borussia was able to repair the damage, perhaps hoping for a replay, so the game was called off. Three weeks later, the DFB decided the home club was responsible for the equipment and awarded both points to Bremen. It may have been a correct decision, but it was typical, very hard Gladbach luck. Bayern, meanwhile, had lost (as always) at Kaiserslautern, but suddenly found themselves back in the running thanks to a rotten piece of wood. And that, somehow, was also typical.

One reason the Reds from Munich were (and are) not loved has to do with what Germans call *Bayern-Dusel* – meaning luck, especially of the variety that seems undeserved. While Gladbach were denied again and again in Europe by the strangest of incidents, Bayern appeared to waltz across the continent with a song on their lips. Their first European Cup final, in 1974, was as good as lost when a superior Atlético Madrid side at long last went ahead after 114 minutes. But seconds from the final whistle, Schwarzenbeck got the ball, 28 yards from the Spanish goal. The defender who statistically needed more than 19 games to find the net once tried a desperate shot that skidded across the pitch and crossed the line inches inside the post. Bayern won the replay, admittedly in great style, 4-0.

In 1975, goals by Franz Roth and Gerd Müller beat a Leeds team that dominated the match and had a Peter Lorimer goal disallowed in controversial circumstances with the score 0-0. A year later, Bayern met St Etienne in the final. The French hit the woodwork twice, but again only Bayern scored. The *Daily Mail* mentioned something about the 'parasites of football' and this was an idea that was also beginning to take root in Germany itself.

Because the other problem with Bayern was that they seemed to take success for granted. When Beckenbauer talked his club into hiring Udo Lattek, he explained: 'As a footballer, you develop a sense for winners. And I think Lattek is a winner.' Well, he was proved right, but that only made this attitude more frustrating to onlookers. Especially since Bayern didn't even appear to appreciate winning. When the team lifted the 1973 league title, Paul Breitner was photographed dancing naked by a swimming pool. He was reprimanded for such unseemly behaviour and angrily retorted: 'At this shitty club, they can't even celebrate!' A year later, Bayern won the championship again, and only 1,500 fans showed up for the party. 'Maier tucked away the trophy as if it were a new household appliance for his wife,' one newspaper noted.

Such strange lack of interest was only made worse by the fact that when Bayern triumphed, they often did so decisively: by eight points in 1969, by 11 in 1973. Their only league title of the decade that was decided on the last day turned out to be anti-climactic, too. Schalke travelled to Munich in 1972 for a true final, trailing Bayern by only one point. The match ended 5-1.

Finally, it also became obvious that Bayern worked under better conditions than Gladbach. There was more money available in a metropolis like Munich, and when the vast Olympic Stadium was built for the 1972 Games, Bayern found themselves able to accommodate 80,000 people for their big matches, while Gladbach were stuck with a tiny, uncomfortable ground. This is not to say that Bayern actually made use of the money that was coming in due to their European success. During the 1970s, it was other clubs that spent big. Bremen signed five established players for the 1971-72 season and were dubbed 'the million-mark side'. (Those five managed 37 goals between them, but Gerd Müller alone found the net 40 times in 34 league games during a record-breaking season.) Even Gladbach bought more mature players than the Bavarians, from Ludwig Müller and Sieloff to the Danish contingent Ulrik Le Fevre, Henning Jensen and Allan Simonsen.

No, Bayern found most of their stars cheap and young, often because they had connections. Uli Hoeness and Paul Breitner signed for them in 1970, a few months after both had given 1860 their pledge. The joint change of opinion came about because Udo Lattek joined Bayern, and he had coached both of them as members of the national youth team. And why was it that Bayern offered the prestigous job to a little-known man like Lattek in the first place? Because Franz Beckenbauer had urged them to do so. In other words, the slap of 1958 cost 1860 three future World Cup winners.

Four years later, Max Merkel alerted Bayern to a good youngster who wasn't yet 19 and played for a tiny club in Westphalia. So it happened that the club snatched Karl-Heinz Rummenigge, who would win two European Footballer of the Year awards, for DM17,500. Inter later paid 650 times that for him. Merkel, by the way, was coaching 1860 when he noticed Rummenigge, but he figured this once-proud club was by now too small for Rummenigge's talents.

However, Bayern knew that the days of stars for peanuts would soon be over. So they were planning ahead. In 1966, the club appointed the league's very first business manager, Robert Schwan, who also doubled as Beckenbauer's personal agent, another first in German football. Put simply: Bayern were smart. And smart people who plan ahead, expect to be successful and have luck to boot are seldom loved. Particularly, as we shall see, when one of them is Uli Hoeness. From the early 1970s on, sympathy was not something Bayern could count upon – until in 1999 they would become the unluckiest European Cup finalists ever. Though in typical fashion, they then blew even this golden opportunity to win people's hearts.

11

VICTORY TURNS SOUR

THE TRIALS OF HELMUT SCHÖN

IT WAS NO FOUL. Uwe Seeler later recorded that, after riding a challenge from Frankfurt's inside-right Georg Lechner, he had 'suddenly felt a ferocious kick, as if I was being hacked down by an elephant', but Lechner swore he never even touched Seeler. His claim was supported by the referee and also by those fans standing nearest to the pitch. They said there was no kick, just a sound like the crack of a whip and then Seeler's scream. Finally, Frankfurt's team physio explained what had happened: 'What Seeler thought was a kick was actually the intense pain triggered by the tearing of the player's achilles tendon.'

It was mid-February 1965, and Seeler's misfortune shook the nation. He was West Germany's most popular footballer, and abruptly his career seemed over. At least that's what most people thought, because back then not many players came back after tearing an achilles tendon, and hardly any at the age of 29.

Seeler's many fans were shocked, for instance a 31-year-old master baker by the name of Siegfried Klinsmann. Although he was living in Swabia now, he had grown up north of Berlin, which is why he was a fervent Hertha supporter. Yet he idolised Seeler and once his sons would be old enough to listen, he'd tell them again and again what a great player this man was. But nobody was more shocked than Helmut Schön. News of Seeler's grave injury reached him at his Wiesbaden home, and the man who always chose his words carefully claimed to have been 'mortally shattered'. He had been the national coach for less than four months and already problems were piling up so fast he felt suffocated.

First he'd had to argue with the DFB's officials until he was blue in the face to have them revoke their ban on 'soldiers of fortune', meaning players with clubs in Italy. Thus Helmut Haller, Karl-Heinz Schnellinger and Horst Szymaniak were allowed back into the fold. Some two years after they had last played for their country, they arrived just in time for West Germany's crucial World Cup qualifier against Sweden in Berlin. Then the match itself, played in November 1964, proved a major disappointment. Munich 1860's Rudi Brunnenmeier opened the scoring, but five minutes from time Sweden equalised. Aptly, the goal was scored by none other than the hated Hamrin – booed for 90 minutes by fans who hadn't forgotten the 1958 World Cup. The result meant West Germany had to beat Sweden in the away match to qualify for the tournament in England. But they hadn't won on Swedish soil since 1911.

Now, nine months before this vital game in Stockholm, Schön had lost his most important player. He tried to replace Seeler with Walter Rodekamp of Hanover, and the striker actually scored the winner against Switzerland. But matches against England and Brazil were lost without West Germany finding the net. There was only one solution. Schön needed Seeler, achilles tendons be damned.

All through the summer of 1965, Seeler worked out like a man possessed. He lost weight to ease the strain on the patched-up tendon, he ran across beaches for hours on end so that the deep sand would help him rebuild muscles and Adi Dassler gave him a specially designed boot that made it possible for him to start playing again. On August 28, four weeks before the Sweden game, Seeler was back in Hamburg's starting line-up. He then played three matches for his club, scoring twice. However, he was clearly unfit. The Hamburg physio warned Schön that Seeler was not up to a make-or-break international, while the national team's masseur told the press: 'If I was responsible, Seeler would not play. Have you seen him jump?'

The player himself felt bad and hinted he could be of no help to the team. Meanwhile, there was another decision no one could take off Schön's shoulders. What about Franz Beckenbauer? Schön had tried out the youngster only once – in a friendly against Tommy Docherty's Chelsea. West Germany had lost 1-0, with only Beckenbauer impressing the coach. But should he give a 20-year-old his international debut in a decisive qualifier away from home?

When West Germany trotted out on to the Stockholm pitch on September 26, 1965, Uwe Seeler captained the side, and Franz Beckenbauer was the right-half. Those weren't the only surprising risks Schön had decided to take. Peter Grosser of 1860 Munich was pencilled in as inside-right, and he too had never played for his country before. For the first and last time in his life, Helmut Schön carried a good-luck charm in his pocket. He knew that if this match wasn't won, it would be his fault and his alone.

A minute before the interval, goalkeeper Hans Tilkowski misjudged a cross and Torbjörn Jonsson put Sweden ahead. Schön shook his head and rose. He turned and began walking in the direction of the dressing-room, preparing his half-time team talk. At that moment, Seeler flicked on a Schnellinger cross for Brunnenmeier. The goalkeeper blocked Brunnenmeier's shot, but the ball reached Duisburg's Werner Krämer, who levelled the score from close range. With nine minutes gone in the second half, Grosser, the other debutant, went past a defender on the right wing and delivered a low cross that Sweden's goalkeeper should have collected but instead only pushed away. Uwe Seeler lunged forward and poked the ball in to win the game. West Germany were on their way to England – and to becoming a footballing superpower.

The West Germans arrived in England on July 8, 1966 in good spirits. The team had won five preparation matches on the trot, and since Helmut Schön had given his players three weeks off in all since June 1, the squad felt relaxed and eager to play. Also, they were under no pressure. West Germany were 14-1 outsiders to lift the Jules Rimet trophy – even the Soviet Union were expected to do better. When a journalist asked the man working as the West German squad's interpreter, guide and general attaché who would win the tournament, the answer came back immediately: 'England.' That man was Bernd Trautmann.

Helmut Schön was worried, but not about the football. The man who had lost his home and many other, less tangible, things to the war was very well aware that his team represented a country which only 26 years previously had reduced London to rubble. Again and again he drummed the idea into his players that the most important thing, more important than winning, was to behave like gentlemen and sportsmen. So impressive were Schön's lectures that even 30 years later, Hans Tilkowski would tell me: 'The main thing was that we left a good impression. Back in 1966, the appearance and the behaviour of the team were essential.'

For the World Cup, West Germany would line up in something resembling a 4-2-4, with Horst-Dieter Höttges,

Wolfgang Weber, Willi Schulz and Karl-Heinz Schnellinger in defence; Franz Beckenbauer in midfield; Sigfried Held and Uwe Seeler in attack. The remaining positions went to strikers Lothar Emmerich or Albert Brülls, and Helmut Haller or Wolfgang Overath, both of whom were capable of playing in midfield as well as up front.

They played Switzerland off the park, winning 5-0, which led the *Daily Mirror* to claim: 'Show us a better team than the Germans, and you'll have the World Cup winners.' Four days later, such praise seemed premature. West Germany hit the crossbar twice but couldn't score against ten Argentinians, while the South Americans had only one dangerous shot at goal, brilliantly saved by Tilkowski. Beckenbauer was called 'phlegmatic and arrogant', Haller allegedly lacked 'fighting spirit and the will to attack'. Then West Germany met Spain at Villa Park and deservedly fell behind after 24 minutes. A defeat would have put them out of the World Cup, but they rose to the occasion and began to dominate the match. Perhaps surprisingly, the 47,000 crowd cheered on the Germans, especially after Emmerich levelled the score with a ferocious shot from an impossible angle. With six minutes left of a nerve-racking encounter, Uwe Seeler's lethal finishing finally saw his side through to the quarter-finals.

Much has been written about West Germany's ugly match with Uruguay. The facts are that two South Americans were sent off and West Germany won 4-0. Near-facts are that the first German goal was a fluke (Haller deflected in Held's shot after 12 minutes), that Uruguay were the better team for much of the first half and that they might have won had they scored early or been allowed to finish the game with 11 men. The former was prevented by Tilkowski, who tipped a shot against the crossbar after four minutes, and Schnellinger, whose handball on the line a few dozen seconds later strangely went unpunished. The latter did not happen due to the South Americans' temper.

There was bad blood from the word go. Uruguay's striker Hector Silva hacked down Schulz as he protected his goalkeeper Tilkowski, then made a silly attempt at kicking the ball out of the goalie's hands, instead connecting with Tilkowski's head. And so it went on. Horacio Troche was sent off for kicking Emmerich, yet the German's agony had a touch of melodrama about it. ('That was Emmerich's best moment in the match,' a German journalist noted sarcastically.) On his way off, Troche slapped Seeler in the face. Then Héctor Silva kicked Haller for what must have been the fifth time and was also dismissed by referee James Finney.

It was back to football in the semis. West Germany's reserve goalkeeper Sepp Maier got to see his idol Lev Yashin in the flesh, as Schön's side met the Soviet Union at Goodison Park. For the first time, the Germans were booed as they came on to the pitch, but the team was undaunted and played well. Haller, the best man on the field besides Yashin, made it 1-0; Beckenbauer scored the second. The USSR pulled one back, but the better side prevailed. Wembley it was for the Germans and a shot at the Jules Rimet trophy. There were smiles all around, but one of the broadest did not belong to a player: Adi Dassler had gone to Ashbourne in Derbyshire to investigate the traditional Shrove Tuesday football match and had dug up an age-old, mouldering football boot which he proudly took home to display in his semi-private museum. The worth of a trophy is always relative.

Who would be a coach? Helmut Schön, that calm and level-headed man, was pacing up and down in his room trying to solve at least two major problems he had with the World Cup final against hosts England. One, who was to play in goal? Hans Tilkowski had hurt his shoulder badly in the semi-final and would only be able to play in pain. Yet neither of the two reserve keepers – Bayern's Sepp Maier and Bremen's Günter Bernhard – had more than four internationals under his belt, and so Schön decided to go with the veteran Tilkowski.

Second, how was Beckenbauer to be used? With hindsight, Schön should perhaps have agreed with his assistant coach Dettmar Cramer, who argued that it would rob West Germany of a major creative force to have Beckenbauer mark Bobby Charlton. Then again, Beckenbauer readily agreed when Schön gave him orders to follow England's playmaker – and hindsight is a perfect but useless vision. As Overath later said: 'Looking back, there were so many things we could have done differently. Schnellinger played against Alan Ball, but maybe he should have played against Geoff Hurst instead. When it's over, you always know what you should have done.'

As it turned out, it wouldn't be over for a very long time, but, as everyone now knows, Hurst's hat-trick won a 4-2 victory for England in extra time. What is perhaps not so well understood is that Germany did not hold a grudge about the outcome, and the controversial third goal in particular. Only one of the Germans really felt robbed on account of that goal. And all of them were proud to have made the final at all, were glad to have given England such a good game and admit that the trophy went to the better side. In 1996, I talked to many members of the 1966 West German squad and their comments all struck similar notes.

Weber: 'Too much has been said about the third goal. England have entered the annals of football history as worthy world champions.' Seeler: 'The English team was exceptional and worthy of the title. We accepted the outcome the way good sportsmen should do, and the whole tournament was a fantastic experience for us all.' Maier: 'The linesman said the ball was in, so that was that. I'm not bitter, no way! It was a huge success for us to be in the final in the first place.' Overath: 'England had a great side. We accepted this defeat, and I hope our conduct brought credit to the German team.'

Only Tilkowski couldn't get the third goal out of his system. Then again, he had an excuse: 'One of the reasons why I still feel deeply about the third goal is that it was the third time in a few weeks I had been unlucky, each time on British soil,' he recalled in 1996. 'First we lost 1-0 to England and had a good goal disallowed. Then, in May, I was in the Cup-Winners' Cup final with Borussia Dortmund, and Liverpool's equaliser should have been chalked off, as the ball had gone out of play. Still, the English and German players have remained close. I'm still friends with Gordon Banks, Geoff Hurst and Alan Ball.'

In West Germany, the homecoming players were greeted as heroes, even though they brought no trophy with them. Apart from Haller, that is, who had kept the match ball. This was no secret – dozens of pictures were taken over the years with Haller and his souvenir and there is a nice shot from after the final that shows him shaking the Queen's hand with the object of play firmly tucked under his left arm. Yet 30 years later the *Daily Mirror* made an absurd fuss out of finally 'revealing' who had 'stolen' the footballing equivalent of the crown jewels and their reporter even wrote a book about the whole 'investigation'. Haller was more or less forced to return the ball, but he still didn't feel bitter. 'Look at it this way,' he said. 'It's because of the third goal that people still talk about us. You stay in people's minds that way.' He could have added that history would see to it that the Germans got their revenge. Many times over. They didn't even have to wait long.

On June 1, 1968, West Germany defeated England 1-0 in Hanover. It was only a friendly, but many years later Franz Beckenbauer had this to say about the game: 'It was the first time in history we had beaten the English. Guess who scored the goal? Yes, I did. It was a real piledriver. No, come to think of it, it was a crappy deflected shot with my left foot.' He smiled, then added: 'That was when we realised we could really beat the English and lost some of the respect we had had. And we just took it from there.'

Two years and two weeks after the Hanover game, Beckenbauer again scored against England, but this time it was in the quarter-final of the 1970 World Cup in Mexico. West Germany probably sent a better squad to this tournament than they had done four years earlier. Schön still had eight stalwart players from the Wembley final. But now Sepp Maier had established himself in goal and Jürgen Grabowski was available in attack. There were also Schalke's Reinhard Libuda, known as 'Stan' for his version of the Matthews step-over, and, of course, Gerd Müller. Both of them had scored in Germany's 3-2 win over Scotland that had earned the side the tickets to Mexico.

But there was still one gifted player absent from the squad: Günter Netzer. Schön considered him unfit, and this might have been true, as Netzer had been able to play through the last weeks of the league campaign only by taking painkillers. Still, it was an open secret that the two men – who liked each other immensely as people – didn't see eye to eye when it came to football. Schön simply preferred Overath, the reliable team player, to Netzer, the unfathomable soloist.

West Germany got to the quarter-finals by beating Morocco, Bulgaria and Peru, at times in irresistible fashion. Still, England were of a different calibre, and some players were so fazed by the prospect of meeting their nemesis that they approached Schön and suggested they should take it easy against Peru so that Germany could play Brazil rather than England. (Of course, Schön was the one national manager in German football history who wouldn't even think about doing such a thing.) In the build-up to the match, Schön proved he could be stubborn. He took Beckenbauer aside and said: 'Franz, you'll take care of Bobby Charlton again!' Before Beckenbauer could object, Schön added: 'But don't be his guard dog. Play your game, move forward and make him follow you.' Beckenbauer would do just that, and it turned the game.

Beckenbauer later said: 'I think the English had nobody to blame but themselves. For all practical purposes, we weren't even on the field for the first 60 minutes. England dominated the game and took a deserved 2-0 lead. Actually, they could have been another two goals up. We just weren't there. But England allowed us back into the game, and when we scored the first goal a sudden jolt went through our side, and everybody stepped up a gear.'

The man who scored that vital first goal was Beckenbauer himself, shooting past Peter Bonetti from just outside the penalty box after 69 minutes. Nine minutes from time, Seeler lobbed the goalkeeper with an extraordinary header and in extra time Gerd Müller, inevitably, scored the winner. Why did West Germany come back? The various arguments have been put forward time and again, but after all is said and done, it was probably just one of those football days. Beckenbauer scored out of the blue at a crucial moment, as great players often will, no matter how hard you try to stop them. The goal altered the psychology of the game, especially as it was played in inhuman weather conditions.

In any case, the reason a book on German football must refuse to delve into this matter at length is that the dramatic England game would forever be overshadowed by the wild, tense and tragic semi-final against Italy, dubbed the 'Game of the Century' by almost all Germans, all Italians (*partita del secolo*, they call it), all Mexicans (there's a plaque at the Azteca Stadium in Mexico City to commemorate the match) and numerous other people around the globe. The reason this is debatable is that it was also a scandalous game.

As with the Uruguay match in 1966, the facts are known. Italy went ahead early, Karl-Heinz Schnellinger equalised in the final minute of normal time, coming from nowhere and lunging towards a Grabowski cross. In extra time, Müller made it 2-1, five minutes on, Italy equalised. The great Luigi Riva then scored his side's third, Müller levelled again seven minutes later. In the 112th minute, an unmarked Gianni Rivera side-footed the ball home from ten yards out, and Italy had won 4-3.

The match had everything you can ask for, at least during extra time. Because it's almost forgotten now that the regular 90 minutes were quite drab. The tired Germans, exhausted by the quarter-final of three days previously, tried everything they knew, but the Italians sat on their early lead and put every man behind the ball with a cold-bloodedness approaching cynicism. That, of course, is perfectly within the rules. The rest was not.

The Germans, themselves called 'great actors' by Argentina manager Juan Carlos Lorenzo in 1966, were subjected to play-acting the like of which has seldom been seen since. Hardly five minutes passed before another Italian was lying on the ground, not moving a limb for endless seconds. The West German radio commentator became so exasperated that at one point he was moved to remark: 'I can make out that Burgnich has just perished in the penalty area.' There was also an awful lot of kicking going on, all of it unpunished, as it was throughout this celebrated tournament. With 16 minutes gone, Beckenbauer was hacked down in the box, but there was no penalty. The same happened after roughly an hour. Five minutes later, Seeler went for a loose ball in the penalty area but was grabbed by the shirt. Then Müller only needed to stab the ball in but was pushed away. Still no penalty.

Beckenbauer, who suffered a severe bruise on his shoulder and had to play through the second half and extra time with his arm tied to his chest, remembers that as early as the interval,

Fritz Walter with the Jules Rimet trophy in 1954. *Getty Images*

Walther Bensemann, German football's key pioneer and the founder of *kicker*, who fled the Nazis and died in exile. *Ullstein*

The DFB's Felix Linnemann (left), a football progressive but political fellow-traveller. *Ullstein*

Football training by route march and communal singing. Germany's first national coach Otto Nerz (with glasses) imposes his own style on the squad, November 1936. *Ullstein*

Otto Siffling in action against Denmark May 16, 1937, when his five goals helped create the *Breslau-Elf* legend. *Ullstein*

Schalke's Fritz Szepan and Ernst Kuzorra, the unrivalled superstars if the 1930s, mark their testimonial in 1950. *Ullstein*

Fans pack Schalke's Glückauf-Kampfbahn ground for their first game (against Düsseldorf) following the lifting of the ban over their 'professional' status in 1931.

Sepp Herberger (left) is interviewed by the unexpected hero of the 1954 World Cup triumph in Berne, the radio commentator Herbert Zimmermann. *PA*

The most famous *Tor!* of all. Helmut Rahn's left-foot shot has beaten Gyula Grosics and West Germany are the shock winners of the 1954 World Cup. *Ullstein/DPA*

The massed ranks of the Brigade of Guards are indifferent to Uwe Seeler's despair after West Germany's 4–2 extra-time defeat at Wembley. Coach Helmut Schön (right) follows him off. *Ullstein/Sven Simon*

Gerd Müller brings Germany level at 3–3 in extra time of their thrilling but controversial 4–3 defeat against Italy in the 1970 World Cup semi-final. *Ullstein/Horst Müller*

The breaking of the Bundesliga scandal on 6 June, 1971. The Offenbach president Horst Gregorio Canellas (centre) rolls the tape to the consternation of his guests. *Ullstein/DPA*

Trauma for Helmut Schön as Jürgen Sparwasser secures East Germany's 100 per cent winning record over the West in 1974. Sepp Maier and Berti Vogts reflect. *Ullstein/DPA*

The heart of Bayern Munich's triumphant progress in the seventies:
Gerd Müller, Sepp Maier and Franz Beckenbauer. *Ullstein/Werek*

Lutz Eigendorf, allegedly murdered by the
Stasi after defecting to play for Kaiserslautern.
Ullstein/Rowell

Günter Netzer's farewell cameo for Gladbach,
the 1973 Cup final win over Cologne. *Ullstein/
Witters*

Jürgen Klinsmann was (above) part of the West German team that won the 1990 World Cup and the unified German team that won the 1996 European Championship. As a manager (below), he managed the German national team to a third-place finish in the 2006 World Cup. *Alamy*

It's 1908 all over again as Germany succumb to England in Munich, 1 September, 2001. *Alamy*

The celebrations begin as Bastian Schweinsteiger raises the World Cup
after Germany's triumph in the 2014 final in Rio de Janeiro, Brazil. *Alamy*

Jürgen Klopp's Dortmund side unleashed, with spectacular results,
counter pressing of a rarely seen intensity in the Bundesliga. *Alamy*

After managing one of the game's all-time great teams at Barcelona from 2008 to 2012, Pep Guardiola took a year-long sabbatical before returning to manage Bayern Munich from 2013 to 2016. Under his stewardship, Bayern won the Bundesliga every season, as well as two domestic doubles. *Alamy*

Ralf Rangnick at RB Leipzig. Known as the 'Godfather of the gegenpress', he developed his ideas from the likes of Valeriy Lobanovskyi and Arrigo Sacchi, and is widely credited, in turn, for influencing the work of Jürgen Klopp, Thomas Tuchel, Julian Nagelsmann and Ralph Hasenhüttl. *Alamy*

Hansi Flick celebrates victory in the 2020 Champions League final. Having joined Bayern Munich as an assistant coach in 2019, Flick became manager in April 2020 and led the team to the treble – only the second time in history that a European club has achieved the feat in two different seasons, matching the 2014/15 Barcelona side. *Alamy*

his team-mates were shaking their heads, not knowing what was going on. And even after West Germany had finally done the seemingly impossible and equalised in the 90th minute, the players remained suspicious. Just prior to extra time, an unsmiling Gerd Müller approached Beckenbauer and quietly told him: 'We are being cheated.'

The referee was Arturo Maldonado Yamasaki, who had received so much praise after being in charge of West Germany v Yugoslavia at the 1962 World Cup. Presumably, this was again just one of those football days, and Yamasaki had a very bad one. He refereed diabolically and to the Germans' detriment. This is not to say that West Germany would have reached the final without him, but it explains why the team were regarded at home – for the second time in four years – as unlucky losers, even the moral victors. Sixty thousand people gathered to welcome the squad on their return.

Indeed, by late 1970, you could make a case that West Germany were playing entertaining football (they were the second-highest scorers in 1966 and 1970, behind Portugal and Brazil respectively), but that they were being denied again and again by unlucky circumstances. In other words, the good guys played in white. However, they would finally achieve their much-deserved moment of glory in 1972, and from then on it was going to be a different matter altogether.

This is the line-up of the third truly legendary national team in German football history, universally regarded as the best side Germany ever had:

Goalkeeper	Sepp Maier (Bayern)
Sweeper	Franz Beckenbauer (Bayern)
Right back	Horst-Dieter Höttges (Bremen)

Centre back	Georg Schwarzenbeck (Bayern)
Left back	Paul Breitner (Bayern)
Midfield	Uli Hoeness (Bayern)
Midfield	Günter Netzer (Mönchengladbach)
Midfield	Herbert Wimmer (Mönchengladbach)
Right wing	Jürgen Grabowski (Frankfurt)
Centre forward	Gerd Müller (Bayern)
Left wing	Sigfried Held (Dortmund)

It was the team that won the 1972 European Championship and received glowing reviews even from the usually reserved foreign press. So thick came the showers of praise that one could be forgiven for thinking those plaudits must have been aimed at a football side representing Brazil rather than Germany. *The Times* made out 'elegance and inventiveness', *Corriere dello Sport* detected 'imagination and genius', while *L'Equipe* simply said: 'This team has no equal in Europe.' *La Libre Belgique* even spoke of a new *Wunderteam*.

None of this was hyperbole. Not since Breslau in 1937 had a German side played so fluently, light-footedly and quite simply beautifully. The final against the Soviet Union, held in Brussels and won 3-0, was such a one-sided affair that even Herbert Wimmer, whose job it was to cover the miles in midfield Netzer couldn't be bothered with, was allowed to score following a pass from Jupp Heynckes. Heynckes? Now wait a minute, his name is not listed above . . .

The interesting thing about 1972 is that it's not really the team that contested the final which has acquired mythic status in Germany. In fact, many people don't even know that Erwin Kremers (Schalke) and Jupp Heynckes (Mönchengladbach) were playing on the wings instead of Grabowski and Held. And there are quite a few football fans who will struggle to come up with the team West Germany played in the semi-final (Belgium) and what the result was (2-1). That's because the near-perfect performance Helmut Schön's team gave in the final has been overshadowed by a game that was, contrary to popular belief, not half as good as the USSR match. The game in question was the first leg of the quarter-final, played at Wembley against England.

In the weeks leading up to the game on April 29, 1972, there were few signs that West Germany was about to witness the second most famous 90 minutes of its national team's history, surpassed only by the 1954 final. Actually, everything concerning the team was upside down. First, the Bundesliga scandal threatened to damage football's reputation. Bielefeld's licence was revoked two weeks before Wembley, and the internationals Bernd Patzke, Reinhard Libuda and Klaus Fichtel were blacklisted as crooks. Regulars such as Weber, Vogts and Overath were injured, forcing Schön to go with the two inexperienced youngsters Hoeness and Breitner, and of course with Netzer. Finally, the Bayern stars who were the backbone of the side came to London with bitter defeats in their luggage. Within three days, their club had been eliminated from the Cup-Winners' Cup by Rangers and then beaten heavily at Duisburg.

Schön sensed he was working with a group of doubting men. Thus he gave them none of the usual build-up, stressing the importance of the match and urging everybody to give his all. Instead, he encouraged a light-hearted spirit in the camp, had the team mainly play matches during training sessions and took the whole squad to the theatre to see a comedy. On the morning of the game, the players were so relaxed they cancelled the customary stroll on their own authority and staged ball-juggling contests on the hotel's lawn instead.

England approached the match very differently. Led by an awesome Netzer, who was so overpowering that even the partisan crowd applauded many of his moves, West Germany played football that night, while England laboured. Netzer would, as if on silent command, often fall back into the sweeper's position, covering for Beckenbauer, who was then free to roam into the space opening up before him. West Germany won 3-1. Hoeness opened the scoring, but Francis Lee equalised 13 minutes from time. Then Bobby Moore brought down Held in the box and Netzer converted the penalty. In the final minute, Gerd Müller, despite being surrounded by half the England team, scored one of his trademark goals to settle things.

There was not a shadow of a doubt that the much better side had won. And yet, as the journalist Ulfert Schröder pointed out: 'Victory wasn't as commanding as the historians would later claim.' The English, despite being outplayed, never gave in, and Gordon Banks almost saved Netzer's penalty. Still, the win carried so many myth-making ingredients – from the mere fact that it was Germany's first-ever on English soil to the romantic picture of Netzer surging through midfield, his flowing mane illuminated by the floodlights – that it became an instant classic. 'Football from the year 2000' was how *L'Equipe* described the performance of the West Germans almost before the sweat had dried.

Two years before the World Cup that was going to be hosted by West Germany, the country's national team appeared otherworldly and indomitable. Surely, a triumph over the world's best teams was inevitable, barring unexpected developments.

It was five days before West Germany's first game at the 1974 World Cup, against Chile. To the casual observer, everything seemed quiet at the West German camp in rural Malente, 60 miles north of Hamburg. Which was only natural, as it was almost three o'clock in the morning, and professional footballers less than a week away from competing for the biggest prize in their sport will certainly value peace and rest and go to bed early.

Only this was no ordinary camp. Actually, everything about it was quite extraordinary.

To begin with, the camp resembled a high-security prison and was guarded like one. Following the terrorist attack during the 1972 Olympics that had cost nine Israeli athletes their lives, and in view of the danger posed by the Red Army Faction terrorist group, the police had intensified their security precautions. They patrolled the premises at Malente with guard dogs, there were sharp-shooters and helicopters everywhere. Indeed, a few players would soon grow sick of the constant supervision. Beckenbauer sneaked out to meet an actress filming nearby. Sepp Maier and Uli Hoeness drove to Hamburg without leave to meet their wives – in a car with defective brakes.

Inside the camp, things were even worse. On that particular night shortly before the start of the tournament, nobody was yet in bed despite the small hours, and neither peace nor rest were to be found anywhere. In one room, Helmut Schön stood beside two packed suitcases. He had just told the head of the German delegation that he was sending all 22 of his players home. FIFA had already been informed that there might be changes to the provisionally nominated West German squad, he explained. Either that, or he, Schön, would go.

In another room, Paul Breitner was sitting on his bed, a packed suitcase of his own in front of him. He had just told his team-mates that he was going home, since the coach had named him as a ringleader and would suspend him anyway. Now Netzer, Overath, Müller and Hoeness were taking turns trying to convince him to stay. Finally, Müller decided only Beckenbauer could help and went to find the Kaiser.

Which wasn't easy. Beckenbauer was in a third room, talking on the phone to Hermann Neuberger. Neuberger was the vice-president of both the DFB and FIFA, and the man in charge of organising the 1974 World Cup. 'Our final offer is DM75,000,'

Beckenbauer told Neuberger. 'You can't have more than 70,000,' Neuberger replied. Beckenbauer promised to pass this on and hung up. It was now becoming likely, he thought, that neither he nor his team-mates would play in this tournament – or, for that matter, any other.

At the root of this bizarre mess was, of course, money. The German FA had neither spoken to the players about a bonus for winning the World Cup, nor had they disclosed the sum they had in mind. That was, Helmut Schön and many others at the DFB felt, the gentlemanly and traditional way of doing things. Footballers weren't supposed to represent their country for money. However, the squad had learned that the Italians had been promised DM120,000 per head for winning the World Cup. The Dutch would be paid DM100,000 – and they were living the high life in their camp, sharing a hotel with their wives and lots of hangers-on. The West Germans, peeved at having been locked away in this gulag in Malente, started talking money to while the time away. Finally, they dispatched their captain Beckenbauer to ask Hans Deckert, head of the delegation, about the DFB's plans. That's how 'Malente Night' began.

Deckert said the idea was to pay every player DM30,000 for winning the title. The players considered this sum an affront and countered with a demand for DM100,000. Deckert increased his offer to DM50,000, the players lowered theirs to DM75,000. And so it went on, all through the evening and deep into the night. Beckenbauer, Höttges, Netzer and Overath were negotiating for the team. With every meeting and discussion, Schön grew increasingly irritated. In the second of his three autobiographies, published the following year, Beckenbauer said that the national manager at one point told the four: 'All I ever hear from you is money, money, money! That is bad form.'

For the first time, Schön realised that this was a new generation of footballers, far removed from the Fritz Walters and Uwe

Seelers. He heard their words, but he could not understand what they were saying. Finally, he just rose and left. Upstairs, he heard Breitner bickering loudly. On the spur of the moment, he opened the door and told the player: 'Cut it out right now! You are undermining everything!' With that he locked himself in his room and concocted the plan to send everybody home and play the tournament with second-stringers.

Meanwhile, Neuberger had been woken up in his Hamburg hotel with the news that chaos had broken out in Malente. He phoned Beckenbauer, who then presented Neuberger's offer of DM70,000 to the players and suggested a vote. The result was 11 for and 11 against. Still anybody's game. At that moment, Beckenbauer decided the course of the 1974 World Cup for the first but not the last time. He told the squad to accept the offer, and after a while they decided to follow their captain. Beckenbauer informed Schön and Deckert that the matter had been settled. Then everybody went to bed.

Five days later, the 'bad form' Schön had spoken of was in evidence on the football pitch too. West Germany defeated Chile 1-0, but with a performance which drew catcalls from the Berlin crowd. They then beat Australia 3-0 in Hamburg, yet that match was nothing to write home about either. Towards the end, Beckenbauer gave the ball away and was hissed at from the stands. The player lost his composure and spat in the direction of the crowd.

Schön was getting more and more depressed. His side didn't behave like representatives of their country, they lacked team spirit and were playing without inspiration. Some said it was because Netzer wasn't in the side, but Schön didn't think that was the problem. On the contrary. He had not really forgiven Netzer for moving to Real Madrid in defiance of his demand that everybody who wanted to play in the World Cup should stay put in the Bundesliga, under the watchful eyes of the national coach. Also, Netzer had compounded his position by not telling Schön in person about the move. Instead, the coach learned that Netzer would leave for Spain from a journalist during a visit to the theatre.

Another problem with Netzer was that it seemed as if the Bayern players preferred to have Overath on the pitch. And the Cologne playmaker had been one of the few bright spots during the Australia match. That's why Schön made only one minor change for West Germany's next match. It was the final group game of the first round, and since the West Germans had already qualified for the next stage the only thing at stake was first place in the group. Or that's how it should have been. Instead, West Germany's third game at the 1974 World Cup meant more to Helmut Schön than almost any other he had ever played or watched. It also meant a lot to the country and it would turn out to be the most memorable of the whole tournament for Germany.

It was a cruel joke indeed. The only World Cup East Germany ever qualified for was the one played on West German soil. As if to extend the punchline, the two teams were then drawn in the same group to play the last match of the preliminary round against each other. At first it seemed as though the furore surrounding the game would be damped down by the fact that the East Germans, too, had already secured their place in the next round. But as it turned out, that only added fuel to the fire.

The West Germans, huge favourites, seemed entirely unsure of how to approach the game. They knew their Dresden-born coach wanted – no, needed – to win this match at all costs. They also knew that nothing short of a convincing victory was expected of them. 'That's why we will win!' bragged the country's largest tabloid on the morning of the game. But a draw was enough to stay in first place in the group, and under normal circumstances that would have meant sitting back and letting the opposition attack.

So Schön's side began the match cautiously, like men playing a game they didn't know the rules of. The GDR players, on the other hand, appeared strangely relaxed, as if they had been waiting for this day for a long time and were now going to enjoy it. They weren't at all the heartless, pig-headed class enemies they had been made out to be. Whenever Konrad Weise brought down Gerd Müller, he helped the striker up, saying: 'I hope you're not hurt.' As the game wore on, the atmosphere became more and more surreal. Just before a corner, Beckenbauer said to Jena's Harald Irmscher: 'I'm afraid I'll have to grab your shirt now.' Whereupon the East German smilingly replied: 'I'm afraid you won't be able to.'

In the very first minute, Schwarzenbeck's back pass was a bit short and West Germany were lucky Sparwasser didn't get to the ball. Cologne's Heinz Flohe went close in the third minute, then Grabowski had a great chance and Müller hit the post. But slowly and irreversibly, the West German game came apart. Beckenbauer cursed his team-mates, yelled at them, began to call for every ball. 'We are playing for Helmut Schön!' he had told the team before the kick-off, but now everybody was playing for and by himself.

Twenty minutes from time, Schön brought on Netzer for Overath. But by that time the match had become such a mess that Netzer later remembered how he had warmed up as far away as possible from the bench, praying he would not be called upon. Netzer had been on the pitch for seven minutes when one of the most famous goals in German football history decided the match. A crossball found Jürgen Sparwasser running towards Vogts and Schwarzenbeck. The ball bounced and Sparwasser headed it into his path, which wrong-footed the defenders. They scrambled after the striker, each lunging forward to block the shot. Sepp Maier made a strange attempt to do the same, turning his head away as if fearing to be hit in the face. With three West Germans at his feet, Sparwasser elegantly lobbed the ball in.

As the ball hit the back of the net, the huge Hamburg ground fell completely quiet – or almost completely, since 2,000 East German fans (carefully selected by the party) cheered, wildly waving their tiny flags. Schön just stared into the void opening up before his eyes. When referee Barreto Ruiz of Uruguay ended the match, the West Germans strolled coolly across the pitch, as if impassionately accepting defeat. Beckenbauer and Irmscher, Vogts and Kische swapped shirts, though not on the pitch – the two East Germans knew their party people would take a dim view of them fraternising with the capitalists. Then the team went to the dressing room and sat down in silence. Schön eyed his players for a moment before icily saying: 'We will have to talk about this.' With that, he left.

There is a conspiracy theory that says West Germany lost to the GDR on purpose to avoid meeting Holland, Brazil and Argentina in the second group stage. This must rank among the most preposterous claims ever made in connection with football. Not because taking it easy under certain circumstances would have been beneath the brave sportsmen of West Germany – see 1970. And not even because Group 3 (with Holland and Sweden) and Group 4 (with Italy and Argentina) wouldn't be completed until the following day, meaning their standings weren't known.

No, it was because the GDR were no normal opponents, and the game wasn't just another match but an occasion with deep historic resonance. Just consider that there is no German book about the final, the game that won the World Cup, but quite a few about this encounter. (They carry titles such as *90 Minutes of Class War* and *Where Were You When the Sparwasser Goal Was Scored?*) The East German FA would never consent to another match, thereby preserving a perfect record. The West German players would never really shake off the stigma of this loss. And Helmut Schön would never be the same coach again.

In the 24 hours after the GDR match, a chain of events was set in motion that would ultimately decide the World Cup. First, Helmut Schön came close to cracking up. While the team left for Malente and a major binge, he gave a brief post-match press conference, looking ashen and very old. Then he was driven to the camp. He arrived at one o'clock in the morning, finding the players drunk out of their minds and the room thick with cigar smoke. 'This is not going to help,' he said with contempt. 'We train at ten, then we leave for our new camp in Kaiserau to prepare for the next round.' He locked himself in his room. The next morning, he refused to have breakfast with the team.

The DFB were worried. Hermann Neuberger considered promoting assistant coach Jupp Derwall at least to share Schön's duties as head coach. The manager of the camp took Beckenbauer aside and told him Schön was in no shape to organise the move to Kaiserau. So Beckenbauer orchestrated the squad's departure for the new camp. At Kaiserau, a press conference was scheduled for the afternoon. More than 100 journalists from all over the world had assembled to ask Schön about the GDR match. But Schön was unable to talk. Again he had locked himself in his room, with just a single light on, apathetically picking at some food, mashed up for him as though he were a child. The DFB called off the press conference, and howls of protest went up among the media. They asked the veteran writer Hans Blickensdörfer to speak to Schön and make him change his mind.

'He was in a bad way,' Blickensdörfer later recalled. 'He was clearly a man in need of a prop.' So the writer suggested Schön should take Beckenbauer along for support. That was the turning point. It may be taking things too far to claim, as some have done, that Beckenbauer now took over the team, but he certainly became a figure of crucial importance. At the press conference, Schön hardly said a word, while Beckenbauer gave the impression of a man in command. He was open, sincere and calm, and his remarks on the team's performance led to a restructuring of the side. Gladbach's Rainer Bonhof and Frankfurt's Bernd Hölzenbein would now come in, while Uli Hoeness – heavily criticised by Beckenbauer – was excluded from the starting line-up for the next match. Günter Netzer was no longer even considered, as it was obvious Beckenbauer preferred Overath as the main man in midfield. It was now a whole new World Cup.

West Germany improved against Yugoslavia, winning 2-0. Then they played a wonderful match with Sweden, running out 4-2 winners. Finally, a hard-fought 1-0 win despite a penalty miss on a rain-soaked Frankfurt pitch against a brilliant Poland side got West Germany into the final. Clearly, they were now a different team. They still hadn't rediscovered the comradeship and sheer class that had carried them in 1972, but they willed themselves into playing decent football through determination – and fear. Fear of letting down the coach yet again, fear of becoming laughing stocks for life by following the GDR debacle with another costly defeat. They knew they weren't a unit, but at least they now had a partnership of convenience that made victory possible. Sepp Maier had played awesomely against Poland, Gerd Müller was scoring as usual and Beckenbauer was in great form and had become the boss both on and off the pitch. There was only one thing that could possibly come between these men on a mission and the World Cup – a better team.

That team should have been the Dutch, of course. Splendidly led by Johan Cruyff, Holland were undeniably the best side in the tournament, and a little over a year before the World Cup final, Ajax Amsterdam had soundly beaten Bayern Munich 4-0 in the European Cup. (Sepp Maier would forever claim that this was the worst game of his career and that he should have saved all four of the Dutch goals.)

Yet in the end it was probably precisely this supposed superiority that cost Holland. Much has been made of Holland's 'Total Football' in 1974 and the originality of their style of play. In reality, however, the Dutch and the West Germans were very much alike (even more so if the latter had had a fit Netzer who was compatible with their team plan). In the final, the two sides mirrored each other very accurately – West Germany's equivalent of Arie Haan was Beckenbauer, their Willem Suurbier was Breitner, their Johnny Rep was Grabowski, and so on. And it's not as if the West Germans did not change positions frequently, as both the second goal and the golden opportunity missed by Berti Vogts, arriving from nowhere, would prove. The only major difference was that Gerd Müller was no Johan Cruyff, just a super-reliable finisher. And that was not exactly a draw back, as one would see.

The West Germans felt they had no reason to fear Holland, provided they finally played according to their capabilities – and provided they could control Cruyff. Schön and Beckenbauer decided Gladbach's Berti Vogts should take care of that, and they even organised a training match in which the reserve team portrayed Holland. Günter Netzer – who else? – was asked to mimic Cruyff and he made Vogts look very poor. Schön and Beckenbauer gulped, but could do nothing except hope that final rehearsals have to go wrong to make it all right on the night.

A minute into the final, Cruyff ran away from Vogts with ease, then was tripped by Hoeness in the box. Johan Neeskens converted the penalty with brute force, and it was 1954 and an uphill struggle all over again for West Germany. But, as in 1954, the team gritted their teeth and displayed resilience, while the opposition – inexplicably, given that this was a World Cup final – began to show off. 'We wanted to make fun of the

Germans,' Rep told the writer David Winner many years later. 'We didn't think about it, but we did it.' Of course this is a cardinal footballing sin, even under normal circumstances.

The Dutch failed to score their second, and suddenly Hölzenbein ran into the Dutch penalty area. Wim Jansen made a poor attempt at a tackle and missed the ball. Hölzenbein knew what to do in such situations. As Beckenbauer later said: 'He ran against the player's leg and immediately went down. That was his speciality. Shortly before, he had stopped Bayern from reaching the Cup final by doing that.' (Thirty years later, Beckenbauer told Hölzenbein at an official banquet that he had forgiven him for the dive in the Cup semi-final, adding: 'You made up for that in the summer, when you went down again.' Hölzenbein was not amused.) Referee Jack Taylor pointed to the spot and Breitner levelled the scores.

Now the Dutch ran into trouble. Neeskens couldn't get past Bonhof, Rep was helpless against Breitner, Cruyff was contained by Vogts. Suddenly Beckenbauer was the star. When West Germany were awarded a free-kick on the edge of the penalty box, he ran up as if to bend the ball around the wall – but then delivered an artistic chip that forced a good save from Jan Jongbloed. Two minutes before half-time, Bonhof raced down the right wing and delivered a sharp, low cross that wrong-footed the Dutch defence. Müller, his back to goal, trapped the ball, turned and slammed it into the far corner past a static Jongbloed.

During the interval, the Dutch regained their composure. They dominated the proceedings for most of the second half and the longer the match lasted, the more overwhelming their superiority became. (Though it has to be said that Müller scored a legal goal on the hour that was wrongly disallowed.) The West Germans were fading fast, four days after the Poland match on that almost swampy surface, and it took great saves from

Maier, goal-line clearances from whoever was available and the assistance of the post to get to the final whistle with the lead still intact. Beckenbauer and Cruyff swapped shirts. There was hardly any ill-will between the West German and Dutch players – that would come later. For the time being, the Germans' natural rivals were France and Austria, while the Dutch still considered Belgium the side they mustn't lose to.

West Germany had lifted the World Cup for the second time, only two years after winning the European Championship. All seemed well. In Hanau, a 15-year-old Rudolf Völler was asked in school to write an essay on what he wanted to do with his life. Now, that was easy. 'I want to become a German international!' Völler wrote. 'Too much imagination,' his teacher scribbled beneath the essay before telling his pupil: 'Maybe you're going to make it as a corner flag.' Völler was certain he'd come through, though, and he was convinced that playing for Germany was an honour. Only a few years later, however, people would no longer be so sure about that.

There was already a sour taste to the 1974 triumph. These men weren't like the players of 1954, 1966, 1970 or even 1972. They were men who had got the business done after first severely disappointing both the country and their benign coach. As Cruyff and his team-mates walked dejectedly off the pitch, it was suddenly no longer clear who the good guys were. Fittingly, all laughter and merriment died out that same evening. It was the beginning of the decline.

At around 8pm on July 7, 1974, the World Cup-winning West German team arrived at Munich's Hilton Hotel for the ceremonial post-match banquet. Sepp Maier saw the Bavarian prime minister and, as was his wont, greeted him jovially. Whereupon a DFB official quite rudely told the goalkeeper to behave according to protocol. As the players made their way through the lobby and into the dining room, they looked for their wives but could only make out those of the officials. Finally they found Susi Hoeness and sat down with her at the table. Suddenly, a waiter materialised and asked her to leave, saying he was under orders from Hans Deckert to exclude the players' wives from the banquet.

A major shouting match broke out that escalated into a row when Deckert reprimanded Hoeness: 'At this place, things are orderly and disciplined. It's not for you to demand things you're not entitled to.' According to Beckenbauer, Hoeness then said 'Save your breath', but we can assume his choice of words was more direct, as he and his wife immediately left the room. Beckenbauer and many others followed him and spent the night in downtown bars and discos, far away from the DFB officials. 'Germans can organise a World Cup perfectly and crush even the strongest opponent through unflagging discipline,' Sepp Maier said. 'But we don't have the faintest idea about holding a party.'

That night, a disgusted Gerd Müller retired from international duty, an idea he had entertained ever since the DFB torpedoed what would have been a lucrative move to Barcelona the previous summer. Wolfgang Overath and Jürgen Grabowski followed the next morning. Breitner did the same a few months later. Schön himself would have stepped down, had it not been for Hermann Neuberger, now the DFB's president. Neuberger pleaded with the coach to stay, and Schön finally consented to carry on until Argentina 1978.

His team, still built around the core of players that had won the World Cup, reached the finals of the 1976 European Championship, with Holland, Czechoslovakia and hosts Yugoslavia. This was one of the great forgotten tournaments. In the semis, West Germany came back against Yugoslavia from two goals down to win 4-2 in extra time, thanks to a hat-trick from Cologne's Dieter Müller on his debut. The Czechs beat Holland

3-1, also after extra time, in a game that was so rough that referee Clive Thomas sent off three players, two of them Dutch.

The final was exciting end-to-end stuff of, according to *L'Equipe*, 'hitherto unknown dimensions'. It was a pity that there were barely 30,000 people in the huge Marakana, which could hold 110,000. If the final went to a replay, Hermann Neuberger feared, nobody at all would show up. Add to this Helmut Schön's concerns – who said 'a third game would be murderous' – and the solution was obvious: only hours before the game kicked off, the DFB asked UEFA, the tournament organisers, and the Czech FA to change the rules and decide the final on penalties if there was no winner after 120 minutes. At first, the rule change seemed of little importance, as the Czechs quickly jumped to a 2-0 lead. But Dieter Müller pulled one back and, in the final minute of normal time, Hölzenbein headed home a Bonhof corner. Extra time yielded no goals, and so West Germany got their first taste of what a shoot-out can do to your nerves.

They had such problems finding five takers, perhaps because some players had come off the pitch still thinking there would be a replay, that the crowd grew restless and booed the men in white. Franz Beckenbauer, in his 100th international, said his shoulder was hurting but agreed to take the fifth penalty. Hoeness, probably recalling the spot-kick he missed against Poland at the 1974 World Cup, said he would rather not. At this point, goalkeeper Maier volunteered, whereupon Hoeness changed his mind. It was 4-3 to the Czechs when he stepped up. Hoeness blasted the ball over the bar and then Antonin Panenka beat Maier with his famous trick shot to win the trophy for his country. 'Perhaps we have won more friends this way,' mused a Frankfurt newspaper, 'as yet another victory may have brought the team close to being regarded as footballing superhumans.'

The almost-superhumans were further reduced to mere mortals, and poor mortals at that, during the 1978 World Cup.

Schön had lost his last flair player in April 1977, when Franz Beckenbauer announced he was joining New York Cosmos and was promptly given the cold-shoulder by the DFB. True, Schön had then found some rising stars, such as youngsters Hansi Müller and Karl-Heinz Rummenigge, but, in general, the squad he took to Argentina was a group of grafters.

The World Cup began and ended with a stir. Hermann Neuberger invited a former Nazi fighter pilot, Hans-Ulrich Rudel, exiled in South America, to the team's camp in Ascochinga – while closing the door to Günter Netzer, who was working for a newspaper. This scandal caused a row in the German press that only died down when the football began, because that was even worse.

Schön's side delivered no fewer than three scoreless draws, but still almost made the final. Facing Holland in the vital second match of the second group stage, West Germany led 2-1 and were giving their best performance of the tournament. There were only six minutes left on the clock when the Dutch finally levelled the score. Then Hölzenbein had a brush with Dick Nanninga. Only the Dutchman was booked and when he complained about this, the referee sent him off. Hölzenbein later said Nanninga had hit him in the stomach, Nanninga said Hölzenbein had grabbed him by the nose. Obviously, things were starting to get strained between the two sides.

The draw against Holland meant the best West Germany could now hope for was reaching the third-place play-off by beating Austria. The Germans hadn't lost to their unloved neighbours since 1938 (officially since 1931), which weighed heavily on the once-proud Austrians. But initially, little seemed to change on June 21, 1978 in Cordoba.

Rummenigge put the West Germans ahead, but then Vogts beat his own goalkeeper and Hans Krankl scored Austria's second. Hölzenbein managed to equalise, and for most of the second half it appeared West Germany were about to collect their fifth draw in six matches. Then, three minutes from time, two Austrians simultaneously became folk legends – even in Germany. The first was Hans Krankl, who scored his country's winner and then raced on to the running track with the facial expression of a man who had just won the lottery. The second was radio broadcaster Edi Finger, who went over the top as the ball went in, howling like a madman before first declaring that he was going crazy, then describing how he was kissing everyone in sight.

The West German newspapers spoke of 'disgrace' and 'downfall', and Austria's 3-2 victory entered the history books as 'the Shame of Cordoba'. Thus the players who had caused Helmut Schön so much grief since 1974 handed their outgoing coach a singularly bitter parting gift. 'I'm convinced that my successor will get the job done,' he said. 'But he might be facing problems. My biggest fear is that the road to football as total showbusiness will lead to the Harlem Globetrotters. I hope the young players are not being brought up that way.'

It is doubtful whether Sepp Herberger would have shared such pessimism. He had always moved with the times and never saw the point of lamenting things you couldn't change. Even at 79, Herberger followed football fervently. In fact, on April 27, 1977, he phoned Schön to discuss that evening's friendly against Northern Ireland. Herberger was watching an initially dour match on TV when he began to have chest pains. His doctor called an ambulance. As West Germany took control of the game (they won 5-0), Herberger told his wife, Eva: 'Give me my tracksuit and Uwe Seeler's checked sports shirt. Trust me, I'll be back.' For once, he was wrong. Herberger died in the early hours of the next morning. He was buried in his beloved dark-blue tracksuit with the DFB badge.

12

COLD GLORY

ULI HOENESS AND BAYERN'S GRIM DECADE

GÜNTER NETZER WAS LOOKING for a job. He had left Real Madrid and seen out his playing career with Grasshoppers Zürich. Now it was early 1978, and a man approaching his mid-thirties should formulate some new goals for his life. Going into coaching had never been an option for Netzer. He could not see himself taking one of those courses where some balding DFB teacher explains how to improve a player's stamina – no. But football was all he'd ever learned, and so Netzer's eyes darted around the Bundesliga map to find a club that was on the rise and could use his nous.

Hamburg showed all the signs of being upwardly mobile. They had won the Cup-Winners' Cup in 1977 and added some formidable players since. Ivan Buljan, for instance, signed from Hajduk Split. And Kevin Keegan, whom Netzer would one day call 'the most perfect footballer I have ever seen'. Yet despite such talent, Hamburg were doing abysmally. The team was stuck in mid-table, miles behind Cologne, who were on their way to lifting the 1978 title under Hennes Weisweiler (who had been forced to flee Barcelona after hitting on the brilliant idea of substituting Johan Cruyff away at Sevilla against the superstar's wish). Hamburg had lost, shame of shames, at home to their city rivals St Pauli, and to Saarbrücken, both of whom would be relegated. Keegan wasn't scoring, mainly because he was often playing as a midfielder, despite the presence of such flair players as Felix Magath and Georg Volkert, who should have been ideal providers to feed his goal-scoring instincts.

Netzer contacted the club to see if there was some work for him. What he had in mind was helping out with the match programme, but Netzer so impressed club president Paul Benthien that he was offered the post of business manager. The former 'rebel' said yes and set about turning things around. The crux of the matter, Netzer soon learned, was that the core of the team which had won in Europe remained an impenetrable clique who resented the arrival of the newcomers Buljan and, especially, Keegan. They didn't even return the Englishman's greetings when he entered the dressing room, and the Turkish coach Arkoc Özcan, who'd replaced Rudi Gutendorf only a few months earlier, wasn't doing anything about it.

In June 1978, the dreadful season over, Netzer fired Özcan. The man he had in mind to replace him was the Austrian Ernst Happel. But Benthien hummed and hawed at the prospect of following Özcan with another man untried in the Bundesliga. An additional problem was that Happel didn't have the coaching badge required by the DFB. And so Netzer settled for none other than Branko Zebec. For good measure, he also offloaded three key players – all forwards. The replacements Netzer signed came from the Second Division: 1860's Jimmy Hartwig, Hanover's Bernd Wehmeyer and Essen's fearsome centre-forward Horst Hrubesch. Hrubesch would now partner Keegan up front and Hamburg never looked back.

Keegan and Hrubesch – one a diminutive whirlwind with a perm, the other a giant monster with straggly, thin hair – netted

30 goals between them, and Hamburg won the 1978-79 title having scored the most goals and conceded the fewest. They were now a force to be reckoned with and would remain so for a few years. But only for a few. Thus began the new pattern that was to characterise the Bundesliga during the 1980s and 1990s. There would always be two clubs fighting for the title, but one of them could not muster up enough energy, nerves and reserves to sustain quality football for more than three or four seasons. The other club was Bayern Munich, and they could go on forever.

One big-name player whom Netzer could have signed early in the 1978-79 season, but didn't, was Uli Hoeness. The former European champion and World Cup winner was going through a difficult time at Bayern, partly because he and his chum Paul Breitner were constantly scheming against the coach Gyula Lorant, partly because the once-deft forward was plagued with recurring knee problems. Netzer was on his guard and demanded a thorough medical from Hoeness before offering him a contract. Probably with good reason, Hoeness denied Netzer such proof of his fitness, and so he was not signed by title hopefuls Hamburg but loaned out to newly promoted Nuremberg in late October. He appeared in only 11 games for them and by March 1979 it was clear that the playing career of Uli Hoeness was over. He had just turned 27.

The nation did not exactly mourn the loss of a great and successful player, because Hoeness was never a favourite with either fans or the press. His biography, published in 1975 by the usually over-courteous *kicker* magazine, reads in parts like a precursor of the mean-spirited exposés that would not become fashionable for another decade or so. 'His career radiates the cold glory of a computer,' it said. 'There are players who play for the crowd, allowing themselves to be stimulated or depressed by it. Others just play the way they think it should be done, no matter if the people in the stands like it or not. And then there are players who play for the bench, because that's where the coach is sitting. A prime example is Uli Hoeness.'

What this is saying between the lines is that Hoeness always did things for a purpose, according to a plan, and for his own, private agenda. More often than not, that agenda centred around money. In early 1974, he said: 'If we win this World Cup...' What? We will be immortals? We will be among the greats of the game? No. 'If we win this World Cup we are set up for life.' Even Paul Breitner, no bright-eyed idealist himself, could only marvel at these particular talents of his friend. 'Without him, I wouldn't make a penny outside football,' Breitner said. 'It's unbelievable how Uli Hoeness develops ideas if something can be made into a business.'

The butcher's son from Ulm had always been like that. At school, he was the head boy and ran the school magazine, and of course he passed his exams. He was already captaining West Germany's junior team by then, and whenever he had a good game, he'd see to it that the local press would hear about it. His coach at Ulm later remembered: 'There was never a single day when I didn't have the impression he knew exactly what he wanted.' Hoeness signed for Bayern in January 1970 (immediately phoning the largest Ulm paper to spread the news) and was seen driving a new car shortly afterwards. Two years later he moved into his own house, a few months after that he announced he was going to marry and offered exclusive pictures plus an interview for DM25,000. He was not yet 23 years old.

At Bayern, Hoeness encountered Franz Beckenbauer, whose father had once said footballers were too stupid to save money, and not a few problems. 'His excessive self-assurance was unpleasant for people at first,' his mentor Udo Lattek said about those first months. Beckenbauer even felt compelled to take the young man aside to urge him to concentrate on football and reprimand him for his 'doggedness'. In short, not many people liked Uli Hoeness, not even team-mates. (Günter Netzer once called him a 'bandit', after Hoeness allegedly made Netzer look bad in an international in early 1974 to get him thrown out of the squad.) That's why it came as a shock to most people when Bayern president Wilhelm Neudecker announced in early 1979 that the man to replace Robert Schwan as the club's business manager was Hoeness.

Hoeness knew money, that much was for certain, but did he have the instinct, the tact, the experience, the connections that were needed? The uncertainties which suddenly surrounded Bayern intensified a few weeks later when Neudecker surprisingly resigned from his post. The reason he gave was growing insubordination on the part of the squad. That sounded bad enough, and there were now many who feared for the club's future, although what really triggered Neudecker's move would turn out to be of an even graver nature.

While all this was happening, the club's famous football team was in the midst of a terrible slump, highlighted by an awful 4-0 defeat at home against relegation fodder Bielefeld. Bayern had finished the previous two seasons in 12th and seventh place. The reshuffling upstairs and the humiliations on the pitch taken together made it seem in the spring of 1979 as if the club was on its way to becoming just another chapter in the history books, not unlike Nuremberg or Schalke.

Then, on March 24, 1979, the team travelled to Mönchengladbach, as if just for old times' sake. Nobody expected much from the match, yet Karl-Heinz Rummenigge scored three and Bayern crushed their former rivals 7-1. They lost only two of their remaining 11 games, which was not enough to catch Hamburg, but it was a sign of life. On the last day of the season, Bayern played at Hamburg, who had already been crowned champions. Keegan cancelled out Bayern's lead, but ten minutes from time Rummenigge won the game. Somehow, that was the beginning of the 1980s, Bayern's decade.

And another thing happened on that day which buried the 1970s for good and heralded a new, sadder age. It had less to do with the people who played the game than with those who watched it. It all started in the infamous 'Block E' at Hamburg's ground, which was crammed full with fans eager to celebrate their team's first title since 1960. The block was meant to hold 3,500 people, but on this glorious day there were close to 5,000 standing on the terraces. Many of them were crushed against the fence – on top of which, according to the customs of the time, were half a dozen rows of barbed wire. The fans began to tear at this obstacle, until a part of the fence gave way. This caused a sudden stir in the block, as a few people climbed through the hole and spilled on to the running track. More and more pushed and jostled to follow them, until a giant wave of bodies crashed against the small opening in the fence. In all, 71 people were injured, four of them needing intensive care. It was no Hillsborough and no Heysel, but the Hamburg near-disaster would leave its mark on the collective psyche throughout the 1980s, since 'the trail of blood', as one paper called it, introduced a decade of ugliness, both on and off the pitch.

I come from a city that is not unlike Newcastle. The club that defines this city sells well over 55,000 season tickets these days and annually tops the attendance averages. 'It's always been like this,' people will tell you. 'We even had well over 25,000 people in the early 1970s, in the Second Division.' Right. 'This place,' they will animatedly add, making a flourishing gesture that takes in the whole ground, 'was always packed.' Wrong.

The thing I remember most vividly about the early to mid-1980s is feeling completely lost, standing on a half-empty terrace, a group of about 50 neo-Nazi thugs goose-stepping around and waiting for the police to arrive to get the action going, with some drab game trying to develop on the pitch below. Well, at least it was better than the away games, which could always be quite risky affairs. Especially if you had a punk hairdo and wore torn jeans. Many people must have felt as forlorn as I did, even those with more conservative hair and better clothing. My club, Dortmund, drew 42,000 people on average in 1976; ten years later that was down to 22,500. Even when mighty Bayern came to town in 1985, barely 30,000 watched the match – the capacity then being 54,000.

I'm self-critical enough to consider the possibility that my feelings and those of others like me were partly to do with the fact that the club was not doing well. However, all the statistics point elsewhere. The Bundesliga as a whole had an average attendance of 27,625 for the pivotal 1977-78 season, the best figure since 1964-65. Then it all went downhill. For the next eight years, there was a consistent decline, until the league hit rock bottom in 1985-86. The average attendance for that year was 18,400 – a shocking figure when you consider it was almost as low as that of 1972-73, the season after the Bundesliga scandal had broken and fans fled the game in droves.

Of course the violence was a problem. A 16-year-old Bremen boy was killed when the Hamburg hooligan gang the Lions attacked a group of Werder supporters. Hertha Berlin supporters destroyed a Turkish shop and the sickeningly named Hertha fan group Zyklon B (the gas used to murder inmates of the Nazis' concentration camps) set fire to a train that was bringing them home from an away game. Right-wing Dortmund fans attacked a pub run by a former BVB player, who died a few months later from the injuries he sustained. That was all in 1982.

Musings on the sources of this phenomenon are probably misplaced in a football book. It would take a sociological tome to discuss them, and too many trees have already lost their lives because somebody set out to do just that. Most of those investigations fall short, because the tempting idea to link hooliganism with society at large poses more problems than it solves. After all, hooliganism intensified in many countries at around the same time, regardless of the peculiarities of their respective football histories or social mores, regardless of whether they had conservative or socialist, stable or chaotic governments.

What is certain, however, is that in Germany the rise of hooliganism fitted the general mood of existential angst. From the mid-1970s to the mid-1980s, West Germany was a country on the verge of becoming collectively neurotic. First there were the terrorist acts carried out by the RAF (Red Army Faction). In 1977 alone, two high-ranking businessmen, Jürgen Ponto and Hanns Martin Schleyer, and the chief federal prosecutor were assassinated. Paranoia gripped everyone, eventually leading to the election of a more conservative government in 1982.

There was also the fear of an impending nuclear conflict, intensified by NATO's decision to station medium-range missiles aimed at the Soviet Union in West Germany. Spearheaded by the Green Party, there were demonstrations and sometimes physical conflicts everywhere. In October 1983, nearly three million people took to the streets across the country. Soon the movement against nuclear energy would also organise itself and become so militant that clashes with the police force became commonplace. Into this pervading atmosphere of vague fear stepped football hooliganism, as if to remind people that even at the places of escapist entertainment there was ultimately no escape.

Still, what made the 1980s the Dark Ages was not just the violence. The football itself was, if anything, an even bigger problem. All through the 1970s, it seemed, every team had its fair share of flair players and mavericks. Not just Beckenbauer and Netzer. Cologne had the stylish Wolfgang Overath and the gifted Heinz Flohe. The Austrian Hans 'Buffy' Ettmayer floated across the pitch at Stuttgart and was joined by Hansi Müller, whose coach once said: 'A ball hit his shin. Otherwise his socks would have remained spotless, just like the rest of his strip.' Jürgen Grabowski was the showman at Frankfurt, and Lorenz Horr at Berlin, while Willi Lippens – known as 'Ente' (the Duck) – never delivered a cross for Essen or Dortmund as long as there was another opponent within sight he could dribble around.

Suddenly, these people were gone, to be replaced by the sort of players who would garner West Germany a very bad name indeed during the 1982 and 1986 World Cups. Hans-Peter Briegel (aptly nicknamed the Roller), Bernd and Karl-Heinz Förster, Guido Buchwald, Wolfgang Rolff, Norbert Eder, Uwe Reinders. All of them internationals, all of them hard-working and very average. Once, such players would have done the dirty work for the stars – like Schwarzenbeck did for Beckenbauer, or Herbert Wimmer for Netzer. Now, they were the stars.

'The players of today...' Buffy Ettmayer would hiss in the late 1980s, then finish the sentence with a scornful grunt. 'Even their calves are calloused, because they are tackling all the time.' Indeed, things were often as rough on the field as they were in the stands. In late 1979, Duisburg's Paul Steiner broke Heinz Flohe's leg as if it were made of glass. Flohe never played professional football again. Less than two years later, Bremen's Norbert Siegmann delivered a flying tackle on Bielefeld's Ewald Lienen that slit the latter's calf. The cut was ten inches long and so deep you could clearly make out muscle tissue and tendons. Lienen went into shock the instant he saw his leg, thus he hardly felt the pain and hobbled towards the Bremen bench, hurling insults at coach Otto Rehhagel, certain that his opponent had acted under orders from above. That may have been true. In 1975, Rehhagel had been suspended by the DFB and fired by Offenbach for loudly instructing his players from the sidelines to scythe down Frankfurt's Bernd Hölzenbein during the Hesse derby. Siegmann, meanwhile, explained the foul on Lienen by pleading: 'I can't play like Beckenbauer.'

The main problem with this sort of football was that it proved successful. West Germany reached two World Cup finals in a row, and while nobody at home liked what they saw, there was no arguing with the naked results. And the same held true for club football. In 1979, there were three West German teams in the semi-finals of the UEFA Cup (now the Europa League); a year later they took all four places (Mönchengladbach, Stuttgart, Bayern and the eventual winners, Frankfurt). That is the only occasion when all the semi-finalists have come from one country, but Germany was not even content with that record – they had five teams in the competition that year, Gladbach having qualified as holders, and the fifth side, Kaiserslautern, also reached the quarter-finals.

Between 1979 and 1983, no fewer than eight teams from the Bundesliga would play in European finals and in 1983 Hamburg became the second German team to lift the European Cup, beating Juventus 1-0 in the final. The match, tellingly, was decided through a long-range strike from Felix Magath, probably the technically most accomplished footballer in the Hamburg side.

Still, most true fans would have been willing to put up with the threat of violence and the numbing football. What was too much to take was the dominance of Bayern Munich. The Reds won seven championships between 1980 and 1990, usually four or more points ahead of the team in second place. The nadir was probably reached on a miserable Tuesday evening in April 1986. Werder Bremen led Bayern by two points when the teams met on the penultimate day of the season. Predictably, it was an extremely dire match – until the 88th minute.

Rudi Völler played the ball into the box and it hit Bayern's Sören Lerby on the chest or the shoulder. However, the referee pointed to the spot, whereupon the Bayern bench emptied as if on command and pandemonium broke out. Scores of fans listening at home could not believe their ears: at long last, Bayern had lost their cool and, it seemed, their proverbial luck. A controversial penalty in the dying minutes of a crucial game – given against the Munich giants. How extraordinary. Bremen's Michael Kutzop, the country's premier penalty taker, stepped up. He'd scored seven times out of seven from the spot that season. During a spell with Offenbach, he'd put away 22 penalties in a row. But this time, he hit the post. Four days later, Bremen lost away to Stuttgart, whereas Bayern beat Gladbach 6-0 to claim the title on goal difference.

The worst thing about Bayern's string of successes was that nobody really knew how they did it. Because while many observers loved (and still love) to place money firmly at the root of all evil by claiming that the club simply bought everyone who promised to be a half-decent footballer, the facts don't bear this out. The first German club to break the DM1 million barrier for transfers was not Bayern but Cologne, for the Belgian Roger van Gool in 1976 ('You could have got a Van Gogh for that much,' said the president of Cologne's city rivals Fortuna). The first club to break the DM2 million barrier was Hamburg (for Kevin Keegan in 1977). The first club to pay more than DM3 million for a player was Frankfurt (for the Hungarian Lajos Detari in 1987). In fact, until a new century dawned almost all of the landmarks in this particular field belonged to clubs other than Bayern. Dortmund were the first to pay more than DM10 million (for Heiko Herrlich in 1995), Leverkusen the first to go beyond DM15 million (for the Brazilian Lucio in 2000).

No, Bayern did not extend their empire through money, or at least not through money alone. Actually, for quite a few years playing the big spender was never even an option for the club, as they just didn't have the necessary funds. Neudecker's resignation in 1979, it soon turned out, had little to do with the players staging a palace revolt. In truth it was a desperate last-gasp attempt to forestall an impending investigation by the internal revenue authorities. This dodge proved fruitless – Bayern were found guilty of tax evasion and had to pay DM2.5 million, while four individuals, Neudecker and Schwan among them, were fined a combined DM400,000.

Today, such sums would be considered small change, but in 1979 Bayern had made a profit of less than DM220,000. Furthermore, at the next AGM, in March 1980, the new president Willi Hoffmann had to admit the club was already some DM3 million in the red. This was serious stuff inded in a country where clubs are not owned by companies or men with deep pockets and where the national FA can and does exclude financially unhealthy clubs from professional leagues. There were even hints in some quarters that Bayern were on the brink of bankruptcy, and while it wasn't quite that bad it would take Bayern until 1984 and the sale of Karl-Heinz Rummenigge to Inter to balance the books. (Officially, the club received some DM11 million for the striker, but rumours persist that the actual sum was closer to DM18 million.) Yet still Bayern managed to spend the 1980s and parts of the 1990s going from strength to strength on the field, while all challengers sooner or later fell by the wayside. The key might be that Bayern had Uli Hoeness.

One of the first signings Uli Hoeness made on behalf of the club was that of his younger brother Dieter, who joined Bayern for considerably less than DM200,000 from Stuttgart in 1979. Initially, many people whispered the word 'nepotism', as the awkward, balding giant seemed a less than ideal heir to Gerd Müller and partner for Karl-Heinz Rummenigge. But Dieter Hoeness went on to score 64 goals in his first four seasons with

Bayern, and he would also produce many legendary moments for the club. There was, for instance, a game against Braunschweig in 1984, when he scored five goals in barely 20 minutes. Above all, however, there was the 1982 Cup final, one of the (strangely few) truly legendary finals in the history of the German cup competition.

Bayern met Bavarian rivals Nuremberg and were two goals down at half-time. Worse, it appeared that Dieter Hoeness would have to go off. He was bleeding heavily from a head wound sustained during a collision with Nuremberg's Alois Reinhardt after less than a quarter of an hour. Still, Uli pleaded with his brother to stay on, and Dieter did so, heavily bandaged. In the second half, Dieter first set up two goals with his bleeding head and then put the game beyond doubt by making it 4-2 in the final minute – with a header.

In many ways, the unlikely rise of Dieter Hoeness exemplifies how Bayern did business under Uli Hoeness. For most of the 1980s, the key players at the club were men like Klaus Augenthaler, Wolfgang Dremmler, Bernd Dürnberger and Hans Pflügler. None of them was even remotely in the same footballing class as a Beckenbauer, a Breitner or a Rummenigge, but all were reliable, all imbued with a winning mentality, and all came cheap.

In order to illustrate the sort of line-up with which Bayern dominated the league, one only needs to look at the 1982 European Cup final in Rotterdam. Fans of Aston Villa will remember that their team beat Bayern 1-0 that night. But can they come up with the names of the Germans they defeated? Yes, Breitner and Rummenigge were on the pitch, but there were also nine others – men like Manfred Müller, Hans Weiner, Wolfgang Kraus, Günter Güttler and Kurt Niedermayer. Even German football fans recall these players only hazily, which is probably just as well.

With such limited but determined men, the Bayern teams of the 1980s finally delivered the technocratic, boring football they had been accused of during the 1970s (when they did not play that way). Partly, it was just a sign of the times. But partly it also reflected the character of Uli Hoeness, who was quickly becoming the most important man at the club. The idea that one should perhaps sign exciting foreign stars or flair players just to offer the crowds value for money or simply to play the game the way it should be played – this idea wouldn't reach Bayern Munich until Franz Beckenbauer became closely involved in the club's affairs. For Uli Hoeness, 'value for money' meant trophies and titles, and the more trophies one could collect for less money, the better.

This, then, is a fairly accurate picture of the man who came to shape the biggest club in the country for the following two decades, thus becoming one of the most influential men in German football full stop. But it is not a complete picture. Uli Hoeness, the cool, stone-hearted calculator who is only interested in results (on the pitch and on the balance sheet), was the man the public knew and often disliked. But there was another side to the man. Because Hoeness was not only Bayern's brain, he also proved to be its heart and soul.

In February 1982, Uli Hoeness was the sole survivor of a plane crash that killed three of his best friends. 'That day, the sunny boy in me died,' Hoeness later said, but people who know him well claim it was rather the egotist in him that died. Under his guidance, Bayern slowly and often secretly would now also become what the writer Dietrich Schulze-Marmeling has called a 'welfare organisation'. No German club played more benefits and did more to raise money for those in need than Bayern. And when Markus Babbel left the club for Liverpool under less than amicable circumstances in 2000, he always let it be known he would never speak badly of Hoeness. 'Among the top clubs in

Europe, Bayern are the most humane,' Babbel said. 'They have always shown generosity when there were problems. Take Alan McInally, who became an invalid and didn't have any insurance. The club said: "We'll give you severance pay." They practically gifted him the money. Our business manager is somebody you can talk to about such things.'

McInally's is not an isolated case. In April 1988, Bayern's Danish striker Lars Lunde was badly injured in a car accident. It was obvious he would never play top-level football again, but Hoeness did everything he could to help the player – and not only financially. For weeks he put Lunde up in his own home and would do something similar many years later when Mehmet Scholl needed help, though in his case it was psychological rather than physical (the player was going through a divorce and had, by his own admission, serious attitude problems). Hoeness was also the driving force behind rescuing Gerd Müller from his alcoholic daze, when he first set up his former team-mate in a detox centre, then offered him a job at the club despite many warning words from others.

But now that Alan McInally has entered the picture, one has to point out that not everything went according to plan for Bayern in the 1980s and early 1990s and that Hoeness was sometimes forced to act against his conviction and buy bigger. That was because Bayern simply could not replace Rummenigge when he left for Italy. The list of people they brought in is long and exotic: the Welshman Mark Hughes, the Yugoslav Radmilo Mihajlovic, the Scot McInally, the Colombian Adolfo Valencia, the Frenchman Jean-Pierre Papin. They all joined Bayern between 1987 and 1994 and they all failed (with the exception of Hughes, who left for Manchester United), which gained the club the nickname 'the strikers' graveyard'.

The reason Bayern felt forced to bring in manpower in attack was that they just couldn't repeat their 1970s triumphs in

Europe, regardless of how dominant they were in the league. Usually it was the British teams that caused them headaches. Liverpool beat Bayern on the away goals rule in the semi-finals of the 1981 European Cup. A year later it was Aston Villa in the final. In 1983, Alex Ferguson's Aberdeen proved too strong in the Cup-Winners' Cup. The following year, Tottenham defeated Bayern in the UEFA Cup. Finally, in 1985, Everton put them out of the Cup-Winners' Cup.

Then came the most traumatic night in Bayern's history so far. On May 27, 1987, they faced Porto in the European Cup final played in Vienna. The Germans were odds-on favourites, and Uli Hoeness proclaimed 'the dawning of a new, great era'. The club's then president, Fritz Scherer, even prepared his victory speech in advance, and he seemed to be proved right when Ludwig Kögl put Bayern ahead after 25 minutes. But 12 minutes from time, a low cross skittered through Bayern's penalty area. Standing with his back to the goal was Porto's Algerian striker Rabah Madjer, who had scored a famous goal against the West German national team five years earlier. Madjer lifted his leg and elegantly back-heeled the ball into the net. Two minutes later, Porto made it 2-1 against a Bayern team still in shock, and it was all over.

Even a decade later, Uli Hoeness would label this loss the worst defeat of his life (unaware that a much more shocking game with the same scoreline was yet to come). That, however, was not how many people in West Germany felt. Madjer's back-heel is still one of the goals I can most clearly visualise, and I still vividly remember hearing muffled cries of joy through my room's open window, coming from our neighbours, who all rejoiced at the artistry of the goal – and the fact that Bayern had been on the receiving end of it. Because by this time, just about everybody had become sick to the core of Bayern Munich, the football club that always won. Or almost always.

The first club to challenge Bayern's domestic supremacy in the 1980s was Hamburg. At first it seemed as if the season following the 1979 title would represent a major setback for the team built by Netzer and led by Keegan. On April 19, 1980, the side travelled to Dortmund as league leaders, level on points with Bayern. The match ended in a 2-2 draw, after Hamburg had been two up. More significant, however, was the furore surrounding coach Branko Zebec on that day.

Zebec had left his home early in the morning to get to the team's coach by car. Or rather, that's what he had tried to do. Following some idiosyncratic manoeuvres by Zebec, the police stopped the car and breathalysed its driver. Zebec's blood-alcohol level turned out to be an unlikely 3.25 mg/ml (the current legal level in Britain is 0.8) and he lost his driver's licence on the spot. Still, he made it to the game – though not a sober man. Television cameras caught him falling asleep on the bench and then almost tumbling over. That Zebec was a boozer was not news to Netzer and his club. They had shielded this part of his personality from the media for as long as possible, safe in the knowledge that he was an excellent coach nonetheless and usually got the job done. Now, however, Zebec's alcohol problems were common knowledge, which placed added pressure on the team.

Five weeks later, Hamburg lost out on two trophies within four days. On May 24, they were defeated at Leverkusen, which practically gifted Bayern the championship, then on May 28, they lost a depressing European Cup final to Nottingham Forest. Afterwards, the players decided to drink their sorrows away. Zebec watched in disgust, because there was still one game to be played in the league and, who knows, Bayern might stumble and present Hamburg with an unexpected chance to catch up after all. Once home, Zebec cancelled a training session, publicly declaring: 'I do not train with drunks.' That was too much for the players to take, coming from a man whose alcohol consumption had caused them many embarrassing moments. A rift developed that would never heal. 'We always stood by the coach, even after what happened in Dortmund,' Manfred Kaltz said. 'That's why I was very disappointed by his remark.'

Seven months later, in December 1980, Zebec again sat on the bench intoxicated. Netzer had to support him as the coach made his way to the press conference. No other Hamburg official was anywhere in sight, and that signalled the end of Zebec's time at the club. He was replaced by the man Netzer had wanted all along – the Austrian Ernst Happel. A few months earlier, the DFB had granted Cologne's Rinus Michels an exemption from the coaching-badge rule, and Netzer figured what applied to a Dutch coach should also apply to an Austrian.

When Happel arrived at Hamburg, Keegan had already left for Southampton, and the only major acquisition the club had made was – Franz Beckenbauer. The Kaiser, 35 years of age, would make only 28 appearances in two seasons with Hamburg, but he would win another championship. Because while the 1981 title went to Bayern again, Happel then guided his team to triumph in 1982, three points ahead of Michels' Cologne.

Ernst Happel was a strange man. He chain-smoked. He loved wine. He gambled. He had a reputation for being very tough on his players, yet most of them revered him. He was even tougher on journalists, all of whom he passionately disliked, yet most of them hung on his every word. He was known as 'the Grumbler' due to his perpetually sullen appearance, but at the same time he possessed a fascinatingly dry sense of humour, hidden behind mumbled oddities. His former team-mate Max Merkel once said: 'Happel speaks five languages. Usually at the same time.' He was also a great tactician, but unlike most such men he preferred attacking football. In short: it was not easy to work Happel out. What was certain was that he turned out to be one of the most influential and respected coaches in all of German football history.

Hamburg repeated the triumph of 1982 in 1983, on goal difference ahead of up-and-coming Werder Bremen. The same year, they also won the European Cup against Juventus and seemed poised for true greatness. Then things very slowly began to come apart. Hrubesch left for Standard Liège and was not successfully replaced. The unlikely dark horses Stuttgart claimed the 1984 championship on goal difference from Hamburg, but for both clubs this season would prove to be the last hurrah for quite some time. Happel's Hamburg finished fifth and seventh the next two years. Then, in 1986, the coach received a letter from his doctor. The first few lines mentioned something about cancer and Happel didn't bother to read the rest of the letter, throwing it away with a shrug. When a sympathetic journalist asked him about it later, he cut him off: 'Ah, get lost! If I've got cancer, well then I've got cancer. What the hell?' At the end of the season, he moved back to Austria, finally becoming the country's national coach.

Also in 1986, Günter Netzer left Hamburg. 'I guess the reason why I've been able to endure the business that is professional football for so long,' he charmingly but patently incorrectly said, 'is that I don't know much about finances.' With that parting shot, he went off to work in advertising and, massively successfully, the sale of broadcasting rights, while also becoming a popular and award-winning TV pundit. Within a few months, Hamburg had lost the man who had turned the club around and the man who had coached them to the biggest triumph in their history. The golden years were over. In September 1988, sad news from Zagreb reached Hamburg. Branko Zebec had died at the age of 59. Four years later, on November 14, 1992, Ernst Happel followed him. He was 66.

When Hamburg descended into the netherworld of mediocrity, the baton was picked up by a highly unlikely contender, Werder Bremen. The reason why Bremen – never a superpower, regardless of their sensational 1965 championship – managed to defy Bayern against all odds set an instructive example. Bayern were able to win, or at least stay in contention, no matter what turmoil might have been going on behind the scenes. They hired and fired coaches, wasted energy through bickering and infighting and withstood often fierce animosities within the team. Other clubs couldn't do that. For them to be successful, it took perfect, stable set-ups: a president who knew his place; a level-headed business manager; a coach who enjoyed free rein. Once one link weakened, it would be all over. That's what happened at Hamburg and what would happen at Cologne, Stuttgart and Dortmund. The prime example, however, remains Werder Bremen.

In 1970, the calm, softly spoken Franz Böhmert (an anaesthetist by trade and previously the team's physio) was elected president of Bremen. Initially, the club's idea was to spend lots of money and hire big-name coaches to acquire success. That backfired badly. After years of mid-table obscurity, Bremen were relegated in 1980, having conceded 93 goals in 34 games. More than halfway through the next season, they signed a new coach, Otto Rehhagel, to get them back into the top flight. And 20 months later, the quick-witted, quick-tongued and loyal Willi Lemke (a politician by trade) became the club's new business manager. This triumvirate – Böhmert, Lemke and Rehhagel – would stay together for almost 14 years.

The main figure was Otto Rehhagel. Like Weisweiler, Rehhagel had been a notoriously thuggish defender during his playing career, and a reputation of being hard-working but little else followed him for a while during his first years as a coach. He took Dortmund back into the Bundesliga in 1976, but was given the boot two years later after his side lost 12-0 at Gladbach. (Naturally, given the result, there were rumours that the Dortmund players had let themselves be bought to help Gladbach chip away at Cologne's superior goal difference. According to Dortmund's Manfred Burgsmüller: 'We did not try to help Gladbach win the title. But the club needed to save face, and Rehhagel was the pawn that had to be sacrificed.')

Later stints at Bielefeld and Düsseldorf proved equally brief and unsuccessful, but at Bremen his fortunes changed dramatically. Fourteen months after being signed by a Second Division team, Rehhagel found himself celebrating qualification for the UEFA Cup. From then on, his word was law, his every decision backed by Böhmert and put into practice by Lemke. Bremen was a place where such an autocracy (soon dubbed 'Ottocracy') could work. It's a relatively small, intimate, down-to-earth city. Rehhagel's biggest advantage, however, was that the Bremen press proved as sleepy as the rest of the city. Nobody tried to dig up scandals, nobody panicked when the team lost a few matches. In fact, most journalists came to fear press conferences, knowing they'd be in for a verbal hiding from Rehhagel for even the slightest criticial remark.

It was an unusual situation, but that suited a coach who loved to do things that ran contrary to popular football wisdom. One of Rehhagel's favourite moves was to find older players who appeared to be over the hill. Such landmark signings included the Austrian Bruno Pezzey (28), Mirko Votava, Michael Kutzop (both 29), his former Dortmund player Burgsmüller and Klaus Fichtel (both 35). None of these men was signed just for one season or so to add some experience. Votava stayed for nine years, Burgsmüller for five, Fichtel for four. 'There are no old or young players,' Rehhagel used to snap at people foolish enough to question the hiring of pensioners, 'there are only good or bad players.'

It's true that Rehhagel didn't have much choice at cash-strapped Bremen. He was interested in signing a young Christian Ziege and a then unknown Brazilian called Jorginho, but the players' respective agents settled for Bayern and Leverkusen instead. It's also true that Rehhagel did find a few youngsters. He signed 21-year-old Karl-Heinz Riedle from Blau-Weiss Berlin in 1987. And five years earlier, he had found a quite remarkable player.

Rudolf Völler was lucky in that his family whole-heartedly supported his football madness. (Well, save for the uncle who didn't like long hair.) His father Kurt, a lathe operator and later storeman, coached the youth teams at little TSV 1860 Hanau, and when the two of them came home after a training session they often finished off the evening with a round of table football. In 1975, Hanau's Under-16 team played a tournament hosted by local rivals Steinheim. In four games, Kurt Völler's team scored ten and let in none. All ten goals were scored by only one player, and that was Kurt Völler's son. 'I knew then he was exceptional,' Kurt Völler said many years later.

Rudolf was also exceptional in that nothing ever seemed to go to his head. Not ten goals in Steinheim. Not when he scored as a 17-year-old for Offenbach in only his fourth professional match. Not even when he was signed by 1860 Munich in 1980 and scored 37 goals in as many second division appearances for them a year later. In 1990, when he was an international superstar with Roma, he was invited to a reunion party by his former school class. Völler boarded a plane, walked into a small Hanau clubhouse and sat down with hairdressers and car mechanics to relive the good old times. He couldn't stay too long, though, because there was a training session the next morning.

In 1982, Otto Rehhagel signed this player from 1860, who needed the money. (If you're still keeping count, this is the fourth World Cup winner Bayern's rivals lost to fate.) It didn't take Völler long to settle in and become much-loved 'Rudi', not only at Bremen but throughout the country, making him the only player apart from Seeler (and maybe Fritz Walter) who was universally liked and never booed anywhere. In his very first season with Bremen, Völler became the league's top scorer and Footballer of the Year. He was 23.

Consequently, Rehhagel's Werder team began to challenge for the title. They finished fifth in 1982, then second in 1983, losing out to Hamburg on goal difference, then fifth again. Clearly, something was up: Werder had played Bayern Munich six times in the league since being promoted, and they had lost only once. This trend continued in 1984-85. Halfway through the season two Völler goals helped beat Bayern 4-2, and Bremen were only a point behind the leaders. They never caught up, but suddenly football fans across the country sat up and took notice. The stage was set for the 1985-86 season, a year many people still haven't forgiven Bayern Munich for.

On November 23, 1985, Bremen played at Bayern. Rehhagel's team were top of the table, three points ahead of the title-holders. With 16 minutes gone, the home team were 1-0 up, but suddenly a pass found Rudi Völler, who raced upfield, with only Bayern's sweeper and captain Klaus Augenthaler standing between him and the goal. Völler pushed the ball past Augenthaler, but the defender tackled nonetheless. The only object he could hope to hit was Völler's right leg. And that's what he did. Thus Bremen lost Völler (for all but two games of the rest of the season), the match and, many claimed, the title. For months afterwards, Augenthaler would be subjected to the worst kind of insults wherever he played, but that was no consolation for Rehhagel's team.

All was not yet lost. There was still the small matter of the rematch and the sad story of Kutzop's missed penalty we have already mentioned. When Rudi Völler came on 12 minutes from time, it was his first appearance since Augenthaler's foul in

Munich. And it was his cross that led to the disputed penalty in the dying moments. For an instant it seemed poetic justice was making a major comeback in German football. Then Kutzop's shot hit the post and a week later Rehhagel was no longer 'King Otto' but 'King Otto the Second', a cruel nickname indicating he couldn't finish in first place.

But oh yes he could. Not in 1987, when Bayern waltzed to their third championship in a row, but in 1988 the Bundesliga heaved a collective sigh of relief. Despite the sale of Völler to Roma, Rehhagel's Bremen dominated the league, thanks in no small part to the heroics of young Karl-Heinz Riedle, who scored 18 goals. Bremen's captain, Mirko Votava, ecstatically exclaimed: 'We have broken Bayern's supremacy!'

It was wishful thinking. Bayern won the next two campaigns rather easily to end a decade that had earned German football few friends. There seemed to be doom and gloom wherever you looked. Attendances were recovering only very slowly and Bayern's dominance had long surpassed the point of being merely irritating. The national team hadn't won anything since 1980 and often carried so much dead wood that the new national coach – none other than Franz Beckenbauer – once actually burst out laughing when reading the line-up. Finally, the clubs were no longer doing well in Europe. Despite the absence of English clubs after Heysel, only four German sides reached European finals between 1984 and 1991, and the only one that won was Bayer Leverkusen. Their 1988 UEFA Cup final win over Espanyol gave them the odd distinction of becoming the first team to win a European trophy before they had won a domestic one.

The main reason for this was the lira – Italian clubs robbed the Bundesliga of whatever talent there was. Between 1984 and 1992, Thomas Berthold, Andreas Brehme, Hans-Peter Briegel, Thomas Doll, Stefan Effenberg, Thomas Hässler, Jürgen Klinsmann, Jürgen Kohler, Lothar Matthäus, Andreas Möller, Stefan Reuter,

Karl-Heinz Riedle, Karl-Heinz Rummenigge, Matthias Sammer and of course Rudi Völler all moved to Serie A. Even Bayern Munich could not compete with the bottomless coffers of the country south of the Alps. However, they did become rich by German standards through the sales of their stars and so hit upon a new strategy.

Beginning in the late 1980s, Bayern would buy young players who had proved themselves at other Bundesliga clubs. A few years on, these players would be sold to Italy at a hefty profit and the cycle started anew. Uli Hoeness defended these tactics by saying Bayern were, in a way, sharing their Italian millions with others, helping them to stay afloat. But the rest of the Bundesliga argued that the Munich giants were now buying not just to strengthen their squad but also to bleed their competitors dry. Between 1986 and 1989, Nuremberg's Hans Dorfner, Stefan Reuter, Roland Grahammer and Manfred Schwabl went to Bayern. Nuremberg dropped from fifth place in 1988 to 14th in 1989. Then Bayern found a new victim. Within seven years, more than half a complete team moved from Karlsruhe to Munich: Michael Sternkopf, Oliver Kreuzer, Mehmet Scholl, Oliver Kahn, Michael Tarnat and Thorsten Fink.

That's why the 1990s were thought likely to bring more of the same, more titles and more riches for the haves (Bayern), more bad football and problems for the have-nots (everybody else). Yet the big change was already under way. Just as in England, the end of the 1980s saw the beginning of a wholly unexpected boom decade. Just as in England, television played a major role. Unlike England, however, the Bundesliga had neither a Hillsborough nor a Taylor Report. Instead, the events that kick-started Germany's boom were of a cultural, political and even footballing nature.

At 5.15pm on July 23, 1988, the Bundesliga completed the first day of its 25th season. Bayern beat Frankfurt 3-0, Bremen beat Hamburg 2-1. Business as usual. Until 6.50pm. At that moment, a stubby man with a Keegan-like perm appeared on television, squinting through glasses, grinning animatedly. Most people had never seen him before and probably presumed his past career included brief stints in 1970s soft porn films. (Which was not so far from the truth – he had recorded two Euro-trash singles under the pseudonym Uli Mario, both of which bombed.) He was called Ulrich Potofski, and he was about to present the biggest football show ever seen on German television, more than three hours long, covering every game from every possible angle and even a few impossible ones.

The reason the show was so drawn out was that it would be interrupted by commercials (with an hour gone, only one match had been shown), something that had never happened before. Because for the first time, the nation's favourite pastime was no longer the property of public service broadcasting only. Potofski was working for Radio Tele Luxembourg Plus, a private TV station that had acquired the rights to the Bundesliga from UFA (a major German film company). UFA, in turn, was a company that bought broadcasting rights to whatever might catch people's fancy, then licensed them at a profit. UFA had paid the DFB DM40 million for the Bundesliga games in 1988, more than double the sum public service stations had come up with in 1987.

It wasn't until the conservative government under Chancellor Helmut Kohl came to power in 1982 that private broadcasting even came on to the political agenda in West Germany. It was legalised in 1983, and in late 1984 SAT1 (owned by the Kirch media group) and then RTL Plus (owned by the Bertelsmann conglomerate) went on air as the first private stations in the country. Their offerings were patchy, to say the least. Silly Hollywood films, cheap game shows and cheaper skin flicks were all they could initially offer to compete with the public service stations, who stubbornly believed in the value of their 30-year head start. Soon, however, the commercial stations decided to bid for the one card that would transform their hand – football.

Predictably, the going rate for televising the game skyrocketed. It rose from DM40 million in 1988 to DM80 million in 1991, when the Kirch Group's pay-TV station Premiere got in on the act. A year later, RTL Plus and Bertelsmann lost the rights completely to Kirch, as UFA's competitor ISPR joined the race and parted with DM700 million for five years' worth of Bundesliga football. Even that proved to be only the beginning. In 2000, Premiere introduced its digital pay-TV and pay-per-view station Premiere World, which broadcast every league match live. That coup cost Kirch some DM750 million, annually.

This no-holds-barred scrapping on the television market brought money pouring into the clubs. More important, however, was that it changed perceptions of how good Bundesliga football was. The men and women presenting the game on RTL, SAT1 and Premiere were not reporters, they were entertainers. They didn't present programmes, but 'shows'. In other words, they were not merely following the games but selling them.

A few years earlier a typical commentary had sounded roughly like this: 'Bayern again . . . Matthäus . . . Dorfner . . . to Wohlfarth . . . and goal. That was quite a good move, and the 11,500 in attendance are . . . happy.' Now it became more like this: 'And Frankfurt are on the attack yet again, a beautiful flick by Uwe Bein, and here comes the turbo, the baby-faced killer, the prodigal son, the supremely elegant Andreas Möller, there's no stopping him, and look at this – wow! What a pass, and goal, goal, goal!! It's Anthony Yeboah again, the black pearl has scored another scorcher and the huge crowd is going crazy!'

As if on command, private television soon found itself presented with characters and events worthy of such overdrive.

The 1988-89 season, RTL's first year of football, was marked by off-field shenanigans surrounding Bayern Munich and Cologne. Bayern were by now coached by Jupp Heynckes, a guarded, businesslike man who suffered the misfortune of blushing in front of cameras. (In fact, his face was quite reddish to begin with, which led his players to dub him 'Osram', after the lightbulb company.) Cologne were coached by Christoph Daum, a witty, fast-talking showman, eight years younger than Heynckes.

Daum had been only a mediocre player for Cologne's reserve team, but he brought a wholly new approach to coaching. He was very interested in the scientific side of football, and his hobby horse was motivational psychology. Later in his career, at Leverkusen, he would get his players to run across broken glass (to tell them one could do the unthinkable), hand them spoons (to teach them they were eating from the same bowl, figuratively speaking), lecture striker Ulf Kirsten on how vacuum cleaner salesmen went about their job (they try again and again) and make his team train in the middle of the night (no sensible explanation given).

At Cologne, his first major coaching post, he decided he had a good team, built around playmaker Thomas Hässler, defender Jürgen Kohler, goalkeeper Bodo Illgner and striker Thomas Allofs. The problem, Daum felt, was that everybody in the league, including his own team, nurtured a mortal fear of Bayern and the deep-seated belief that no one could beat them. The cure, Daum figured, was to lead by example.

'Heynckes invites bad luck,' Daum trumpeted, his protruding eyes darting this way and that, giving him the air of a dangerous madman. 'He always loses out at the last moment. Why should this ever change?' Then he got personal: 'The weather map is more interesting than a talk with Heynckes.' The man thus attacked just didn't find it in his character to retort, and so Bayern's business manager Uli Hoeness became the club's anti-

Daum spokesman. He even accompanied Heynckes on to a popular sports show, where he exchanged verbal jabs with Daum while Heynckes largely watched and probably wondered what the world had come to.

Of course, the television people loved the hullabaloo, and even the fact that Bayern proved stronger than Daum – winning in 1989 and 1990, both times ahead of Cologne – couldn't really dampen the new enthusiasm. Because on July 8, 1990, West Germany won the World Cup in Italy, introducing a new wave of football fever. And a few months earlier, on November 9, 1989, the Berlin Wall had come tumbling down, resulting in a state of collective national euphoria and the belief that the future could only be bright.

13

FORWARDS AND UPWARDS

THE STRANGE WORLD OF THE GDR

WHEN MIKHAIL GORBACHEV BEGAN rebuilding the social and political structures of the Soviet Union in 1985, the hardliners running the German Democratic Republic resolutely opposed any notions of reform. In fact, in late 1987, the head of state Erich Honecker visited West Germany and was met according to the normal rules of protocol, which signalled to the world that the Federal Republic had at long last acknowledged its eastern neighbour as a sovereign state. The USSR may have been reeling, but the GDR stood as firm as ever.

But not for long. Gorbachev's politics of *perestroika* (relaxation) spread like wildfire through the eastern bloc, and soon Hungary and Czechoslovakia in particular guarded their western borders less rigidly than before. During 1989, more and more East Germans entered the West German embassies in Budapest and Prague, seeking political asylum. In September and October alone, almost 40,000 of them were allowed to enter West German territory.

At the same time, the ruling Socialist Unity Party (SED in German) was celebrating the country's 40th anniversary. Outside East Berlin's Palace of the Republic, tens of thousands gathered to demand change. The army, the police and even the secret police (Stasi) dispelled the crowds with brute force – but they were back in even greater numbers two days later. For a brief moment, the possibility of a terrible bloodbath hung in the air, as SED officials discussed the option of sending tanks on to the streets, as they had done in 1953. They decided against it, and the end of the GDR was now only a matter of time.

On October 18, Erich Honecker was forced to step down from his post. His successor, Egon Krenz, attempted to pacify the demonstrators by announcing a general amnesty and an investigation into the wrongdoings of the Stasi. It was too little, too late. On November 8, the whole Politburo resigned and a day later the frontier crossings between West and East Germany were opened. It would be another 11 months before reunification (historically a misnomer, but it has become the accepted term for the GDR's entry into the Federal Republic) was to become fact, but for all practical purposes, November 9, 1989 marked the end of the four-decade history of East Germany. And, of course, the four-decade history of East German football.

That history may very well be one of the game's most fascinating tales still waiting to be told properly. The reason it has proved to be a matter almost too complex to tackle is that it cannot be understood outside the context of its political and social setting. Most of the things that happened in and around East German football seem utterly bizarre and often downright incredible to someone who has grown up in a completely different society, which invariably invites misconceptions.

One such misconception is that East German football was awful and spectacularly unsuccessful. Granted, one could argue strongly at least for the latter. The GDR's national team never qualified for a European Championship and just once for a World Cup. Only three East German clubs ever reached a European final, only one won – and they were all in the Cup-Winners' Cup, the weakest of the three European competitions. After all, when Carl Zeiss Jena reached the final in 1981, it was only after squeaking past Newport County in the quarter-finals.

Yet there is also evidence to the contrary. The GDR's clubs may have seldom won, but they were no lightweights. Fiorentina, Inter, Leeds, Porto, Juventus and Barcelona all lost, if not the tie then at least one game, to Dresden and Rostock (the two clubs that would qualify for the Bundesliga in 1992). Magdeburg won the 1974 Cup-Winners' Cup against none other than Milan. The result was 2-0, and the East Germans could have had more. Oh, and the other three teams Jena beat on the way to their final were Roma, Valencia and Benfica.

The national team, on the other hand, were known as the 'world champions in friendlies'. That's because the side often played well but usually lost their nerve when it counted most. They beat Cruyff's Holland, Beckenbauer's West Germany and Platini's France; they drew with Brazil, Argentina and England. Yet it was never quite enough.

In 1963, the GDR eliminated World Cup finalists Czechoslovakia from the European Championship, winning 3-2 on aggregate against a side featuring Josef Masopust, Jan Popluhar and other stars who had shone in Chile. Yet the team didn't make it to the 1964 finals because they could only draw with Hungary in Budapest. (Two Hungarian goals should have been disallowed and East Germany's winner in the last minute was dubiously ruled out – the Yugoslavian referee was banned by UEFA.) All they needed to qualify for the 1976 European

Championship quarter-finals was one victory against Iceland, but they drew at home and lost away. They missed out on the 1980 European Championship because they couldn't hold a 2-0 lead against Holland. During the qualifiers for Euro 88, they dropped a vital point to the Soviet Union only because of a terrible goalkeeping blunder ten minutes from time. In short, whenever there was a qualifying campaign, you could bet the GDR would end up one point short.

The problem may have been rooted in the GDR's football philosophy, which discouraged the development of individual stars and instead focused on team play. That is not to say there were no stars. The most spectacular East German player was probably Jena's Peter Ducke, who was often compared to his contemporary Péle. (A crucial difference being that Ducke was such a notorious hothead that he often showered a lot earlier than his team-mates did.) Then there was Joachim Streich, who set so many scoring records for club and country that he was known (in the west) as 'the Gerd Müller of the east'.

And yet there is a grain of truth to the tired, ugly cliche that said east European sides were 'collectives' made up of 'automatons'. Dresden's Matthias Sammer began flirting with trouble when, as a youngster, he started to display leadership qualities. 'One day, the squad players were given new boots,' he later recalled. 'Mine were the only ones that didn't fit. They were three sizes too large. It was pure harassment, as individualism wasn't tolerated.' This approach often proved detrimental when the chips were down. The most famous example is Hans-Jürgen Dörner's failure to carry his Dynamo Dresden side through a mere 30 minutes of football during a Cup-Winners' Cup tie at Bayer Uerdingen in 1986. Dresden had won the first leg 2-0 and they led 3-1 at Uerdingen after an hour. Then the roof fell in, and the West Germans scored six goals. A club history published in 1993 says: 'After the final league game, Dörner was told to see [club director] Horst Arlt. "Starting on Monday, you're a youth coach." This directive was unequivocal. The career of the best East German sweeper was over.'

One area where East Germany excelled was youth football. They won major tournaments in 1965 and 1970, the European Championship in 1986 and came third in the World Youth Cup in 1987. When the Wall fell in 1989, representatives of Bundesliga clubs dashed eastwards, knowing there were countless well-trained youngsters to be picked up. And they were right. Proven players like Andreas Thom, Ulf Kirsten, Matthias Sammer and Thomas Doll were the most eagerly sought possessions to be prised loose. But equally important were kids like Jörg Heinrich, Steffen Freund, René Schneider, Carsten Jancker, Thomas Linke, Alexander Zickler, Jens Jeremies and René Tretschok – all products of the GDR's youth set-up and all future winners of the European Championship and/or the Champions League.

So what was it that prevented the country's clubs, its national team and its many exceptional prospects from making good on their promises? The answer: everything that was around them, especially politics. In order to understand what went wrong with East German football, one has to understand an apparent paradox. Some of the Communist Party people who ruled the country viewed football in a similar way to the Nazis, and some others ran the league not unlike America runs its baseball or gridiron leagues.

Manfred Ewald was the head of the GDR's Gymnastics and Sport Union (DTSB) and the president of the country's National Olympic Committee, the most powerful man in East German sport. His motto was: 'Sport isn't private amusement, it is social and patriotic education.' The nation's largest youth magazine had formulated this idea as early as 1954, arguing: 'The athletes in the German Democratic Republic have to understand that they must learn to win competitions for the cause of our workers' and peasants' state.' All this sounded strangely like the otherwise taboo Nazi rhetoric of the past generation, and the consequences were the same: losing was forbidden and sports that carried the risk of losing were frowned upon.

Thus Ewald viewed football with the same suspicion as the fascists had done. The game ranked only 14th on the list of sports the DTSB deemed worthy of support, way behind everything that could guarantee Olympic medals. Which is why a very young Michael Ballack was urged to take up speed skating after the customary sports medical examination in kindergarten revealed his build suited this sport. Who knows, football might even have died a quick death in the GDR. That's what happened to ice hockey, when Ewald decided in 1969 that the sport would no longer be financed. Six of the eight clubs went under immediately, creating the surreal situation that for the next 20 years, the GDR's ice hockey championship was fought out between only two teams.

Unlike ice hockey, however, football was very popular with the people – and especially with selected party big shots, who considered the football club of their city their private property. 'They tried to enhance their reputation in populist fashion through the game,' Ewald wrote in his autobiography, not a little disdainfully. 'That's why they felt called upon to develop and carry out their own ideas, independent of our plans. They used the financial means put at their disposal for completely the wrong objectives. These functionaries viewed their teams in the same way that medieval princes saw their court ballets.'

As powerful and as ruthless as Ewald was, he could do little against the men this tirade was aimed at. Men such as Rostock's Harry Tisch (later head of the country's federal trade union) or Berlin's Erich Mielke (head of the Stasi). And so East German football would rumble onwards, torn between differing directives, tugged this way and that by conceited party bosses, unloved by men in suits who would have preferred it if youngsters had taken up swimming or weightlifting. No surprise, then, that things got chaotic, scandalous or simply weird. Usually all at the same time.

Strangeness crept in early. As mentioned, the old clubs – denounced as 'bourgeois' – were disbanded after the war, replaced by 'sporting groups' (SGs) which would soon evolve into communal, multi-sport clubs that were linked with certain lines of production and dubbed 'company sporting groups' (BSGs). In the early 1950s, these BSGs were given generic names to denote ties with a certain line of industrial production. No more Borussias: now it was Chemie (chemical industry), Aufbau (construction industry), Stahl (steel workers), Lokomotive (state railways) or Wismut (ore mining). Less obviously heroic occupations received exhortations as their new names such as Empor (upwards!) for public servants and Vorwärts (forwards!) for the army. The tricky area of the media was represented by clubs called Rotation (from the German word for 'rotary press' – *Rotationspresse*) and, of course, Dynamo became the name associated with both official and secret police.

One would think that old habits would die hard and that East German football fans would have been unwilling to part with clubs that had been in existence for half a century. But the party went about its business swiftly and thoroughly. Few stories illustrate this better than the drama surrounding Dresden. Helmut Schön's famous SC Dresden had become SG Dresden-Friedrichstadt in 1946. Four years later, Friedrichstadt met Zwickau at home, in what was practically a play-off for the championship of the GDR. It was the inaugural season of the country's Oberliga, the first nationwide league on German ground. (In fact, the second division, which came to be known as *DDR-Liga* from 1950 on, covered the entire country as well, meaning East Germany was way ahead of the West in this regard.) Going into the last day of the season, Friedrichstadt and Zwickau were level on points.

There were 60,000 people in attendance, cheering on their beloved and legendary team regardless of the new name it had been forced to carry. Friedrichstadt's squad still included Schön and its icon, Richard Hofmann, and the team had scored 86 goals in 25 games so far. Zwickau, on the other hand, was an entirely new, artificial club, the product of an arranged marriage between three teams. (Ominously, one of these teams had come from Cainsdorf – 'Cain's village'.) Helmut Schön would later suspect the Soviets had demanded that socialist Zwickau were to beat bourgeois Friedrichstadt, and the events of the day seem to support this claim.

Friedrichstadt went ahead after three minutes. Then the Zwickau players began brutally kicking their opponents, with the referee turning a blind eye. No substitutions were allowed then, and at half-time the home team were down to ten men. 'A few times,' Schön remembered, 'the pitch had to be cleared of fans who were so enraged they invaded the field.' When the final whistle went, it was 5-1 to Zwickau and all hell broke loose. Thousands invaded the pitch and one Zwickau player was badly beaten up. Mounted police finally restored a semblance of order.

A few weeks later, orders came from above to dismantle SG Friedrichstadt and send the players to BSG Tabak (Tobacco) Dresden. Richard Hofmann, who had once been banned from the national team for allowing his image to be used in cigarette advertising, escaped the ignominy of playing for a cigar factory by retiring. Schön and most of the other Friedrichstadt players fled the country.

Clubs and footballers now became playthings. In late 1954, Empor Lauter beat Rotation Babelsberg and suddenly found themselves topping the table. That was remarkable, because Lauter was a village of only 8,000 inhabitants in the Erzgebirge (ore mountains), not far from the Czech border, and the club couldn't count on too much support from the local mining factory. Such unplanned success irked the Rostock politician Harry Tisch, who felt his city was much more deserving of a good football club. And so he decreed that Empor Lauter's team be moved to Rostock. As simple as that.

Lauter's players were carried northwards by train – at five o'clock in the morning, so that the locals wouldn't catch wind of what was happening. Some, however, had spotted removal vans and attempted to block the roads. Kurt Zapf, the team's captain, remembered: 'The fans tried to knock the vans over and police had to intervene. We were regarded as traitors.' Four players refused to move to Rostock, but the majority figured they had no choice. On November 14, the new club – Empor Rostock – played its first game. It would later evolve into Hansa Rostock.

A similar story was unfolding in Dresden. The football-mad city, robbed of SG Friedrichstadt, had been given a new team – Volkspolizei (People's police) Dresden, soon to be known as Dynamo Dresden. Seventeen players from 11 different cities were delegated to Dresden to form the nucleus of the new squad, and only three years later, in July 1953, that team won the East German title. This didn't sit well with Erich Mielke, who ran the Stasi from his offices in Berlin. Because while Dresden now had two teams in the nationwide league (Rotation, later Einheit, had been promoted), Berlin lacked a single prestigious football club. Mielke announced Dynamo Dresden would relocate to Berlin and become Dynamo Berlin on November 21, 1954. The few players who remained in Dresden, mostly youngsters and reserves, were allowed to play Second Division football. In 1955, the weak team was relegated even further. Dynamo Dresden didn't return to the top flight until 1962.

In the 1960s, the relocation or renaming of teams became less common, but the compulsory transfer of individual players increased. That was because the DTSB and Manfred Ewald, already exasperated by the failures of the national football team, decided that success could only be achieved by what was called 'concentration of performance'. As of January 1, 1966, 11 selected clubs were made independent of their multi-sport parent organisations and were turned into clubs solely for football. Thus Dynamo Berlin now became FC Dynamo Berlin, Empor Rostock spawned FC Hansa Rostock and the football divison of Aufbau Magdeburg was named 1. FC Magdeburg. These clubs were known as 'focus clubs', the most important of them being Berlin, Dresden, Leipzig, Jena, Frankfurt/Oder and Magdeburg. They were supposed to be supplying the national team with talent and to that end every promising player was ordered to play for one of these teams.

Only two well-known players ever refused to heed such instructions. One was Jürgen Croy, who kept goal for perennial strugglers Zwickau. Many politicians would have loved to see him in Dresden's goal, but Croy didn't want to leave Zwickau, and his then national coach Georg Buschner convinced the officials that for a goalkeeper it was actually advantageous to play in a team that was forced to defend a lot. The other player was Rostock's Gerd Kische. 'When Rostock were relegated,' Kische recalled, 'the East German FA said: "Either you go to Berlin or Jena, or you won't play for the national team."' Kische, stubborn and strong-willed, refused. He was blacklisted for three months, then it was Buschner again who lobbied in the player's favour. However, Kische had so annoyed the East German FA they were looking for ways to bully him. Finally, in 1981, his unpleasant divorce from a former Olympic middle-distance runner provided the FA with the cause they had been looking for. Kische was banned from the national team for good and Hansa were ordered to release him.

Still, most footballers just packed their bags and moved when commanded to do so. Yet while such string-pulling from above turned the players into marionettes, they weren't robots, and the matches themselves remained immune from overt influence, at least for 15 years. Take the crazy season of 1964. There were two Leipzig teams in the top league, Lokomotive and Rotation. The party came to the conclusion that only one major force was needed in the city and so the best players from the two teams were ordered to create a new side, SC Leipzig (in 1966 they would be renamed 1. FC Lokomotive Leipzig). The remaining players – outcasts, has-beens and never-would-bes – joined an older club, BSG Chemie Leipzig, and were allowed to make up the numbers in the top flight. A surefire relegation candidate if ever there was one.

Predictably, Leipzig won the championship that season, two points ahead of Empor Rostock. Unpredictably, it wasn't SC Leipzig that triumphed, but lowly and ridiculed BSG Chemie, nicknamed the 'Rest of Leipzig'. I'm not sure if there's ever been a more sensational and unexpected outcome to a season anywhere in Europe in the past century. (If so, I'd like to hear about it.) Chemie won both games against SC, who ended up in third place. Erich Mielke's beloved Dynamo Berlin came eighth. You could almost see Manfred Ewald tearing out his hair over this unruly sport.

And it would get even crazier, if that's possible. Because in the 1970s, Dynamo Dresden made a major comeback, and all championships between 1971 and 1978 went to either Dresden (five titles) or Magdeburg (three). The club was an exception in many respects. It had fiercely loyal fans, who guaranteed Dynamo would top the average attendance lists year in, year out. Dresden often drew 25,000 people – other teams were happy when they reached the 10,000 mark.

The club also had its fair share of maverick players. There was the elegant Hans-Jürgen Dörner, who hated running and tackling almost as much as he hated interfering politicians. There was

Klaus Sammer, father of Matthias, whom a Stasi file described as 'ideologically useless'. Or what about Frank Lippmann? In late 1985, he drove home from a party, rather drunk. He crashed into another car, panicked, and fled the scene of the accident. Unfortunately, he'd rammed a police truck transporting prisoners. Naturally, the police presumed the collision was an attempt to help the convicts escape and ordered a large-scale man-hunt for poor Lippmann that involved tracker dogs, helicopters and the secret police. (Lippmann was a marked man from that day on. He sought political asylum in West Germany the night after Dresden's disastrous 1986 match in Uerdingen.)

It's a minor miracle such characters could survive, even blossom, in East German football, where rules were strict. In fact especially strict at Dresden. In the 1970s, the team was coached by a man who has come to shape many people's ideas of what a typical GDR coach was like, Walter Fritzsch. Fritzsch was a maniacal bureaucrat, who was obsessed with pre-planning and analysis. He gave each of his players a notebook and told them to write essays about every competitive match they played. Four days after the match, he would then collect the notebooks and compare the players' impressions with how he had seen the game. Fritzsch also monitored his charges' every move. He took his wife along to away trips, telling her to stand next to the hotel bar and count the beers each player drank, while he himself mooched around the lounge, meticulously noting every single lit cigarette.

Still, such rigid regimentation wasn't the most stifling aspect of football at Dresden and elsewhere. Worse was the supervision carried out by the Stasi and party people. The Stasi would recruit undercover agents, known as *Informelle Mitarbeiter* ('informal collaborators') among the players, whose job was to spy on their colleagues and immediately report undesirable behaviour. One such IM was the international Gerd Weber. In late 1980, Weber travelled with Dresden to Enschede in Holland for a UEFA Cup tie against Twente. After the game, representatives of the West German club Cologne contacted Weber and his two friends Matthias Müller and Peter Kotte, offering them contracts if they fled the GDR. Weber, as a secret employee of the Stasi, should have blown the whistle immediately, but that would have meant trouble for Müller and Kotte. Also, Weber was interested.

He asked Cologne for time to think about it and returned home. There, Weber discussed the matter with Müller and Kotte, who were unwilling to take the risk. Weber, on the other hand, felt inclined to accept the offer. However, it was too late. On January 22, 1981, Weber, Müller, Kotte and seven other people, among them Weber's fiancée, were arrested by the police. The players were banned from top-class football and Weber spent 11 months in prison.

Weber must have racked his brains to find out who had betrayed him. After all, he was an IM himself, and he had kept his mouth shut. It turned out much later that the Stasi had been more devious than Weber could have imagined. They covered every angle by having IMs spy on other IMs. One of Müller's best friends, not a footballer, had also been an undercover Stasi man, and as soon as he had learned enough to gather that Weber was really trying to escape, he informed the police.

There were many such IMs at clubs. (In the late 1980s, both star strikers at Dynamo Dresden were Stasi informants: Thorsten Gütschow and Ulf Kirsten.) Their number had increased dramatically after March 21, 1979. That was the day Lutz Eigendorf, a Dynamo Berlin player, had not returned to the team's hotel in Kaiserslautern, where Dynamo had played a friendly on the previous evening. Erich Mielke was livid. After all, Dynamo Berlin were his club, a club as close to the Stasi as one could get. According to eyewitnesses, Mielke went into a fit of rage and yelled: 'Eigendorf will never play in the Bundesliga!'

But he did. Eigendorf played 61 league matches for Kaiserslautern and Braunschweig. Then, on March 5, 1983, he was killed in a car crash. It appeared to be an accident, brought about by Eigendorf driving under the influence of alcohol. However, his friends said he was not a drinker, and doubts remained. Almost two decades later, a German filmmaker unearthed new evidence, including secret Stasi files which indicated that up to 50 agents had been following Eigendorf's every move. The film leaves almost no doubt that the Stasi killed Eigendorf, but as yet no one has been charged with his murder.

It's hard to assess how strong the grip of the Stasi and the party really was and how deeply infiltrated the clubs had become. At all events, West Germans always feared the worst. When Bayern Munich were drawn against Dynamo Dresden in the 1974 European Cup, they initially planned to stay in Dresden before the second leg. At the last minute, however, club president Wilhelm Neudecker claimed: 'Dresden is situated 116 metres above sea level. Munich is 567 metres above sea level. This difference might turn out to be detrimental to our performance and two days in Dresden do not suffice to acclimatise ourselves.' So the team spent the night before the game in the West German town of Hof and travelled to their Dresden hotel only on the day of the game. Of course, everyone knew this asinine excuse was only masking Bayern's fear that they would be poisoned or spied on. Even the West German press spoke of 'arrogance' and 'paranoia', pointing out that Bayern had badly let down their huge contingent of fans in the East. Many years later, Uli Hoeness apologised for what he called 'an over-reaction'.

And yet, while this story is often told, its punchline is not widely known. Because as idiotic as Bayern's fears may appear, they weren't completely unfounded. On the day of the match, the hotel parlour in which the visitors held their team talk was bugged, which resulted in the surreal situation that Dresden's coach Walter Fritzsch heard a knock on the door just as he was briefing his Dynamo team. A man in a dark suit handed Fritzsch a piece of paper and left. The coach studied the note, then turned around and said: 'Let us now talk about Bayern's line-up and their tactics.'

But lest this picture of East German football becomes too sinister, it should not be forgotten that many of the players thoroughly enjoyed playing the game and truly believed in their country. When clubs like Dresden played in Europe, the footballers found delight in the wonders of the capitalist world, curiously checking out the shops. But most of them were not in awe and only a few seriously contemplated escape. True, in some cases that was because they had to fear for the well-being of relatives they would have to leave behind, but in other cases it was simply because their life at home wasn't exactly desperate. In the context of their society, they were privileged men, even well-off. To some, it was enough to taste the western world every now and then when on European duty. And sometimes, that little bit was more than enough.

In 1977, Dresden travelled to Liverpool. As usual, the team went to the movies. As usual, an official was stationed at the entrance of the cinema to make sure no one sneaked out. Normally, this man had a quiet job, but on this evening he soon noticed a few players strolling towards him. Traitors trying to desert the republic? No. The cinema was showing Steven Spielberg's *Jaws*, and many players' stomachs just weren't used to Hollywood horror fare.

Still, as the 1980s came along, football became less and less fun. Erich Mielke had got sick of Dresden and Magdeburg grabbing all the silverware, and he now exerted his influence. More and more good players were ordered to play for Dynamo Berlin. The referees were aware that Mielke had a say in which official would be singled out for one of the much-craved trips into western Europe to referee an international, and they knew better than to cross him. Thus it came about that Berlin would be awarded a penalty when they needed one, or would have an opponent's goal disallowed during moments of crisis. Berlin went on to win the next ten league campaigns, often under dubious circumstances. 'We had the best players,' said midfielder Rainer Ernst, who was there for all those titles, 'but when you saw many of the decisions that went our way, you did begin to question things.' Even their own fans sensed something was foul: Dynamo's average attendance fell from more than 15,000 at the start of the Eighties to around 5,500 by the time the GDR closed for business.

Fittingly, it was during the political upheaval of 1989 that Berlin's dominance was finally broken. Led by the impressive strikeforce of Gütschow and Kirsten, Dynamo Dresden won the championship a solid eight points ahead of Mielke's men. They repeated the triumph in 1990. By that time, Dynamo Berlin had changed their name to FC Berlin to prepare for the impending arrival of democracy and German unity. It was to no avail: the team finished fourth and was still hated by the whole country. Defiantly, they later picked up the name Dynamo again, though that didn't do them much good either.

The 1990-91 season was to be the final one of GDR football. After that, it was decided, the top two teams would join the Bundesliga and six others would go into the second division. Coached by the West German Uwe Reinders, Hansa Rostock defied all expectations and won the title, with Dynamo Dresden second. These two clubs, then, would soon no longer play teams called 'Stahl' or 'Lokomotive', but fight it out with European Cup winners like Bayern or Hamburg. They would no longer play in front of 5,000 at Jena or 4,000 at Riesa, instead they would face 40,000 in Dortmund or 35,000 in Stuttgart. They would no longer deal with dour party people and secret Stasi men, but would have to come to grips with hard-nosed business people and nosy journalists.

They would also soon find out that the politicians' talk of 'brothers and sisters' in a unified German nation was an empty concept to the younger generation, particularly in the west. Nearly every West German born after 1960 had grown up regarding the GDR as what that country had always wanted to be – a foreign state. Much more foreign, in fact, than France or England or Italy. Soon clubs like Dresden and Rostock would find themselves greeted by chants of 'Put the wall back up' when they played in the west. The physical borders between west and east were torn down, but they had been replaced by a psychological one that observers would soon term 'the wall in our heads'.

In short, handling unification was a difficult mission for the football clubs from the former GDR to begin with, even before economics entered the picture. And they made it an impossible one. By the time the new, pan-German Bundesliga kicked off, the eastern clubs had already been stripped of their best players. In 1990 alone, Dresden lost Ulf Kirsten to Leverkusen, Matthias Sammer to Stuttgart and three other regulars to Fortuna Cologne. The DM6.1 million the club received in transfer money was soon wasted by officials either taken to the cleaners by western 'advisers' or eager to fill their own pockets. Then agents descended on Dynamo, selling mediocre players for outrageous sums. The club also got entangled in a ruinous sponsorship deal, besides electing a shady (western) president who spent more time in courtrooms than in boardrooms.

By 1994, Dynamo were DM16 million in the red. When the team finished the Bundesliga season in last place, the DFB denied the club a licence for the second division and demoted it to regionalised amateur football. If Hansa Rostock hadn't clawed their way back up that year, Germany's top flight would have been an entirely western affair again. But even so the former GDR was quickly becoming a barren footballing wasteland, instead of the 'blooming landscapes' Chancellor Kohl had promised at the beginning of the decade. Most clubs had to make do with substandard squads who played in decrepit grounds and were watched by few fans, often in an atmosphere polluted by racism and the threat of violence. Meanwhile, across the western border that was no longer visible but still distinct, a boom was in full swing.

That boom would widen the divide between eastern and western clubs until it became a chasm. If you had opened a newspaper in the second half of 2013, shortly after the first all-German Champions League final, you would have found only nine clubs from the former GDR among the country's 56 more or less professional sides. And very many of them were teams most non-Germans had never heard of. You would have to turn a lot of pages to find familiar names such as Lokomotive Leipzig and 1. FC Magdeburg, then both in the fourth division.

Today, the situation has improved. One former *Oberliga* club is even in the Bundesliga, the idiosyncratic but very popular 1. FC Union Berlin. The former powerhouses Dresden and Magdeburg have stabilised, both financially and in footballing terms, and now oscillate between the second and third division. After 11 seasons at the third level, Hansa Rostock won promotion in 2021. And then there is Leipzig. The city currently has three teams in the upper regions of the league pyramid. All of them prove, each in its own way, how complicated football in the east was and can still be.

Consider that fourth-division Lokomotive Leipzig is not really the club of old by this name. The old Lok Leipzig changed its name to VfB Leipzig in 1991 to honour Germany's first national champions and demonstrate that the club saw itself in the tradition of this pre-GDR team. This new VfB Leipzig went into administration in 2004 and stopped competing in organised football. Which is why a number of fans formed a new club and called it, guess, Lokomotive Leipzig. This new Lok slowly climbed up the divisions and came very close to winning promotion to the 3. Liga (a third nationwide league created in 2008) in the chaotic COVID-19 summer of 2020. One year later, VfB's long-winded insolvency proceedings finally came to an end, allowing the team to merge with – are you still with me? – the new Lok to form a club that will probably be called 1. FC Lokomotive Leipzig VfB e.V.

The second Leipzig club that is doing rather well is Chemie Leipzig, also in the fourth division. However, this is not the two-time GDR champion but a team formed as recently as 1997. In 2021, this new Chemie could have been en route to winning promotion to the 3. Liga if the season hadn't been aborted on account of coronavirus when Chemie were in third place.

The third Leipzig club is, of course, playing in the Bundesliga. It fielded the second-best team in the land in 2017 and then again in 2021, when it also reached the Cup final. However, there are those who insist that this is not really a club from the east, a discussion we have to lead in a later chapter.

14

ROOM AT THE TOP

THE NINETIES BOOM AND ITS FALLOUT

GERMANY IS A ONE-SPORT country. We do not even have terms like 'summer game' and 'winter game', as this would somehow suggest there is a time of year when another sport takes over from football, which is a ludicrous idea. For the first eight decades of the 20th century, the only truly major German sports figure who was not a footballer was the cherished boxer Max Schmeling, world heavyweight champion from 1930 to 1932. In all the other events that most people consider 'major' – the golf and tennis grand slam tournaments, the Tour de France, the Formula One world championship – no German had ever won anything, while the footballers were among the world's elite.

And yet, even though it may test the imagination, there was a time when not a few experts thought football was finished as the be-all and end-all of German sport. As we have seen, the Bundesliga's average attendances hit a historic low during the 1985-86 season and this blow came at the worst possible moment for the game. In 1985, Bernhard Langer won the US Masters at Augusta. The same year, the swimmer Michael Gross captured the public's imagination by grabbing no fewer than six titles at the European Championship. And Boris Becker, only 17 years of age, won Wimbledon. Suddenly there were non-footballing sporting heroes wherever you looked, none more influential than young Becker, the Bayern Munich fan.

Becker's unexpected triumph sparked a tennis boom in Germany. In his wake there was Steffi Graf, who started her singular career with victory at the French Open in 1987. A year later, West Germany lifted the Davis Cup; in 1991, Michael Stich won Wimbledon. Kids all over the country threw away their football boots and took up racquets, while their parents began spending their evenings following five-hour-long clay-court matches played on the other side of the world. They could do this because television quickly discovered the new market and began to broadcast tennis in ever greater quantities. Ten years earlier, live coverage of the Wimbledon tournament would usually only start with the semi-finals; now I found myself watching Becker play Ivan Lendl in Indian Wells (wherever that was) at two o'clock in the morning, fielding phone calls from my aunt, a Schalke fan, who wanted to know under which circumstances players are allowed a second serve.

It was madness. By 1993, there was more tennis on television than football for the first (and only) time in history. Of course, the end was already in sight: there was no one to follow Becker and Graf and more and more viewers woke up in the morning, slumped in their chairs, the TV still on, wondering what had got into them. Still, make no mistake, tennis was a serious threat to football.

As late as 1993, the noted essayist Helmut Böttiger wrote: 'Tennis has superseded football as the central German sport. The cultural identity of Germans is about to change.' He then, almost pityingly, mentioned how Chancellor Kohl had fought to get a picture taken of himself and Diego Maradona at the

1986 World Cup, thinking that being associated with football greats was good publicity. 'In reality,' Böttinger said, 'nobody cared any more.'

Even though it is admittedly difficult to recognise a revolution when you are right smack in the middle of it, Böttiger should have known better. After all, he had just witnessed the pivotal 1991-92 season, whose events surpassed even the wildest imagination of the TV people who hoped football could be sold as gripping, prime time entertainment. He had also seen how the mightiest club in the land had been outdistanced in the first race for the fleshpots. It was goodbye Indian Wells, hello Champions League.

The seeds were already being sown in 1990-91. For the first time since 1984, the league title was won by a complete underdog – 1. FC Kaiserslautern. They managed to ward off Bayern, mainly thanks to their partisan crowd, which turned Kaiserslautern's ground (officially the Fritz-Walter-Stadion, more commonly known as the Betzenberg) into a bear pit. Countless visiting teams ran up an early lead there, then lost their cool during the final minutes, often because they noticed the referee had turned a bit pale and was adding on six or seven minutes of stoppage time. 'Games last for 90 minutes,' the saying went, 'except at Kaiserslautern. There, they last until the home team has won.' Perhaps because Udo Scholz, the flamboyant master over the stadium's PA, would sometimes intentionally announce a wrong minute for a substitution to lure the referee into believing there was something wrong with his clock.

A year later, for the first time in history, fans could watch league matches on a regular basis live on television, thanks to the subscription channel Premiere. Right on cue, 1991-92 evolved along lines not even the entertainment pros at the private TV stations would have dared to script. To begin with, Bayern disintegrated. It was the first year the club really started becoming

'FC Hollywood' – a headline-generating machine that was a dream come true for the tabloid press. As the on-field disasters piled up – six defeats in the first 14 games, a 4-2 Cup exit at home against Second Division Homburg and an ugly 6-2 defeat at Copenhagen in the UEFA Cup – bickering and in-fighting got out of hand. Jupp Heynckes was fired, his successor Sören Lerby lasted only five months, then Erich Ribbeck came in and guided the team to a ridiculous tenth place. So bad were things at Bayern that the club asked Franz Beckenbauer and Karl-Heinz Rummenigge to join the board of directors. Both were elected vice-presidents, but that didn't really steady the ship. On the contrary.

The title was fought out between three teams and not decided until four minutes from time on the last day of the season, when Guido Buchwald's header gave Stuttgart a 2-1 win at Leverkusen and pinched the championship from under the noses of the favourites Frankfurt and dark horses Dortmund. Yes, even to be in contention was something of an achievement for Dortmund. Only eight years after being practically bankrupt and only six years after avoiding relegation thanks to a goal deep into injury time, the tradition-laden club from the Ruhr had – not for the last time – miraculously managed to turn things around. The man most responsible for the team's great 1991-92 season was a former Stuttgart player who had had some success coaching in Switzerland but was virtually unknown in his home country: Ottmar Hitzfeld.

The drama of that season fuelled the football frenzy even more, coupled with the fact that Bayern's dominance appeared to have been broken for good. The club spent DM22 million on new players to prepare for 1992-93 and even brought Lothar Matthäus home from Italy, but it did them little good. Otto Rehhagel's Bremen won the championship and their business manager Willi Lemke hinted that the Bundesliga was no longer a 'Bayern versus the rest' league. 'We have now outstripped

Bayern in footballing terms, while Dortmund have done so financially,' he gloated.

And that was indeed the major repercussion of 1991-92. By finishing tenth, Bayern missed their turn at the trough on the first occasion that the TV stations handed out enormous amounts of money to cover European football. For the UEFA Cup ties involving German teams, a new (and short-lived) system was installed. All money would go into a pool from which clubs were to be paid depending on how far they made it. And thus Dortmund's second-place finish turned out to be a blessing in disguise. They reached the 1993 UEFA Cup final (losing to Juventus), but more important was that no other Bundesliga side even made it to the quarter-finals. From March on, all the money in the pool was pocketed by Dortmund – DM25 million in all.

Stuttgart, meanwhile, blew their chances of earning riches in the new Champions League. Christoph Daum's team won the first leg of the first round tie 3-0 against Leeds and lost the return match 4-1. That should have seen them through on away goals but Daum committed a serious blunder when he brought on a fourth foreigner at Elland Road. Normally, that meant automatic disqualification, but surprisingly UEFA settled on a play-off on neutral territory – a solution regarded as sensible in Stuttgart but scandalous everywhere else. Justice prevailed, the English side won and Stuttgart's 1992 title turned out to be a hollow triumph. Matthias Sammer had left for Italy and Daum's reputation at the club would never recover from the ill-fated substitution. He was given the boot in late 1993 and sought exile in Turkey.

Dortmund's new financial power meant they were now in a position to rival the salaries paid in Italy. They became the first German club to bring back German star players in large numbers. Stefan Reuter, Jürgen Kohler and Andreas Möller all joined them from Juventus between 1992 and 1994, Matthias Sammer was rescued from what he considered solitary confinement at Inter, Karl-Heinz Riedle returned from Lazio. In addition, Dortmund bought the Brazilian Julio Cesar and the Portugese Paulo Sousa, also from Juve. Such a collection of egos would have resulted in chaos at a club like Bayern, but Dortmund had Ottmar Hitzfeld, who was now regarded as the best man-manager in German football.

Dortmund's time had come. The club won two championships (1995 and 1996), the Champions League (1997) and even the Intercontinental Cup (the precursor of the Club World Cup). The balance of power within German football appeared to have been altered once and for all. Giants Bayern Munich had now hardly won anything domestically since the Wall had fallen. Their last Cup victory dated from 1986 and they had lifted only one league championship in six seasons. And they had brought it all upon themselves.

In the early 1990s, Bayern began making very debatable signings indeed. That's not to say that all of the people who joined them failed as footballers, as the Brazilian Bernardo did (signed for DM2 million in May 1991, loaned out in September, never to be seen again in Munich). Rather, quite a few of Bayern's prestigious transfers were found wanting when it came to questions of character, and many proved to be disruptive influences. There was, for instance, the narcissistic midfielder Stefan Effenberg, signed from Mönchengladbach. He joined Bayern in 1990, and then said: 'We will win the championship because the other teams are just too dumb.' He added: 'Kaiserslautern can only do throw-ins and corners' – then promptly proceeded to lose the title to precisely that club. In 1992, having won nothing, he went to Fiorentina together with his pal Brian Laudrup. In Italy,

Effenberg first lost Serie A status with his new club and then also a friendship, when he borrowed Laudrup's brand-new Mercedes SL without bothering to tell the owner about it.

Bayern's next *faux pas* was called Thomas Berthold. He came from Roma in 1991 but spent more time first in hospitals, then on golf courses, than at the training ground. He was called a malingerer behind his back, and Bayern's treasurer remarked bitterly: 'Berthold is one of the best-paid amateur golfers around.' Finally, Bayern banned him from the squad and Berthold watched an entire season from the stands. His role as trouble-maker was assumed by the eccentric Mario Basler. When Basler left Bremen, he claimed: 'Fifteen out of 20 players at this club are glad to see me go.' That ratio didn't improve at Bayern and after three troublesome years the club suspended him following a late-night brawl in a restaurant.

And yet all the capers indulged in by these men paled into insignificance compared to the damage done by a player Bayern re-signed in 1992: Lothar Matthäus. The Herzogenaurach boy led Germany to World Cup victory in Italy, was twice World Footballer of the Year and in 1990 even won an honour seldom handed out to soccer stars, World Sportsperson of the Year. But was he a revered icon in his home country? Never. Or at least not until the waning seasons of his active career, when he reinvented himself as a 38-year-old elder statesman who – importantly – kept his mouth shut.

Before that, Matthäus was known as 'the loudspeaker'. 'He has to get his two cents in even if we're only discussing the menu,' Erich Ribbeck moaned when he was Germany's assistant coach. Matthäus came across as an egomaniac with a penchant for the media spotlight. At the 1980 European Championship, when he was only 19, Matthäus and his girlfriend loved posing for the cameras, and Matthäus once said to her: 'Come on, Silvia, give me a French kiss for the photographers.' Also, and many people have forgotten this, for a very long time he wasn't regarded as a particularly impressive performer, only as an average if dogged defensive midfielder. When he left for Italy in 1988, the largest German weekly called him 'an ageing child star', suggesting a failed talent was seeking one last, fat cheque.

But at Inter, under coach Giovanni Trapattoni, he improved dramatically and finally broke through during Italia 90, at almost 30 years of age. In 1992, Matthäus damaged his cruciate ligament and Inter let him go back to Bayern, thinking his time was up. 'I used to be a big-mouth, but I'm a different person now,' Matthäus said on arriving in Munich (for once not speaking of himself in the third person), before going on to prove the opposite. He teamed up with a former Swiss beauty queen by the unlikely name of Lolita Morena, and their relationship kept the tabloids very busy indeed. Within a few months, he also made headlines with two tasteless altercations. At an airport, he leeringly invited a team of female basketball players to check out the physical credentials of his Colombian team-mate Adolfo Valencia, saying: 'The black guy has the biggest one of us all.' Then, at the Oktoberfest, he allegedly snarled at a Dutch tourist: 'Hitler must have overlooked you.'

One magazine characterised Matthäus as 'a child of our times: ambitious, assiduous, superficial, media-trained. But a complete professional.' Yet soon he also became quite unprofessional. When Jürgen Klinsmann – a baker's son with a heavy Swabian accent and yet the most cosmopolitan of all German players – signed for Bayern in 1995, he and Matthäus immediately became sworn enemies. The striker was probably merely annoyed at Matthäus's limitations, but Matthäus appeared to hate Klinsmann's guts, because he tore into his team-mate at every opportunity. Finally, his delusions of grandeur got so out of hand that he suggested he and Klinsmann should settle their dispute live on television. The national coach Berti Vogts was forced to intervene. He realised the Klinsmann–Matthäus strife was tearing Bayern apart, and did not want the same to happen to his national side. He banned Matthäus from Euro 96.

At first, that didn't stop the little Franconian. He continued to bark and boast, until his Bayern team-mates sent a fax from the German camp in England to Franz Beckenbauer, pleading with the Kaiser to make Matthäus shut up. Then, it seems, reality dawned on Matthäus. He'd got himself thrown out of the national team – the one side he'd always wanted to play for, no matter what the circumstances. For the remaining years of his playing career, he tried to stay out of the limelight and the papers as much as possible. Slowly, things calmed down at Bayern, and the club could concentrate on football again.

There were two reasons why Matthäus was allowed to go on his damaging rampage unrestrained. One was that Beckenbauer had had a soft spot for him ever since Italia 90 and took Matthäus under his protective wing. The other was that Bayern didn't find the right coach for the club's collection of hot-headed, mistrustful stars. And even if they hit upon one who could deal with the playing staff, there was still the matter of celebrities such as Beckenbauer (president since late 1994), Rummenigge and Hoeness meddling with squad affairs.

In 1995, Bayern even appointed Bremen's Otto Rehhagel. It was clear as daylight that the thin-skinned man who had been 'King Otto' up north would have problems working under a Kaiser and dealing with Munich's mad media, but the club were so desperate they closed their eyes and hoped for the best. Rehhagel lasted only 11 months, then Beckenbauer took over again and at least won the UEFA Cup. The Rehhagel disaster not only plunged Bayern further into crisis, but also castrated Werder Bremen. After nine top-five finishes in 13 years, Bremen were helpless without Rehhagel and sank like a stone.

In 1997, Jürgen Klinsmann finally got the championship he'd wanted so much when Bayern fought off new rivals

Leverkusen. But on the first day of the next season, Bayern met Rehhagel again, now coaching newly promoted Kaiserslautern. Surprisingly, Kaiserslautern won 1-0 at Bayern. Unbelievably, this victory would prove to make the difference that season, as Kaiserslautern lifted the 1998 title two points ahead of Bayern – the first and probably last time a promoted team pulled off this feat in Germany. Clearly, Bayern had to come up with a new plan, and they couldn't afford to make another mistake. They had now won only two championships in the 1990s, they had just been made to look silly by Rehhagel's collection of unknowns and veterans, and they could feel a new pursuer breathing down their necks – Leverkusen.

This highly unfashionable club had always had the backing of the Bayer pharmaceuticals company, but that had never secured them the league title they wanted so much, only a Cup victory in 1993. Even that was marred by the fact Leverkusen beat the much-loved outsiders Hertha BSC in the final in Berlin. Hertha's reserves, that is, or their 'amateurs', to use the football parlance of the time. Very few cheers went up when Ulf Kirsten, the prolific striker who was then seen as Gerd Müller's only true heir, celebrated his only trophy with a west German side.

Leverkusen were desperate for success and – perhaps even more – for acceptance. In 1993, they landed a major coup when they signed Germany's golden-boy-cum-black-sheep Bernd Schuster from Atlético Madrid. Bayer's go-getting business manager Reiner Calmund figured some glamour was badly needed, but he got more than he bargained for. Schuster arrived at Leverkusen with five fighting dogs, ten bodyguards, 15 horses and legs that were now 33 years old. For a while, he handled himself well (once scoring a famous goal from the halfway line), but during the 1995-96 season he came to blows with coach Erich Ribbeck. Finally, Ribbeck pencilled in the very slow midfield maestro as sweeper – with predictably awful results. While Leverkusen were edging nearer and nearer to the relegation zone, the Schuster strife became a full-blown scandal. The player was banned from the squad but won a court injunction that forced Leverkusen to allow him to train with the team.

One man watching all this in disbelief was Rudi Völler. He had been signed from Marseille in 1994, the idea being that he would see out his career at Leverkusen, then take over as director of football. That was fine with Völler, who wanted to return home because his daughter had just started school in Offenbach – and because he finally wanted a league title, something he had not managed at Bremen, Roma or Marseille (the French club finished top of the table in 1993, but were subsequently stripped of the title). Instead, he found himself in a nightmare situation. Leverkusen finished seventh in his first year, then seemed poised for the drop in his second. It was Völler's last season as a player, and on this farewell tour he received mammoth flower bouquets and thunderous applause wherever he went. Only points were hard to come by.

In what amounted to a relegation play-off, Leverkusen met Kaiserslautern, featuring Völler's fellow World Cup winner Andreas Brehme, on the last day of the season, with Bayer needing one point to stay up at the expense of the visitors. Kaiserslautern went ahead, but Leverkusen equalised nine minutes from time, sparing Völler the humiliation of finishing his career with a relegated side. After the final whistle, Völler and Brehme circled the ground, arm in arm, both men in tears.

That day – May 18, 1996 – was an interesting one. For as long as people cared to remember, there had been six fixed points in the Bundesliga: the four founder members Hamburg, Cologne, Frankfurt and Kaiserslautern, who had never been relegated from the league since its inception in 1963, plus Bayern and Mönchengladbach, who were considered honorary founders.

That's how it had been for over three decades – but now things were changing.

Frankfurt were relegated with Kaiserslautern and two years later the same fate befell Cologne. That left Hamburg as the sole survivor of the original old-guard quartet. Then, in 1998-99, the unthinkable also happened to Gladbach: on back-to-back weekends the once-proud club first conceded eight against neighbours Leverkusen, then seven at Wolfsburg. During the Netzer days Gladbach fans hardly knew these clubs even existed – now they were sending the Foals to the Second Division.

Some people argued that this upheaval was the much-feared and often-predicted outcome of the Bosman ruling and the fact that most of the money raining down on the league was siphoned off by a select few, big-city clubs. Ten years after the watershed 1985-86 season, average attendances had risen by well over 10,000 to 29,100 in 1996, and the 30,000 mark would soon be shattered. In 1999, Dortmund became the first club to draw over 60,000 people per game, thanks in part to the construction of the largest terrace in Europe, arguably the world (it holds almost 25,000). That same year, however, half of the league drew fewer than 27,000 per game. The gap between the haves and the have-nots was widening, ran the argument, and teams from smaller towns like Kaiserslautern and Gladbach would no longer be able to compete with clubs from big cities, or those that had the support of powerful companies.

Proof of this, it seemed, could be found in the rise of Hertha Berlin and VfL Wolfsburg. The former used to be habitually in financial trouble. It was so bad in the early 1990s that Hertha trained on a field owned by the British Army, which they had to vacate weeks prior to the annual polo tournament so as not to ruin the grass for the horses. Hertha spent large parts of the decade in the Second Division (in 1987 and 1988 they had even fought it out with Spandau, Tasmania 73 and Zehlendorf in the amateur Third Division), often in danger of being given the boot by the DFB for not adhering to their financial rules.

Then the marketing and TV rights company UFA (part of the Bertelsmann group) decided there was too much untapped potential to let Hertha rot. In 1994, UFA helped the club erase a DM4 million deficit in return for marketing rights, and two years later they granted the club another DM6 million to buy new players, followed by an additional DM9 million the season after. In order to protect this investment, UFA's managing director Rolf Schmidt-Holz joined Hertha's supervisory board, even briefly becoming its chairman. 'We don't make a secret of the fact,' he said, 'that in the long run we intend to make a profit from football.' In case you were wondering, 'we' meant UFA, not Hertha.

All of this sounded very bad to the ears of traditionalists. The situation was compounded when Hertha were promoted in 1997 with VfL Wolfsburg, a club previously considered to belong in the third division (they had played there from 1977 to 1992) but which was backed by the Volkswagen company, resident in Wolfsburg. In addition, Leverkusen – under new coach Christoph Daum – finished second in 1997 and would turn out to be long-term contenders. Soon, Uli Hoeness would say that, besides Leverkusen, he considered Hertha and Wolfsburg the most serious future threats to Bayern's supremacy because of their close ties with men who knew the marketplace. Leverkusen, Hertha and Wolfsburg! The first known as the 'pill makers', the second perennial laughingcstocks, the third a club that didn't even exist when Nuremberg had already been champions six times. By the way, where were Nuremberg? In the *Regionalliga* (third division), playing Bayern Munich Amateurs, that's where.

However, rash conclusions about how things will shape up are often just that – rash. As we have seen, Kaiserslautern came back from the Second Division to deny Bayern. Frankfurt, Cologne and Gladbach would return too. As would, in 2001, Nuremberg. Then there was Freiburg. Operating on a shoestring budget in a small city with a small ground (its capacity was marginally increased to 25,000 in 1999), the club held its own all through the 1990s and into the new century. Led by a highly admired coach, Volker Finke, and a president who was so invisible he wasn't even seen at the ground (the late Achim Stocker used to follow his team via teletext to ease the strain on his nerves), Freiburg made a trademark of churning out promising youngsters and playing fluent, technically accomplished football – actually, they do it to this day, even though Finke left in 2007.

Or what about the word that struck terror into so many hearts – Unterhaching? This club from a town so close to Munich that it's almost a suburb was promoted to the Bundesliga in 1999, playing in a ground that held 15,000 to the sounds of a Bavarian marching band, with a squad that included only three foreigners and only two players anyone had ever heard of (the 33-year-old Ludwig Kögl and an Albanian international, Altin Rraklli).

So, were the combined effects of Bosman and TV money really making the Bundesliga a two-tier league, divided into the rich and the rabble? Perhaps not. Freiburg proved (and continue to do) that you can compete if you do your job well. What has changed is probably the margin for error in the lower regions. Dortmund could afford to sign Thomas Hässler and then decide he was past it, while the Freiburgs and even the Kaiserslauterns had to make doubly sure they did the right thing.

But has it ever been different? In the 1960s, big and famous clubs like Dortmund, Nuremberg and Hamburg slowly but steadily went under, while newcomers like Bayern and Gladbach collected the silverware. For most of the 1970s, the Bundesliga looked like today's Primera División, in which only two teams battle it out, and during the 1980s it was sometimes even three-tiered: Bayern, one temporary challenger, the other 16.

What was indeed new during the 1990s was that it became hard to tell who would rise and who would sink. Freiburg jumped to third, then were relegated two years later. Kaiserslautern were promoted, won the title, then barely qualified for Europe. Dortmund were fourth in 1999, then almost got relegated the following season. Schalke slumped to 13th place in 2000, then jumped straight back into contention.

Put differently, during most of the 1990s things moved so fast that even Bayern Munich could no longer afford to make too many blunders with regard to their coaching and playing staffs. Finally, Bayern did something right and contacted Ottmar Hitzfeld. Hitzfeld had taken a year off after winning the Champions League with Dortmund in 1997, because pressure from the media, interference from above and the stress that came with keeping his stars under control had taken their toll. His hair was greying, his features were becoming haggard, his digestive system was a mess. But the sabbatical worked wonders, and the day Hitzfeld arrived at Bayern the club's fortunes took a radical turn for the better.

As if a fairy had brandished her magic wand, peace and harmony descended. Gone was not only the edgy atmosphere but also the defensive football first introduced at Bayern by the Hungarian Pal Csernai (1979-83) and carried to new extremes by Giovanni Trapattoni (1994-95 and 1996-97). Hitzfeld's team now delivered the attacking game Beckenbauer had always demanded, and they won the 1999 title by 15 points from Leverkusen.

With a good team, a great coach and a calm boardroom, Bayern could now be almost certain of success in the league and thus diverted their attention to the Holy Grail – the European Cup they hadn't won since 1976. On May 26, 1999, Bayern Munich met the team of Hitzfeld's friend Alex Ferguson in the Champions League final in Barcelona. Manchester United trailed to a Mario Basler free-kick, but, of course, two famous injury-time goals from Teddy Sheringham and Ole Gunnar Solskjær denied Bayern the cup known as Big Ears.

A fellow writer watched this final in a Cologne pub that was frequented by both Germans and Englishmen. 'It was weird,' he later told me. 'The Germans all rooted for Manchester, the English were all urging Bayern on!' It was natural, not weird, as Bayern were as unloved in their own country as Manchester United were in theirs. But the instant Ole Gunnar Solskjær scored the winner, the mood changed. It seemed too cruel to lose a match under such circumstances, even if the losers were Bayern. Also, after winning three European Cup finals they should have lost, the once lucky Bayern had now lost three they should have won. Hitzfeld took defeat in his stride, and the image of this gentlemanly coach congratulating Ferguson despite being hit so hard altered the picture some people had of Bayern as a club of cold egotists.

The wave of sympathy was large – but Bayern wasted little time fighting it back. It was almost as if the club relished its bad-guy image and did whatever it could to nip compassion in the bud. Because only two years after Barcelona, there were again cries of desperation that Bayern had a pact with the devil and that somebody must put an end to their lucky streak.

On the last day of the 1999-2000 season, Bayer Leverkusen needed only a draw at lowly Unterhaching to win their first championship. The visitors' 23-year-old midfielder Michael Ballack, newly acquired from Kaiserslautern for DM8 million, opened the scoring after 20 minutes. Unfortunately, it was an own goal and the team that had the title as good as wrapped up proceeded to lose 2-0. While a sad Christoph Daum hugged his inconsolable young son at Unterhaching's tiny Sportpark, Bayern were celebrating their 16th championship a few miles down the road. 'I'm sorry for Leverkusen,' said Uli Hoeness.

Daum answered: 'It would be nice if Hoeness really means this, but I don't think he does.' He was alluding to a statement from Hoeness that had deeply hurt everyone at Leverkusen. 'Daum will never in 100 years finish ahead of us,' Hoeness had said about Bayern's old foe.

Twelve months on, history almost repeated itself. Bayern played a nonchalant league campaign, losing an improbable nine matches, as they quite openly concentrated on Europe. With three games to go, Schalke were unexpectedly topping the table on goal difference, with Bayern second. Schalke then beat Wolfsburg, while an 87th-minute goal at Leverkusen kept Bayern in the race. A week later, both sides were drawing their matches – until injury time. Then Schalke conceded a goal and seconds later Bayern scored their winner. They now needed only a point from their last match at Hamburg, while Schalke had to beat Unterhaching and hope for a miracle.

It was May 19, 2001. Schalke fell behind 2-0 and 3-2, but they came back to win 5-3. Ninety seconds after Schalke's Danish striker Ebbe Sand had scored the fifth goal, Hamburg made it 1-0 against Bayern in the final minute of regular time. When Schalke's match finished, fireworks went off, thousands stormed the pitch and players and officials gave jubilant interviews, most with tears in their eyes. The famous club from the Ruhr had not won a national championship since 1958.

Meanwhile, four minutes into injury time in Hamburg, the home side's goalkeeper Mathias Schober – born near Gelsenkirchen and a fervent Schalke fan – picked up a back pass. Bayern were awarded an indirect free-kick in the Hamburg penalty area. Eight Hamburg players formed the wall, while Schober readied himself to spring forward and parry the shot. The referee indicated that this was going to be the last action of the game, and thus the whole season. Unmoved, Stefan Effenberg – who had rejoined Bayern in 1998 to finally win something – called up defender Patrik Andersson. Andersson had never scored for Bayern before. Yet Effenberg told him: 'Knock it in, and then we'll go home.' With that, he nudged the ball and Andersson knocked it in.

Four days later, Bayern also won the Champions League final against Valencia, despite falling behind early, despite missing a penalty after seven minutes and then two more in the shoot-out. However, most German fans watched the joyous celebrations unsmilingly. 'Had the Spanish been paying attention,' a Berlin paper commented with an air of resignation, 'they would have picked up their losers' medals straight away.' In Munich, people sensed that the nation only grudgingly respected Bayern's achievement and felt no reason to be happy about it. Sarcastically, a Munich paper lectured the other clubs: 'Bayern make the Bundesliga a bit more attractive, even if you wish them relegation. And if the league enjoys more prestige, that's also your prestige. The Bundesliga can't be as poor as it's judged if it produces Europe's best side.'

Typical Bayern arrogance, many thought, and they remembered the words of Leverkusen's goalkeeper Adam Matysek. Upon learning of Bayern's late equaliser at Hamburg, Matysek shrugged his shoulders and said: 'It's always the same load of crap.'

But crap or no crap, football was back as the undisputed king of German sport by the end of the 20th century. In 1994, Michael Schumacher became the first German to lift the Formula One world championship, three years later Jan Ullrich became the country's first Tour de France winner. Both events triggered off hysteria and intensified interest in motor sport and cycling. But there was no comparison with the mid-1980s tennis craze. As the 20th century's final whistle sounded, 56 per cent of all sport coverage on radio dealt with football, while no other sport even broke the six per cent barrier. And television? In 2001, a German subscribing to Premiere could watch every single Bundesliga match live. They could also watch every single Champions League match, no matter who was involved. Throw in six to seven live games on any given weekend from Spain, Italy, England, Austria and at times even Argentina, and following football had become a chore more time-consuming than even the most drawn-out five-set marathon on clay.

And all this while the Bundesliga was slowly but surely falling behind the other big leagues in Europe in terms of glamour, quality and especially success, as the Munich paper's remark about being judged to be poor indicates. In club football, the decline was gradual and not yet very pronounced as the new century began – when Bayern lifted the Champions League in 2001, few fans would have suspected that this would be the last European trophy won by a German team for more than ten years. However, it was a different matter as regards the national team. Around the turn of the century, Germany was having years you wouldn't wish on your most despised enemy. And worse was still to come.

15

INTO THE ABYSS

FROM DERWALL'S DISGRACE TO
THE DAUM AFFAIR – AND BEYOND

ACCORDING TO THE DFB's unwritten rules, Helmut Schön's successor in 1978 was his assistant, Jupp Derwall. Derwall would go on to have a better won-lost record that either of his legendary predecessors. He managed the team for two and a half years before first tasting defeat. His reign brought prestigious victories over old rivals Austria (four times) and new rivals Holland (twice). Less than 24 months after being made head coach, he won the European Championship, then he reached the final of the World Cup in 1982. In June 1984, his team was 90 seconds away from qualifying for the semi-finals of the European Championship in France. Then the Spaniard Antonio Maceda unexpectedly headed his side to victory. Immediately, the DFB did the unprecedented and unthinkable – they fired Jupp Derwall.

This, the bare skeleton of the Derwall saga, might lead the casual observer to believe that by 1984 the West Germans had become so cocky and sure of success that one unlucky defeat was enough to get the national coach the boot. However, this was not at all the case. The writer Norbert Seitz nicely summed up the core problem of the Derwall era with the line: 'Not every win is a gain.' Indeed, though non-Germans may be surprised by this, what Derwall, unknowingly, taught the country was that there are things that are more important than winning.

The spirit of the game, for instance. Who could ever forget the scandalous first-round match between West Germany and Austria at the 1982 World Cup in Spain? A narrow victory for the West Germans would have seen both sides through at the expense of Algeria, who had sensationally beaten a stilted West German side nine days earlier. Horst Hrubesch put West Germany ahead after 11 minutes, then Wolfgang Dremmler was denied by Friedl Koncilia in the Austrian goal, but from then on the match became an orgy of back passes and time wasting, as neither of the two teams made another serious attempt at goal. Some politely chose to dub the drama a 'non-alignment pact', but most observers didn't mince words. West Germany's largest tabloid spat *Shame on you!*, former international Willi Schulz labelled all 22 players 'gangsters' and the TV commentator covering the match, or whatever it was, lapsed into the murmur of a funeral speech. 'What's happening here is disgraceful and has nothing to do with football,' he whispered in a broken voice. 'You can say what you want, but not every end justifies every means.'

Still, that's exactly what the players and especially the coach claimed when confronted with the accusations from home. 'We wanted to progress, not play football,' said a shockingly unmoved Derwall, unwittingly offering a succinct explanation of what made him tick. Dremmler proved he was a true Bayern player by snapping: 'I can't worry about the prestige of German football. I'm a professional.' And Lothar Matthäus explained: 'We have gone through. That's all that counts.'

Only it wasn't. One of the World Cup books, published by a popular national newspaper, later proclaimed: 'This victory was worse than a defeat,' before going on to say: 'Money. It's only about money. Never before have German football fans been told with such insolent directness that they shouldn't really count on being offered matches worth seeing. That's not the object of the competition.' The fans were also told that their opinion didn't count for much in a more direct way. When German supporters gathered in front of the squad's hotel to get the team to justify themselves, the players threw water-filled balloons at them from the windows of their luxury suites. Many of these people had been following the national team for a long time, had become used to hearing praise for both the players' and the supporters' behaviour in 1966, 1970 and 1972 – and now this.

What came to be known as the 'Disgrace of Gijón' was the 170th international by Germany or West Germany that Richard Gaulke attended. The superfan from Monheim, near Cologne, was well-off but not rich, yet he followed the national team almost everywhere and was so well-known that he stayed in the team's hotel and called players or coaches by their first names. On the day after the Austria game, he kept telling anyone within earshot that he was 'upset, very upset' by what had happened. Later, the 67-year-old went to a restaurant called *Las Delicias*, a ten-minute drive from the hotel. He noticed a few reporters and joined their table. Richard Gaulke repeated he was upset. Then he turned blue in the face and collapsed. He was dead before the ambulance reached the hospital.

Maybe it's a good thing Gaulke didn't have to see the Spanish newspaper that referred to the match as *El Anschluss*, as if it was only expected of Germany and Austria to spitefully collaborate, as if no one in Europe had ever noticed how bitter the rivalry between these two countries was. Or should that be 'once was'? The Austrian Hans Krankl, who had gone bonkers four years earlier when his goals beat Germany, now shrugged off all complaints about his side not trying to score an equaliser: 'We made the next round. And I don't give a damn about the Germans.'

Two weeks after the scandal in Gijón, the West German side suddenly found themselves presented with a golden opportunity to make good. Their semi-final against France became one of the most exciting matches in World Cup history, as Derwall's men came back from a 3-1 deficit ten minutes into extra time to level the match with a fine bicycle kick from Klaus Fischer. Then they won on penalties. It was a lucky victory, but at least and at last the West Germans had been part of a game worth seeing. Did this pacify the angry fans and the seething journalists? No. The 1982 West German team were so resourceful they even managed to blemish their only courageous performance.

With 55 minutes gone, the score was 1-1. Michel Platini accelerated past three opponents and tried a shot at goal that cleared the bar by two or three yards. The ball was collected by the French fans, standing behind the goal of West German keeper Harald Schumacher. The fans were in a good mood, singing loudly, as their side was playing fluent football. They refused to give the ball back and the referee handed Schumacher a replacement ball for the goal-kick.

Schumacher carried the new ball back to the box, then suddenly pretended to throw it into the stands behind the goal. It was a strange gesture. The TV commentator let out a laugh and called the goalie 'a joker', obviously interpreting the move as meaning 'Do you want another ball?' The French fans weren't so sure. Some laughed, some cheered, but most felt there was an element of aggression about the gesture that was uncalled for. The goal-kick was taken to a chorus of boos.

Less than 60 seconds later, Platini played a wonderful chip that split the defence and set substitute Patrick Battiston free. The only two West Germans to react quickly were wing-back Manfred Kaltz and Schumacher. Both raced towards the point, a few steps outside the area, where the ball was going to land. But neither had any chance of beating Battiston to it.

Battiston had his eyes on the ball because he knew it was going to bounce and he couldn't afford to miss it. However, he must have briefly looked up to determine where Schumacher was, because when he made contact with the ball, he pushed it gently past the goalkeeper. It missed the post by a yard or so, but Battiston never saw that. The instant he touched the ball, everything went black.

Schumacher had never stopped charging, perhaps foolishly thinking he could reach the ball, maybe fearing he would be lobbed, probably not caring at all. In any case, he knew that a collision was inevitable, because just prior to crashing into Battiston he did a little jump and turned his upper body in order to ease the impact. Ease it for himself, that is, as the helpless Battiston was hit in the face by Schumacher's hipbone with full force, immediately going down unconscious. The TV commentator spoke of a 'terrible incident', but he also said that 'Schumacher had to risk everything, and these things can happen'. That's also how the goalkeeper himself has always viewed it. Even 15 years later, he said to me: 'Given the same circumstances, I'd do the same thing again. Believe it or not, I was really only trying to get to the ball.'

This might be true, but it misses the point. The problem was not that Schumacher had committed a foul, and an ugly one at that. He could always claim that from his point of view it was a 50/50 ball. The problem was not that Schumacher was not booked. (Today, such a foul warrants a red card, but in 1982 a yellow would have been more likely, especially at a tournament where Diego Maradona was kicked relentlessly.) The problem wasn't even that the French were forced to use up their substitutes.

The real problem was that Schumacher had added another, darker dimension to Matthäus's credo that going through was all that counted. He had accepted the possibility of severely injuring Battiston and regarded this as a professional attitude. Obviously, for this West German squad winning was the only thing that counted, and everything else – sportsmanship, conduct, reputation, expectations of fans – was nonsense from a forgotten era.

As Battiston was lying on the ground, with half a dozen team-mates around him who were beginning to fear for his life, Schumacher stood impassively at the edge of the six-yard box. His body language said: get the guy off the pitch so that I can take the goal-kick. When he later learned that Battiston had lost two teeth, he snapped: 'There's no compassion among professionals. Tell him I'll pay for the crowns.'

'It was arrogance taken to new extremes,' the writer Ludger Schulze notes in his history of the German national team. And the author Dietrich Schulze-Marmeling says that at this moment 'the image of the ugly German came back to life'. Well, it could still get worse. Because after West Germany had lost the final to Italy, the side returned home expecting to be hailed as the second best team in the world. Instead, the squad was met with frosty silence if not outright disgust. The rift between the team and the country it represented further deepened when Derwall let it be known he wouldn't accept any responsibility. He concocted a conspiracy theory that said the West German press had intentionally decided to spread 'negative coverage' and accused it of 'latent cruelty and treason'. He was now a man whose days on the job were numbered.

Only ten years after being repeatedly praised for both its conduct and its marvellous football, the West German team were playing badly, behaving worse and fast becoming lepers not only in foreign countries. The 1982 World Cup made a large number of fans who were at an impressionable age around that time lose interest in the national team and concentrate completely on club football. The 'club before country' attitude had always been widespread among Germans, a people rife with regional rather than national pride, especially after the war, when patriotism became a taboo. Now that stance was not merely widespread, it was the norm.

Who was to blame? Of course there were the players, who had quickly made Helmut Schön's portentous forecast a reality. The new men in white plainly only cared for themselves, with little regard even for their team-mates. During half-time of the 1982 final, Uli Stielike and Karl-Heinz Rummenigge engaged in a shouting match, and after the tournament Stuttgart's Klaus Allgöwer announced his international retirement, citing the disruptive influence of Paul Breitner as one reason.

Yes, Breitner was back in the side, talked into coming out of exile by Jupp Derwall. Derwall had done so because he felt there wasn't enough class available to him, but while it was true that West Germany no longer had quality in depth, the coach himself had done a lot to cut the supply. Even in the early 1980s, there were still a few West German players capable of playing aesthetically pleasing as well as effective football. Hamburg's Felix Magath, for instance, or Uli Stielike. The latter is not highly regarded outside of Germany and Madrid, but he used to be an imaginative midfielder at Gladbach, which was why Real signed him in 1977. In the national team, however, he was often pencilled in as sweeper despite his lack of pace, which forced him to interpret the role much more defensively than his predecessor Beckenbauer had done. Magath was even made to play on the left wing during the World Cup, though he was neither a dribbler nor a crosser.

And then there was Cologne's Bernd Schuster, arguably the most talented German player since Beckenbauer and Netzer. He was only 20 when he went to Italy for the 1980 European Championship. It was a dreadful tournament (dubbed 'a hideous disfigurement of football' in the official West German account), which the Germans won because they played two decent halves while no other team could produce more than one. The first came against Holland and brought three goals, all scored by Klaus Allofs, all involving Schuster. The second was in the final against Belgium, which they won 2-1, and it produced the first goal, made by Schuster again.

Young Schuster could have been the answer to many of West Germany's problems. So good was he that Barcelona came in with an offer only three months after the European Championship. Schuster had fallen out with his club coach and so the country's best prospect went abroad at a tender age indeed. Schuster stayed in Spain for 13 years, proving he feared nothing and nobody when he moved from Barça to Real Madrid – and then from Real to Atlético Madrid (the only other man who played for all three clubs is Miquel Soler). Later, the Spanish press voted him the best foreigner of the previous 25 years, ahead of Johan Cruyff.

Yet this unique talent played only 21 matches for his country. Admittedly, he was a difficult man to get along with, often rashly speaking his mind. He also stood out from his colleagues in that he preferred a quiet evening playing Bach on the piano with his wife Gaby to hanging out with his team-mates. This wife was a blonde beauty who would pose more or less naked for a men's magazine, but she was also a determined, clever wheeler-dealer who doubled as her husband's agent. All of which was too complicated and too unfamiliar for the other players, who shunned him, and for the national coach, who never learned how to handle him.

After a game between West Germany and Brazil in Stuttgart in May 1981, Hansi Müller invited the squad to his place for a housewarming party. The only player who did not attend was Schuster, who immediately went back to his hotel because he had to catch an early flight to Barcelona. In Müller's house meanwhile, Derwall got increasingly worked up over the fact that Schuster was the only member of the squad who wasn't there, socialising – and drinking – with the rest of the team. Late at night, the phone rang in the Schusters' hotel room, waking the couple. Gaby answered, listened for a while and then told her husband: 'It's Derwall. He's drunk.' The national coach said Schuster shouldn't bother about travelling to the next international and gave him a general, slurred mouthful.

From that day on, Schuster was no longer particularly interested in playing for the national team. For a time he made sporadic comebacks, if the fancy took him and he was fit. In 1986, Franz Beckenbauer even pleaded with him to play at the World Cup. The reply came from Gaby Schuster – and she wanted DM1 million for her husband's participation. It tells you something about how desperate the DFB was back then that president Hermann Neuberger – he of the DM70,000 offer in 1974 – actually asked Adidas to supply the money. Adi Dassler's son Horst told Neuberger to close the door on his way out.

And so a match with Belgium in February 1984 remained Schuster's last for Germany. He was then not yet 25 and just about to enter his prime. Less than four months later, the European Championship came round again, and this time it was an exhilarating tournament, but an uninspired West Germany did not come to the party. A few days after they were eliminated by Spain, Jupp Derwall was history. Officially, he stepped down, but it was an open secret that the German FA had at last broken with tradition and fired a national coach.

After that defeat by Spain, the French paper *Libération* wrote: 'German football, this brute animal, deserved to be drowned in its own urine.' That might have been a crude way of putting it, but it echoed a sentiment felt everywhere. The national team was caught in a downward spiral, morally bankrupt and shockingly sluggish on the pitch. Hermann Neuberger knew there was no way he could save Jupp Derwall's hide. He also knew there was no point in looking for a replacement among the DFB coaches. Men like Derwall's assistant Erich Ribbeck were encumbered with the shame of 1982 and had no credibility whatsoever. What he neeeded was a respected man from the outside, a role model.

Beckenbauer. Oh, how Neuberger would have loved to have him run the national team. Alas, the Kaiser had left everyone in no doubt he was not interested in coaching. In fact, after following the 1982 World Cup with the media, Beckenbauer had told everybody willing to listen: 'One of the things I realised was that I would never make a good coach.'

Neuberger's second choice was Helmut Benthaus, who had just won the Bundesliga title with Stuttgart. But Benthaus was on holiday in Canada and couldn't be reached. Also, he was under contract at his club. Then, on June 22, 1984, two days after the Spain game, Neuberger was given an unexpected lifeline. The country's largest tabloid *Bild* hit the newsstands with the headline *Franz: I am ready*.

'Franz', of course, was Beckenbauer, and he suddenly seemed to express an interest in taking care of business. The only person left in the cold about this new development was Beckenbauer himself. The newspaper article was pure fabrication, produced out of thin air by the paper's sports editor in co-operation with Beckenbauer's agent Robert Schwan, who figured that if he couldn't talk the Kaiser into becoming the national coach he could at least put so much public pressure on him that it would leave him no choice.

Neuberger and Beckenbauer met during the European Championship final and reached an agreement that the Kaiser would take over the team until Benthaus could get out of his contract. As it turned out, Stuttgart had a disastrous 1984-85 season, Benthaus went to Switzerland and Beckenbauer was there to stay, not the last time an interim coach unexpectedly became the national manager for good.

'At the time, my son asked me: "Dad, did you really have to do that?"' Beckenbauer later said. 'No, I didn't have to. If anything, I felt a moral obligation. Everything I had, I owed to football. But I didn't want to live from and through something that had lost its credibility.' Credibility was almost the only thing Beckenbauer brought to the job. Technically, he wasn't even allowed to train the team as he didn't have a coaching badge, so the DFB labelled him 'team supervisor' instead of 'national coach'. And this supervisor didn't have much of a team, either. 'I considered what I had seen in the Bundesliga,' he said a decade later, 'and I realised that there wasn't much apart from the proverbial German virtues: fighting spirit and solid defending. Nothing much was to be found in midfield, only Rudi Völler and Rummenigge for the attack. It really wasn't a lot.'

In Beckenbauer's opinion, there were no two ways about it. An early exit from the upcoming 1986 World Cup was all but guaranteed, the thing that counted was rebuilding for the future. He was also painfully direct about this. He openly admitted that the players in his squad were 'no artists, just reliable men, most of them blind'. ('Blind' is German football parlance for unimaginative.) One day, long after the tournament had ended, he sat in a hotel room doing a magazine interview. While giving his account of the 1986 World Cup and the performance of his players, he suddenly broke into fits of laughter. When the journalist asked why, the Kaiser said: 'Well, can you believe we reached the final of a World Cup with these players?'

Yes, it was unbelievable and yes, Beckenbauer's cast of blind men had done just that – through luck and the 'proverbial virtues' the coach had decided to rely on. Again they beat France in the semis, this time fair and square (Battiston gave away the free-kick from which Andreas Brehme opened the scoring) before succumbing to Maradona and the rest of the Argentina team. And even that was close. A Schumacher blunder and a marking error gave the South Americans a 2-0 lead.

But then, as if trying to defy their coach's opinion of them, the West Germans willed themselves into playing above their abilities. Rummenigge scored and then Völler equalised eight minutes from time. West Germany had now come back from two goals down in the final of a major championship for the third time – no other team had done this even once. (Even more extraordinary, as in 1958, they had reached the latter stages after trailing in each of their three group games – a feat also unmatched by any other country.)

Rightfully, Maradona decided the game with a fine pass that found Jorge Burruchaga, who pushed the ball past a vacillating Schumacher. Still, West Germans were content. The football had certainly not been great, but at least the team had not embarrassed the country again. Or not on a scale comparable to 1982. Because the 1986 campaign did have its share of unpleasant distractions.

Uli Stein was sent home from Mexico, after calling Beckenbauer a clown. The goalkeeper, angry that he wasn't playing, had become convinced there was a plot against players who didn't have endorsement contracts with the team's sponsors, Adidas. While this may seem a bit paranoid, Stein was certainly not the only member of the squad bearing a grudge. When Beckenbauer called Dieter Hoeness an 'idiot', the Bayern striker shot back: 'I know how well equipped I am upstairs and how well you are. You're not the one to call me an idiot.' Young Olaf Thon, realising he wouldn't get a game, said: 'I can't learn anything here. I want to go home.'

Beckenbauer himself frequently lost his temper when speaking to journalists and even his own press officer. On the evening before the final, Beckenbauer tendered his resignation to a stunned Neuberger, arguing he wasn't diplomatic enough to handle public relations. Probably it was just that Beckenbauer was still learning on the job, trying to find out how to discipline players and feed journalists, while keeping his impatience with both groups of people under control. He would never become as eloquent and composed as Schön had been, but he was learning fast.

And indeed, on a balmy summer evening four years later in Turin, a different Beckenbauer was standing on the sidelines, waiting for referee José Roberto Wright's final whistle. He now wore a suit, which signalled respectability had been added to credibility, and glasses, which hinted intellect was meeting competence. He was also almost unnaturally calm. When the match ended, Beckenbauer strolled over to the opposing coach, Bobby Robson. The two spoke for a moment, wishing each other luck for the lottery about to begin. Then they shook hands.

It was 1-1 after extra time between West Germany and England in the 1990 World Cup semi-final, and penalties now had to determine who was to meet Argentina in the final. The match was the closest and most evenly fought West Germany would play in the tournament, the two sides matching each other strike for strike, tackle for tackle. They even both hit the post once, but thanks to misses from Chris Waddle and Stuart Pearce in the shoot-out, it was the Germans who went through.

Beckenbauer's new-look team was brimming with talented players such as the naturally exuberant Jürgen Klinsmann, Rudi Völler and Karl-Heinz Riedle. It boasted a surplus of flair players, such as Uwe Bein, Thomas Hässler, Pierre Littbarski and Andreas Möller; and there were no-nonsense, dynamic craftsmen such as

Jürgen Kohler, Klaus Augenthaler and Lothar Matthäus. It was, plainly, the best team at a tournament which, also plainly, was full of sub-par sides lacking either talent, nerve or team spirit.

That said, West Germany's campaign was unusual in that the team did not improve during the course of the tournament, as they used to do. After putting 12 goals past Yugoslavia, Colombia, the United Arab Emirates and Holland, the Germans failed to score more than one goal in any of their last three matches, and none of them came from open play. This probably had to do with the nature of the whole World Cup: most sides apparently decided they were so bad they had to shut up shop and hope for penalties.

In the final, Argentina put everybody behind the ball, and when that didn't work well enough, they played it dirty. On 65 minutes, Pedro Monzón was sent off for bringing down Klinsmann. It was a foul, no doubt about that, but the Swabian made the most of it – which gave him a reputation as a diver and would lead to a memorable press conference at White Hart Lane.

The West Germans were so much in command even their defenders took their turn to squander chances. Guido Buchwald was cynically cut down in the box, but the referee Edgardo Méndez waved play on. Five minutes from time, Rudi Völler half-dived, half-stumbled in the area, and this time Méndez pointed to the spot (he'd probably had enough of the match).

Lothar Matthäus was the designated penalty taker, but – there's German planning for you – he had to change the boot on his favoured right foot during the interval and felt uncomfortable in it. So Brehme stepped up and placed the ball just inches inside the post. As the team paraded the trophy around the ground, Franz Beckenbauer silently walked across the pitch, hands in his pockets, the shiny medal dangling from his neck. He seemed completely oblivious to the tumult around him, a man at peace with himself. He was no longer the centre of attention but a sympathetic yet detached bystander. That's because he felt the team had won the match, not Franz Beckenbauer. It was also because he knew it was his last night in charge of the national team and he had managed to go out on the highest note you can possibly strike.

During the minutes he circled the lush Rome grass lost in thought, Franz Beckenbauer looked like a man deserving of the name 'Kaiser', a gentleman worthy of having held in trust Helmut Schön's heritage. The next day, he was the unpredictable, cheeky Beckenbauer again, the coach who would call his players 'blind' to their faces and who would later, as club president, term Bayern's teams 'pub sides' or 'full of players with feet of lead'. At the press conference, his tongue was too fast again, and he said: 'I'm sorry for the other countries, but now that we will be able to incorporate all the great players from the East, the German team will be unbeatable for a long time to come.'

This famous, and famously stupid, prediction put unnecessary pressure on Beckenbauer's successor, a man who would have had a hard time following the Kaiser's example even without such bragging parting shots. His name was Berti Vogts, and only 11 months after the World Cup final his Germany team lost at home – to Wales. The 'long time' was over in a hurry.

Berti Vogts's period of service was at least as turbulent and controversial as that of his fellow Rhinelander Jupp Derwall – probably more so. Both men preferred a comradely approach in dealing with their players and were to pay for that with disciplinary problems that often undermined team spirit. Both were under the misconception that being a football manager was mainly about sport, thus they turned out to be complete failures in the public relations department and grew increasingly thin-skinned when questioned by the media.

Helmut Schön had always lived by Herberger's maxim that ultimately the coach was responsible for whatever happened.

Beckenbauer had updated this concept by pointing out that, at least every once in a while, players have a hand in things, too. Derwall and Vogts, however, seldom allowed themselves or their squads to be criticised. Instead they tended to pass the buck and blame outside forces – the press, society at large, referees, FIFA. And so Derwall and Vogts had very little going for them. However, there was one big difference between the two: Derwall at least got results.

The two World Cups Germany participated in under Vogts, USA 94 and France 98, were embarrassing affairs marked by bad football and appalling behaviour. In 1994, Germany almost blew a 3-0 lead against South Korea, mindlessly belting the ball away after being pulled back to 3-2. Fifteen minutes from time, Vogts took Stefan Effenberg off the field and brought on the defensively more solid Thomas Helmer. As Effenberg walked off the pitch, the German fans loudly cheered his substitution and the player gave them the finger in response.

It wasn't such a dramatic gesture. After all, Beckenbauer had spat in the direction of the supporters in 1974 without serious consequences. But the new DFB president Egidius Braun was a man who often seemed to value the example set by the players and the social responsibility of the DFB higher than results and standings. 'Many fans from Germany paid a lot of money to follow us in the US,' Braun said. 'And there are many German-born Americans who may never have the chance to see Germany play again. There is no excuse for insulting these people.' Effenberg was ordered to pack his bags and leave the continent immediately. 'For as long as I'm coaching this team,' Vogts insisted, 'Effenberg will not play for Germany again.' Two weeks later, his team were beaten by Bulgaria in the quarter-finals. It was Germany's earliest exit from a World Cup since 1962.

Four years on, it was Vogts himself who caused discomfort at home. Germany were eliminated from France 98 by Croatia, again in the quarter-finals. The match was open, with the Germans delivering one of their better performances, until Christian Wörns was sent off for a blatant and nasty foul on Davor Suker. No German journalist covering the match, whether for television, radio or print, found anything wrong with the referee's decision.

The players thought differently. Wörns called Suker 'an actor', the sending-off 'a joke' and the Croats' style of play 'provocative'. Vogts, however, surpassed everyone. He hinted the referee had acted under 'orders from above', muttering something about the Germans 'having been too successful in the past'. Disgusted by this lack of sportsmanship, the most influential German tabloid, *Bild*, urged Vogts in a headline to *Stop whining!* and called for his head. Even the reserved *kicker* bemoaned the squad's 'petty and paltry' behaviour.

It is sometimes claimed that Vogts's biggest drawback was that he simply lacked Beckenbauer's Midas touch, and that he was unlucky. A book published for the German FA's centenary cites as an example that Vogts 'reached second place at the 1992 European Championship in Sweden, yet there was much more malice than applause. That was because the title was won by the Danes, who were only allowed to play in the finals because Yugoslavia had been excluded for political reasons, and who arrived straight from their summer vacations, having supposedly trained on fast food during their brief preparation.'

What this account fails to point out is that Germany were lucky to even have survived the group stage – they lost 3-1 to Holland and drew with the CIS (as the disintegrating Soviet Union was briefly known) only thanks to a goal in stoppage time. In other words: for the third time in ten years the team had made a final without earning it. That was what really triggered the malice.

Even the argument that Vogts was the right man at the wrong time, taking over the team just as German football began to suffer from long-overlooked structural problems, is not entirely convincing. It's true that there was very little young talent coming through during Vogts's reign, but he himself had secretly predicted exactly that during his time as the DFB's main youth coach back in the 1980s. Not only had he failed to inform the public that some dire years might lie ahead, as Beckenbauer had once done, he also did very little to correct the problem – until shortly before his reign ended, as we shall see. Instead of going with hungry hearts and young if limited legs, he relied on the 1990 stalwarts who were beyond their peak and would never again surprise any opponent. The side he took to France 98 was still built around Jürgen Kohler, Thomas Hässler and Jürgen Klinsmann. As if it wasn't enough to have the pundits ridicule the squad as 'Jurassic Park', Vogts then lifted his ban on Lothar Matthäus, the very ban which had had such a morale-boosting effect in 1996. The 37-year-old Matthäus laboured across the pitches of Lens and Montpellier, until arriving in Lyon, where he gave the ball away to Suker, who then ran past Wörns. Or tried to.

Vogts's excuse for rebuilding only hesitantly was so obvious he didn't even have to state it. Between 1966 and 1992, Germany had reached the final of five World Cups and four European Championships. Consequently, expectations were high, and not only those of fans, writers or officials. Every new national coach felt the pressure, unspoken or voiced, to do at least as well as his predecessor. And if that predecessor was Franz Beckenbauer, no longer simply called 'the 'Kaiser' but 'the shining light of German football', well, let's just say it would be useful to win some silverware pretty quickly. It would not be the last time that a national coach felt under so much pressure that he delayed doing the inevitable until it was almost too late.

This curse of success also played a role in forestalling the development of new talent, because it's human nature to avoid change, especially when you don't see the need to change. And for a long time, German football didn't see it. As late as 1997, two Bundesliga clubs held both European trophies (Dortmund the Champions League, Schalke the UEFA Cup) while the national team was officially the best on the continent. And despite the tennis boom, still large numbers of kids joined football clubs. In a big country like Germany, people were confident that enough of these kids would turn into stars, the way they had always done. Only, they didn't.

Something had indeed changed – the game. The 'proverbial virtues' that had carried Germany through so many crises in the past – fitness, organisation, self-belief – no longer made the difference, because the world had caught up. Organisation and discipline was no longer a German speciality, it was everyone's bedrock. Germany had missed the bus, probably thinking it was the driver's duty to wait, not theirs to hurry up. While other nations moved forward and attempted to improve, the Germans firmly sat on their laurels and kept on doing what they had always done. This was particularly conspicuous in youth football, where the smaller clubs kept feeding the bigger ones with 14- and 15-year-olds who knew how to win games – be resilient, don't try anything fancy, make the best kid sweeper – but who couldn't play.

Indeed, the sweeper system Germany had been playing for almost a quarter of a century proved to be a particularly potent stumbling block. In the late 1990s, it was still de rigueur at almost every club, from the battle-scarred seniors down to the rosy-cheeked beginners. There is nothing inherently wrong with the system. In fact, you could argue it's theoretically the most flexible formation for a team. A good defence built around a talented sweeper can quickly react to what's happening during a match. If the team is under pressure, the sweeper may play behind the full-backs. If attack is the order of the day, he may move in front, utilising the channels opening up in midfield.

The sweeper may also decide to form a flat back three with the other central defenders, to orchestrate an offside trap or have his team move upfield to deny space to the opposition.

The problem is, that's an awful lot to ask of just one man. The system works best when the sweeper is nothing short of superhuman – quick on his feet and in his head, technically gifted yet fearless, at least useful in the air and good at tackling, someone who not only reads the game perfectly but then knows how to process this information and react accordingly. Oh yes, and he also has to be a leader of men.

There have been players who could do all these things, or most of them. Franz Beckenbauer, Italy's Franco Baresi, Holland's Danny Blind. But they don't grow on trees, not even in a country as densely wooded as Germany. And so the question 'Who is our sweeper?' has tortured every national coach since Beckenbauer hung up his boots. Helmut Schön tried Manfred Kaltz and, in desperation, even Bochum's Franz-Josef Tenhagen and Georg Schwarzenbeck. Derwall tried Cologne's Bernd Cullmann and Uli Stielike, besides half a dozen others, then even Rainer Bonhof and Stuttgart's Bernd Förster. Beckenbauer tried Matthias Herget and Holger Fach (both from Uerdingen), then even Thomas Berthold. Finally, he settled on Klaus Augenthaler, hoping for the best.

And Vogts? In 1998, he was so desperate, having lost all his potential sweepers to injuries, that he made a pilgrimage to Canossa (Munich) to make up with Matthäus and have him sweep up at the World Cup. It was the beginning of the end for the national coach. Derwall, Beckenbauer and Vogts all toyed, at one time or another, with the idea of abandoning the sweeper system in favour of a flat back four. They were all knowledgeable enough to realise that the liberos available to them were first and foremost defenders, uncomfortable on the ball. Asking such men to build from the rear either invited disaster or slowed the game down, because it forced the creative midfielders to fall back and carry the ball upfield themselves. But in the end, two things prevented the national coaches from making radical changes.

First, the system had proved successful in the past, and not only Germans are notoriously averse to altering their habits. Second, the flat back threes and fours that became the latest rage in international football after Italia 90 demanded that you have defenders who could think, plan and act on their own – without the help of a father figure called sweeper. Such independent-minded players were not common, however, as every young German player had come up through youth teams built around a tall, commanding kid reverently known as 'the last man'.

And one other thing happened that tricked Germany into thinking everything was still OK, further slowing down the inevitable process of restructuring. Berti Vogts, widely regarded as luckless, happened upon a final ace up his sleeve.

In October 1993, Matthias Sammer was the man anchoring Dortmund's midfield, asked to do everything because he seemingly could: close the gaps, set up the strikers, score himself. Then the club's sweeper, the Australian Ned Zelic, succumbed to one of his many injuries, and coach Ottmar Hitzfeld asked Sammer if he'd be willing to play a game or two in that position. Sammer quickly became the best sweeper the country had had since Beckenbauer. In some respects he was even better than the Kaiser, because while he lacked Beckenbauer's elegance and finesse, he brought a fiery determination to the job, complemented by a readiness to take risks.

There was a day in September 1995, when Dortmund were running into problems against Eintracht Frankfurt. Sammer looked over to the bench to make eye contact with Hitzfeld, trying to get his approval to shake things up. Hitzfeld knew Sammer's judgment was excellent, so he just nodded. From that moment on, Sammer was all over the pitch, forsaking his role in defence for that of a quasi-playmaker. His team conceded three that day, but they scored four.

At that time, Sammer was not yet the Germany sweeper, as this role had fallen to Matthäus. Sammer played in midfield during the 1994 World Cup, and he was so good that some pundits claimed Germany were only eliminated because he had to sit out the Bulgaria match with a calf problem. As had been the case at Dortmund, it took an injury to the regular sweeper to make the coach try something new.

In January 1995, Lothar Matthäus tore his achilles tendon. Vogts pencilled in Sammer as libero for a Euro 96 qualifier in Sofia, the much-anticipated clash with Bulgaria. Again Germany lost, 3-2. But everyone who saw the game was thrilled by how well they had played. The team then won nine out of ten, including a 2-0 win over Italy, a 3-1 victory in the return match against Bulgaria and a 1-0 defeat of Holland in Rotterdam. When Matthäus was fit again, in November 1995, he had lost his place in the side to a better player and a man more beneficial to team spirit. Vogts could afford not to pick Matthäus and then, when the player protested in vitriolic terms, to ban him outright. Germany were ready for Euro 96.

It would be Vogts's tournament, his sole moment of glory, as much as Sammer's. The coach made all the right decisions at the right moments. Sometimes, as in the case of Oliver Bierhoff, with a little help. The old-fashioned target man had made his international debut only some four months prior to Euro 96, having broken through at Italy's Udinese surprisingly late in his career (he was 27 at the time). Vogts was unsure whether or not he should include Bierhoff in the squad, until his wife told him: 'Take him along. He'll repay you.'

Vogts's biggest contribution to his side's success at Euro 96 was that he managed to create team spirit. His dismissal of Matthäus and his constant repeating of the phrase 'There are no stars; the team is the star' kept the players relaxed and made them a close unit, in the face of seemingly endless misfortune. Kohler was badly injured a mere 15 minutes into the tournament, then Mario Basler, Fredi Bobic and Jürgen Klinsmann were sidelined. Finally, Steffen Freund tore his cruciate ligament in the semi-final, while Möller and Reuter were booked for the second time and thus suspended for the final. Things were so bad that Vogts nominated his two reserve goalkeepers as outfield players and was forced to contest the final with four men who were clearly not fit.

Yet the Germans did not complain. They didn't blame higher forces, referees or their opponents, instead accepting the blows fate had dealt them and getting on with business. Which was probably due to the presence of Sammer and Klinsmann, both possessed of an almost eerie fighting spirit, both consummate professionals and complete team players. Sammer in particular rose to the occasion and carried the team. Whenever Germany got into trouble, he stepped up a gear and did more than was asked of him. He broke the deadlock against Russia after an hour, when he suddenly appeared in the opponents' penalty area, got on the end of a Möller pass and scored Germany's crucial first goal. It virtually secured the team's passage into the next round – where Sammer netted again, this time the winner against Croatia in a bad-tempered quarter-final. And that set up the most dramatic match of the tournament, against England.

After Alan Shearer had put England ahead after only three minutes, Sammer had his hands full shoring up the backline, but he was so successful at it that full-back Thomas Helmer found the time to race upfield with a quarter of an hour gone. He laid the ball off to Stefan Kuntz, who equalised. Some observers would later claim that this goal planted doubt in the minds of the English players, as if they were suffering from a complex about playing Germany, borne out of too many defeats in vital matches over the past 26 years.

This idea probably sprang from the pre-match coverage in the English tabloids. Their prevalent usage of war imagery, to be found in tasteless headlines full of words such as 'Blitzkrieg', 'Kraut' and 'tanks', at first deeply irritated the Germans. They seemed baffled by the notion this was not just a game of football but something harking back 50 or more years. Six years before Euro 96, Franz Beckenbauer had remarked: 'I have always wondered why people read so many different aspects into a football match. In England, war correspondents seem to get their say whenever their team plays us.' Since then, it seemed, things had only got worse. The largest German political weekly, *Der Spiegel*, was not even angry at the choice of words to be found in England's tabloids, just dumbfounded: 'Compared to the *Sun*,' it said, 'our *Bild* newspaper is almost a herald of sophisticated disposition.'

The interesting thing about this scenario was that, from a German viewpoint, there was hardly any rivalry between the two teams (let alone the countries). 'Germany v England is something special,' Stefan Reuter once remarked, 'because both teams have a lot of tradition, and often there's a lot at stake. But it's not a rivalry, no way.' To the Germans, playing England was like playing Italy or Brazil – prestigious, high-profile games, but nothing to get all fired up about. The fact that the English appeared to nurture feelings of resentment either because of the war or because of Germany's many (and often lucky) triumphs, didn't make much difference. After all, almost every other European country also had reasons to feel like that, and did.

If the Germans had, in footballing terms, a true 'rival', it was by now Holland, and even that had started out as a pretty one-sided affair. After Cruyff's side lost the 1974 World Cup final to Beckenbauer's team, there was no true animosity between the players or the fans. Wim van Hanegem didn't attend the after-match banquet, explaining 'I don't like Germans', but he was an exception. During the following decades, however, matches between the two countries grew increasingly heated and emotionally charged with each passing year. The instigators, it has to be said, were the Dutch. As Simon Kuper noted in *Football Against the Enemy*: 'The Dutch hysteria rather bewilders the Germans.'

The two sides met again at the 1978 World Cup, when – as mentioned – Nanninga and Hölzenbein almost came to blows. Two years later, during Euro 80, the official tournament book made out 'a curious aversion' characterising the match between Holland and Germany, while Karl-Heinz Rummenigge complained of Dutch 'roughness, sometimes going beyond what is permissible'. Johnny Rep hit Harald Schumacher in the stomach, according to the goalkeeper. In 1988, a late Marco van Basten goal put West Germany out of the European Championship on home turf. 'It wasn't just football,' said Holland's coach Rinus Michels, 'it was also a quarrel and a fight.' Still, Hermann Neuberger said: 'The better team won.' And Michels stated: 'Now we can stop talking about 1974. This was our revenge, and we have won.'

Only it wasn't 1974 that was the problem. In his book on Dutch football, *Brilliant Orange*, David Winner says: 'Over the following years, the intricate crossover between football- and war-related feelings shaded into something much darker. Ronald Koeman admitted he had used as toilet paper the shirt he had swapped with Olaf Thon. When Holland and Germany met in Rotterdam in 1989, a Dutch banner scandalously compared Lothar Matthäus to Adolf Hitler.'

Now the Germans were getting a bit restless themselves. If the English wanted to get all gung-ho, then so be it. But the Dutch were too close to home. Besides, the English would never

go as far as showing their contempt by spitting at Germans, as
Frank Rijkaard did during the 1990 World Cup. Within less
than two minutes, he did so three times at Rudi Völler – twice
on the pitch and a third time as both men left the field having
seen red cards (in Völler's case, for nothing). Actually, there's no
indication that Rijkaard's act was motivated by anti-German
feelings. He knew Völler from Italy, and both men respected
each other. Five months later, when Milan played Roma,
Rijkaard apologised and said he'd lost his head, explaining he'd
been under emotional pressure, having separated from his wife
shortly before the World Cup.

That, however, was lost on most German fans. A Dutchman
had spat at a German (and at the one who was almost impossible
to dislike despite his hairdo), which could mean only one
thing: it was the war and the Nazis and Hitler all over again.
That Germany managed to win this game, largely thanks to a
courageous performance from Jürgen Klinsmann, was sweet
indeed and would see to it that the match now ranks as the
most memorable since Wembley 1972 in German football lore.
But it left a sour taste. Games between Germany and Holland
had clearly degenerated into something that only marginally
concerned football. And that, of course, was an invitation to the
hard core of mindless German neo-Nazi hooligans to enter the
fray. From then on, there was bad blood on the pitch, very literal
blood off it.

Yet on that mild evening in June 1996, the Germans were not
facing their true rivals Holland, just classic opponents England.
Having equalised through Kuntz's stab, they would now play
the rest of the game with cool heads and clear minds, leaving
all that emotional fuss to their opponents, until the English got
too keen on winning or too afraid of losing. That was the theory,
and though it was a desperately close-run thing, Germany's win
on penalties did indeed seem to confirm that the football world

352

still played more or less by their rules, even with Berti Vogts in charge. Four days later, Germany beat the Czech Republic in the final. As always, they fell behind 1-0, but 20 minutes from time Vogts brought on Oliver Bierhoff. He repaid his coach by first levelling the match, then scoring the golden goal five minutes into extra time.

In the weeks following the final, Matthias Sammer would win a lot of trophies – he was voted Footballer of the Year both in Germany and the whole of Europe – but what he needed most he couldn't get: his physical health. In August 1996, he underwent surgery to correct a knee problem. It was the start of an agonising series of failed comeback attempts and more operations, one of which resulted in a disastrous bacterial infection. After Euro 96, Sammer played only 19 more league games for his club, and four more internationals. In July 2000 he officially retired and became head coach at Borussia Dortmund. He was only 32.

Two years after being crowned the best team at Euro 96, Germany were the most disappointing team at the World Cup. Another two years on, and they were arguably the worst team that showed up for the European Championship in Holland and Belgium. Had the international game ever witnessed a faster or more spectacular crash to earth up to that point? France may come to mind. They won the 1984 European Championship and came third at the 1986 World Cup, then failed even to qualify for the next two major tournaments. But the French were always known as a side that had its ups and downs, not as one of the nations that always did reasonably well, like Brazil, Italy – or Germany.

Germany's downfall, then, was by and large unprecedented, which may explain why it quickly went beyond the national team, plunging the whole of German football into a crisis whose characteristics were strangely un-German: disorganisation, lack of professionalism, self-doubt and frantic activity of the headless chicken variety. It was much worse than it had been even under Derwall, probably because the traditionally slow-moving DFB had misread or ignored both the writing on the wall and the signs of the times. Then, when decisions could be put off no longer, there were too many to make about too many different things.

During the 1998 World Cup, German thugs ran riot in the streets of Lens, beating and kicking a French policeman, Daniel Nivel, to within an inch of his life. Egidius Braun was horrified and discussed the idea of withdrawing the team from the competition with his fellow officials. When Vogts learned about this – not from Braun himself, it appears – he threatened to resign immediately. Braun stuck with Vogts, but in the light of later events he would have done the reputation of German football more good had he followed his initial instincts.

When Germany went out against Croatia with such bad grace, a German paper printed a resignation letter, asking Vogts just to sign it and go home. It was a bit like 1984 all over again, but Braun was no Neuberger. Such impertinence from the press made him only more determined to close ranks around the coach. Yet the ranks had already come unstuck and the general was in a state of panic. Vogts completely lost his head, begging Stefan Effenberg to come back (the second time he had recalled a man 'banned for life') and declaring he would at long last abolish the sweeper system.

Germany played with a flat back four for exactly 45 minutes. It was the first half of a friendly with Malta. During the interval, with the score 1-1, Vogts abandoned the new system and Germany went on to win 2-1. Three days later, they were outclassed by Romania, escaping with a lucky draw. Effenberg performed like a man whose mind was on something else, and during the following week he suddenly declared his resignation from international football, saying he needed 'more time with the family'. It was a slap in the face for Vogts and he did the only thing he could do – he grabbed his coat.

At the same time, the DFB was preparing for a general meeting that was to bring far-reaching reforms. The commercialism of the 1990s had left the governing body little choice but to break with a century-old tradition. Clubs would finally be allowed to become limited companies by detaching their professional football division from the parent organisation and turning it into a fully fledged business. (Prompting Bayern Munich to delete the antiquated abbreviation 'e.V.' from their badge.) This in turn made it possible to float clubs on the stock market, and only two years later Borussia Dortmund would become the first German club to do just that. Yet the DFB gamely tried to formulate a rule preventing rich individuals or conglomerates from buying and selling clubs as if they were merely an object of speculation. The officials were working on a statute designed to ensure that 50 per cent of a plc's voting shares plus one share had to remain with the parent club (the so-called '50+1' rule, more about which in the next chapters), when suddenly their attention was diverted to Vogts and the national team.

Now it was Braun's turn to panic. He began what one newspaper later labelled 'a grotesque win-a-manager tombola' by apparently phoning everyone whose name he found in his notebook. For the first but not the last time, every German coach with any kind of reputation – Christoph Daum, Jupp Heynckes, Ottmar Hitzfeld and Otto Rehhagel – was under contract and/ or unwilling to become the captain of a sinking ship. So Braun phoned the Englishman Roy Hodgson, offering him the job. A day later, he called again and told Hodgson he had changed his mind. Then he rang Paul Breitner. Breitner, who had never coached a senior team in his life, agreed to take over. Fifteen hours later, Braun contacted him again, now with the news that there was opposition within the DFB and that he had to take his offer back.

So Braun went to Uli Stielike, head of the country's Under-17 team since being fired by second-division Waldhof Mannheim. Stielike agreed and began informing the press of his new role. Braun, meanwhile, was having second thoughts, deciding Stielike was not suave and media-friendly enough. Instead, he figured, the perfect man to issue homilies and enthral the public with his legendary good looks was Erich Ribbeck. Ribbeck had spent the past two years playing golf on a Spanish island and was known among scribes as 'Robinson Crusoe', but when presented with the chance to get the job he felt should have been his back in 1984, he said yes.

Stielike and Ribbeck were introduced at a surreal press conference, highlighted by Ribbeck's assurance that he was still in touch with modern football because he 'used to follow the game by watching television and reading magazines'. It was a Waldorf-and-Statler performance that had one reporter exclaim: 'Welcome to the banana republic of German football!'

Four months after Ribbeck's coronation, Germany suffered their most shocking defeat since going down to Algeria in 1982, losing 3-0 against the US. The North Americans fielded four players active in Germany (one in the Second Bundesliga) and though none was known as an exceptional player, three of them scored. *kicker* headlined *That's enough* – but it wasn't. In July 1999, the US once again kept a clean sheet against Germany, winning 2-0. Still, Ribbeck somehow managed to qualify for Euro 2000 by putting everyone behind the ball and scraping a scoreless draw against Turkey in Munich. Alarms were going off in all corners, but the DFB – and in fact many German fans – felt secure in the knowledge that it had always somehow turned out all right in the past and would do so again. However, the only thing that was about to turn out was that this was a costly misapprehension.

The title-holders scored only once in three matches at Euro 2000. That was in the opener, a clumsy match that pitted Ribbeck's men (average age 30) against Romania (average age 28.8) and produced a 1-1 draw. Then Germany lost to England for the first time in 15 years. The *Sunday People* gave the result as 'Hun-Nil', but the majority of the English press was less warlike this time. 'It felt good to beat the Germans,' David Downing recorded in *The Best of Enemies*, 'but was there any real significance to the result?' The implication was that both teams had played depressingly poorly, and that the Germans in particular were so inept that it was taking all the fun out of showering them with torrents of vitriol. Who takes any pleasure in flogging a dead horse? Well, the Portuguese, that's who. They fielded nine second-stringers against Germany and won with ease, 3-0.

It was by far the worst showing of a German national side at a major tournament since 1938. There was now no denying the country's representative team was knee-deep in a mess. The largest German sports weekly carried on its cover a photograph of Zinedine Zidane, with the caption: 'This is a footballer.' Next to it was a picture of a Bratwurst in a football kit, with the caption: 'This is a German international.'

And it wasn't just Ribbeck (who was forced to step down immediately) and the national team that were coming under fire. The Bundesliga, increasingly characterised as a mediocre competition, was dragged into the affair as well as the clubs, who were accused of giving any mundane foreigner a game before employing an aspiring young German and paying only lip service to the cause of the nation's XI – when, of course, the main problem was that there were no aspiring young Germans. As if on cue, Energie Cottbus were promoted and would, in April 2001, become the first club to field 11 foreigners in a Bundesliga match.

The first, and in the end only, club to bow to such public pressure was Bayer Leverkusen. They agreed to grant their coach Christoph Daum his life's wish by letting him out of his contract to run the Germany team. However, Leverkusen stipulated that this would have to wait a year, so that the club had time to find a capable replacement. In the meantime, Leverkusen's director of football would steer Germany through the churning waters. His name was Rudi Völler. Völler wasn't a coach by any stretch of the imagination. But he was almost as respected as Beckenbauer had been in 1984, and he was even more popular than the Kaiser. No one would criticise him for bad results or bad football, not when he was new to the job and only there for one year anyway.

In short: the DFB appeared to have things halfway under control again – and not before time. The 36 professional clubs, awash with television money and beginning to think in global dimensions, had been unhappy for quite some time about being ruled by an amateur body. They even toyed with the idea of a breakaway league, which left the DFB little choice: in late September 2000, the organisation that had regulated every aspect of the domestic game for a century allowed the clubs to form a 'League Association' and take over the running of the top two divisions, through a company they called the *Deutsche Fussball Liga* (German Football League) or DFL.

All this must have been very hard to swallow for the former conservative politician and VfB Stuttgart president, Gerhard Mayer-Vorfelder. In a few months he would follow the ailing Egidius Braun at the helm of the DFB, thus fulfilling the ambition of a lifetime spent lobbying for posts and prestige. But the presidency of the DFB was no longer what it used to be. 'German football now rests on two pillars,' he commented on the formation of the League Association, though he knew very well that his pillar did not support the shiny new parts of the building, but rather the dusty annexes where you could find referees, part-timers and a national team in decline. Yet as it would soon turn out, the DFB's long history of controlling the entire game in Germany, from the very top to the very bottom, was to be of profound importance for the future.

However, Mayer-Vorfelder had no way of knowing this at the turn of the century. While he was still wondering what to do with the cashed-up and cocky professional clubs, the biggest scandal since the bribe drama of 1972 shook the country. In September 2000, a Munich tabloid published an article on Daum that dug up a bit of new dirt about an impending lawsuit instigated by a former, slightly shady business partner, and lots of old dirt about Daum leaving his wife for a glamorous singer. It also included a strange half-sentence, which could have been interpreted as linking Daum with drug use. No one took any notice. But on the first day of October, Uli Hoeness gave an interview in which he asked the DFB to reconsider making Daum national coach. Hoeness said that if a journalist could hint Daum was taking cocaine without being challenged, 'then that makes me wonder'. He went on: 'If someone can produce proof of this, I can't ignore it. Then Mr Daum cannot become the national coach.'

Hoeness never said that he himself was accusing Daum of having a drug problem, but that's how his words were widely interpreted. Instantly, Hoeness became the league's public enemy No 1. He was booed and attacked at grounds, then he received death threats. Daum, meanwhile, appeared to stay calm amid the storm raging around him. He pleaded innocence, but dismissed the suggestion that he allow his hair to be analysed for traces of cocaine on the principle that 'the accuser has to prove the guilt of the accused'.

But only one week later, Daum suddenly changed his mind and consented to a laboratory examination of a hair sample. Why he did so has never been fully explained. Daum himself later said he had been somehow misled: 'I thought I could get away with it.' On Friday, October 20, Daum and his friend, the Leverkusen business manager Reiner Calmund, were handed the results of the test. The two men opened the letter, read the contents, then looked at each other. 'This can't be!' Daum cried. Calmund slowly said: 'You need help.'

Early the next morning, October 21, Daum boarded a plane to Florida before news of his positive test reached the press. While he was in the air, Rudi Völler was asked to take care of yet another team, temporarily. As Völler sat on the bench watching Leverkusen beat Dortmund, it dawned on him that he would soon relinquish this Bundesliga job to a better-trained man, but that he was now the national coach for good.

16

INTERLUDE

IT WAS THE DAY after Elvis entered Sun Studios to record his first single, and the boy's father was at work. Of course he was conscious of his duties, but since hardly anybody else had gone to work on this Tuesday he could have used the occasion as an excuse to stay home and ease the strain on his disc, which was so damaged sitting down was an ordeal. But no, he went to work and sat down. Maybe it was his way of saying that he still gave a damn about football.

So it was mother Antonie who did the best she could to guide her eight-year-old son through streets that were so thick with people you could literally not topple over, even if you lost consciousness. (Which did happen quite a few times that day.) But finally she and he had to stop. People now stood not just shoulder to shoulder but ear to ear, and there was no headway to be made. The boy could see nothing more than what must have seemed like a sea of backsides, and tears welled up in his eyes.

Then, abruptly, a man grabbed him around the waist, lifted him up and put him on top of a construction workers' shack, many of which were scattered around the ruins. Suddenly, the boy hovered far above everyone else and could clearly see the men all these people had come to see. This being the days before television, the only one he readily recognised was Fritz Walter. He also thought to himself that the Coupe Jules Rimet was a lot smaller than he had imagined.

It was the first but not the last time Franz Beckenbauer was that close to the biggest trophy in football. Twenty years and two days later he was lying in a pool feeling dizzy on account of the champagne while he listened to his team-mates' sarcastic rendition of the song 'Holland wins the World Cup'. And 16 years and one day after that, he was taking a leisurely stroll across the pitch while his players were celebrating like kids. Like eight-year-old kids, in fact.

On this day – 8 July, 1990 – Franz Beckenbauer had won the World Cup for the third time. First as a fan, then as a player, now as a coach. He was, as a book called *Der Kaiser* soon claimed, 'on the pinnacle of triumph' – with nowhere to go, no new summit to climb. At least that's what everybody, Beckenbauer himself included, thought.

But then, ten years later, it was July yet again, the 6th. In a few moments, FIFA president Sepp Blatter would announce which country had been awarded the 2006 World Cup. Franz Beckenbauer had spent years flying around the globe to promote the German bid, apparently using only the charm of his Shirley Temple persona (as an American magazine had once characterised his mixture of naivety and calculation we will soon have to come back to) in order to woo the world. Yet even Shirley's golden locks would never sway the original wheeler-dealer, it was felt. Sepp Blatter wanted South Africa, so South Africa it was going to be.

Yet when Blatter finally entered the platform and walked to the lectern, he smiled the tired but knowing smile of a man who has just seen a feared opponent coming from behind again. He said: 'And the winner is – Deutschland.'

17

A WHOLE NEW BALL GAME

REVOLUTION AND RENAISSANCE

CONTRARY TO WHAT GIL Scott-Heron (whose father was
Celtic's first black player) once predicted, the revolution was not
only televised, it was even broadcast live. Late on a cold but not
chilly Saturday night, a few days before Christmas 1998, a curly-
haired presenter welcomed a few million viewers to the latest
edition of a popular German sports show. He stood in front of
a tactics board when he introduced his main guest on the show,
a 40-year-old man dressed in a dark suit and wearing the type
of rimless glasses John Lennon made popular. After the polite
applause from the studio audience had died down, the presenter
said: 'For years, we've been talking about flat-back fours and
zonal marking. One has the feeling there is almost something
like awe when this system is discussed. There are still very many
people watching this show who say: I don't really understand
what this is all about.' He then gestured towards the tactics
board and asked his guest: 'Could you briefly explain it to us?'

The guest's name was Ralf Rangnick. In the great tradition of
German football coaches, he loved England. In fact, Rangnick

had once played for Southwick in the Sussex County League while studying English in Brighton. What was less traditional about Rangnick was that this stint was almost the highlight of his active career (he would never play higher than the third division) and that the football person he found the most fascinating and inspiring did not come from England or Italy or Spain – but from the Ukraine.

In the mid-80s, as a player-manager with the tiny Swabian club Viktoria Backnang, Rangnick had once played a training match against Valeriy Lobanovskyi's Dynamo Kyiv side. Many years later, he would call this irrelevant game his 'epiphany'. Dynamo had no sweeper. There was no man-marking. When Backnang were in possession, the entire Kyiv team moved into the direction of the ball, as if pulled by invisible strings. Their pressing was so intense that you felt suffocated deep in your own half. They even had what would later come to be known as a holding midfielder in front of the back four, a very young Oleksiy Mykhaylychenko.

The amazing thing about this demonstration of modern football was not that it left a deep impression on a thinker and tinkerer like Rangnick. The amazing thing was that almost one and a half decades later, the concept was still so alien to Germans that Rangnick was asked to explain it live on television with the help of a tactics board. At the time, he wasn't even a Bundesliga coach, just someone who was slowly making a name for himself because his team – small, unfashionable Ulm – was doing well in the second division by playing a different game than everyone else.

The idea that a team could be a lot more than just the sum of its parts was not entirely new to the millions who were watching Rangnick that night in late 1998. After all, Volker Finke had kept Freiburg in the Bundesliga for a number of years mainly through smarts and organisation, through what he termed 'concept football'. It simply meant having a plan, unlike those clubs who signed star players and then hoped they would make the difference. (Finke ridiculed this widespread approach as 'hero football'.)

However, for a long time people regarded Finke – another man who'd never played professionally – simply as a coach who was forced to be inventive because he lacked the money to buy good players. The idea that his model was not born of necessity but actually the way forward for everyone didn't take root until the late 1990s, when the nagging feeling began to spread that German football was somehow outdated. Hence the request for Rangnick to 'briefly explain' all that stuff about 'flat-back fours and zonal marking' on television.

He got for his effort what all innovators get – scorn and derision. The tabloids heard the Swabian accent, saw the Lennon glasses and the suit and immediately gave Rangnick the sarcastic nickname 'The Professor'. Then national coach Erich Ribbeck let it be known he was 'disappointed by this exaggerated debate about tactical systems. For instance when a colleague is selling platitudes on television in a manner as if the Bundesliga coaches were a bunch of dimwits.'

But Rangnick would forge ahead and finally break into the mainstream, not least because a club based just 20 miles from his home town of Backnang made a terrible mistake. That club was VfB Stuttgart. Between 1996 and 1998, the team captured the country's imagination with a refreshing attacking game. Under a young coach by the name of Joachim Löw, Stuttgart won the Cup in 1997 and reached the Cup-Winners' Cup final a year later, which they narrowly lost to Chelsea. Despite this success and the team's entertaining football, VfB did not extend Löw's contract and so the coach left in the summer of 1998.

The decision quickly proved to be a disaster, as Stuttgart went through no less than three coaches in the span of only ten months.

Finally, the situation was so unsatisfactory that a desperate VfB approached a man who had never played or coached at this level before and who had just been denounced as a wiseacre by the Germany manager. In May 1999, Ralf Rangnick had at last made it to the Bundesliga.

'The modernisation of the German game began in the south because of some influential coaches,' Frank Wormuth once told me. At the turn of the century, he was Joachim Löw's assistant, and in 2008 he became the DFB's chief coaching instructor. 'One was Volker Finke at Freiburg. Another was Wolfgang Frank, who coached Mainz. And of course Rangnick. It wasn't as if there were no young, progressive, modern coaches in Germany in the 1990s. Many coaches at the lower levels had really good ideas.'

What these and like-minded men needed to really change the game in Germany were mainly three things. First, better and differently schooled players. Then a role model who would prove that you could stir things up in a massive way and have success with it, preferably with a really big team. And, finally, a large-scale attitude change, a new way of looking at football. In time-honoured fashion, what helped bring all three about was a series of disasters.

It began with the 1998 World Cup. In the wake of that tournament, shortly before Rangnick appeared on television and explained modern, ball-oriented defending, Berti Vogts had finally convinced the DFB to launch a 'Talent Promotion Programme'.

It was based on the models of youth development that were up and running in France and Holland. The DFB hired 400 additional youth-football coaches, then it gave each of its 21 regional associations the equivalent of £800,000 to improve the scouting and schooling at the Under-13 level. Finally, the DFB spent an additional £1.3 million on 120 youth-football bases across the country where boys and girls between the ages of 13 and 17, specifically those not already affiliated to a big club, could work with qualified, salaried coaches. In other words, it was not so much an elite programme but aimed at the grassroots level.

Two years later, under a different national coach, there was the next humiliation, a lot worse than France 1998. And so, following Euro 2000, the DFB, traditionally a sworn enemy of radical solutions, realised that the original programme wasn't radical enough. The next two years were spent devising what came to be known as the 'Extended Talent Promotion Programme'. It was presented to the public in July 2002 and launched two months later. The number of youth-football bases was increased to 390, the number of salaried coaches rose to 1,170 and the DFB promised to spend £8 million per year on this project for an unlimited period of time.

But that wasn't all. Because you have to add to this the amount of money which the country's 36 professional clubs spend on talent development. In 2015, a national radio channel produced a feature on the massive changes in German youth football and estimated that the clubs had invested 'more than a billion euros' (£730 million) in their academies since the turn of the century. It quoted Oliver Ruhnert, then-manager of the Schalke Academy, as saying: 'In the past, clubs too often considered youth development the fifth wheel, but now it's become a central element.' There were a number of reasons for this dramaric change in attitude. One was that most German teams simply could no longer afford to compete with English or Spanish clubs on the transfer market even for lesser quality, let alone for star players.

It was one of the repercussions of the so-called Kirch Crisis which rocked German football in 2002. Leo Kirch was the entrepreneur behind Premiere World, which gave him control over the digital TV market and therefore also over the clubs' balance sheets. In 2000, *Forbes* magazine had listed him as one of the world's most powerful billionaires, but only one year later it had become clear that the business of getting Germans to pay money for watching football on TV was much more problematic than Kirch thought.

German fans were not used to paying the kind of sums to watch live football that had become normal in England. In 2001 you could still buy a seat to watch reigning Champions League winners Bayern Munich for a mere £8 and fans had fought so hard to retain terracing that the DFB had been granted an exemption from UEFA's all-seater rule for domestic competitions. Kirch was unable to convince more than 2.5 million people to invest in his expensive decoders. There was no way he could break even, not when he had just agreed to pay the league more than £1 billion over four years for the broadcasting rights.

Only the most acute business minds saw what was happening, and the officials who monitored Germany's professional clubs were not among them. They continued spending money as if they could just print some more. (And at least one could: Borussia Dortmund, the most mindless spenders around the turn of the century, simply went public and earned more than £100 million literally overnight.) The bubble finally burst shortly before the 2002 World Cup, when Kirch Media and its subsidiaries went into administration, plunging the domestic game into the financial crisis that would prompt most clubs to reconsider their spending habits.

And there was another factor which very literally forced the clubs to change: the DFB. Throughout this book I have poked fun – not always mild fun – at the deep conservatism and the distrust of commercialism that has shaped so much of German football history throughout the 20th century. But sometimes the laugh is on the joker. Because just when the outlook was the bleakest, precisely those antiquated amateur structures helped turn the game around in more ways than one. There was, for instance, the 50+1 rule we'll meet again.

But there was also the fact that the game's governing bodies – primarily the DFB, but now also the DFL – held much more power over the clubs than in other countries. The licensing procedure which was introduced when the game turned professional back in the 1960s was still in place. It meant that the clubs annually had to apply for a Bundesliga licence by opening their books and proving they were solvent. It also meant that the DFB and the DFL could withhold this licence if they felt that a club didn't meet certain requirements.

In 2001, the DFB decreed that only clubs that ran a youth academy, or Centre of Excellence, would be granted a Bundesliga licence. A year later, this new rule was extended to cover the Second Bundesliga, too. It even specified how many players eligible for a German national youth team had to be in the squads, how many coaches and physios the club had to employ, how the clubs had to interact with local schools and so on.

Put differently, throughout 2002, the DFB sowed seeds that were meant to completely change the footballing landscape, from the lowest local level all the way up to the professional game. Nobody could guarantee that this huge effort would yield the desired results, but in a country as large and as football-mad as Germany, chances were fairly good that one day, years down the road, you could harvest a crop of excellent, modern players. When former Bundesliga goalkeeper Jörg Daniel, the director of the project, presented the 'Extended Talent Promotion Programme' in September, he said that one stated aim was to make sure nobody would slip through the net anymore. 'If the talent of a century happens to be born in a tiny village behind the mountains,' he said, 'we will from now on find him.'

His resolve was probably strengthened by the story of Miroslav Klose, who had won his first cap for Germany the previous year.

Despite his obvious talent, Klose had never played youth football for a big club, let alone for a German junior national team. In fact, he played amateur football in the fifth division until he was 21, when a Kaiserslautern scout finally spotted him by chance. If Klose had lost interest or self-belief along the way and taken up a regular job after finishing school, Germany would have missed out on the player who scored more World Cup goals than anyone else in the history of the game.

Ironically, it was not least this man – the prolific striker Klose – who unwittingly erected one last, temporary stop sign on the road to revolution. That's because two months before the 'Extended Talent Promotion Programme' kicked into gear, Germany reached yet another World Cup final, thanks to the goal-scoring heroics of Klose (and the goalkeeping heroics of Bayern's Oliver Kahn). It was a tremendous success that would soon put near-fatal pressure on the national coach.

It was, however, a freak result achieved through resilience and luck at a freak tournament, the 2002 World Cup in Japan and South Korea. Germany reached the final without having to play a single traditional superpower. Instead, Rudi Völler's team squeezed past Saudi Arabia, the Republic of Ireland, Cameroon, Paraguay, the United States and South Korea.

The football was hardly exciting. During the closely-fought quarter-final against the US, Germany's new bogey team, television commentator Marcel Reif begged for the final whistle 'on humanitarian grounds'. When at last it sounded, the writers next to Reif hit their keyboards to damn Germany's qualification for the semi-finals as an injustice.

'*Dusel* is our biggest fan,' said the *Westdeutsche Allgemeine Zeitung*. (*Dusel*, you may recall, refers to unearned luck.) The *Süddeutsche Zeitung* sarcastically labelled Völler's tactics – nominally and at long last a version of 4-4-2 – 'a flat back one', which was to say that Germany's strategy amounted to hoping

Kahn could keep another clean sheet. 'This time the side doesn't deserve to be supported,' said the Ruhr football paper *Revier Sport*. But seldom before had the media misjudged the public mood so thoroughly. While Reif felt personally offended by the team, tens of thousands of Germans poured on to the streets to celebrate with abandon. The police reported 'scenes of South American exuberance'.

Bizarrely, the nation went crazy during this lukewarm World Cup. (Or at least what passed for crazy until a much hotter World Cup came along.) Almost 20 million people followed the Paraguay game on television – at 8.30 in the morning. A Berlin factory producing 10,000 flags a day could no longer keep up with demand. In Cologne, an entire Under-10 team went into a barber's shop and asked for mohawks like the one Spurs midfielder Christian Ziege sported. Germany had not seen anything like it in its recent history.

Or maybe it wasn't really bizarre. After all, this was the first tournament since 1966 which the Germans entered as outsiders, with more than half a dozen other countries more strongly fancied. The life of the underdog, many people found out, could be fun. Equally important was that the squad coached by the folk hero Völler contained only one strong, somewhat unpopular character – goalkeeper Kahn. And he was disliked in many quarters essentially only because he played for Bayern Munich and because his will to win bordered on the unhealthy.

Even the team's biggest star, Michael Ballack, appeared affable and modest. Next to him were players like Klose and Oliver Neuville, so shy they whispered more than they spoke; or Christoph Metzelder, the 21-year-old defender who was thrown on to the world stage only a few summers after he had regularly enchanted the occupants of old people's homes by playing the clarinet in an amateur band. In short: there was no Schumacher, no Effenberg, no Matthäus, not even a Berthold or Basler.

On the last day of the World Cup, a tournament of many firsts had three more left in store. One was that Germany met Brazil in the final, a team they had never previously played at the World Cup. The second was that Völler's team played good football for the full 90 minutes, their best performance in years epitomised by Leverkusen's skilful Bernd Schneider. The third was that the blunder that decided the final was committed by Kahn. On 67 minutes, he failed to hold a Rivaldo shot, and Ronaldo put the rebound away. No one could blame Kahn for Ronaldo's second, 12 minutes later, but that was no consolation – his one mistake had cost the World Cup.

When the match ended, the goalkeeper slumped by the goalpost, and maybe there was yet another first – the first time many Germans felt sorry for Kahn. No fewer than six of his team-mates lifted themselves from the ground and walked over to console him, then came Völler, then even referee Pierluigi Collina and Brazil's Cafu.

It isn't very often that the man who fumbles to lose a World Cup final is the hero. But the next day, when the German squad landed at Frankfurt airport, a roar went up as Kahn stepped off the plane. For a second, he squinted at the cheering masses as if suspecting this could be a cruel joke. Then he lifted a bandaged hand to acknowledge the applause. For a man who hated losing so much, it must have been an irritating moment.

It was also a symbolic moment. Seven weeks before the World Cup final in Yokohama, a fiendishly expensive Dortmund team had lost the UEFA Cup final (against Feyenoord in Rotterdam) and a brave Bayer Leverkusen team had been defeated in the Champions League final (by Real Madrid). True, both clubs had ample reason to consider themselves unlucky. But the message of those days in May and June of 2002 couldn't have been clearer: the Germans, once feared for finding ways to win when it counted, would have to learn how to lose.

Times were rough, and they would get rougher. Not only for the national team but also for the Bundesliga, which became increasingly unfashionable and unsexy in the new millennium. Outside of Germany, that is. Because while foreigners tended to regard the league as lacking stars and glamour, German supporters flocked to domestic games in ever greater numbers. During the first decade of the 21st century, average attendance rose from 31,000 to 42,500 – which made the Bundesliga the best-supported football league in the entire world. The German fans obviously liked their league precisely because it was different from the hyped top flights in England or Spain.

For one, it was far more fan-friendly than any of the other big leagues. The tickets were cheaper, there were still terraces (not to mention proper beer) for those who were partial to this and a lot of football on free terrestrial television. The Bundesliga still had all that because supporters were determined to fight for what they considered their rights – in 2001, they even organised a mass boycott that eventually forced a private television station to move its football show to a much earlier time slot.

The main reason why football fans in Germany took it for granted that their voices should be heard was – again – German football's long tradition of amateurism and anti-commercialism. The mere idea that someone could actually own a club was utterly incomprehensible to many Germans. That is why the vast majority of them whole-heartedly supported the 50+1 rule, even though it effectively discouraged entrepreneurs or benefactors from giving their clubs money. (Basically, the rule amounts to telling an investor: please gift us cash, but don't even dream of telling us what to do with it.)

This deep-rooted idea, that clubs are not meant to be businesses but representative of a community, was and is equally prevalent among club officials. In late 2012, I interviewed the entire Borussia Dortmund board for a *FourFourTwo* cover story and asked them why clubs back the 50+1 rule even though it appears to run counter to their interests by making investments unattractive.

'Whenever you have investors, some kind of corporate demeanour begins to engulf the club,' chairman Hans-Joachim Watzke replied. 'And that's not our mentality. The German fan wants to have the feeling that he is a part of the whole. In England, the fan is now basically a customer and can by and large live with that. But if you tell a German supporter that he's just a customer, he's going to kill you. He has to feel connected to the club and that's only possible through the 50+1 rule, because when you really get down to it, the parent club's members are still in control. Of course we run the limited company autonomously, but if the members one day think I should leave, they can sack me.'

But it wasn't only what happened off the pitch that made the Bundesliga so attractive to German fans, it was also what happened between the lines. An old cliché says that German football is more defence-minded, less daring than the game in England or Spain. The figures, though, have never borne this out. Take the one easily available statistic which most obviously indicates attacking football, goals per game. Starting with the 1990-91 season, the Bundesliga outscored the other popular leagues in Europe (England, France, Italy and Spain) in every single year all the way through to and including 2015-16. We are talking about 26 consecutive seasons here, such an improbably long streak that you can rule out the vagaries of chance as an explanation.

Even more importantly, while the other top leagues were increasingly monopolised by a select few big clubs, the Bundesliga became, if anything, even more competitive. During the first ten years of the new millennium, no less than five different clubs were crowned league champions. This didn't happen despite Bayern's exalted position but because of it. Even the best and richest teams will have off years when they need to rebuild or reconsider their approach. When, say, Barcelona have such an off year in Spain, Real will most likely win the league, and vice versa. But when Bayern had an off year, it was all up for grabs.

The first team to take advantage of the situation should have been Leverkusen. With only three games left to play in the 2001-02 season, Bayer led Dortmund by five points and a vastly superior goal difference. Obviously, there were to be new champions and ones who had not only never won the title before but who were also delivering the best and most entertaining football by a mile.

Leverkusen played an attack-minded game that at times looked like an updated version of the Dutch 'Total Football' of the 1970s. Whereas Bayern and Dortmund relied on expensive signings and a Hollywood-esque star system, Leverkusen's football stood and fell on the performance of every single player. And yet they, like the Dutch of old, did have a star. Michael Ballack had scored 15 Bundesliga goals by April, even though he lay deep behind the German-born Turkish international Yildiray Bastürk, who fed the strikers. Ballack had scored a third of those goals with his head, as if he were a target man. He had also made eight goals for his team-mates, as if he were a provider. And he had already been booked 12 times (and sent off once), as if he were an out-and-out ball-winner.

Leverkusen didn't just come within an inch of finally winning the league, they also reached the Cup final and knocked out Liverpool and Manchester United en route to the Champions League final. However, both finals were lost and Dortmund inexplicably, not to mention undeservedly, crept past Bayer in the final three weeks to win the Bundesliga title by one point. These events prompted the press to give Leverkusen the nasty nickname *Vizekusen*, or 'Neverkusen' in England.

However, in reality the campaign was a tremendous achievement of which the club was (and still is) rightfully proud. Borussia Dortmund, by comparison, may have looked for the moment like glorious victors. The dark truth, though, was that delusions of grandeur had already plunged the club into a vicious circle of having to go into debt in order to buy stars who would bring success and with it the Champions League money that was needed to pay off other debts.

In the off-season, Leverkusen lost two key players to Bayern – Ballack and the versatile Brazilian Zé Roberto – and the Munich giants waltzed to the 2003 title, 16 points ahead of Stuttgart. In the greater scheme of things, though, more momentous was the fact that Dortmund failed to win direct qualification for the Champions League by failing to hold a lead at home against lowly (and already relegated) Energie Cottbus on the final matchday.

Three months later, Borussia were beaten – on penalties, no less – by Club Brugge in the third qualifying round. The club was thus relegated to the much less lucrative UEFA Cup and dropped out of Europe entirely in late November. The club president told a newspaper that rumours of impending bankruptcy were 'absurd' and that 'wage restructuring' would do the trick. But behind the façade things looked very different. It now dawned on the men in charge that they had entered an arms race with an opponent they could never beat, Bayern Munich, and that losing the race might mean losing the club.

And so it wasn't Dortmund that seized the moment when Ottmar Hitzfeld's magic began to wane and the Bayern machine occasionally misfired in 2003-04. Instead, a good old foe made an unexpected comeback. A stubby striker from Brazil by the name of Ailton scored 28 goals, which nobody had done in more than two decades. He was rewarded by becoming the first foreign player to be named Germany's Footballer of the Year. (Back in the days of Kevin Keegan and Allan Simonsen, only Germans could win this honour.) And his team – none other than Bayern's 1980s *bête noire* Werder Bremen – were rewarded by lifting the first league and Cup double in club history.

As far as Bayern were concerned, this amounted to insolence and they retaliated with a vengeance, winning back-to-back doubles under new coach Felix Magath in 2005 and 2006, something nobody had ever done before in Germany. And ahead of the 2007-08 season, the club assembled such an all-star team – the French winger Franck Ribéry, the Italian marksman Luca Toni and Miroslav Klose were signed for an estimated £41 million – that yet another double was the almost inevitable outcome. Kahn set a record by conceding only 21 goals during the league season, as Bayern topped the table from the first matchday all the way through to the last.

Well, this doesn't really sound like a competitive league, right? That's true. But the reason Bayern invested so heavily in the summer of 2007 was that they had just finished the season in a silly fourth place, while the title was decided between Bremen, Schalke and Stuttgart. Two derby defeats down the stretch, at Bochum and Dortmund, cost Schalke the title. Bremen also lost two of their final four games and somehow the youngest team in the league, VfB Stuttgart, ran away with the championship.

And things became even crazier in the season after Bayern had invested so much money. There was, for instance, a newly promoted team that won eight out of nine games between early October and late November to climb into first place. That in itself was sensational enough. But it was the identity of this team that turned the winning streak into an international news story – TSG 1899 Hoffenheim.

This first calls for some geography. Many readers are probably familiar with Heidelberg. Some 20 miles southeast of Heidelberg is a town called Sinsheim, home to 35,000 people. Since 1972, Hoffenheim is a borough of Sinsheim, though that doesn't really mean it's a part of it. Because from Sinsheim you have to travel another three miles to reach Hoffenheim. But don't drive too fast, lest you pass through the hamlet without noticing it, as less than 3,300 souls live here.

Why and how this village team made it to the Bundesliga is, of course, a story that has a lot to do with money. When foreign journalists descended upon Hoffenheim in 2008-09, many of them reported home that the club's rise had been monitored by 'owner Dietmar Hopp, a billionaire' and some even called this man 'the German Roman Abramovich'. It never failed to deeply enrage Hopp. For one, of course he wasn't the owner. (He wasn't even on the board.) Second, he had played youth football at the club way back in the 1950s. The local butcher gave young Hopp a can of sausages whenever he scored a goal. Could Abramovich tell such a tale of his Chelsea days?

When, in 1989, Hopp learned that his old team had been relegated to the eighth division, he figured he could put some of his money to good use by helping this small club in a poor region. Of course, he had no idea that he would eventually part with hundreds of millions of pounds. Or that, in the summer of 2006, a well-known Bundesliga coach would agree to join Hoffenheim, then in the third division, just because he was given *carte blanche* and trusted with building a young, modern, offence-minded team. The name of this coach was Ralf Rangnick and he took the village team to the top flight within a mere two years, well ahead of schedule.

So Hopp was basically just an old-fashioned, classic German patron, not totally unlike Jean Löring or Klaus Steilmann, who had once taken other small clubs – Fortuna Cologne and Wattenscheid, respectively – all the way to the Bundesliga simply because they loved them. Yet some fans saw Hoffenheim's rise as further proof that the people's game was in danger of becoming the billionaire's game, and they started to target Hopp. Over time, the conflict deepened until both sides looked equally silly and stubborn. Some of the ultras' chants and banners overstepped the mark, but it didn't help that Hopp refused to turn a blind eye like football people normally did. In August 2011, he even put loudspeakers in front of the away stand which blasted shrill sounds at the travelling fans whenever they raised their voice against Hopp. Some years down the line, this strife would spiral so completely out of control that only a global pandemic could stop it.

By that time, though, the great Hoffenheim fairy tale had already turned somewhat sour. It started the way these things always start – when Hopp, who had the money, and Rangnick, who had the plan, fell out with each other. The first signs that there might be no happy ending appeared as early as the second half of the 2008-09 season that had begun so well. After the winter break, Hoffenheim suddenly sank like a stone and finished seventh.

However, that didn't mean that Bayern had suppressed the insurgency. Because now VfL Wolfsburg, coached by former Bayern manager Magath, slowly climbed up the table. Wolfsburg! The club was not exactly loved by German fans because, like Leverkusen, they had been granted an exemption from the 50+1 rule, seeing as how the Volkswagen company was the reason the city, let alone the club, existed in the first place. But now they did the one thing that will always greatly improve your standing in Germany – annoy Bayern. It had taken a while, but Uli Hoeness's bold claim had become true: Wolfsburg were finally a serious threat.

More than that, as it would turn out. For emotional purposes, the race was decided on April 4, 2009, when Bayern travelled to level-on-points Wolfsburg. The upstarts won 5-1 and the final goal of the game encapsulated one of the most astounding Bundesliga seasons of all time. Wolfsburg's Brazilian Grafite dribbled his way through half the penalty area, kept possession against four defenders plus the goalkeeper and then cheekily back-heeled the ball across the line like a Rabah Madjer for the new millennium. Seven weeks later Magath lifted the championship trophy with a slightly incredulous look on his face. 'We had the third-youngest team in the league,' he said. 'It's more than just unusual that these young players were able to cope with the pressure during the final weeks.'

Oh, and another thing about this season was totally crazy. For the first nine months, the name of Bayern Munich's coach was . . . Jürgen Klinsmann. The story of how he got there is the story of how the Germans reinvented themselves, so let's rewind the clock a bit.

By 2003, the national team had lost all momentum and a lot of goodwill from the World Cup in Asia. During the qualifying rounds for Euro 2004, Völler's team drew at home with Lithuania and away to Scotland. Tellingly, the most memorable game was a poor 0-0 in Reykjavik against Iceland on September 6. The starting XI had an average age of 27.9 and Völler would soon give a very young wing back by the name of Philipp Lahm his first cap, so a little progress had been made. But only in passports, not on the pitch.

As Völler sat down for a post-match interview with German television, he caught the closing statements from pundit Günter Netzer, who was understandably unhappy about the team's performance. When the interview began, Völler launched into a tirade that ranks alongside Giovanni Trapattoni's 1998 speech as one of the legendary temper tantrums.

The national coach used the word 'shit' three times. For good measure, he added 'filth', 'rubbish' and 'baloney' before accusing the interviewer of being tipsy. It was great entertainment and

Völler was actually lauded by many people for being honest and not putting up with everything. But it was also revealing. A few months before a major tournament and less than three years before the World Cup in Germany, the national coach was under enormous pressure because the team was plainly not good enough for either event. What had gotten under Völler's skin was that the pundits had complained about German football having reached another 'low point' on Iceland. Who knows, perhaps Völler lost his cool because deep down he knew that the low point was yet to come?

As early as 2000, when Germany was awarded the 2006 World Cup, free thinkers like Paul Breitner and Bernd Schuster had suggested that the national team should approach the coming tournaments – the 2002 World Cup and Euro 2004 – with an eye to the long term and accept setbacks, even a possible failure to qualify, as steps towards building a team that could compete when it counted, in 2006. Of course, both men had been immediately declared dangerously neurotic psychopaths, but as the big event drew nearer more and more people wondered if maybe Breitner and Schuster had been right. The need to win had been stronger than the need to rebuild and now time was running out.

That is why the voices who pleaded with Völler to call up a few youngsters to his Euro 2004 squad grew louder, just so that they could learn. The national coach was initially reluctant, but ten days before the tournament began, he took a leap of faith. The German Under-21 side had lost two out of three games at the European Under-21 Championship, but some of the players had done well. Völler decided to take two of them along – Bayern's Bastian Schweinsteiger and Cologne's Lukas Podolski, both 19 years old.

The two made their debuts in Germany's final preparation match – a 2-0 defeat in Kaiserslautern at the hands of a young and inexperienced Hungary team. It was a noteworthy game because it was meant to commemorate the 50th anniversary of the 'Miracle of Berne'. And because Hungary's coach was none other than Lothar Matthäus. And because this embarrassing game would prove to be a fitting send-off for the national team.

For the second time in a row, Germany failed to win a game and exited a European Championship at the group stage. For the second time in a row, Germany were beaten by a reserve team: in the final group match, the Czech Republic, which had already gone through, made nine changes to the starting XI – and still won, 2-1. Twelve hours after the final whistle, Rudi Völler stepped down from his post. Two years before the World Cup on home soil, Gemany had neither a team nor a national coach.

What followed was even more absurd than 1998's 'grotesque win-a-manager tombola'. The tournament was still underway when Ottmar Hitzfeld announced he wasn't ready and had to 'recharge the batteries first'. Christoph Daum told the press he was unavailable, too. According to a *kicker* poll, 24 per cent of the magazine's readers were now ready for a radically new solution and said Arsène Wenger should replace Völler. Yet the Arsenal manager said: 'It's true that I had a chat with Franz Beckenbauer. But my contract runs until 2005. I am not free.'

The next man to decline the offer was Otto Rehhagel. Then it was Jupp Heynckes. Then Guus Hiddink, Felix Magath and Morten Olsen. The magazine *Der Spiegel* published a piece that said: 'Have you always wanted to do something for your country? And save German football on the side? Then send us your application for the post of national coach. Time is tight.'

Nobody said it loud, but it was obvious. Every coach worth his salt knew that the 2006 World Cup was going to be a disaster of epic proportions and nobody was interested in ruining his reputation by being the man who had to oversee this doomed project. When Hitzfeld told *kicker* 'I'm not saying I'll never do the job', you almost suspected that everybody was simply waiting for a naive fall guy in order to clean up after him and start anew once this inconvenient World Cup was over and done with.

They found the fall guy in the most unlikely place – in Huntington Beach, California. That's where Jürgen Klinsmann lived since finishing his career in 1998. (Save for a brief stint with Orange County Blue Star at the fourth level of the US game under the nom-de-foot Jay Goppingen.) It wasn't unfitting that Klinsmann had chosen to move to a beach city. No, not because he had toyed with his image during his first press conference at Tottenham Hotspur by asking: 'Is there a diving school in London?' It was rather that he had always seemed more American than European anyway. In Germany, they called him a *Sonnyboy*, an anglicism referring – not really admiringly – to a happy-go-lucky hedonist.

The man who found the fall guy knew all about that role. In the summer of 2004, Berti Vogts spent his holidays near Los Angeles and met Klinsmann for dinner. In the course of their conversation, Vogts suddenly realised that Klinsmann held the highest coaching badges – and was genuinely interested in the Germany job. Vogts immediately informed the DFB about this unexpected option and on July 26, 2004, the baker's son who was taught to always ask himself what Uwe Seeler would have done became the ninth (West) Germany manager.

In his first interview as the new man in charge, Klinsmann said: 'I think the team has potential. At the Euros, the players gave their all and did a super job.' That seemed to indicate he had accepted the offer because he was deluded. However, more illuminating were other statements, such as: 'The crucial thing is that the DFB becomes more open in some areas. We're good, even great, in some areas, but in others we can learn from the French, the Japanese, the Americans. A speed specialist is an issue, or a sports psychologist.'

It soon became apparent that Klinsmann had taken over the job precisely because the situation was desperate. It gave him more bargaining power than any national coach had ever enjoyed. The DFB wanted Klinsmann to work together with the experienced Holger Osieck, Beckenbauer's assistant in 1990. Many journalists lobbied for Ralf Rangnick. But Klinsmann chose Joachim 'Jogi' Löw, who was available because his Austrian club, Tirol Innsbruck, had just been dissolved on account of bankruptcy.

Klinsmann also invented an entirely new post – a general manager for the national team – and gave it to his former team-mate Oliver Bierhoff. The DFB accepted by and large whatever he asked for, even reintroduced red shirts for the national team, until Klinsmann came up with another new position in early 2006 – a director of football for the DFB – and intended to give it to a man called Bernhard Peters. He was the coach of the national field hockey team.

Who knows, maybe the DFB would have agreed to this choice as well, but now *Bild* had enough, a newspaper that was traditionally critical of Klinsmann because he had always refused to cooperate with the tabloids. 'You can't be serious, Mr. Klinsmann!' *Bild* headlined on 1 February. And only two days later, the paper spoke of a widespread 'rebellion against Klinsi's hockey coach'. The DFB finally drew a line, felt that the revolution had gone too far already and made Matthias Sammer the director of football.

It was a decision Klinsmann would not forget, but for the time being there was nothing he could do. By February 2006, he had no bargaining power left. He had promised the DFB a younger team and had delivered: in only his second game in charge, a high-profile match against Brazil in Berlin, Klinsmann fielded a flat-back four with an average age of 22 and was rewarded with a 1-1 draw. He had also promised attacking football and had delivered that, too: in five matches at the 2005 Confederations Cup, Germany scored 15 goals and thrilled the crowds with highly adventurous football.

But Klinsmann had also promised a team that could win the World Cup. And he hadn't delivered that. In late 2005, Germany were beaten by Slovakia and Turkey. And on March 1, 2006, the side suffered a terrible 4-1 defeat in Italy. Klinsmann kept repeating his mantra, that his team would be ready on the day that the World Cup began, but the doubts grew daily.

When Germany played the United States in Dortmund on March 22, it was an open secret that this was a must-win game for Klinsmann. As then DFB president Theo Zwanziger later disclosed in his autobiography, the feeling that the revolution had failed was so strong that he was prepared to fire the national coach only 79 days before the World Cup and replace him with Sammer. After a tense and scoreless first half, Schweinsteiger's free-kick sailed past friend and foe and into the far corner. Germany won 4-1. Klinsmann smiled his *Sonnyboy* smile.

The significance of the 2006 World Cup cannot be overstated. It was a pivotal moment in our football and social history. Perhaps in our history, full stop. On the day it began, the German team wasn't the only thing that was ready. As if on cue, a long period of cold, miserable weather ended and the sun came out for a solid four weeks, which was one reason why the tournament came to be known as the *Sommermärchen* – the summer (fairy) tale.

When the DFB had bid for this World Cup, one of the selling points was that a reunified Germany would present itself to the world and show people what a modern, friendly, peaceful country it was, more than six decades after the war. Even the men and women who prepared the bid cannot have imagined how thoroughly their dream would come true. As early as June

18, the BBC's Laura Smith-Spark marvelled: 'Isn't it funny how 10 days of football can change so many people's ideas about other nations? I never expected to hear so many voices from around the world say how great the Germans are. I also didn't expect the World Cup to be quite such an international love-in.'

That the Germans turned out to be a fun-loving, hard-partying nation of pleasant people surprised almost everyone, including the Germans themselves. More precisely, what surprised the Germans was a phenomenon that would soon be labelled 'new patriotism'. Until this World Cup, the majority of Germans had frowned upon displaying allegiance to the national team in ways that were considered totally normal in other countries. But a few weeks before the tournament started, you suddenly spotted some cars with German flags. A day later, their number seemed to have doubled. Then it quadrupled.

By the time the World Cup kicked off, black, red and gold was everywhere, especially on the public squares where countless people followed the games on giant screens. The Germans had another anglicism for this – *Public viewing* – and it became a national obsession. Six years later, when Germany met Italy during Euro 2012, more than 500,000 people watched the game on an area in Berlin that measured 77,000 square metres and was known as the 'Fan Mile'.

Even the coverage was a success. Eight years after Rangnick had been ridiculed for his zonal-marking lecture on television, the same public-service broadcaster (*ZDF*) now hired a young coach as a pundit and put him in front of a shiny touchscreen to explain the teams' tactics. The man, who had just kept Mainz in the Bundesliga against all odds, proved to be such a natural in front of cameras and talked with such wit and charm that he became one of the secret stars of this World Cup – and won a prestigious television award. Like Rangnick and Klinsmann, he came from the Stuttgart area. His name was Jürgen Klopp.

But who knows how much of this would have happened if Klinsmann hadn't been true to his word? His team was young, his team played attacking football – and it came close to winning the whole thing. Germany were one hundred seconds away from a semi-final penalty shoot-out with Italy when Andrea Pirlo's brilliant no-look pass found Fabio Grosso, who curled his first-time shot into the net.

Despair was deep but brief. For Germany and for German football, this World Cup was about more than trophies and silverware. Which is why the most emotional encounter of the entire tournament was a game most non-Germans have long since forgotten – the second group match, against Poland. Even though the Germans didn't have to win and could have sat back and waited, Klinsmann's players kept attacking with a passion that was almost palpable up in the stands – and the fans there loved them for it with an intensity that gave even neutrals goose-bumps. But Celtic's Artur Boruc, the Polish goalkeeper, made save after save. In the final minute, Klose and Ballack both hit the crossbar. It was maddening.

Then, 50 seconds into stoppage time, the substitute David Odonkor raced down the right wing and sent in a cross which Neuville, who had come on for Podolski, pushed past Boruc from close range. 'Unbelievable scenes are happening here, on the German bench and in the stands,' the hoarse-voiced television commentator reported, meaning the wild celebrations that followed. The first German player to reach Odonkor and wrap his arms around him was Klose, born in Opole, a city on the river Oder in Poland.

This goal – or rather, its protagonists – highlighted another important aspect of this World Cup. For the first time, the foreign media noticed that German football was changing in more ways than one. Odonkor, the son of a Ghanaian man, was black, just like squad member Gerald Asamoah. Podolski was born in Silesia, just like Klose. Neuville came from Switzerland, his grandfather was Belgian, his mother Italian, his father German.

The foreign press would have been even more surprised had they paid closer attention to Germany's Under-21 team. The class of 2006 included men like Gonzalo Castro (born in Germany to Spanish parents), Ioannis Masmanidis (born in Germany to Greek parents), Marvin Matip (born in Germany to a German mother and a Cameroonian father) or the orphan Nando Rafael, who had lost his parents in the Angolan Civil War.

More than six decades after the war, Germany was not only reunified, modern, friendly and peaceful, it was also a normal west European society in that it had become truly multi-cultural. In fact, Klinsmann's side could have easily had an even more diverse background. Because there was a national team that had only narrowly missed out on qualifying for this World Cup and which often featured five or six players who would have been eligible for Germany. This team was, of course, Turkey.

Today, there are 2.8 million people in Germany who have a Turkish background. For a long time, it was almost unthinkable that one of the footballers among them would choose to represent Germany, the country of his birth, rather than Turkey, the country of his ancestors. But this has changed since the turn of the century. In the summer of 2013, Yildiray Bastürk (who, remember, opted to play for Turkey) told me: 'There are various reasons why more and more German-Turkish players decide to represent Germany. An important one is that they think they'll get better schooling if they are German junior internationals. Of course the DFB also made more of an effort to enlist such players. But generally you have to say that it just had to happen sooner or later. Many members of the third generation [the grandchildren of the Turks who came to

Germany as so-called guest workers] feel more German than Turkish. All my nephews and nieces speak German much better than they speak Turkish. That more and more players with a migration background now choose to represent Germany is normal, really. It had to happen.'

In September 2006, two months after the World Cup, one such member of the third generation, a delicate Gelsenkirchen boy by the name of Mesut Özil, made his debut for Germany's Under-19 team against Austria. One day, the fact that he had chosen to play for Germany would dominate the headlines and lay bare simmering racist resentents. But that day was many, many years in the future. At the next World Cup Özil would be a member of an even better, even more modern and even more entertaining German team and a key player for the national coach.

However, this coach was not Klinsmann. On July 12, three days after the World Cup final, he had announced he would not extend his contract. 'I feel empty and burnt-out,' he said. 'The players know that the project we have gotten off the ground is not dependent on one person. And they have always assured me that in case of my departure Jogi Löw would be the right man to continue on this path.' And with that he went back to Huntington Beach.

If you mull over the changing fortunes of German football during the past two decades, sooner or later it strikes you how closely the rise and fall and rise of the national team and Borussia Dortmund mirror each other. Both sides won a major European title (their last to date) within 12 months of each other in the second half of the 1990s. Then they reached – and lost – finals in 2002 and 2008, both times on the back of largely middling performances, before suddenly taking off and capturing the public's imagination in 2010. Not to forget that both went through arguably the biggest crisis in their history in late 2004, early 2005.

If you then contemplate the situation some more, you realise that this correlation isn't really surprising. Through large parts of the 1990s, Dortmund were desperately trying to buck the trend and become what the Bundesliga had until then failed to produce: a strong, perennial rival of Bayern Munich. The problem was that the only concept of how to go about this seemed to be to out-Bayern Bayern. In a mixture of desperation and megalomania, Dortmund spent ridiculous amounts of money and became arguably the most commercial club in the country, epitomised by the fact that they are still the only major German club listed on the stock exchange, together with chemical companies, internet startups or soft drink producers. (Actually, they were the only one until July 2019. That's when Unterhaching, then in the third division, went public as well.)

Dortmund's house of cards collapsed during 2003-04. At the end of this financial year, the club admitted to have accumulated debts totalling £100 million. Only a few weeks after Rudi Völler had stepped down as national coach and plunged the Germany team into a deep crisis, Dortmund's president was forced to resign and it became apparent that nothing less than survival was at stake. The deciding day was March 14, 2005. On this Monday, 444 small-time investors came together in a cheap, ugly building made of corrugated sheet at Düsseldorf airport to listen to a Borussia Dortmund representative.

These sceptical men and women had loaned the club money through an investment fund. Now they were being told that Dortmund could no longer meet the instalment agreement simply because there was no money left. Finally, they were asked to agree to a deferring of these payments. If they voted no, they were informed, Borussia Dortmund would be bankrupt with immediate effect. After more than six hours of questions and explanations, the investors agreed to the bailout plan the club had drawn up. At 3.30pm – the time when most Bundesliga games kick off on a Saturday – the club was saved.

But of course that was only the beginning. Now Dortmund were forced to reinvent themselves, or at least radically change their entire approach, something Bayern Munich never had to do in their recent history. In so doing, Borussia followed a model similar to that of the national team. Partly out of necessity, partly through conviction, the club decided to trust young, cheap or even homegrown players who would hopefully offset their lack of experience with passion and enthusiasm. But it wasn't easy and it took time and courage.

In 2008, for instance, Dortmund surprisingly reached the Cup final against Bayern Munich. There was a talented centre back in the squad, 19-year-old Mats Hummels. But coach Thomas Doll put him on the bench and played Christian Wörns (35) and Robert Kovač (34) at the heart of the defence. Two Luca Toni goals won the game for Bayern. It might have been the moment when Dortmund's board realised you can't forge new paths with an old type of coach. Five weeks after the Cup final and five weeks before Germany reached the Euro 2008 final, Dortmund announced they would replace Doll with Jürgen Klopp.

The ensuing revolution in Dortmund was greatly abetted by the fact that the two Talent Promotion Programmes had begun to yield results. Spectacular results. Germany had won nothing whatsoever in youth football since 1992 (when the Under-16s beat Spain in the final of the European Championship). But in mid-2009, the country became the first nation to simultaneously hold the three major continental titles at the junior level. The Under-17s (built around offensive midfielder Mario Götze), the Under-19s and an Under-21 side that included Özil, Hummels and goalkeeper Manuel Neuer had all won the European Championship.

Suddenly there were almost more excellent young players than you knew what to do with. And suddenly coaches were no longer afraid of placing trust in them. In early 2011, Dortmund would play – and win – a crucial game away at Bayern with a team that had an average age of 22.3 years. In the same season, no less than four Bundesliga clubs (Mönchengladbach, Kaiserslautern, Freiburg and Hannover) that were either expecting to fight relegation or actually doing so decided to try youngsters in the one position where conventional wisdom says you need experience: in goal. The keepers in question were Marc-André ter Stegen (19), Kevin Trapp (20), Oliver Baumann (20) and Ron-Robert Zieler (22). They all came through.

During the ten years that followed the launch of the 'Extended Talent Promotion Programme', the average age of a Bundesliga footballer sunk from 27.6 to 25.3 years. It wasn't just that the young players were much better schooled than the generations before them – it was also that the game had become so much more demanding that young legs possessed an edge. They could run more, run longer and needed less time to rest.

In October 2010, national coach Joachim Löw said: 'Our team at the World Cup was four and a half years younger than our team at the Euros and you could see that we were physically able to play at a higher pace than two years ago.' He was referring to the 2008 European Championship in Austria and Switzerland and the 2010 World Cup in South Africa. And he was right. Although Germany came second in the former tournament and only third in the latter, the World Cup was much more impressive and the real eye-opener as far as the rest of the football world was concerned.

There were some misgivings in the build-up to the World Cup, because Löw first lost his preferred goalkeeper, Leverkusen's René Adler, and then his captain and most important player, Michael Ballack, both of them to injury. But Neuer was a more than capable replacement for Adler, while Philipp Lahm, who was now widely hailed as Germany's most consistently outstanding player, took over both the captain's armband and the leadership role. Finally, none of the kids Löw tried out seemed in any way overawed by the occasion or suffering from nerves. Barely three months after his first international, Bayern's 21-year-old midfielder Thomas Müller tore through the best defences in the world with fearless abandon, often to collect another fine through ball from Özil.

It's not much of an exaggeration to say that the pace and the inventiveness of the German game virtually humiliated England in the round of 16 and Argentina in the quarter-finals. Both opponents conceded four goals, which normally doesn't happen at this level and at these stages of a major tournament. (Though there was a lucky moment for Löw's team when Frank Lampard hit the underside of the crossbar with a terrific shot. However, he was no Geoff Hurst. Which is to say that the linesman miraculously failed to spot that the ball had crossed the line.)

But the German youth movement was stopped in the semi-final and by the same team that had beaten them in the Euro 2008 final, Spain. Löw's players were never able to initiate one of the breath-takingly swift attacks that had overwhelmed England and Argentina, simply because they only rarely had the ball. And if they finally won possession, often near their own penalty area, all they saw was a sea of red shirts quickly shutting off the passing lanes and closing in on them.

It was a style of play Germans had begun to refer to as *Gegenpressing*, literally 'counter pressing'. It basically meant that if a player lost the ball far upfield, his team-mates did not retreat or swarm out in anticipation of a counter attack. Instead they moved further forward to immediately put pressure on the opposing player with the ball. It was a highly effective tactic, because what often happened was that the man in possession was forced to rush his pass and if it was intercepted, it happened in a highly dangerous area of the pitch. But it was also a tactic that demanded an awful lot of running – not to mention a lot of practice – from the players.

Six weeks after the World Cup, Jürgen Klopp unleashed counter pressing of a rarely seen intensity on an unsuspecting Bundesliga. His young team seemed to be constantly in attack, even against strong opposition, and created a plethora of chances. Even though they managed to waste most of them (Dortmund missed all five penalties they were awarded!), Borussia ran away with the league – and won both games against Bayern.

Like the other Bundesliga teams, the Munich giants didn't know what hit them. In the same year Klopp had joined Dortmund, 2008, they had felt their own team could also use a shot in the arm and signed Jürgen Klinsmann, largely on his reputation as a professional revolutionary. It was such a complete mismatch that Klinsmann's brief reign made many people wonder if maybe Löw had been the main author of the *Sommermärchen* all along. But Bayern quickly got over this sorry episode and had a marvellous season under new coach Louis van Gaal in 2009-10.

New signing Arjen Robben, a speedy dribbler, formed a formidable partnership with the other great individualist in the squad, Franck Ribéry, and Bayern came very close to winning the treble. They went into the Champions League final against Internazionale as favourites, even though they were missing the suspended Ribéry, but the savvy, well-organised Italians won 2-0.

And so Dortmund's dominance in 2010-11 came as an utter shock to Bayern's supporters and officials. Worse was to follow. Because Borussia upped the ante in the following season. This time they won three games against Bayern, including the Cup final. They collected 81 points, a record. They went 28 games unbeaten, a record for a single season. Their average attendance of 80,522 was another record. But the most painful moment for Bayern came two weeks after the end of the league season.

For the second time in three years, the club reached the Champions League final. And this one was staged at home, in Munich. The Germans appeared to have won this game three times. First when they took a more than deserved lead against a very defensive Chelsea team with only seven minutes left. Then when they were awarded a penalty in extra time. And finally when they raced into a 3-1 lead in the penalty shoot-out. However, the players whom UEFA president Michel Platini eventually handed the trophy wore blue, not red. An English side had won a final against a German team on penalties – times had well and truly changed.

So, this is the long story that led up to the greatest night in German club football. Perhaps in German football. Because in late June 2012, the national team were eliminated from the European Championship in Poland and Ukraine by their old nemesis, Italy. (Of course in the semi-final, as always.) Suddenly a counter-revolutionary debate sprang up. Some people argued that the Germans, with their proverbial thoroughness, had only swung from one extreme to the other and were now lacking the one thing they had always had, a winning mentality. It wasn't a far-fetched idea. German teams indeed now often looked like Brazil in 1982 – all delicate flair players like Özil and scrawny attacking midfielders like Müller but no muscle men, no target men (which would become a serious problem once Klose finished his career) and, crucially, no silverware.

Put differently, it was about time a German team went all the way. And it was also about time that this team was Bayern Munich. But they needed Dortmund to do it. Twice in a row, a star-studded and expensive Bayern team had been embarrassed by a young side in which nobody had cost more than £4.3 million. Dortmund's secret was – as it always is in these cases – supreme team spirit and team play.

And so Bayern set about combining outstanding individual class with excellent organisation. The man who somehow managed to teach Ribéry how to track back and explain to Robben the concept of a tackle was none other than Jupp Heynckes. Perhaps we'll one day look back on the events of the 2012-13 season and say that the greatest irony of it all was that right smack in the middle of German youth mania, a 68-year-old man who had come out of retirement to do his old pal Uli Hoeness a favour was the one who finally delivered the most coveted prize.

Bayern won the league by pulverising most of the records Dortmund had set. They also won the Cup. They scored 11 goals and conceded none in the quarter-final and the semi-final of the Champions League against Juventus and Barcelona. They were clearly the best football team in Europe, probably the world, during large parts of this season. And yet their knees were trembling when they ran out on to the Wembley pitch on May 25, 2013, to play yet another Champions League final. Because their opponents were the only team they really feared, Borussia Dortmund.

Klopp's team, bolstered by Marco Reus, not only Dortmund-born but Germany's reigning Footballer of the Year, topped a group that included Real, Ajax and Manchester City with what came close to being ease. They needed a lot of luck and two goals in stoppage time to squeeze past Málaga in the quarter-final but then disposed of Real in the semi-final in great style. In the home leg, Dortmund's Polish striker Robert Lewandowski became the first man to score four goals against the Spanish giants in a European game.

A final worthy of the occasion was won by the better team. But it tells you all you need to know that UEFA's man of the match was Robben, who scored the 2-1 winner a minute from time, while the fans voted for Manuel Neuer. They knew that Bayern's goalkeeper had kept his team in the game in the crucial first half hour, when nerves appeared to get the better of the one team that had played in more big games than any other German side.

Despite the drama and the enormity of the occasion, Heynckes looked and sounded much calmer and more composed after the final whistle than a week earlier, when he had broken into tears after the away game at his home town club Mönchengladbach, assuming it had been his last-ever Bundesliga game as player or coach. In all likelihood, Heynckes would have gone into retirement (again) regardless of how the season went, but Bayern had taken the decision out of his hands four months before the Champions League final. In mid-January 2013, the club announced they had secured the services of the most in-demand coach in the world, the Catalan Pep Guardiola, who had built the all-conquering Barcelona side Klopp and numerous others had set out to emulate.

However, Heynckes typically didn't draw attention to himself in his post-match analysis. Instead, he said: 'It was time for the Lahm and Schweinsteiger generation, who are my two captains, to win an international title.' It was not a lightly-made remark. On one level, the outgoing coach was referring to the fact that these players had lost their previous two Champions League finals with Bayern. But he was also addressing growing concerns with regard to the national team. The Lahm and Schweinsteiger generation had now reached the semi-finals at four consecutive major tournaments. It was a fantastic achievement, but more and more people feared that it could never be crowned. After all, the 2014 World Cup would be held in Brazil, and no European team had ever won a title in the Americas. In other words, yet another heartbreaking defeat seemed inevitable, probably in the semis again.

As it turned out, this is not exactly what happened. So why not end this eventful chapter with the biggest event of all, with the pinnacle of Germany's football revolution: the national team's most sensational game at least since the Miracle of Berne, maybe ever? Because while many people were looking away, there was another, very different form of revolution going on. To understand what it was all about and why it would shape the next phase in the history of German football much more than games and goals, we have to come back to the man we met at the beginning.

Seven days after Bayern's triumph over Dortmund in London, Ralf Rangnick was watching an equally tense and momentous game in Lotte, a town in Westphalia roughly the size of Knottingley or Dunscroft. It was a fourth-division play-off that featured a goal five minutes into stoppage time which almost drove Rangnick to despair (and added another 30 minutes to the proceedings). However, after the end of extra time, Rangnick could finally heave a sigh of relief. 'We were stuck at this level for a couple of years,' he told a reporter. 'Which goes to show one shouldn't be planning and defining goals all the time, one should just get on with things.'

Twelve months earlier, Rangnick had added a new facet to his already colourful career by being appointed director of football at two clubs in two countries at the same time. One was based in Salzburg, the other in Leipzig. This second club had the plans and the clearly defined goals Rangnick was alluding to. They were quite simple: go all the way to the Bundesliga and topple Bayern Munich. The biggest hurdle on that journey, Rangnick had found out, was not so much the other teams but the other teams' supporters. They seemed to think that his new club wasn't a club at all.

18

CULTURE WARS

STRUGGLES IN CHANGING LANDSCAPES

AS IF A PANDEMIC wasn't enough. In April 2021, more than a year into the global COVID-19 crisis, 12 of the biggest clubs in Europe announced the formation of a breakaway European Super League to be bankrolled by an American investment firm. The new league was an attempt at ensuring fair competition and preserving the integrity of the game. No, just kidding. Of course it was about 'significantly greater economic growth', as Real Madrid's president Florentino Pérez phrased it in his official statement. After 13 months of games behind closed doors, Real needed money.

The public – and indeed the political – outcry was particularly loud in England, where six of the founder clubs were based, all but one of them under non-English ownership. Fans held protest marches across the country; in Manchester, they even forced the postponement of the high-profile clash between United and Liverpool when Old Trafford was invaded by hundreds of supporters. Pressure groups called for an introduction of the German 50+1 rule, citing Bayern Munich's and Borussia

Dortmund's refusal to join the renegade league as proof that what they referred to as 'fan-owned' clubs were the antidote to a crass commercialism that was threatening to devour football as five generations had known it.

The UK government apparently felt the same, because it went as far as hinting at 'legislative options' to stop British participation in the Super League. If anyone wondered what that could possibly mean, newspapers soon reported that Prime Minister Boris Johnson was considering 'new laws that would hand control of the football clubs over to the fans, possibly based on the German model'. Within three days, Chelsea, Manchester City, Arsenal, Liverpool, Manchester United and Tottenham issued apologies and withdrew from the ESL.

Alanis Morissette would call it ironic. Because while everybody outside of Germany seemed to think the Bundesliga's traditional club model was something to aspire to, the 50+1 rule was openly debated – and questioned – in the country itself. In fact, you could argue that for the previous five or six years, German football's central debate had had nothing to do with how the game was played or who played it – but why it was played in the first place. Sometimes this debate got out of hand, such as when Borussia Dortmund were controversially forced to close the most famous terrace in world football for a game in February 2017 as a brutally visible form of punishment. Or, indeed, on the very last normal football weekend before coronavirus threw everything into disarray in March 2020. That is, provided you can call it normal when referees across the league suddenly stop play and threaten to abort games because of banners and chants directed at Hoffenheim owner Dietmar Hopp. Wait, wait, wait: did someone just say 'owner'? Ah, okay, let's go back again . . .

In 2006, the year of the *Sommermärchen* World Cup that changed so many things, the Austrian energy drink giant Red Bull entertained the idea of taking over a German club, just as they had done with their native Austria Salzburg a year earlier. But which club? The company did what companies do and looked at the numbers. The eighth largest city in the land, Leipzig, didn't have a professional club, so there was a lot of potential. The seventh largest city, Düsseldorf, had a club with a lot of tradition that was treading water in the third division. The third largest city, Munich, had mighty Bayern, but all figures indicated that the other team in town was rather popular as well. And roughly the same situation, the corporate clubhunters concluded, was to be found in Hamburg. So the Austrians decided to buy and then rename either Sachsen Leipzig, Fortuna Düsseldorf, 1860 Munich or – the height of bizarreness – FC St Pauli, the most stubbornly independent, left-wing and anti-capitalist club in Germany, probably Europe, maybe the world.

To their obvious surprise, the Austrians found out that they couldn't buy a German club because there were no owners. They also weren't allowed to change a club's name from, say, Fortuna into Red Bull. And perhaps most surprising of all: the clubs didn't even want Red Bull's money. In fact, the members of Sachsen Leipzig voted to rather go bust (which they eventually did) than get into bed with a foreign corporation. Fortuna Düsseldorf's members also told Red Bull to close the door from the outside, while the company's advances at 1860 Munich and St Pauli were rebuffed as early as the boardroom and never even reached the members (and thus, for many years, the public). Confused by all this antagonism, Red Bull quietly retreated to hatch a new strategy.

Anyone who has read only parts of this book must at this point wonder why someone as savvy as Dietrich Mateschitz, the Austrian billionaire who co-founded Red Bull, didn't seem to grasp the implications of the 50+1 rule. One possible explanation may be that it's such an alien concept to any dyed-in-the-wool businessman that entrepreneurs just can't believe there isn't a way around it. In March 2011, for instance, a Jordanian investor by the name of Hasan Ismaik began to pump a lot of money into 1860 Munich. In May of that year alone, he paid almost £16 million for 60 per cent of the club's shares – only to find out that he still held only 49 per cent of the all-important voting shares. Ismaik would spent the larger parts of the following ten years warring with 1860's board, who were happy to take his money while making sure their cash cow had very little say in how the club was run. In the summer of 2017, the exasperated investor finally filed a complaint with the Federal Cartel Office. 'Unfortunately, I fell into this trap in 2011,' Ismaik admitted. 'I had the best of intentions, I was only trying to help 1860. This rule is a charade. I will use all my powers to have it abolished.'

His move wasn't quite as desparate as it may sound, because this time Ismaik knew what he was doing. He didn't complain about the rule as such – but about the increasing numbers of exemptions. There were the two obvious ones, Bayer Leverkusen and VfL Wolfsburg, who had been granted grandfather clauses early into the rule's history. But it no longer stopped there. Hannover 96's managing director Martin Kind had gone on a one-man crusade against the rule as early as 2007. He didn't have many allies, but he argued so loudly and so stubbornly that 50+1 would never stand a chance in a European court of justice that the league finally created a loophole to silence him.

The rule was amended to say that any person or company that had been supporting a club 'uninterruptedly and substantially' for a period of at least 20 years would be allowed to become the club's owner. Funnily, when Kind tried to invoke this new rule, it turned out he didn't quite fulfil those requirements. However, one person who certainly did was Dietmar Hopp. In early 2015, he jumped at a chance he probably never thought he would get. The man who had poured at least £255 million into unfashionable Hoffenheim over the course of a quarter of a century took over the vast majority of the voting shares to become the first person to ever own a football club in Germany.

And then there were the Austrians. It took the Red Bull brain trust some time to come up with a solution to the conundrum of how to violate the spirit but not the letter of the 50+1 rule, but by May 2009, they had found it. Tried and trusted company employees simply went out and formed their own club, based in Leipzig. They named it *RasenBallsport*, lawn ball sport, so that the abbreviation RB could be used, and created a badge that bore an uncanny resemblance to Red Bull Salzburg's crest, which in turn looked like the Red Bull logo. The most crucial part of the plan, however, was to make sure that nobody from outside could become a member. (In March 2021, some 12 years after RB's formation, the number of club members still stood at only 21.)

Despite all this attention to detail, it remained touch and go whether or not the plan would work, as the new club's close ties to a multinational corporation were not exactly hard to spot, which is why the regional Saxony Football Association (SFV) at first refused to accept the badge. However, at this point RB were still flying very much under the radar. Amateur clubs are not subject to the DFB's and the DFL's rigorous licensing procedures and thus don't come under very close scrutiny. In the end, the SFV admitted RB into organised football. It may not have been the point of no return, but now it all went very quickly. Needless to say, Mateschitz had not the slightest intention of starting at the very bottom of the league pyramid. And so he offered SSV Markranstädt, a small club ten miles west of Leipzig, a cool 350,000 euros if their men's football division would sail under the RB banner for one season. The true target was Markranstädt's first team, which was playing in the fifth division. As RB Leipzig, it immediately won promotion to the fourth level in 2010. While the other teams returned to Markranstädt, this one stayed in Leipzig. And suddenly there it was – a club openly controlled by a corporation right in the middle of what is supposed to be fan-ownership's model country.

But the sailing wasn't smooth. First, there were the opposing fans. They hated RB with a passion never seen before, which is why the new club had to play its first-ever game – remember, in the fifth division! – under police protection. That was in August 2009, away at Jena's reserves. The players were spat at, while the crowd chanted 'Death to RBL'. After the final whistle, the squad walked from the pitch straight to their coach, surrounded by policemen, and drove off without having showered or changed into street clothes. When I spoke to RB fans a few years later, one of them told me: 'I know that everyone hates us. It will pass. They hated Wolfsburg, then Hoffenheim, now it's RB Leipzig. In five years, they'll hate someone else. As long as the aggression remains verbal, I don't mind.'

But it never really passed – and sometimes the aggression didn't remain verbal. In early 2015, about two dozen Karlsruhe fans stormed the hotel at which RB Leipzig were staying. According to eyewitnesses, they were wearing hooded sweaters and some got as far as the dining room before security people stopped them. Only a few months later, the cup game between Osnabrück and Leipzig was abandoned after 71 minutes because the referee was hit in the head by a lighter thrown from the stands that had been aimed at Leipzig's striker Davie Selke. Club representatives later said players and officials had things hurled at them throughout the game and were insulted unremittingly. And in 2017, travelling Leipzig fans were attacked outside Dortmund's ground, while a great number of anti-RB banners, most of them not very tasteful, covered large parts of the famous South Stand. As a penalty, the DFB ordered the entire terrace to be closed for the next home game. Borussia Dortmund complained this penalty was 'a collective punishment against 25,000 spectators, of which the overwhelming majority cannot be blamed or accused', but eventually accepted the decision.

Second, RB Leipzig also met with resistance on the pitch. Some teams seemed to put in an extra bit of effort when they were up against the 'Bulls', as the new club styled themselves. For two years running, Leipzig couldn't get out of the regional fourth division. At the same time, the mothership in Salzburg also found itself in rough waters. Red Bull had won four of the last six Austrian league titles, but repeatedly failed to qualify for the real show, the Champions League. In 2012, the team was even knocked out by F91 Dudelange from Luxembourg, one of the greatest debacles in the history of the Austrian game. Something had to happen. Enter Ralf Rangnick.

Less than a month before the Dudelange drama, the Swabian was signed as director of football for both Salzburg and its German branch. 'I have no doubt that Leipzig will one day play in the Bundesliga,' he told a newspaper in August 2012. 'As the man in charge, I hope it will happen as quickly as possible.' When the reporter argued he could theoretically do it in three years, Rangnick replied: 'That would be a miracle.' In the end, it took him only one year longer. But when RB finally won promotion to the top flight, the bigger miracle was probably that quite a few people welcomed them with open arms. One of the major reasons for this unexpected hospitality was a Catalan coach, or rather: the legacy he had left.

On the face of it, Pep Guardiola's three Bundesliga years were a resounding success. Yes, he failed to claim another European crown for Bayern, losing three Champions League semi-finals, each time against a Spanish side. But, contrary to popular opinion, the club's fans are not so blasé that they don't realise how amazing it is to be among the four best teams on the continent practically by default. And domestically, Bayern Munich went from strength to strength. Guardiola took the treble-winning team he had inherited from Jupp Heynckes and turned it into something even more frightful – a relentless footballing machine that never stopped running. Until he arrived in Munich, Bayern were known to have off-days, sometimes off-seasons, but now they didn't even pause to catch breath.

And yet the majority of Bayern fans were glad to see the back of Guardiola when his contract ran out and he took over Manchester City. They resented the fact that he only seemed to care about what happened between the white lines, disliked how he never interacted with the support in any meaningful way and felt that all his references to the club's culture, history and tradition were just lip service. Maybe it was all just unfortunate timing. Maybe Bayern's field-tested double act would have managed to balance things out. I'm talking about, of course, the club's two key officials: Karl-Heinz Rummenigge, the pragmatic and slightly technocratic rationalist, paired with Uli Hoeness, the impulsive, emotion-driven sentimentalist. But when Guardiola began to rebuild Bayern in his image, Hoeness had other things on his mind than gently reminding the Catalan of the club's ways.

In January 2013, only four weeks after he had travelled to New York with a contract for Guardiola in his suitcase, Hoeness turned himself in to the tax authorities. He disclosed a secret Swiss bank account and admitted to having earned considerable amounts of money from shares and currency dealings for which he had failed to pay income tax. This voluntary disclosure was made in the hope it would grant him exemption from punishment, but eventually the Munich district court decided Hoeness would have to go to trial regardless. Partly because the voluntary disclosure was incomplete, partly because it had been made while investigations were already underway.

Ironically (again, in the Alanis Morissette sense), it was the biggest scandal to rock the German game since Hoeness himself had set the Daum affair in motion in 2000. Hoeness explained the secret account didn't exist to hide or launder money but purely for gambling the stock market. Of course, that didn't make much of a difference to the authorities. On March 13, 2014, he was sentenced to three and a half years in prison for tax evasion on a stupendous scale (at least £23 million). One day later, Hoeness announced he would not appeal against this sentence and immediately stepped down as both president of Bayern Munich, the parent club, and as chairman of Bayern Munich Ltd.

Amidst this turmoil, one could see the first indications that Guardiola had a strange knack for controversial decisions. There was, for instance, the fact that Bayern had just signed the German game's golden boy, Mario Götze, for £32 million thanks to a get-out clause. It looked like a smart deal, not only because this transfer weakened rivals Dortmund. Just weeks before he joined Bayern, *kicker* had attested Götze 'world class' in the magazine's bi-annual and influential rankings. But Guardiola, who had asked Bayern's board to secure the services of the Brazilian Neymar instead, didn't quite seem to know what to do with Götze and where to play him. At the end of the 2013-14 season, his first in Munich, Götze's stats did look sensible (the 21-year-old saw action in 27 league games), but there were some ominous signs, such as the fact that Götze was not a starter when the chips were well and truly down, most notably in the Champions League semi-final games against Real. When the national team left for Brazil to try and win the World Cup against all odds, doubts were suddenly hovering over the country's greatest talent.

But that wasn't the only problem Guardiola's first season created for national coach Joachim Löw. Bayern had begun their campaign with Bastian Schweinsteiger in defensive midfield and Philipp Lahm, arguably the world's best right back at, well, right back. But in late August, Schweinsteiger suffered an ankle injury and the coach moved Lahm into midfield – permanently, as it turned out. When I talked to the player a few months later, he seemed delighted about his new role. 'It didn't come as too much of a surprise for me that I could play this position,' Lahm said, 'because I used to play there in youth football, and I have already helped out in midfield on occasion.'

When it became apparant that Bayern now considered Lahm to be a midfielder, Löw felt forced to follow suit. He had always been a believer in not unnecessarily shuffling people around, and so he first used his captain as a holding midfielder in November, seven months before the World Cup. Not every fan, observer or pundit was happy. Unlike Guardiola, who could play the Brazilian Rafinha at right back, nowhere near as good as Lahm but reliable and experienced, Löw had no obvious alternative. Actually, he didn't have a natural left back, either, and so he opted for four centre backs in defence. The debate raged on until it came to a head almost three weeks into the tournament in Brazil.

In the round of 16, Löw's team came very close to being knocked out by Algeria, winning a nerve-racking encounter 2-1 in extra time. After the game, a reporter asked Per Mertesacker why the pre-tournament co-favourites Germany were looking so 'sluggish and vulnerable'. The Arsenal defender, visibly exhausted beyond the point where he would field such questions politely, replied that he couldn't care less about the performance, said the result was all that counted and launched into a monologue that became known as the *Eistonnenrede*, the ice bath speech. He said there were no 'carnival troupes' among the last 16 at a World Cup and that Germany had given their all against a difficult opponent, adding: 'I'll now take a three-day ice bath and then we'll analyse the game.' When the reporter insisted the match was cause for concern, Mertesacker queried: 'What do you want from us? Do you want a successful tournament? Or do you want us to play beautiful football and get eliminated again?'

Mertesacker's statements were a timely reminder that even the most consistently good team in international football, and that's what Germany certainly were at this point, could not take anything for granted. Sepp Herberger's famous dictum – the next game is always the hardest – was still valid. This next game was the quarter-final against France three days later. For the first time at the tournament, Mertesacker was not in the starting XI – but not because he was still in his ice bath. It was rather that the national coach no longer had to have four centre backs on the pitch. As Löw later said, he had decided his team needed 'a new impulse', and so he played Schweinsteiger and Sami Khedira, the son of a German mother and a Tunisian father, in front of the back four. And Lahm at right back.

'We weren't isolated in the camp, we watched German television and of course there was also the internet, so we were aware that there was a discussion back in Germany about whether I should play in midfield or at full back,' Lahm told me a few months later, when I asked him and his Bayern team-mates Neuer and Müller to relive the events in Brazil. 'There had been reasons why I started in midfield. Sami and Basti had both come back from injuries and didn't have a lot of match practice. But we had always said we would decide upon my position from game to game and this is what happened.' He added: 'People say that we played better after the Algeria game, but I'm not sure about this. Against France we also had some moments where we didn't look so good defensively. It was a good game against a good opponent, but it wasn't totally convincing.' He paused. 'Of course, the one after that was absolutely outstanding.'

Hundreds of pages ago, I brazenly said there are three truly famous, mythical teams in the history of German football. It was easy to be certain about the *Breslau-Elf*, the Heroes of Berne and the 1972 team, because they have stood the test of time. The World Cup in Brazil, on the other hand, is a relatively recent event. Many of the players who took part in it are still active, and it seems strange to call someone a legend who still spends his Saturdays running round in shorts. And yet ... here is the side that took to the field against France in Rio de Janeiro on July 4, 2014:

Goalkeeper	Manuel Neuer (Bayern)
Right back	Philipp Lahm (Bayern)
Centre back	Jérôme Boateng (Bayern)
Centre back	Mats Hummels (Dortmund)
Left back	Benedikt Höwedes (Schalke)
Holding midfielder	Sami Khedira (Real Madrid)
Holding midfielder	Bastian Schweinsteiger (Augsburg)
Right midfielder	Thomas Müller (Bayern)
Central midfielder	Mesut Özil (Arsenal)
Left midfielder	Toni Kroos (Bayern)
Striker	Miroslav Klose (Lazio)

Of course it was not the France game, won 1-0 thanks to an early Hummels header, that makes me think a book about the history of German football must include this line-up. It was 'the one after that', four days later in Belo Horizonte, where Germany faced Brazil in the semis. The hosts were without their best player, Neymar, who had suffered a fractured vertebra against Colombia in the quarter-final. ('I felt it was a pity, because you want to play against the best,' Lahm told me. 'It was sad to see such a great player being sidelined.') Still, his absence alone can't really explain what happened at the Estádio Governador

Magalhães Pinto. Nothing can, because nothing like it had ever happened before or will happen again.

Needless to say, it played a major role in meaning that the Brazilians, devoid of the one player who could carry the team, finally did what had been long overdue: they succumbed to the enormous pressure exerted by a loving but demanding nation. Yet it takes two to tango – or to collapse. A good case in point is the first goal, scored by Müller from a corner after 11 minutes. It seemed to be down to a monumental marking error, as the feared Bayern forward found himself in the proverbial acres of space. But four months later, Müller told me: 'Before the game, our assistant coach Hansi Flick suggested we should try a corner routine. I'm at the near post and then drop back, while Miroslav Klose moves from the far post to the near post. We tried it in the game and it worked. Our markers followed us and because we were moving in opposite directions, they impeded each other. For the spectators it probably seemed as if nobody at all was marking me. But whenever something like this happens at a corner, you can be sure there's a reason for it and that somebody's path was blocked.' He added: 'After the second goal, they lost their heads. You can understand why, there were the expectations and the crowd. But they blindly rushed forward and if you give a team likes ours so much space then, well, it's going to be tough.'

Tough doesn't even begin to describe it. Klose, Kroos and Khedira added four goals in the span of just six minutes. Before half an hour was up, Germany were leading 5-0. In the semi-final of a World Cup. Against Brazil. Commentating for German television was Béla Réthy, a reporter of Hungarian descent who had spent the first 11 years of his life in São Paulo. When Khedira sidefooted the ball into the net for the fifth goal, he didn't say 'Goal!' or '5-0!' or anything of the sort. He just gasped: 'Madness. This is madness. What's going on?'

When I asked Neuer about the atmosphere, which had quickly gone from carnival-like to funeral, he said: 'The people at home could see how demoralised the Brazilians were, because the cameras zoomed in and showed the players' reactions in slow-motion replay. I didn't see much of this, because I was so far away. But their body language told you they were finished. During the half-time break we said we shouldn't become defensive now. We wanted to keep a clean sheet and not change our game.' Lahm added: 'We sat down and said we must not lose focus. We also said that we owed our opponents, the people in the stands and the entire host nation a lot of respect and should not start showboating. We felt the best way of treating Brazil with respect was not changing our approach.'

Everybody remembers that the game finished 7-1. Most people have forgotten that, with 35 seconds left on the clock and the score 7-0, Germany launched a four-against-three counter attack (!) and that Özil had only the goalkeeper to beat. He put the ball wide by just a few inches. Put differently, it could have been even worse. As Réthy said, it was madness. Neuer told me: 'When we got back to our camp, the Brazilian employees were unhappy about the result. But at the same time they were happy for us. The one thing that counted for them was that Argentina mustn't win the World Cup.'

On July 13, the players made sure that the nice people at their remote Campo Bahia base got their most pressing wish. Though it tells you how close the final was that the best player on the pitch was Boateng, the towering defender born in Berlin to a German mother and a father from Ghana. Germany also needed some luck, never more so than when Neuer left his line on 56 minutes to knock away a long ball aimed for Gonzalo Higuain. The goalkeeper did punch the ball clear, but he also crashed into the Argentinian with a reckless force almost reminiscent of Harald Schumacher in 1982, not to mention that it was very difficult to ascertain if Neuer was still in his area when he got to the ball. The Italian referee awarded Germany a free-kick (the only decision he could make in this tricky situation that was definitely wrong) and the game remained scoreless.

A few minutes from time, Löw turned towards the subs' bench and told Götze to get ready. When Klose noticed the national coach was taking him off, he walked over to the referee and shook his hand. While this was happening, Löw stood at the sideline next to Götze. He put his arm around the player's shoulder and said: 'Show the whole world you're better than Messi. Show them you can decide a game.' Five minutes later, the final went to extra time.

After 108 minutes, Schweinsteiger and Sergio Agüero went into an aerial duel and the Argentinian hit the German in the face. Not with his elbow, as often happens in these moments, but with his fist. That's why Schweinsteiger suffered a nasty cut. He was bleeding so profusely that Löw told Dortmund's Kevin Grosskreutz to get into the game. However, Schweinsteiger informed both men that he had no intention of leaving the pitch just because he was looking like a prizefighter after a bout gone wrong. The picture of the bloodied Bayern player would be one of the two iconic images produced by this final, and it would help change people's opinion of Schweinsteiger. He was already a hero for Bayern's fans (who had long since taken to yelling 'Football god!' whenever his name was announced). But until this day the rest of the country had still seen primarily a cheeky rogue in him, the kid who used to be up to all kinds of mischief with his close pal Lukas Podolski. Those days were long gone, though. Schweinsteiger had grown up and grown into a leader.

The other iconic image was, naturally, the goal. With seven minutes left, Chelsea's André Schürrle crossed from the left for Götze, who chested down the ball at the edge of the six-yard box and volleyed home in one fluent motion. Of course he was not better than Lionel Messi, but he had shown the world he could decide a game – and do it with one of the finest goals to ever win a World Cup. 'Nobody deserved it more than us,' Löw said after the game, having at long last stepped into the pantheon of the very greats. 'It was due.'

In the summer of 2014, just one year after two Bundesliga teams had contested a Champions League final at Wembley, Germany were champions of the world for the fourth time. The Bundesliga had just set a new attendance record (43,500 fans per game), was officially the best-supported league on the planet and could lay claim to football's two most talked-about and in-demand coaches, Guardiola and Klopp. Actually, a third was already waiting in the wings, as Guardiola would very soon meet a 41-year-old called Thomas Tuchel. The former Mainz coach was on a sabbatical (a fashionable new trend started by the Catalan himself) and met Guardiola in a Munich restaurant. The chance encounter turned into an improvised tactics give-and-take involving salt shakers and wine glasses that left such an impression on Guardiola that he would urge Bayern to make Tuchel their next coach because this man was clearly going places.

To top it off, the German game had achieved all this, and produced all those talents, with clubs that were still owned by their supporters instead of rich businessmen, and in the most fan-friendly environment known to football in the year 2014. In other words, triumph was total. Germany had reached the utmost pinnacle. Which also meant that there was only one way to go from here . . .

Much has been made of the fact that no club other than Bayern Munich has won the Bundesliga since 2013. There is one major reason for this, and we'll look into it when the 50+1 rule comes into view again. But it is also worth pointing out that, for all

Bayern's undeniable class and sheer quality, German club football would certainly have looked very different during the last decade if one single deal had not been made.

This was, of course, Bayern's signing of Robert Lewandowski from Borussia Dortmund in 2014. The Polish striker had just won his first Golden Boot in Germany and was already considered one of the best forwards in the whole of Europe. But at 25 years of age, he was really only starting. Apart from all the silverware he eventually collected with Bayern, Lewandowski would win more individual honours over the course of the coming years than even his Wikipedia page could hold. The most prestigious was probably 'The Best FIFA Football Award' in 2020, a cumbersome modern alias for the old-fashioned World Footballer of the Year. But for the purpose of this book, it's more noteworthy that Lewandowski went on to break the most unbreakable and hallowed of all German scoring records and would become the only player who could claim to be on the same level as the greatest centre-forward who ever ghosted into penalty areas.

Of course Bayern would have signed some other prolific striker if Lewandowski had stayed put or gone elsewhere. And of course Dortmund did find other finishers, from the Gabonese speedster Pierre-Emerick Aubameyang to Norway's teenage sensation Erling Braut Haaland. But is it really just a bizarre coincidence that less than four months after Lewandowski's departure, Dortmund had sunk to last place in the Bundesliga?

Yes, you read that right. Klopp's team lost eight of their first 13 matches in the post-World Cup campaign, the club's worst start to a season since 1986. The charismatic coach did manage to turn things around after the winter break, even leading his team into Europe again, but the weeks and months in the relegation zone had taken their toll. On April 15, 2015, Klopp held a press conference to announce he would step down at the end of the season even though everyone wanted him to stay. The club's press officer closed the event by saying: 'This is a black day for Borussia Dortmund.'

Yes, there was plenty of gloating down south, where Bayern's supporters rejoiced at the prospect of having gotten rid of yet another pesky rival, like they had done with Gladbach, Hamburg, Cologne and Bremen before. But the party died down shortly after dawn. On April 16, Bayern's team doctor Hans-Wilhelm Müller-Wohlfahrt resigned with immediate effect because, as his press release said, the 'medical department was made primarily responsible' for a defeat in Porto 'for inexplicable reasons'. It was an open secret that Müller-Wohlfahrt didn't see eye to eye with Guardiola, and while the resignation of a physio wouldn't have meant anything for most other teams, it was a totally different matter here: Müller-Wohlfahrt had been working for the Reds for 38 years and was as much a club icon as any player, coach or official Bayern had ever had.

Worse was to follow. On July 10, Schweinsteiger knocked on Rummenigge's door and asked to be released from his contract. He was a few weeks away from his 31st birthday and couldn't seem to get a game anymore. He had spent 17 years at the club, so the CEO immediately granted the player his wish. On the following day, Rummenigge held a press conference – without Schweinsteiger, who was already on his way to Old Trafford. 'We parted as great friends,' Rummenigge said. 'We will certainly properly say goodbye to him during a dinner someday.' He meant well, but the fans were aghast. Someday? A goddamn dinner? How about a testimonial, Mexican waves, tears and bouquets of flowers? No, none of that. Their football god, and the country's World Cup hero, had been forced to sneak off like a thief in the night. For most supporters, there was little doubt who was to blame for what smacked of a total lack of decency. When Guardiola next arrived at the club's training ground, he saw a fan banner that had appeared overnight: 'Our identity is being destroyed.'

Those were quite a lot of rude awakenings for a single year, but 2015 had one more heavy blow left to deal to the game. On October 16, *Spiegel* magazine announced: 'In what could turn out to be the greatest crisis in German football since the Bundesliga bribery scandal of the 1970s, *Spiegel* has learned that the decision to award the 2006 World Cup to Germany was likely bought in the form of bribes. The German bidding committee set up a slush fund that was filled secretly by then-Adidas CEO Robert Louis-Dreyfus to the tune of 10.3 million Swiss francs, which at the time was worth 13 million deutsche marks.'

The bit about the scale of the imminent crisis was a tad grandiose, because the news that officials were sometimes crooked and that World Cups were often awarded in fishy ways (Qatar, anyone?) was hardly news at all. Furthermore, for most fans this revelation was not at all comparable to being told that your players are throwing games. So it wasn't German football as a whole that was plunged into a massive crisis – but most certainly the DFB.

Wolfgang Niersbach, president since March 2012, resigned three weeks after the bribery story had broken, saying he was accepting 'political responsibility' for the affair. However, he was also directly involved, having been the executive vice president of the organising committee back in 2006. Which is why the Office of the Attorney General of Switzerland would some months down the line release a statement saying it was opening investigative proceedings against Niersbach and three other members of said committee for alleged fraud, criminal mismanagement, money laundering, breach of trust and misappropriation. The other three accused were the former DFB president Theo Zwanziger, the former general secretary

Horst R. Schmidt – and the former shining light of German football, Shirley Temple. Sorry, Franz Beckenbauer.

Even now, more than 20 years after this World Cup was awarded, 15 years after it was played and six years after the *Spiegel* report, only very few people really know what happened. Maybe only two. In April 2020, the *Süddeutsche Zeitung* newspaper summed it up thus: 'The central question is quite simple: Why were 10 million francs sent from the chairman of the organising committee, Franz Beckenbauer, to Mohammed bin Hammam, the scandal-drenched Qatari administrator, in 2002? Beckenbauer and Bin Hammam: They are the central figures in this affair, the ones who know everything. They will probably never have to share their knowledge.'

Early in the affair, Beckenbauer professed he had a 'clear conscience', adding: 'We did not bribe anyone. There was no slush fund.' Asked about his bewildering ignorance with regard to those unaccounted-for 10 million francs (back then the equivalent of £4 million), he explained: 'I just signed everything all the time, even blank cheques. There was so much to do. Remember, I was not only working for the World Cup, at the time I was also Bayern's president.' This was very unfortunate, not least for Niersbach, Zwanziger and Schmidt. In April 2020, the Swiss trial against them ended very quietly, when it came under the statute of limitations. The three men are no longer in any immediate danger of being penalised, but now they will have to live with a blemish on their reputations, even though nobody has ever accused them of seeking personal gains – and although their protestations of complete innocence could very well be true.

And the greatest player the country had ever had? To a large degree, Beckenbauer disappeared from the public eye, after having been the most public German for half a century. He quit his various side jobs, such as a pundit for Sky Germany or a columnist for the *Bild* tabloid, and retreated. It infuriated many of the reporters who were investigating the scandal, but it would seem the average fan understood and agreed. In late July 2015, less than three months before the affair made headlines, Beckenbauer lost his son Stephan, aged only 46. Of the five Beckenbauer kids, he had been the one who most closely followed in his father's footsteps, even playing in the Bundesliga for Saarbrücken. At the time of his death from a brain tumour, he was a scout and a youth-team coach with Bayern. Some years later, Beckenbauer, who had always called himself the luckiest man on the face of the earth, told a Swiss newspaper: 'I'm not sure you can ever get over something like that. I think it will stay with you forever.'

Nine months after his son passed away, Beckenbauer underwent complicated heart surgery. Next came a hip operation. Then, in March 2019, he unexpectedly attended Bayern's game against Liverpool (now coached by Klopp) in the Champions League and gave his old Sky cronies an interview at half-time. When the station cut back to the studio, the audience rose as one and roared its approval. This rare case of someone getting a standing ovation who isn't even present seemed to suggest the football nation bore no grudge. Maybe people figured £4 million was such a paltry figure for a World Cup that Beckenbauer must have been telling the truth. Or maybe they just didn't care, figuring he was still and would always be their Kaiser.

Six months and 22 days after *Spiegel* proclaimed the greatest crisis in German football since the 1970s, RB Leipzig beat Karlsruhe 2-0 on the penultimate day of the second-division season. When the final whistle sounded, striker Davie Selke grabbed a huge glass of beer and started chasing Ralf Rangnick. It was not a fair contest. Selke's young legs were too quick; Rangnick stumbled, fell to the ground and was soon soaked in lager.

Not even seven years after the club's formation, Lawn Ball Sport had just won promotion to the Bundesliga. On the downside, there were now going to be no less than four clubs in this 18-team league that were either enjoying an exemption from the 50+1 rule or circumventing it by means that may or may not have been legal. You could almost see Hasan Ismaik gleefully rubbing his hands in anticipation of the day when the rule-makers would have to explain to him why all these people could own clubs but he couldn't buy 1860 Munich. You could also see countless serious and committed fans across the country, not just ultras but regular supporters as well, clench their fists in disgust.

But, you know, it's complicated. For one, there was the very old question of football in the east. This has always been a subject of great interest to foreigners, who wonder what happened to all those teams with fanciful names like Dynamo or Lokomotive that used to capture everyone's imagination in the 1970s or 1980s. Why were they still all playing in some lower league, often after having been reformed in the wake of some financial collapse? Well, it's no mystery at all, and it's not restricted to football. In 2014, a feature produced by *Sport Inside*, a weekly magazine on public-service broadcaster WDR, calculated that a German club could win 108 different national championships in various team sports. During the 2013-14 season, just eight of those titles had gone to clubs from the east (and two of them went to floorball players, which is an obscure indoor sport).

The reason was manifest: according to *Sport Inside*, there were 13,000 large companies in Germany in 2014, but only 1,400 of them were based in the east. Consequently, a study had just found that the economic power in the east was still 30 per cent below that of the west. And this situation has not really changed since. Berlin, which is geographically an eastern city, may serve as a good example. It is a vibrant place and undoubtedly a metropolis like London, Paris, Tokyo or New York. But unlike those places, Berlin is not where money is made. When Klaus Wowereit, the Governing Mayor, coined his most famous phrase in 2003, he was really just stating the obvious: 'Berlin is poor but sexy.' It's debatable whether the second adjective applies to the entire east, but the first does.

And so there were those who considered RB Leipzig's success a welcome shot in the arm for the game on the territory of the former GDR. True, enthusiasm was far from universal. Chemie and Lokomotive, the two local clubs with tradition, resented the newcomers, and Michael Schädlich, the long-time president of Halle FC, spoke for many when he sneered 'RB Leipzig is not eastern football'. (Halle lies 30 miles northwest of Leipzig, though the club's traditional rivals are Magdeburg.)

But time is a good medication for antagonism, and so is winning. In late 2020, a Nuremberg consulting firm conducted a large and intricate study into the popularity of the clubs then in the Bundesliga. In contrast to opinion polls, where fans just say whom they support or dislike, this study took into account some objective factors (such as attendances or, indeed, the number of members) before asking more than 30,000 Germans to subjectively award the 18 teams points in certain categories. There were a few surprises. Bayern, Dortmund and Gladbach came first, as was to be expected, but Leverkusen finished ahead of Schalke, Hoffenheim were more popular than Hertha – and RB Leipzig came sixth overall.

One explanation for this result was that there is a school of thought that regards RB as the great hope of the domestic game precisely because they bend the rules. 50+1, the argument goes, practically cements Bayern Munich's monopoly. When the Reds won the 2020 league title, their eighth in a row, finishing a ridiculous 13 points ahead of Dortmund, the *Süddeutsche Zeitung* rhetorically asked what separated the two clubs. The question was rhetorical because the newspaper knew the answer: '250 million euros.' That's the difference in annual turnover and the reason why Dortmund can't compete with Bayern in terms of wages and will thus forever have to see their Götzes or Lewandowskis leave. Did this mean that RB Leipzig were the only club that could one day break Bayern's stranglehold thanks to Red Bull's deep coffers?

Well, even the gloomy analysis from the *Süddeutsche Zeitung* painted only half of an increasingly bleak picture. The international footballing landscape had changed dramatically a few years earlier, when state-run Qatar Sports Investments took over Paris Saint-Germain and the state-controlled Abu Dhabi United Group bought Manchester City. Until that point, German clubs had been competing in Europe with teams bankrolled by companies or oligarchs; now they were up against clubs financed by countries. When Neymar moved from Barcelona to Paris in the summer of 2017 for almost £200 million, which more than doubled the previous world record, the transfer market spun out of control. Even Dortmund, immensely rich by German standards, could no longer afford to sign proven players from abroad but began to look for talented youngsters who would be sold for a profit some years later.

Was the 50+1 rule simply outdated, no longer tenable in the hyper-modern world of football? Even Bayern seemed to think so. In early 2018, the DFL held a surprise vote about the regulation upon St Pauli's request. Twenty-two of the 36 professional clubs cast their vote (the rest were undecided or abstained). 18 voted to keep the rule intact, four wanted to have it abolished. Although it was a secret ballot, it soon transpired that Bayern had been one of the four. 'I think every club should decide for themselves whether or not to bring in investors,' Rummenigge said. (The other three, according to sources, were Leipzig plus second-division Heidenheim and Fürth.)

So the rule was still alive, but was it well? Another very worrying sign was that two months after this ballot, a clock was stopped. Or rather, it should have been stopped at 54 years, 261 days, 36 minutes and two seconds but was initially kept running, simply because nobody knew what to do with it. It was the league's most famous clock, more precisely: a digital counter. It had been a feature of Hamburg's ground for some two decades and indicated how long this founder member of the Bundesliga had continuously played in the top flight. On May 12, 2018, Hamburg's time was up.

It was not just that Kevin Keegan's old club, a former European Cup winner, had been relegated from the Bundesliga for the first time. What's more, Hamburg had never ever played below the highest level of the domestic game going all the way back to 1919, when three local teams merged to form the modern club. The drama had been a long time coming (in both 2014 and 2015, HSV avoided the drop only via the promotion/relegation play-offs), but it was shocking nonetheless, the more so since other former giants of German football would quickly follow Hamburg downstairs: Nuremberg (2019), Düsseldorf (2020), Bremen and Schalke (2021).

It created a bizarre situation: The once attractive Bundesliga that used to set attendance records left, right and centre had become a one-horse race full of company teams and brave but hardly exciting smaller clubs like Mainz, Freiburg or Augsburg, all playing in modest stadiums. At the same time, the very competitive Second Bundesliga was brimming with big names and clubs with large followings, among them also regional powerhouses like Dresden, Karlsruhe or Rostock and the cult club to end all cult clubs, St Pauli. The mind boggled.

And yet May 12, 2018, the day Hamburg left the building, is not widely remembered as a seismic shift or historic date. That's probably because only a few weeks later more than just a clock was stopped. For a moment, and you know I'm not given to hyperbole, the earth stood still. I even know exactly what time it was.

At 5.53pm on June 27, 2018, I was staring at a large television screen in the Berlin offices of a monthly football magazine. Apart from myself, there was only an intern called Florian to be found on the premises. Everybody else had gone to the public screening the magazine always organises during big tournaments to watch the World Cup in Russia.

'Florian,' I said loudly, 'I really think you should watch this.'

'You know I don't care for them,' he replied.

'That's why you should come and watch this.'

Florian left his desk and walked over to my room. He was 24 years old and a not untypical young German football fan, having become disillusioned with the national team in the wake of 2014. Not because the side had since lost yet another semi-final – at the 2016 European Championship and against France – but rather on account of what he referred to as 'this annoying marketing bubble around *die Mannschaft*', all but spitting out the last two words. It had been some sort of nickname for the German national team in some countries, most notably France and the United States, for some time. But nobody in Germany had called the team that. Some people said *Adlerträger*, eagle bearers, due to the badge on the players' shirts, but even that sounded artificial. Most fans called the national team the national team and that was that.

But one year after the World Cup in Brazil, Oliver Bierhoff (then the general manager of the national team, a job description that was later changed to technical director) announced the launch of an image campaign based around that slogan – *die Mannschaft* would now adorn the team's coach and its clothing and of course the inevitable deluge of official merchandise.

It seemed a bit too corporate, but there was nothing inherently wrong with it. The problem was, again, the timing. Soon, saying 'die Mannschaft' in that sarcastic tone Florian had down pat would become a code word that signalled you disliked all that was wrong with the national team, and of course the scandal-ridden DFB, and wanted no part of it.

And all of a sudden, there was a lot that was wrong with the team. In May 2018, Mesut Özil and Ilkay Gündogan posed for photos with the controversial Turkish president Recep Erdoğan. At least in Özil's case, it was not the first time he had expressed support for Erdoğan. But now, exactly a month before the World Cup, the pictures went viral and caused a lot of criticism. Some of it was valid and appropriately phrased. But a lot of it was triggered by a thinly-veiled mistrust (and maybe a stronger word should be used here) which a certain section of the public had always harboured towards all those players with diverse backgrounds who were now part of the team. If Özil and Gündogan considered Erdoğan their president, the argument went, why were they playing for Germany?

Even that was not really the problem. A public debate about what constitutes nationality in the 21st century, not only but also with regard to football allegiance, would have been long overdue. Countries like France, Holland and even Switzerland (a team that now featured many players with Albanian roots) had already gone through this, but Germany hadn't. The problem was that the DFB, and by extension the men in charge of the national team, more or less did nothing. In early June, Bierhoff simply declared the matter closed ('It's enough now') during a live television interview. On the very next day, Gündogan was loudly booed by German fans during a friendly against Saudi Arabia in Leverkusen. After the final whistle, the Manchester City midfielder, born and raised in nearby Gelsenkirchen, broke down in tears.

Gündogan would continue to play for Germany, unlike Özil. He retired from international duty in July 2018, posting a statement in which he heavily criticised Reinhard Grindel, the man who had replaced Niersbach as the DFB's president. The most scathing of Özil's lines read: 'In the eyes of Grindel and his supporters, I am German when we win, but I am an immigrant when we lose.' Of course this was unfair. He should probably have said something like: 'In the eyes of some fans, I'm a German if we win and an immigrant if we lose – and Grindel and his men have closed their eyes to this situation, pretending it didn't exist.' In any case, it was a sad end to an international career that had seemed so glittering only four years earlier.

So, this was the background to Florian's refusal to watch Germany's final group game against South Korea on June 27. As he came into my office, he saw an American called Mark Geiger stare at a small screen at the side of the pitch in stoppage time.

'What's going on?' Florian asked.

'The referee has just disallowed a South Korean goal,' I explained. 'And now he will find out that it was legal.'

'Wow,' Florian said.

Yes, it was a wow moment. For the first time ever, Germany were eliminated at the group stage of a World Cup. As the reigning title holders, no less, and having reached at least the semi-finals at every major tournament since 2006. To top it off, the defeat at the hands of South Korea even meant that Löw's complacent team finished dead last in what should have been an easy group with Mexico and Sweden. There were no two ways about it, Löw had to step down. This, after all, was the unwritten rule. The quarter-final is the minimum for a German national coach – anything else means you know what you have to do, thank you.

Only Löw didn't resign – and the DFB didn't fire him. Maybe because of his undeniable merits, maybe because there was no one else, maybe because the DFB was a total shambles after the *Sommermärchen* scandal and now the Özil affair. Whatever the reason, it was highly unfortunate. Because Löw now proceeded to ruin, or at least damage, his near-impeccable reputation and track record by making strange decisions. In March 2019, he travelled to Munich to tell Hummels, Müller and Boateng that their services were no longer required because the team needed to be rebuilt, only to recall two of them for the next tournament. Oh, and by piling on debacles of historic proportions.

No, this is not too strong an expression. In November 2020, Germany were beaten 6-0 by Spain, the country's heaviest defeat since 1931. In March 2021, Löw became only the third Germany coach to lose a World Cup qualifier at home. (And the other two men had lost to Portugal and England, respectively, not against North Macedonia.) In June 2021, Germany were knocked out of Euro 2020, rescheduled due to COVID-19, by England in the round of 16. It was the first time that Germany had failed to reach the quarter-finals at two consecutive tournaments.

When Löw rode into the sunset after the England match, he had overseen more games (198) and collected more victories (124) than any German national coach before him. His string of successes until 2016 had been unparalleled not just in German football history, though more important than the numbers was that he had turned a team too often thought of as joyless result-grinders into an attack-minded side full of flair and style. But his erratic late work meant that people breathed a sigh of relief when he finally stepped down and welcomed his successor with open arms.

One is tempted to say this successor was chosen according to one of the oldest DFB traditions, which is the promotion of the national coach's right-hand man to main man. But in this case the story came with a few twists. Hans-Dieter Flick, who never seemed to mind that everyone called him by the diminutive 'Hansi', had been Löw's assistant for many years, but he no

longer held that role when he was finally offered the one job he
had always wanted. In fact, Flick had stepped down as assistant
coach after the 2014 World Cup to become the DFB's director
of football. (Perhaps because Löw kept extending his contracts
and Flick wanted more from life than to concoct corner routines
with Thomas Müller.)

But suddenly, Flick grew restless. After three years with the
DFB, he joined Hoffenheim for another boardroom role that
ended only eight months later, when he became Bayern Munich's
assistant coach. He was 54 and now had to answer to Niko Kovač,
seven years his junior. But the move wasn't as strange as it seems.
Flick knew the club well, having made more than a hundred
league appearances for Bayern between 1985 and 1990. Plus,
there were more and more doubts surrounding Kovač.

The Berlin-born Croat had taken over the team from –
kudos if you saw that one coming – Jupp Heynckes in 2018.
Yes, Heynckes had done his friend Hoeness yet another favour
when the Bayern hot seat turned into a bit of an ejection seat
during the post-Guardiola years. Kovač and his trusted assistant,
brother Robert, had just won the Cup with Frankfurt (against
Bayern), but they always seemed a bit overwhelmed in Munich.
When Bayern lost the Champions League home game against
Klopp's Liverpool that was attended by Beckenbauer, the duo
was living on borrowed time.

In November 2019, one day after a painful 5-1 defeat in –
where else? – Frankfurt, the Kovač siblings were sacked, and
Flick took over the team, as the press release said, 'for the time
being'. It would be the most successful time in the club's long
history, as Flick's Bayern became only the second team in history
(after Barcelona in 2009) to win six major trophies – the league,
the Cup, the domestic and the European Super Cup, the FIFA
Club World Cup and, of course, the Champions League. Six
years after Wembley, the final was another one between two

German coaches, as Flick was up against Paris Saint-Germain and Thomas Tuchel. The game was close and very strange, as it had to be played behind closed doors because of coronavirus. Bayern won 1-0, and when Flick asked to be freed from his contract to take over the national team, Bayern could hardly say no.

There was another strange thing about the Champions League final in 2020: the deciding goal was scored by the French winger Kingsley Coman, not by Lewandowski. The Pole had found the target a sensational 15 times during that season's competition (only one man, Cristiano Ronaldo, has ever done better) and was rewarded with numerous individual awards. However, he was still a year away from the most unlikely of his many achievements.

On May 22, 2021, the last day of the Bundesliga season, Bayern won a last-gasp penalty against Augsburg. The score was 4-2, so the spot-kick was irrelevant for the outcome. Yet the nation held its collective breath. Lewandowski stepped up and converted. Manuel Neuer came running across the entire pitch to celebrate with the striker, who had taken off his shirt to reveal a bare chest. That must be mentioned because a week earlier, when he'd scored his 40th goal of the season to equal Gerd Müller's 49-year-old Bundesliga record, he had worn a shirt that read '4 Ever Gerd'.

He did have a similar shirt with him, though, when he scored from the spot in the final minute to become the sole record holder with 41 goals. Immediately after the game, he rode an elevator to Bayern's club museum, situated on the stadium's third floor, to meet Gerd Müller's wife Uschi and present her with the signed shirt. Before Lewandowski could get a word out, Uschi said: 'You were wasting so many chanes today that I was beginning to believe you were doing it on purpose to not break the record.' Then she added: 'Gerd would have told you: Are you daft, lad? Whenever you have the chance to score, you must score.'

Gerd Müller couldn't give the Pole this piece of advice himself. He was suffering from Alzheimer's and had been living in a nursing home for almost six years. It was almost as if he was subconsciously waiting for someone to finally did what he had done. Because less than three months after Lewandowski had given Uschi Müller the '4 Ever Gerd' shirt, Germany's greatest striker of all time passed away. Oliver Kahn, who had just become Bayern's new CEO, said: 'We are all deeply affected by the news. His achievements will in all eternity form a part of the history of this club and German football as a whole.' Then he added: 'Gerd will forever be in our hearts.'

INDEX

POLARIS
PUBLISHING